Law, Education, and the Place of Religion in Public Schools

This text presents a comparative, cross-cultural analysis of the legal status of religion in public education in 18 different nations while offering recommendations for the future improvement of religious education in public schools.

Offering rich, analytical insights from a range of renowned scholars with expertise in law, education, and religion, this volume provides detailed consideration of legal complexities impacting the place of religion and religious education in public education. The volume pays attention to issues of national and international relevance including the separation of the church and state, public funding of religious education, the accommodation of students' devotional needs, and compulsory religious education. The volume thus highlights the increasingly complex interplay of religion, law, and education in diverse educational settings and cultures across developing and developed nations.

Providing a valuable contribution to the field of religious secondary education research, this volume will be of interest to researchers, academics, and educators with an interest in religion and law, international and comparative education, and those involved with educational policy at all levels. Those more broadly interested in moral and values education will also benefit from the discussions the book contains.

Charles J. Russo is Panzer Chair of Education and Research Professor of Law, University of Dayton, USA.

Routledge Research in Religion and Education

Series Editor Michael D. Waggoner,
University of Northern Iowa, USA

14. **Improving the Pedagogy of Islamic Religious Education in Secondary Schools**
    The Role of Critical Religious Education and Variation Theory
    Ayse Demirel Ucan

15. **A History of Islamic Schooling in North America**
    Mapping Growth and Evolution
    Nadeem Ahmed Memon

16. **Teaching Sexuality and Religion in Higher Education**
    Embodied Learning, Trauma Sensitive Pedagogy, and Perspective Transformation
    Edited by Darryl W. Stephens and Kate Ott

17. **Curriculum Renewal for Islamic Education**
    Critical Perspectives on Teaching Islam in Primary and Secondary Schools
    Edited by Nadeem A. Memon, Mariam Alhashmi, and Mohamad Abdalla

18. **Islamic Religious Education in Europe**
    A Comparative Study
    Edited by Leni Franken and Bill Gent

19. **Teaching Religious Literacy to Combat Religious Bullying**
    Insights from North American Secondary Schools
    W. Y. Alice Chan

20. **Law, Education, and the Place of Religion in Public Schools**
    International Perspectives
    Edited by Charles J. Russo

For more information about this series, please visit: www.routledge.com

Law, Education, and the Place of Religion in Public Schools

International Perspectives

Edited by Charles J. Russo

Routledge
Taylor & Francis Group
NEW YORK AND LONDON

First published 2022
by Routledge
605 Third Avenue, New York, NY 10158

and by Routledge
2 Park Square, Milton Park, Abingdon, Oxon, OX14 4RN

Routledge is an imprint of the Taylor & Francis Group, an informa business

Library of Congress Cataloging-in-Publication Data
A catalog record for this book has been requested

ISBN: 978-0-367-45713-6 (hbk)
ISBN: 978-1-032-06448-2 (pbk)
ISBN: 978-1-003-02497-2 (ebk)

Typeset in NewBaskerville
by Apex CoVantage, LLC

Dedication

To the three generations of women, and little women,
in my life. . . . To my wife and the love of my life, Debbie,
with my undying love, and affection, and devotion, now, always, and forever.
To our wonderful daughter, Emily, an outstanding Mother, with much love.
And, to my granddaughters, Lorelai and Adelaide with much love for the
immeasurable joy they bring to the life of my family.

Contents

Contributors

Mark Anderson, M.Ed., Ph.D., has been the Principal/Head of School at Luther College in Regina, Saskatchewan, since 2007 and President of the Saskatchewan Association of Historical High Schools since 2013. He began his career as a teacher of English literature, international baccalaureate English, and theory of knowledge; he also served as a vice principal for three years. Much of his postgraduate research focused on Canadian education law, the teaching of religion in public schools, and funding independent high schools. He was the 2001 recipient of the Canadian Association of the Practical Study of Law in Education Fellowship.

Paul T. Babie, LL.M., D.Phil., is ALS Professor of the Theory and Law of Property and Director of the Law and Religion Project of the Research Unit for the Study of Society, Ethics, and Law at the University of Adelaide. He was associate dean of law (research) from 2007 to 2017 and associate dean of law (international) from 2017 to 2019. His research involves asking what property is and how it can be justified, if at all, exploring both questions from legal and theological perspectives. He was elected a Fellow of the Australian Academy of Law in 2017.

Chih-Hung Chou graduated from the Department of Law of the National Taiwan University with a bachelor's degree and obtained his master's degree of law from the Fu-Jen Catholic University in 1989 and Ph.D. in 1999. He is currently a professor at the National Taipei University of Education and President of the Taiwan Education Law Association. He served as a commissioner of the Public Service Protection and Training Commission during 1998–2001; secretary-general of the Taiwan Law Society in 1998; editor-in-chief of the *Taiwan Law Review* during 2001–2006; a commissioner of the Central Election Commission during 2003–2009 and 2017–2020; and chairman of the Taiwan Cultural Law Association in 2012–2016.

Paul T. Clarke, M.A., LL.M., Ph.D., is a professor of education at the University of Regina who served as the associate dean of human resources and faculty development from 2014 to 2018. His research focuses on education law and leadership. He is the co-editor of a new book on student radicalization that will be published in 2021.

Nóra Zsuzsanna Csekő-Lengyel graduated from the University of Szeged (M.A. in law) in 2009 and King Sigismund College, Budapest (M.A. in international studies) in 2010. She worked as an adviser in the European Parliament in Brussels from 2009 to 2012; since 2012 she has worked at the Constitutional Court of Hungary. In 2018, she was a visiting researcher at the European Court of Human Rights. She is a Ph.D. candidate at the Doctoral School of Law and Political Sciences of the Pázmány Péter Catholic University, Budapest, where her field of research is the right to education and freedom of religion in Hungary.

Javier García Oliva, LL.M, Ph.D. (cum laude and European distinction), is a senior lecturer in law, a lecturer in Spanish law at the University of Oxford, a teaching fellow at University College London, a research associate at the Centre for Law and Religion at Cardiff University, Profesor Honorifico de la Universidad Carlos III de Madrid, Profesor Visitante del Centro de Derecho Comparado de la Facultad de Derecho de la Universidad de Sevilla, and visiting professor at Schulich School of Law, Dalhousie University. He has published two books and more than 50 articles and book chapters on constitutional law and law and religion.

Balázs Szabolcs Gerencsér, Ph.D., is an associate professor in the Administrative Law Department of the Pázmány Péter Catholic University, Budapest, and has been Director of the PPCU Ereky Public Law Research Center since 2011. He has served as a visiting research scholar in both the United States and Belgium and has had a traineeship at the Council of Europe. He regularly cooperates with international and national nongovernmental organizations. His current fields of research are comparative and European public administration, education rights, language rights, and protection of minorities.

Rev. Dr. Helen Hall studied law at Peterhouse, Cambridge, subsequently earning her M.A. in theology from Durham University and Ph.D. in law from Cardiff University. An associate professor in law at Nottingham Trent University, she is Editor of the *Nottingham Law Journal* and the *Journal of Rights and Justice* and is a member of the editorial board of *Law and Justice*. With Javier García Oliva, she is co-author of *Law, Religion and the Constitution: Balancing Beliefs in Britain* (Routledge, 2017). She has published numerous articles in the field of law and religion and is particularly interested in children's rights and legal issues relating to exorcism.

Pieter W. Huisman, LL.M., D.Jur., is Professor of Education Law at the Erasmus School of Law, Rotterdam, and senior lecturer at the Academy for Public Management, Safety, and Law at The Hague University of Applied Sciences, The Hague, Netherlands. He has practiced education law at the Hobéon consultancy in The Hague since 2014. He is a member of the Dutch Education Council, the main advisory body for the Ministry of Education, Culture, and Science; and the editorial board of the *International Journal for Education Law and Policy*. His main research themes focus on constitutional issues, lawmaking in education, the rights of students, and comparative educational law.

Bilgen Kiral, Ph.D., is an associate professor in the Department of Educational Administration at Aydin Adnan Menderes University in Turkey since 2019. She was a teacher and assistant principal in a primary school from 2001 to 2016 and an assistant professor from 2016 to 2019 at Aydin Adnan Menderes University. She teaches undergraduate- and graduate-level courses in comparative education, Turkish education law, the Turkish educational system and school management, children's rights, and teacher empowerment.

Erkan Kiral, Ph.D., has been an associate professor in the Department of Educational Administration at Aydin Adnan Menderes University since 2017. He graduated from the Institute of Education, Department of Educational Administration and Policy at Ankara University in 2012 and the Justice Department of Law in 2017. He teaches a variety of courses, especially ethics and morals, at the undergraduate and graduate levels. Having written many scientific publications in the field of education administration, he mostly focuses on the leadership of school administrators and its reflections on education.

Heriberto Lozano, M.S., is a graduate of the University of Monterrey with a master's degree in organizational development. With degrees in education and communications, he is a faculty member in the School of Engineering and the Emergency Management Coordinator at the University of Monterrey. He is also an emergency management consultant with the government of the State of Nuevo León. His research and teaching focus on emergency and crisis management in public spaces.

Ricardo Lozano, M.Ed., Ph.D., has a doctorate in educational administration from Texas A&M University and a master's in curriculum development and instruction from Concordia University Texas. He is the former director of graduate studies in education and humanities at the University of Monterrey and has been a professor of education in the United States, Turkey, and Mexico. His research and teaching focus on comparative/international education and teacher preparation programs internationally.

Giovanni Patriarca, Ph.D., is Post-Doctoral Fellow in the Department of Philosophy and Economics at the University of Bayreuth (Germany). He studied political science at the University of Camerino (Italy) and philosophy at the Pontifical Lateran University (Vatican City); earned a diploma in Islamic studies at the Pontifical Institute for Arabic and Islamic Studies–P.I.S.A.I.; and completed his Ph.D. in the history of economic thought at the Pontifical University Regina Apostolorum (Rome). A DAAD-Stipendiat at the Humboldt University in Berlin, he received the 2012 Novak Award. He conducts extensive research on international educational policies and the history of education.

Stefan Philipsen, LL.M., D.Phil., is a senior legal advisor to the Ministry of Education, Culture, and Science and an associated researcher at the Montaigne Centre for Rule of Law and the Administration of Justice of Utrecht University. His research focuses on the protection of fundamental rights in education.

Marta Ponikowska-Stejskal is a lawyer and public policy specialist who is passionate about education law, EdTech, the future of the workforce, and human rights. A Ph.D. candidate in international law at Wyszynski University of Warsaw, she graduated with a double master's degree in law and political science from Warsaw University. She serves as Expert at the Home Renaissance Foundation (UK), as a Central Eastern Europe advisor at the Wonder Foundation (UK), and as a community leader at the Warsaw Women Club.

Boguslaw Przywora, Ph.D., is Chair of the Department of Constitutional and Comparative Law at Jan Dlugosz University in Czestochowa, Poland, and Head of Legal Analysis in Laboratory in its Faculty of Law and Economy. He received his habilitation in law at Jagiellonian University in Cracow; graduated from the School of Ukrainian Law (Lviv University of Ivan Franco in Lviv / Kyiv-Mohyla Academy / Jagiellonian University); and finished postgraduate studies in banking law in the Faculty of Law and Administration at Jagiellonian University.

Jeewan Ramlugun, M.Sc., has a background in higher education teaching, research, and academic administration and has contributed to publications in education and law. He co-founded the Commonwealth Faculty of Research and Advanced Legal Studies (UK), the Ghana Institute of Advanced Legal Studies, and PMNglobal (Geneva). His expertise lies in human resource management and development, with over 20 years of experience in this field. He serves as an honorary development consultant at the African Capacity Building Foundation, engaged in institutional strengthening, skills, and knowledge dissemination projects, with special reference to sub-Saharan parliaments and is a member of the Strategic Studies Group.

Charles J. Russo, M.Div., J.D., Ed.D., is the Joseph Panzer Chair in Education in the School of Education and Health Sciences, Director of its Ph.D. Program, and Research Professor of Law in the School of Law at the University of Dayton. He was president of the (US) Education Law Association in 1998–1999 and was the recipient of its McGhehey (Achievement) Award in 2002. In addition, in 2020 he received Distinguished Scholar Award from the Religion and Education Special Interest Group of the American Educational Research Association. He has authored or co-authored more than 325 articles in peer-reviewed journals; authored, co-authored, edited, or co-edited 74 books (including this volume, his third for Routledge); and has more than 1,100 publications focusing on issues in education law. Russo has spoken extensively on issues in education law in 34 US states and 31 nations on all six inhabited continents. In addition, he edits two academic journals and serves on more than a dozen editorial boards.

Nina Beatriz Stocco Ranieri, Ph.D., is Associate Professor II in the Department of Public Law of the University of São Paulo Law School as the UNESCO Chair on the Right to Education and Senior Researcher at its Center for Public Policy. Ranieri held positions in the São Paulo State's Government and public education, advising international and national entities on aspects of the right to education and education law; she currently serves on São Paulo's State Board of Education. Author of books and articles on Public Law and Education Law and a member of national and international academic editorial boards, Ranieri was elected to the São Paulo State Academy of Education in 2018.

David Ryffé, J.D., M.Phil., is an associate professor of legal studies at the University of Gothenburg, School of Business, Economics, and Law. His research touches upon educational law and constitutional and public law, among other areas. Besides his academic work, Ryffé is also a practicing lawyer and conducts educational activities in private management.

Marius H. Smit, LL.M., Ph.D., is an associate professor in the Faculty of Education, North-West University, South Africa, where he teaches education law and leadership. He is a C2 NRF–rated researcher who has authored 75 academic publications including books, chapters in books, articles in accredited journals, conference proceedings, and other articles. He served on the governing bodies of five public schools for which he provides consultation services. Smit serves on the editorial board of the *Education and Urban Society* and the *International Journal of Educational Reform*, the national committee of the South African Education Law Association, and the national and provincial councils of the Federation of South African School Governing Bodies (FEDSAS).

A. Keith Thompson, LL.B., M.Jur., Ph.D., is Professor and Associate Dean at the Sydney School of Law of the University of Notre Dame Australia. He also continues to practice part time as a consultant and special counsel with a boutique law firm in Sydney and a regional practice with five offices in southwestern New South Wales. He previously worked for 20 years as international legal counsel for the Church of Jesus Christ of Latter-Day Saints in the Pacific and the African continent, where he was principal advisor in the church's educational system after practicing as a solicitor and partner in a commercial law firm in Auckland, New Zealand.

Fatt Hee Tie, LL.M., S.J.D., is a professor at the Faculty of Law, University of Malay, Kuala Lumpur. He has taught in two secondary schools and a teachers' training college for 12 years. He has also taught education law at the Faculty of Education and the Institute of Educational Leadership at the University of Malaya for more than 18 years. Tie was admitted to the High Court of Malaya as an advocate and solicitor in 1994.

Foreword From Michael D. Waggoner, Series Editor

The opening years of the 21st century brought increased attention to religion as an important dimension of culture and politics. Early in this period, the dramatic multi-pronged attacks of September 11, 2001, came as a jolting reminder of the potential for violent action that can have bases in religious motivations. Over the same period, we came to see an increase in religiously motivated activity in politics. In the United States, we see this in the evolution from the Moral Majority movement that emerged as a force in the late 1970s as the beginning of the new religious right. On further reflection, however, we can see the involvement of religion extending much further back as a fundamental part of our social organization rather than a new or emerging phenomenon. We need only recall the religious wars of early modern Europe through to the contentious development of US church and state relations as evidence of the long-standing role religion has played as a source of competing values and beliefs. That said, there has been a significant upturn in research and scholarship across many disciplines relative to the study of religion in recent decades. This is particularly the case in the area of the interplay of education and religion.

While religious education (study *toward formation* in a particular faith tradition) has been with us for millennia, religion education (study *about* religion as an academic subject apart from theology) is more recent. Whereas theology departments proceeded from religious assumptions aiming to promulgate a faith tradition, the religious studies field emerged as a discipline that sought to bring a more objective social scientific approach to the study of religion. The origins of this approach date back to the European research centers that influenced US scholars beginning in the 18th century. The formalization of this trend, however, is a fairly recent phenomenon, as illustrated by the 1949 formation of the Society for the Scientific Study of Religion, with its own scholarly journal, and the creation of religious studies departments across the United States in the wake of the Supreme Court decision in 1963 that allowed teaching *about* religion (rather than *for*) in public education institutions. It was also that same year that the American Academy of Religion was born out of a group of scholars that had since 1909 been meeting under various names related to biblical study.

It is out of this relatively recent increase in scholarly attention to religion and education that this book series arises. Routledge Publishers have long been an important presence in the respective fields of religion and of education. It seemed like a natural step to introduce a book series focused particularly on Research in Religion and Education. My appreciation extends to Max Novick for guiding this series into being in 2011 and now to Elsbeth Wright, for continuing Routledge's oversight.

In the 21st volume of this series, Charles J. Russo brings together legal scholars from around the world for a comparative examination of the law regarding teaching religion in public schools. The 18 nations profiled in this volume each have distinct legal foundations, histories, and formulations, as one would expect. They all, however, reflect in varying degrees some important international agreements that undergird their legal philosophy regarding religion and education. Russo outlines these in his introduction: they include the 1948 Universal Declaration of Human Rights (UDHR); the 1959 Declaration of the Rights of the Child; the 1989 Convention on the Rights of the Child; the 1992 Declaration on the Rights of Persons Belonging to National or Ethnic, Religious and Linguistic Minorities; and the 1994 International Covenant on Civil and Political Rights. Following a common outline, the author(s) of each chapter elucidate the constitutional and legal foundations of education, underscoring protections for freedom of religion and education as well as any litigation within these areas.

Professor Russo sees three basic categories of national approaches: (1) separation of education and religion, (2) accommodation of selective integration of religion and education, and (3) allowing or encouraging integration of religion and education. Those countries mandating some degree of separation of education and religion include the United States, Canada, Brazil, Italy, New Zealand, Spain, Australia, Taiwan, and Mexico. Among those that permit optional teaching about religion are Mauritius, Netherlands, and Sweden. Those nations more favorably disposed to teaching about religion in public schools, including content that is confessional or sectarian, include England, Hungary, Poland, South Africa, Malaysia, and Turkey. The latter two, in particular, require instruction about Islam in public schools.

One emerging topic, Russo suggests, is becoming a challenge across all the countries considered in this volume: human sexuality. The question becomes one over who can or should control curricular content when dealing with issues of human sexuality. For example, he points out that public school leaders must balance teaching respect for the LGBTQ+ community while also respecting those whose value systems, most often deriving from religious traditions, have counterviews. Even in this context, the internal diversity of faith traditions can complicate the discussion as there is rarely unanimity on perspectives. The key here, he underscores, is discussion rather than heated dispute that threatens deeper division.

Dr. Russo concludes with recommendations for teaching religion in public schools that he derives from his analysis conducted across the countries reported in this volume. There are important learnings to be had from these cross-cultural analyses that can improve the work of religion in public schools, whether *about* or *for* or *from*, in many national contexts. This unique volume can contribute greatly to that learning and practice.

Michael D. Waggoner
University of Northern Iowa
Series Editor, Research in Religion and Education

Acknowledgments

As with any book, I must thank many people. Six sets of people were very helpful in assisting me to bring this book to fruition. First, I offer great thanks to my longtime dear friend and colleague, Professor Emeritus Mike Waggoner of the University of Northern Iowa, for encouraging me to proceed with this project and encouraging me throughout the process.

Second, I offer my heartfelt thanks to my editor, Elsbeth "Ellie" Wright, for her always gracious assistance and help in shepherding the proposal through to publication and her associate, AnnaMary Goodall, for the many ways in which she also offered her generous assistance throughout the publication process. I am also grateful to Ganesh Pawan Kumar Agoor, Project Manager at Apex CoVantage, India, for helping to prepare the final manuscript for the publication.

Third, it almost goes without saying that I am grateful to the authors for their valuable contributions to this book.

Fourth, at the University of Dayton, I would like to thank my Dean Ali Carr-Chellman and Department Chair Dr. Dave Dolph in the School of Education and Health Sciences along with Dean Andrew Strauss in the School of Law for their ongoing support and friendship in many ways. Thanks, too, to President Dr. Eric Spina and Provost Dr. Paul Benson for working with my Deans, Chair, and other campus leaders in creating an atmosphere supportive of research, study, and teaching as well as for their friendship and support.

Fifth, I would like to thank those who read this book and reflect on the importance of the topic as they perhaps advance the cause of teaching religion in public schools in order to enhance great human understanding of those whose religious views may be different from their own.

Sixth, but certainly not least, I would like to express my deepest appreciation and undying love to the love of my life, my wife, Debbie, for her ongoing love and support in all of the aspects of our life together in addition to her help in proofreading the text.

Introduction

Being educated about religion continues to play a central role in the lives of many different cultures and billions of peoples through the world. As such, in discussing such matters, this introduction is divided into three sections. The first part of this chapter briefly reflects on the status of both religion and education as essential for human development. In so doing, it illustrates the importance of encouraging political and educational leaders as well as policymakers to promote the teaching of religion in public schools, in the hope that doing so will engender mutual respect not only among students as they grow toward adulthood but also their parents, educators, and societies.

The second part of this chapter highlights key language from the most significant international documents that enshrine both education and religious freedom as a fundamental right. The third part briefly reflects on why it is important for leaders of public schools to permit teaching about religion so that children can grow up with an understanding of and respect for those whose beliefs are different from their own.

The Status of Religion

Religion, typically defined as a belief in some form of a higher being or supernatural power, has seemingly always occupied a central role in the lives of humans and their societies or cultures. Evidence of the importance of religion in human life can be traced as far back as 40,000 years in the hundreds of Paleolithic cave paintings in France and Spain, plus such far-flung locations as Australia, Indonesia, and Mexico. As reflected by the varieties of human belief present in such diverse systems as the polytheistic religions of ancient Egypt, Greece, and Rome, as well as the animistic belief systems and totems erected in much of the rest of the pre-Judeo-Christian, non-Western world, humans all over the world have since time immemorial recognized the need to call on a higher being while engaging in what today might be described as exercising their right to freedom of religion.

At present, millions, if not billions, of people throughout the world continue to acknowledge the need to honor the deities and belief systems of their choices. Yet respect for other religions or systems of belief is often ignored, even outlawed, in some nations and societies. One has but to search the internet or read a newspaper to see how the lack of tolerance of diversity of belief can readily be witnessed in some societies as persistent tensions all too often break out into violence and bloodshed in many global regions. In fact, high-profile stories are often in the news addressing controversies dealing with the status of religion in public elementary and secondary schools, whether allowing it to be taught or permitting students to pray and engage in religious activities.

Against this background of the nascent tensions among the adherents of different religions, this book is designed to help readers to learn to develop better understandings of and respect for the beliefs of others so as to help promote greater cooperation. Consequently, this interdisciplinary, comparative volume, which includes original chapters by leading academicians from 18 selected nations – including at least one country on all six inhabited continents – with expertise in law, education, and/or religion, is designed to serve as a resource for researchers in education, law, and religion as well as policymakers, lawmakers, and students.

While examining legal issues that arise over the teaching of religion in public schools in selected nations, this book intends to provide readers with an enhanced understanding of how and why this practice is being implemented in divergent locations in the hope of promoting mutual tolerance for belief systems other than one's own. In so doing, the chapter authors have made every effort to avoid using technical language by writing in a manner that plainly explains the dynamic relationships between the law, education, and religion. More specifically, the chapters in this volume are designed to enhance the awareness of educators, lawmakers, policymakers, and other interested readers about issues involving the legal status of teaching about religion in schools in selected nations at a time when religious strife appears to be growing in many parts of the world.

Because I do not think any other work exists with the scope and focus of this book, it is my hope that it will stimulate further interest, research, and debate on comparative analyses associated with teaching about religion in public schools at a time when the place of religion is of vital interest in many parts of the world. Moreover, while articles published in both professional and academic journals address the place of religion in state-funded schools, no single work is devoted solely to the topic of legal issues associated with teaching about religion in public schools that is written for interdisciplinary audiences involving educators, lawyers, researchers, and lawmakers.

International Documents

Education as a Fundamental Right

The compulsory education laws of most nations nominally, if not explicitly, operate in a manner consistent with a variety of international covenants, the effectiveness of which is beyond the scope of this volume. Consequently, although not all nations automatically enter international agreements into domestic legislation,[1] the principles in these instruments reflect the long-standing view present for many that the right to education for all children is of utmost importance.[2] In order to develop an understanding of these widely accepted documents, this subsection briefly reviews the key features of the leading instruments on education as a fundamental human right because they form the bedrock for the ideals discussed in this volume.

The Universal Declaration on Human Rights (UDHR), promulgated in 1948, was the first internationally accepted document to enunciate the value of education as a basic human right. According to this Declaration:

(1) Everyone has the right to education. Education shall be free, at least in the elementary and fundamental stages. Elementary education shall be compulsory. Technical and professional education shall be made generally available and higher education shall be equally accessible to all on the basis of merit.
(2) Education shall be directed to the full development of the human personality and to the strengthening of respect for human rights and fundamental freedoms. It shall promote understanding, tolerance and friendship among all nations, racial or religious groups, and shall further the activities of the United Nations for the maintenance of peace.
(3) Parents have a prior right to choose the kind of education that shall be given to their children.[3]

In 1959, Principle 7 of the Declaration on the Rights of the Child reiterated the right to an education, asserting:

> The child is entitled to receive education, which shall be free and compulsory, at least in the elementary stages. He shall be given an education which will promote his general culture and enable him, on a basis of equal opportunity, to develop his abilities, his individual judgment, and his sense of moral and social responsibility, and to become a useful member of society. The best interests of the child shall be the guiding principle of those responsible for his education and guidance; that responsibility lies in the first place with his parents.[4]

Further, Principle 5 of this Declaration maintains that "[t]he child who is physically, mentally, or socially handicapped shall be given the special treatment, education and care required by his particular condition."[5]

The 1989 Convention on the Rights of the Child (hereinafter, Convention) has had a significant impact on the legal duties of educators. While the Convention is perhaps the most expansive instrument to achieve international recognition on the rights of children, many signatories have not acted in keeping with its spirit, let alone its letter, in safeguarding the educational rights of all children.[6]

Among the more than 30 of the Convention's 54 articles impacting on education, Article 3 states that in "all actions concerning children . . . the best interests of the child shall be a primary consideration."[7] It is unlikely that these interests can be met without affording children some right to speak for themselves on a range of social and educational issues, including religion. In this regard, Article 12 claims just such a right in stating that a "child who is capable of forming his or her own views" has a right "to express these views freely in all matters affecting them."[8] Article 13 extends this concept by maintaining that children "shall have the right to freedom of expression including freedom to seek, receive and impart information and ideas of all kinds,"[9] presumably including matters of faith and religion.

Religious Freedom as a Fundamental Right

The same international instruments that discussed education are just as cognizant of the need to maintain religious freedom. In order to develop an understanding of these widely accepted documents, this subsection briefly reviews the key features of the leading international instruments on religion as a fundamental human right.

Pursuant to Article 2 of UDHR:

> Everyone is entitled to all the rights and freedoms set forth in this Declaration, without distinction of any kind, such as race, colour, sex, language, religion, political or other opinion, national or social origin, property, birth or other status.[10]

Article 18 of the UDHR adds what may be the most basic freedom of all:

> Everyone has the right to freedom of thought, conscience and religion; this right includes freedom to change his religion or belief, and freedom, either alone or in community with others and in public or private, to manifest his religion or belief in teaching, practice, worship and observance.[11]

The 1959 Declaration on the Rights of the Child highlights the place of nondiscrimination based on religion starting in its Article 1:

Article 1

The child shall enjoy all the rights set forth in this Declaration. Every child, without any exception whatsoever, shall be entitled to these rights, without distinction or discrimination on account of race, colour, sex, language, religion, political or other opinion, national or social origin, property, birth or other status, whether of himself or of his family.

Article 2

1. States Parties shall respect and ensure the rights set forth in the present Convention to each child within their jurisdiction without discrimination of any kind, irrespective of the child's or his or her parent's or legal guardian's race, colour, sex, language, religion, political or other opinion, national, ethnic or social origin, property, disability, birth or other status.

Article 10

1. The child shall be protected from practices which may foster racial, religious and any other form of discrimination. . . .[12]
2. The most recent instrument on children, the 1989 Convention on the Rights of the Child, expresses similar concerns in its provisions.

Article 14

1. States Parties shall respect the right of the child to freedom of thought, conscience and religion.
2. Freedom to manifest one's religion or beliefs may be subject only to such limitations as are prescribed by law and are necessary to protect public safety, order, health or morals, or the fundamental rights and freedoms of others.

Article 29 General Comment on Its Implementation

1. States Parties agree that the education of the child shall be directed to:
   (d) The preparation of the child for responsible life in a free society, in the spirit of understanding, peace, tolerance,

equality of sexes, and friendship among all peoples, ethnic, national and religious groups and persons of indigenous origin.

Article 30

In those States in which ethnic, religious or linguistic minorities or persons of indigenous origin exist, a child belonging to such a minority or who is indigenous shall not be denied the right, in community with other members of his or her group, to enjoy his or her own culture, to profess and practise his or her own religion, or to use his or her own language.[13]

The Declaration on the Rights of Persons Belonging to National or Ethnic, Religious and Linguistic Minorities, enacted in December 1992, shares many of these same concerns:

Article 1

States shall protect the existence and the national or ethnic, cultural, religious and linguistic identity of minorities within their respective territories and shall encourage conditions for the promotion of that identity.

Article 2

1. Persons belonging to national or ethnic, religious and linguistic minorities (hereinafter referred to as persons belonging to minorities) have the right to enjoy their own culture, to profess and practise their own religion, and to use their own language, in private and in public, freely and without interference or any form of discrimination.
2. Persons belonging to minorities have the right to participate effectively in cultural, religious, social, economic and public life.[14]

More recently, Article 2.1 of the 1994 International Covenant on Civil and Political Rights declares:

Each State Party to the present Covenant undertakes to respect and to ensure to all individuals within its territory and subject to its jurisdiction the rights recognized in the present Covenant, without distinction of any kind, such as race, colour, sex, language, religion, political or other opinion, national or social origin, property, birth or other status.

Further, its Article 18 states:

1. Everyone shall have the right to freedom of thought, conscience and religion. This right shall include freedom to have or to adopt a religion or belief of his choice, and freedom, either individually or in community with others and in public or private, to manifest his religion or belief in worship, observance, practice and teaching.
2. No one shall be subject to coercion which would impair his freedom to have or to adopt a religion or belief of his choice.
3. Freedom to manifest one's religion or beliefs may be subject only to such limitations as are prescribed by law and are necessary to protect public safety, order, health, or morals or the fundamental rights and freedoms of others.
4. The States Parties to the present Covenant undertake to have respect for the liberty of parents and, when applicable, legal guardians to ensure the religious and moral education of their children in conformity with their own convictions.[15]

Importance of Learning About Religion in Public Schools

The purpose of this volume is to enhance educator awareness of issues involving the legal status of teaching about religion in schools at a time when religious strife appears to be growing in many parts of the world. Significant news stories address controversies over public elementary and secondary schools and the status of religion. Consequently, this interdisciplinary, comparative volume is designed to serve as a resource for researchers in education, law, and religion as well as policymakers and students. To this end, the book provides readers with an enhanced awareness of strategies for addressing the status of teaching about religion in rapidly diversifying public elementary and secondary school settings.

About This Book

The status of the legal issues related to teaching about religion in public schools around the world vary. Aware of these differences, this volume includes essays by a representative sample of scholars from 18 nations on all six inhabited continents addressing commonalities and differences on this important and timely topic. The 18 chapters, each concerning an individual country, all of which were authored by accomplished academics and/or jurists, are:

Australia (Paul T. Babie)
Brazil (Nina Beatriz Stocco Ranieri)

Canada (Mark Anderson and Paul T. Clarke)
England (Javier García Oliva and Helen Hall)
Hungary (Balázs Szabolcs Gerencsér and Nóra Zsuzsanna Csekő-Lengyel)
Italy (Giovanni Patriarca)
Malaysia (Fatt Hee Tie)
Mauritius (Jeewan Ramlugun)
Mexico (Ricardo Lozano and Heriberto Lozano)
Netherlands (Pieter W. Huisman and Stefan Philipsen)
New Zealand (Keith Thompson)
Poland (Marta Ponikowska-Stejskal and Boguslaw Przywora)
South Africa (Marius H. Smit)
Spain (Javier García Olive and Helen Hall)
Sweden (David Ryffé)
Taiwan (Chih-Hung Chou)
Turkey (Bilgen Kiral and Erkan Kiral)
United States (Charles J. Russo).

The book concludes with a chapter of analysis by the editor that draws on the various issues addressed throughout the book.

Based on a common outline, I asked these academicians and lawyers to begin each chapter with a brief introduction and a review of the legal/constitutional sources of higher education in the nations they covered. Substantively, the chapters examine the protections available for freedom of religion and the right to education as well as analyses of any litigation protecting religious freedom and the right to education, recognizing that no other nation has nearly the amount of litigation that this topic generates in the United States. Each chapter includes a section on emerging issues before rounding out with a conclusion. Acknowledging that issues vary from one nation to the next, I asked authors to examine the topics as they saw fit while examining the issues from their own points of view. As such, there are some variations in terms of chapter headings even though all chapters generally cover the same topics.

By affording chapter authors some latitude in addressing their topics, it is possible to draw conclusions in a final chapter that can hopefully lead to future dialogue and study. Further, as noted, recognizing the importance of as far-reaching a representation as possible, I was fortunate to be able to ensure that I had at least one nation on each continent or region of the world represented.

As what I believe is the first book of its kind, I hope that this collection of essays will help to enhance a common understanding of the importance of teaching religion in public elementary and secondary schools throughout the world. As the world continues to shrink and interdependence grows, one of the major challenges facing the global community is ensuring the protection of freedom of religion and the right to education for all.

As an important caveat, rather than translating notes and other pertinent information into English, they are often preserved in their original languages. I have done this not only because the underling documents are often unavailable in English but also because translating texts might create difficulties for native speakers who wish to research relevant materials. Moreover, because each of the nations covered in this book uses different systems of legal citation, I have left references in their original form rather than attempt to standardize them under one rubric. Finally, I have preserved minor variations in the different forms of English used throughout the world so that readers can get a flavor of how this seemingly common tongue is used throughout the world, particularly for academicians and attorneys whose first languages are not English.

Notes

1. See the Constitution of the Republic of South Africa 231.3, International agreements: "Any international agreement becomes law in the Republic when it is enacted into law by national legislation; but a self-executing provision of an agreement that has been approved by Parliament is law in the Republic unless it is inconsistent with the Constitution or an Act of Parliament. . . . 233. Application of international law. When interpreting any legislation, every court must prefer any reasonable interpretation of the legislation that is consistent with international law over any alternative interpretation that is inconsistent with international law." Retrieved from www.info.gov.za/documents/constitution/1996/index.htm.
2. For a report on 12 countries (Australia, Belgium, Canada, Denmark, Germany, Iceland, Ireland, New Zealand, Norway, South Africa, Spain, Sweden) that worked to embed the rights of children into domestic law, see Laura Lundy, Ursula Kilkelly, Bronagh Byrne, and Jason Kang, *The UN Convention on the Rights of the Child: A Study of Legal Implementation in 12 Countries* (Belfast: Queens University, 2012). Retrieved from www.unicef.org.uk/Documents/Publications/UNICEFUK_2012CRCimplementationreport%20FINAL%20PDF%20version.pdf.
3. www.un.org/en/documents/udhr/index.shtml.
4. www.un.org/cyberschoolbus/humanrights/resources/child.asp.
5. Ibid.
6. See Editorial, "There aren't as many parties as it seems," June 18, 2017, *Washington Post*, also available at 2017 WLNR 18779445 (stating that "[t]he United States is a signatory to many treaties and agreements it has never ratified, including the U.N. Convention on the Rights of the Child.").
7. http://www2.ohchr.org/english/law/crc.htm.
8. Ibid.

9. Ibid.
10. www.un.org/en/documents/udhr/index.shtml.
11. Ibid.
12. www.un.org/cyberschoolbus/humanrights/resources/child.asp.
13. http://www2.ohchr.org/english/law/crc.htm.
14. www.un.org/documents/ga/res/47/a47r135.htm.
15. www.hrweb.org/legal/cpr.html.

1 Religion and Education in Australian Government Schools

Paul T. Babie[*]

Introduction

This chapter examines the place of and protection for freedom of religion or belief (FoRB) in Australian government primary and tertiary education ('government schools').[1] In order to understand that place, it is necessary to outline the legal foundations for education in Australia and the protection of FoRB in Australian law.

Australia, like the United States, is a constitutional, federal democracy; as such, the legal foundations for education involve an uneasy balance of federal (whether national, or Commonwealth) and state and territorial or regional law and policy. This means that no one unitary source exists in Australia for the foundation of government schools, their funding, and/or for the protection of FoRB and its application to education. Instead, both government schools and the protection of FoRB are established through a piecemeal collection of constitutional, legislative, and common law provisions at both the Commonwealth and state and territory levels.

This chapter contains five sections. The first section outlines the legal status of government primary and tertiary education in the Australian states and territories. The purpose of the second part of the chapter is twofold: (i) it provides an overview of constitutional, legislative, and common law protection for FoRB within the multicultural, multi-faith environment found in Australia; (ii) it examines the judicial application of those protections in the governmental school setting; in fact, though, as will be seen, there is very little judicial analysis. As such, it is necessary to extrapolate from the general approach taken by the courts to the available FoRB protections. The third section briefly touches on emerging issues, suggesting that the courts may soon be required to provide guidance as to how the available protections operate in government schools. The final section briefly concludes.

The Legal Foundation for Education and Religion

Australian students generally begin school with a kindergarten or preparatory school year and then undertake 12 years of primary and secondary schooling. While ten years of schooling is generally the minimum, there is some variation among states and territories as to school starting and leaving ages.

A fundamental distinction exists in Australian law between government and nongovernment[2] primary[3] and tertiary[4] education. State legislation provides the framework within which both educational levels operate.[5] Notwithstanding Australia's state and territorial foundation for government schools, though, significant funding for both government and nongovernment schools comes from the states and territories as well as from the Commonwealth.[6]

Commonwealth legislation provides for primary and secondary school funding on the basis of the Schooling Resource Standard (SRS), 'a measure of the amount of public funding needed by each school to meet the educational needs of its students'.[7] Once the requirements of the SRS are met, funding depends on the state or territory entering a bilateral agreement with the Commonwealth for minimum state and territory funding requirements. Moreover, s 22A of the Australian Education Act 2013 (Cth) requires that states and territories must meet or exceed minimum funding contribution requirements for both government and nongovernment sectors as a condition of receiving Commonwealth funding.[8] State and territory governments have discretion to fund above these requirements.[9]

The legal foundation for religious education differs based on the type of school. Thus, secular nongovernment schools usually eschew specifically religious education in favour of broader cultural, social, and historical studies subjects. The majority of religious nongovernment schools appear to advocate a values-based approach to religious education, with a greater or lesser focus on evangelism or proselytism depending on the individual school. Perhaps the greatest single difference between such schools and government schools is the religious backdrop to instruction and the corresponding intensity of explicitly religious activities such as chapel, devotions, prayers, or similar activities during nonteaching time as part of the school day.[10]

Special Religious Instruction (SRI), while available in all Australian government schools, receives variable treatment depending on the state or territory.[11] South Australia provides a broadly representative example of Australian state government approaches to SRI.[12] Provision for religious education in South Australian government schools is made by the Education Act 1972 (SA), with the content and conduct of religious education in government schools provided for by the Education Regulations 2012 (SA) made under the Act.[13]

Among other things, the Regulations provide for the establishment of standing committees[14] and school-specific Religious Education Committees[15] as well as for the development of course modules for distribution to schools.[16] Most significantly, government schools also provide for the conduct of both 'religious education' and 'religious seminars' in schools,[17] which are typically 'opt-out/opt-in' at the discretion of parents, or outside of school hours. If students opt out, in some cases ethics courses may be offered as substitutes for SRI.[18]

The Protection for and Judicial Analysis of Freedom of Religion or Belief in Education

What protections exist for FoRB in the Australian government school context one finds scattered across constitutional texts, Commonwealth and state and territory legislation, and the common law. This part considers each in turn, including the applicable judicial treatment.

Commonwealth and State Constitutions

Australian constitutional texts establish two types of protection for FoRB in the government school environment: express protection found in the text itself and a freedom implied from that text for political communication.

Express Protection

Section 116 of the Australian Constitution provides four guarantees for FoRB:

> The Commonwealth shall not make any law for establishing any religion, or for imposing any religious observance, or for prohibiting the free exercise of any religion, and no religious test shall be required as a qualification for any office or public trust under the Commonwealth.

Tasmania's Constitution Act 1934 (Tas), s 46, provides a similar protection:

> (1) Freedom of conscience and the free profession and practice of religion are, subject to public order and morality, guaranteed to every citizen.
> (2) No person shall be subject to any disability, or be required to take any oath on account of his religion or religious belief and no religious test shall be imposed in respect of the appointment to or holding of any public office.

The High Court has interpreted s 116 as a limitation on the legislative and executive power of the Commonwealth as opposed to a broad protection of an individual right.[19] Taking a similar approach, the Tasmanian Supreme Court calls s 46 a 'historical puzzle'[20] that 'does not, in terms, confer any personal rights or freedoms on citizens'.[21] As such, ss 116 and 46 seem to provide, at best, no more than a qualified guarantee for FoRB.

It is difficult to say what protections ss 116 and 46 may create in the government school educational context; s 46 has never been applied to that setting, and only the establishment and religious test guarantees of s 116 have been so applied.

In *Attorney-General* (Vic); *Ex rel Black v. Commonwealth* (*Defence of Government Schools*) (*DOGS* case), the High Court held that Commonwealth funding of nongovernment schools does not constitute 'establishing [a] religion' for the purposes of s 116.[22] In *Williams v. Commonwealth* (*School Chaplains* case),[23] the Court held that a religiously affiliated chaplain funded by the Commonwealth to provide a government school chaplaincy program did not violate the religious test for a Commonwealth office guarantee of s 116. The Commonwealth's funding was 'insufficient to render a chaplain engaged . . . the holder of an office under the Commonwealth'.[24]

Taken together, the *DOGS* and *School Chaplains* cases constitutionalise interaction and cooperation between the state and religious schools, providing for a 'semi-permeable membrane' or 'imaginary wall' rather than an impenetrable barrier between church and state: 'Metaphorically, the flow of Commonwealth largesse to religious institutions is permitted; what is blocked is the reverse passage of religious entanglement with Commonwealth affairs'.[25]

The most significant guarantee found in s 116, though, that for free exercise, has never been applied in the educational setting. Indeed, since federation in 1901, only three High Court decisions have dealt with the free exercise guarantee,[26] confirming the same test enunciated in *Krygger v. Williams*:

> To require a man to do a thing which has nothing at all to do with religion is not prohibiting him from a free exercise of religion. It may be that a law requiring a man to do an act which his religion forbids would be objectionable on moral grounds, but it does not come within the prohibition.[27]

The judicial use of this test means that laws regulating matters that have 'nothing at all to do with religion'[28] and laws that have as their effect the infringement of religion but do not 'discriminate against religion generally'[29] do not violate this prohibition. It therefore seems, at a minimum, that in the government school setting, s 116 protects against at least direct infringements of FoRB, as well as attempts to establish a defined state religion, to which observance must be given and of which one must be a member in order to hold a public office.

Of course, an individual right to FoRB must be understood as operating within the wider community. For this reason, limitations may justifiably be placed on the former to protect the interests of the latter. In *Adelaide Co of Jehovah's Witnesses Inc v. The Commonwealth*, Latham CJ said that

> the protection of any form of liberty as a social right within a society necessarily involves the continued existence of that society as a society. Otherwise the protection of liberty would be meaningless and ineffective. It is consistent with the maintenance of religious liberty for the State to restrain actions and courses of conduct which are inconsistent with the maintenance of civil government or prejudicial to the continued existence of the community. The Constitution protects religion within a community organized under a Constitution, so that the continuance of such protection necessarily assumes the continuance of the community so organized. This view makes it possible to reconcile religious freedom with ordered government. It does not mean that the mere fact that the Commonwealth Parliament passes a law in the belief that it will promote the peace, order and good government of Australia precludes any consideration by a court of the question whether or not such a law infringes religious freedom. The final determination of that question by Parliament would remove all reality from the constitutional guarantee. That guarantee is intended to limit the sphere of action of the legislature. The interpretation and application of the guarantee cannot, under our Constitution, be left to Parliament. If the guarantee is to have any real significance it must be left to the courts of justice to determine its meaning and to give effect to it by declaring the invalidity of laws which infringe it and by declining to enforce them. The courts will therefore have the responsibility of determining whether a particular law can fairly be regarded as a law to protect the existence of the community, or whether, on the other hand, it is a law 'for prohibiting the free exercise of any religion'.[30]

Thus, it remains unclear the extent to which any of the guarantees contained in s 116 may apply to religious education in the government school setting. But whatever their application, given the level of funding for SRI in state and territory government schools, there does seem the potential for increased concern about the protection of FoRB. And it does seem clear that the Commonwealth may justify both the limitation of some rights inherent in FoRB as well as the funding for the teaching of SRI as justifiable and consistent with the provision of ordered government and the protection of the existence of the community. Indeed, it may be that this pragmatic judicial approach to s 116 allows the Commonwealth legislative and executive branches to reach a functioning outcome with the states and territories, thereby balancing the community interest against the individual right to FoRB in the provision of government school education.[31]

Implied Freedom of Political Communication

In addition to the express guarantees identified in the text of the Commonwealth Constitution, and perhaps the Tasmanian Constitution, the High Court has also found implied by the text a protection for freedom of political communication.[32] This may provide some additional scope for the protection of FoRB in government schools. In *McCloy v. New South Wales*,[33] the High Court stated the implied freedom as

> [a] qualified limitation on legislative power implied in order to ensure that the people of the Commonwealth may 'exercise a free and informed choice as electors'. It is not an absolute freedom. It may be subject to legislative restrictions serving a legitimate purpose compatible with the system of representative government for which the Constitution provides, where the extent of the burden can be justified as suitable, necessary and adequate, having regard to the purpose of those restrictions.[34]

In *Attorney-General* (SA) *v. Corporation of the City of Adelaide*,[35] the High Court ruled that

> some 'religious' speech may also be characterised as 'political' communication for the purposes of the freedom. . . . Plainly enough, preaching, canvassing, haranguing and the distribution of literature are all activities which may be undertaken in order to communicate to members of the public matters which may be directly or indirectly relevant to politics or government at the Commonwealth level. The class of communication protected by the implied freedom in practical terms is wide.[36]

The ambit of the implied freedom of political communication seemingly expands, then, so as to cover religious communication.[37]

Of course, limitations are inherent to expression for the purposes of maintaining the community's interest in being free from harmful speech. As with the rights in s 116, then, the High Court has established a three-question standard by which to test the justifiability of limitations that may be placed on the implied freedom by either the Commonwealth or the states:

> Does the law effectively burden the freedom in its terms, operation or effect?

If 'no', then the law does not exceed the implied limitation and the enquiry as to validity ends.

If 'yes' to question 1, are the purpose of the law and the means adopted to achieve that purpose legitimate, in the sense that they are compatible with the maintenance of the constitutionally prescribed system of representative government? This question reflects what is referred to in these reasons as 'compatibility testing'.

The answer to that question will be in the affirmative if the purpose of the law and the means adopted are identified and are compatible with the constitutionally prescribed system in the sense that they do not adversely impinge on the functioning of the system of representative government.

If the answer to question 2 is 'no', then the law exceeds the implied limitation and the enquiry as to validity ends.

If 'yes' to question 2, is the law reasonably appropriate and adapted to advance that legitimate object? This question involves what is referred to in these reasons as 'proportionality testing' to determine whether the restriction which the provision imposes on the freedom is justified.

The proportionality test involves consideration of the extent of the burden effected by the impugned provision on the freedom. There are three stages to the test – these are the enquiries as to whether the law is justified as suitable, necessary, and adequate in its balance in the following senses:

suitable – as having a rational connection to the purpose of the provision;

necessary – in the sense that there is no obvious and compelling alternative, reasonably practicable means of achieving the same purpose which has a less restrictive effect on the freedom;

adequate in its balance – a criterion requiring a value judgment, consistently with the limits of the judicial function, describing the balance between the importance of the purpose served by the restrictive measure and the extent of the restriction it imposes on the freedom.

If the measure does not meet these criteria of proportionality testing, then the answer to question 3 will be 'no', and the measure will exceed the implied limitation on legislative power.[38]

Neither the implied freedom, nor the standard for assessing limitations that may be placed on it has been tested in the educational setting. It may be assumed, though, that the freedom, if it does extend to religious belief and speech in the form of worship, may both protect religious speech within the government school setting and prevent proselytising as a justifiable limitation imposed on such speech.

Legislative Protections

Two forms of legislative protection exist for FoRB: bills or charters of rights enacted by the states of Victoria and Queensland and by the Australian Capital Territory, and Commonwealth and state and territory antidiscrimination legislation. While neither form of protection has been expressly applied in the educational setting, this section considers the judicial application of each to FoRB generally.

Legislative Bills or Charters of Rights

The Human Rights Act 2004 (ACT), the Charter of Human Rights and Responsibilities Act 2006 (Vic), and the Human Rights Act 2019 (Qld) protect a range of fundamental human rights,[39] including express protections for freedom of thought, conscience, religion, and belief as well as the rights of minorities to enjoy their own cultures, religions, and languages.[40] In addition to these specific religious rights, the legislation protects the rights to equality before the law,[41] life,[42] privacy,[43] peaceful assembly and association,[44] expression, taking part in public life,[45] and liberty and security of the person.[46] These rights apply only to individuals[47] and 'may be subject to reasonable limits set by . . . laws that can be demonstrably justified in a free and democratic society'.[48]

Surprisingly, citizens have made little use of the rights protected by these legislative bills or charters of rights.[49] Indeed, there is very little judicial analysis of any of the rights protected, and none at all of the FoRB protections. It remains to be seen, then, how protections might apply to FoRB generally, and in the educational setting specifically. It seems likely, though, that should they be used, the protections would provide the same sort of protections for those who seek to exercise religious freedom or to be free from proselytising in government schools as are found in s 116 of the Constitution. And, as with s 116 and the implied freedom of political communication, the rights protected by these legislated bills of rights are subject to reasonable limitations as part of ordered government.

Antidiscrimination Legislation

Commonwealth and state and territory human rights and antidiscrimination legislation provide negative protections and positive obligations in respect of equality. Commonwealth equality protections (known as 'federal discrimination law') protect every Australian against unlawful discrimination[50] pursuant to four principal enactments: the Racial

Discrimination Act 1975 (Cth), the Sex Discrimination Act 1984 (Cth), the Disability Discrimination Act 1992 (Cth), and the Age Discrimination Act 2004 (Cth).[51] While the proposed Religious Discrimination Bill 2019 (Cth) is currently before the Commonwealth Parliament,[52] federal discrimination law currently provides no positive protection against discrimination on religious grounds.

The states and territories,[53] however, provide comprehensive protection against defined grounds of discrimination, including FoRB.[54] This legislation both prohibits discrimination against individuals on the basis of a professed religious belief[55] or the lack of such a belief[56] while exempting religious orders, bodies, or institutions generally, including religious and nonreligious educational institutions, allowing for discrimination on prohibited grounds necessary for the religious purposes of the order, body, or institution.[57]

While the exemptions take on paramount importance in nongovernment religious schools in relation to the hiring of teachers,[58] in government schools the equality and nondiscrimination principle provides protection for religious expression and for the freedom from proselytising for those who hold no religion. Yet, these protections have been raised in only one case involving the government school setting. That case, *Aitken v. Victoria,* involved a challenge to the use of SRI in Victorian government schools, was ultimately unsuccessful, and provides no guidance as to the application of nondiscrimination in the government school setting.[59] The litigation did, however, prompt a change in Victorian government policy, making SRI opt-in/opt-out in after-school hours.[60]

At best, we can assume that the rights protecting discrimination on religious grounds may prevent attempts at proselytising in the government school environment. It is likely, though, that the most significant outcome of challenges pursuant to antidiscrimination legislation will be to pressure governments to alter their policies concerning SRI, as has been the case in Victoria, which no longer prohibits ethics courses for those students who opt out of optional SRI.[61]

Common Law

While the Australian common law contains no express recognition of rights,[62] canons of statutory interpretation provide limited protection through a 'common law bill of rights' and the principle of legality.[63] These norms apply to legislation that may purport to limit a specific right, such as FoRB. In assessing a statute that seeks to limit FoRB, a court will consider whether it does so in clear and unambiguous terms.[64]

In assessing ambiguous legislation, the courts favour constructions that are most in conformity with Australia's treaty obligations concerning the right in question.[65] As with constitutional and legislative protection for

FoRB, there exists no judicial analysis of the application of these canons to the government school setting. It may be assumed, then, that should the courts be called on to analyse legislation pursuant to these canons, they will do so in accordance with these general principles.

Emerging Issues

While at first blush FoRB in Australian government schools appears to be the subject of a panoply of robust constitutional, legislative, and common law protections, deeper analysis reveals two clear failings with each source. First, Australian courts have demonstrated limited interest in making broad use of these protections against legislative and executive encroachments on FoRB. The second failing follows from the first. There is no judicial analysis at all of the operation of these principles in the educational context, with the exception of the *School Chaplains* case and *Aitken v. Victoria,* both of which provide no guidance as to the application of s 116 or antidiscrimination legislation to the government school setting, respectively. As such, each of the possible sources of protection remain just that: possible sources of protection.

There is little doubt, though, that the courts will soon be called on to analyse the way in which the constitutional and legislative protections apply in the government school setting. Fairness in Religions in School (FIRIS), which operates in New South Wales and Victoria,

> is a group of parents and citizens who want education about religions in state schools that is:
>
> - Delivered by teachers employed by education departments without bias, using materials in the Australian Curriculum
> - Respectful of the secular nature of state schools
> - Consistent with Australia's multicultural society
> - Inclusive, not divisive or discriminatory
> - Committed to fostering citizenship.
>
> . . .
>
> FIRIS supports the NSW Department of Education's statement that 'schools are neutral grounds for rational discourse and objective study', and that public schools should not be arenas for 'opposing political views or ideologies'. The Department allows religious organisations to do things other organisations cannot.[66]

Similarly, the Humanist Society of Victoria (HSV) seeks 'to ensure that religious privilege/overreach/discrimination does not infringe the rights of people who do not identify as religious to be able to access, as well as to provide, spiritual care'. The HSV has been involved in litigation in Victoria and supports similar actions in New South Wales, the object of which is to require that government school chaplains may be of any or of no faith.[67]

Conclusion

As the number of challenges brought by FIRIS, HSV, and similar organisations increase, it seems less likely that governments will, in every case, seek out-of-court settlements. Rather, it seems very likely that Australian courts will be forced to make use of the constitutional and legislative protections for FoRB in the government school setting. Such guidance, so long in coming, will be welcome.

Cases

Adelaide Company of Jehovah's Witnesses Inc v. Commonwealth (1943) 67 CLR 116
Aitken v. State of Victoria [2013] VSCA 28
Aitken v. State of Victoria Department of Education & Early Childhood Development (Anti-Discrimination) [2012] VCAT 1547
APLA Ltd v. Legal Services Commissioner (NSW) (2005) 224 CLR 322
Attorney-General (SA) v. Corporation of the City of Adelaide (2013) 249 CLR 1
Attorney-General (Vic); Ex rel Black v. Commonwealth (*DOGS* Case) (1981) 146 CLR 559
Australian Capital Television v. Commonwealth (1992) 177 CLR 106
Brown v. Tasmania [2017] HCA 43
Canterbury Municipal Council v. Moslem Alawy Society Ltd (1985) 1 NSWLR 525
Christian Youth Camps Ltd v. Cobaw Community Health Service Ltd [2014] VSCA 75
Church of the New Faith v. Commissioner of Pay-Roll Tax (Vic) (1983) 154 CLR 120
Clubb v. Edwards; Preston v. Avery [2019] HCA 11
Corneloup v. Launceston City Council [2016] FCA 974
Cottrell v. Ross [2019] VCC 2142
Grace Bible Church v. Reedman (1984) 36 SASR 376
Hogan v. Hinch (2011) 243 CLR 506
Kapoor v. Monash University (2001) 4 VR 483
Kruger v. Commonwealth (1997) 190 CLR 1
Krygger v. Williams (1912) 15 CLR 366
Lange v. Australian Broadcasting Corporation (1997) 189 CLR 520
Lemon v. Kurtzman, 403 U.S. 602 (1971)
McCloy v. New South Wales [2015] HCA 34

Minister for Immigration and Ethnics Affairs v. Teoh (1995) 183 CLR 273
Nationwide News Pty Ltd v. Wills (1992) 177 CLR 1
OV & OW [2010] NSWCA 155
Re Bolton; Ex Parte Douglas Beane (1987) 162 CLR 514
Stephens v. West Australian Newspapers Ltd (1994) 182 CLR 211
Theophanous v. Herald & Weekly Times Ltd (1994) 182 CLR 104
Unions NSW v. State of New South Wales (2013) 88 ALJR 227
Williams v. Commonwealth (*'School Chaplains Case'*) (2012) 248 CLR 156

Notes

* Some of the material in this chapter has appeared earlier in the following: Paul Babie and Benjamin Mylius, 'The Future of Religious Freedom in Australian Schools', *International Journal of Education Reform*, 21(2012), 173; Paul Babie and Benjamin Mylius, 'Religious Education in Australia', in Derek Davis and Elena Miroshnikova (eds.), *The Routledge International Handbook of Religious Education* (London: Routledge, 2013), 23–31; Paul Babie and Benjamin Mylius, 'The Constitution, Religious Education, and the Future of Religious Freedom in Australian Schools', in Charles J. Russo (ed.), *International Perspectives on Education, Religion and Law* (London: Routledge, 2014), 97–110; Paul Babie, 'The Concept of Freedom of Religion in the Australian Constitution: A Study in Legislative-Judicial Cooperative Innovation', *Quaderni di diritto e politica ecclesiastica* (2018), 259; Paul T. Babie, 'The Ethos of Protection for Freedom of Religion or Belief in Australian Law', *University of Western Australia Law Review*, 47(2020), 64.

1. In Australia, 'public education' is referred to as 'government schools'.
2. Variously referred to as 'independent', 'religious', 'church' or 'private', depending on the particular school.
3. 'Primary' schools correspond approximately to US elementary schools, typically catering for students from Reception to Grade 6 or 7.
4. Secondary schools typically cater for students from Grade 7 or 8 to Grade 12 or 13.
5. The South Australian legislation, which is representative of the state legislation, is the Education Act 1972 (SA) and Education Regulations 2012 (SA).
6. The Commonwealth legislation which applies to all states is the Australian Education Act 2013 (Cth) and the Australian Education Regulation 2013 (Cth). The South Australian legislation is the Education Act 1972 (SA) and Education Regulations 2012 (SA). See also Australian Government Department of Education, Skills and Employment, *How Are Schools Funded in Australia?* Retrieved from www.education.gov.au/how-are-schools-funded-australia; Australian Government Department of Education, Skills and Employment, *Australian Education Act 2013*. Retrieved from www.education.gov.au/australian-education-act-2013.
7. Australian Government Department of Education, Skills and Employment, *How Are Schools Funded in Australia?*
8. Ibid.
9. Ibid.
10. Emma Rowe, 'Religion in Australian Schools: An Historical and Contemporary Debate', *The Conversation*, August 24, 2017. Retrieved from https://theconversation.com/religion-in-australian-schools-an-historical-and-contemporary-debate-82439.

11. See, e.g., Education and Training Reform Act 2006 (Vic) s 2.2.11. See also Anna Halafoff, *The Multifaith Movement: Global Risks and Cosmopolitan Solutions* (Dordrecht: Springer, 2013), 137–161; Renae Barker, 'Explainer: What the Law Says About Religious Instruction in Schools', *The Conversation*, March 3, 2014. Retrieved from https://theconversation.com/explainer-what-the-law-says-about-religious-instruction-in-schools-23608?; Anna Halafoff and Gary Bouma, 'It's Time to Replace Religious Instruction with Worldviews Education in Australian Schools', *Multifaith Education Australia: Resources for SRI Educators*, October 1, 2019. Retrieved from www.multifaitheducation.com.au/2019/10/01/op-ed-its-time-to-replace-religious-instruction-with-worldviews-education-in-australian-schools/#more-1174.
12. Relevant legislation in the states and territories includes the Education Act 2004 (ACT), the Education Act 1990 (NSW), the Education Act *2015* (NT), the Education (General Provisions) Act 2006 (Qld), the Education Act 2016 (Tas), the Education and Training Reform Act 2006 (Vic), and the School Education Act 1999 (WA).
13. See Department of Education and Children's Services, South Australian Government, *Administrative Instructions and Guidelines: Section 3: Religious Activities in Government Schools*, 2013. Retrieved from www.saasso.asn.au/wp-content/uploads/2013/04/Administrative-Instructions-and-Guidelines-Section-3.pdf.
14. *Education Regulations 2012* (SA) Pt 7.
15. Ibid.
16. Ibid.
17. Ibid.
18. Rowe, 'Religion in Australian Schools'.
19. *Attorney-General* (Vic); *Ex rel Black v. Commonwealth* (*DOGS* Case) (1981) 146 CLR 559, 605.
20. Tasmanian Constitutional Law Reform Project, *The Current Constitution*, 39–40. Retrieved from https://wikis.utas.edu.au/display/TCLRP/The+Current+Constitution#FootnoteMarker39-0.
21. *Corneloup v. Launceston City Council* [2016] FCA 074, [38].
22. *Attorney-General* (Vic); *Ex rel Black v. Commonwealth* (*DOGS* Case) (1981) 146 CLR 559.
23. *Williams v. Commonwealth* (*School Chaplains* Case) (2012) 248 CLR 156.
24. Ibid., 110.
25. Tom Frame, *Church and State: Australia's Imaginary Wall* (Kensington: UNSW Press, 2006), 7–9, 103–104; Peter Macfarlane and Simon Fisher, *Churches, Clergy and the Law* (Sydney: Federation Press, 1996), 32 (citing *Lemon v. Kurtzman*, 403 U.S. 602, 613 (1971)).
26. *Krygger v. Williams* (1912) 15 CLR 366; *Adelaide Company of Jehovah's Witnesses Inc v. Commonwealth* (1943) 67 CLR 116; *Kruger v. Commonwealth* (1997) 190 CLR 1.
27. *Krygger v. Williams* (1912) 15 CLR 366, 369.
28. Ibid.
29. *Church of the New Faith v. Commissioner of Pay-Roll Tax (Vic)* (1983) 154 CLR 120.
30. *Adelaide Co of Jehovah's Witnesses Inc v. The Commonwealth* (1943) 67 CLR 116, 131–132.
31. See Laura Grenfell and Sarah Moulds, 'The Role of Committees in Rights Protection in Federal and State Parliaments in Australia', *University of New South Wales Law Journal*, 41(2018), 40.
32. *Nationwide News Pty Ltd v. Wills* (1992) 177 CLR 1; *Australian Capital Television v. Commonwealth* (1992) 177 CLR 106; *Theophanous v. Herald & Weekly Times*

Ltd (1994) 182 CLR 104; *Stephens v. West Australian Newspapers Ltd* (1994) 182 CLR 211; *Lange v. Australian Broadcasting Corporation* (1997) 189 CLR 520; *APLA Ltd v. Legal Services Commissioner* (NSW) (2005) 224 CLR 322; *Hogan v. Hinch* (2011) 243 CLR 506; *Unions NSW v. State of New South Wales* (2013) 88 ALJR 227; *Attorney-General (SA) v. Corporation of the City of Adelaide* (2013) 249 CLR 1; *McCloy v. New South Wales* [2015] HCA 34; *Brown v. Tasmania* [2017] HCA 43; *Clubb v. Edwards; Preston v. Avery* [2019] HCA 11.

33. *McCloy v. New South Wales* [2015] HCA 34, [2].
34. Ibid. (footnotes and citations omitted).
35. *Attorney-General (SA) v. Corporation of the City of Adelaide* (2013) 249 CLR 1, 43–44, 73–74.
36. Ibid.
37. See also *Clubb v. Edwards; Preston v. Avery* [2019] HCA 11.
38. *McCloy v. New South Wales* [2015] HCA 34.
39. See Andrew Byrnes, Hilary Charlesworth and Gabrielle McKinnon, *Bills of Rights in Australia: History, Politics and Law* (Sydney: UNSW Press, 2008), 109–114; Carolyn Evans and Simon Evans, *Australian Bills of Rights: The Law of the Victorian Charter and ACT Human Rights Act* (Chatswood: LexisNexis, 2008); Matthew Groves and Colin Campbell (eds.), *Australian Charters of Rights a Decade On* (Leichhardt: Federation Press, 2017).
40. See, e.g., Human Rights Act 2004 (ACT) ss 14 and 27.
41. Ibid., s 8.
42. Ibid., s 9.
43. Ibid., s 12.
44. Ibid., s 15.
45. Ibid., s 16.
46. Ibid., s 18.
47. Ibid., s 6.
48. Ibid., s 28(1).
49. Nicholas Aroney, Joel Harrison and Paul Babie, 'Religious Freedom Under the Charters', in Matthew Groves and Colin Campbell (eds.), *Australian Charters of Rights a Decade On* (Leichhardt: Federation Press, 2017), 120. This is changing; see *Cottrell v. Ross* [2019] VCC 2142; Lisa Martin, 'Blair Cottrell Moves to Appeal Conviction Over Mock Beheading Video', *The Guardian*, July 10, 2019. Retrieved from www.theguardian.com/australia-news/2019/jul/10/blair-cottrell-moves-to-appeal-conviction-over-mock-beheading-video.
50. Australian Human Rights Commission, *Federal Discrimination Law* (Australian Human Rights Commission, 2016). Retrieved from https://humanrights.gov.au/our-work/legal/publications/federal-discrimination-law-2016.
51. To this list could be added a fifth: the Fair Work Act 2009 (Cth).
52. See Australian Government, Attorney-General's Department, *Religious Freedom Bills – Second Exposure Drafts*. Retrieved from www.ag.gov.au/Consultations/Pages/religious-freedom-bills-second-exposure-drafts.aspx.
53. Anti-Discrimination Act 1977 (NSW), Equal Opportunity Act 1984 (SA), Equal Opportunity Act 1984 (WA), Discrimination Act 1991 (ACT), Anti-Discrimination Act 1991 (Qld), Anti-Discrimination Act 1996 (NT), Anti-Discrimination Act 1998 (Tas), Equal Opportunity Act 2010 (Vic).
54. A list of the prohibited grounds, representative of State and Territory regimes, found in the Equal Opportunity Act 2010 (Vic) s 6, includes age, breastfeeding, employment activity, gender identity, disability, industrial activity, lawful sexual activity, marital status, parental status or status as a carer, physical features, political belief or activity, pregnancy, race, religious belief or activity, sex, sexual orientation, an expunged homosexual conviction, and personal

association (whether as a relative or otherwise) with a person who is identified by reference to any of the these attributes.

55. See, e.g., Equal Opportunity Act 2010 (Vic) s 6(1)(n). In Victoria, discrimination on the basis of a characteristic of a person's religion is also prohibited: Equal Opportunity Act 2010 (Vic) s 7(2)(b), (c); *Kapoor v. Monash University* (2001) 4 VR 483.
56. See, e.g., Equal Opportunity Act 2010 (Vic) s 4(1).
57. See, e.g., Anti-Discrimination Act 1977 (NSW) ss 31A, 31K, 46A, 49ZO, and 56; Sex Discrimination Act 1984 (Cth) ss 37, 38; Equal Opportunity Act 1984 (SA) ss 50, 85ZM; Equal Opportunity Act 1984 (WA) ss 66(1), 72, 73; Discrimination Act 1991 (ACT) ss 32, 33, 46; Anti-Discrimination Act 1991 (Qld) ss 41(a), 90, 109; Anti-Discrimination Act 1996 (NT) ss 30(2), 37A, 51; Anti-Discrimination Act 1998 (Tas) ss 51, 52; Equal Opportunity Act 2010 (Vic) ss 39, 81, 82, 83, 84. See also Fair Work Act 2009 (Cth) ss 153(2)(c), 195(2)(c), 351(2)(c), 772(2)(c); Sex Discrimination Act 1984 (Cth) s 37(a), (b), (d), and 38.
58. For the judicial treatment of the exemptions as concerns FoRB, see *OV & OW* [2010] NSWCA 155; *Christian Youth Camps Ltd v. Cobaw Community Health Service Ltd* [2014] VSCA 75.
59. In a challenge to SRI in Victorian government schools, the Victorian Civil and Administrative Tribunal (VCAT) found no discrimination: see *Aitken v. State of Victoria Department of Education & Early Childhood Development (Anti-Discrimination)* [2012] VCAT 1547. An appeal against this decision was dismissed by the Supreme Court of Victoria Court of Appeal: *Aitken v. State of Victoria* [2013] VSCA 28 (February 22, 2013). Another challenge was settled before it was decided by the VCAT: see Joe Sehee, 'HSV Plays a Part in Successful Chaplaincy Challenge', *Humanists Victoria*, April 30, 2019. Retrieved from https://vichumanist.org.au/practical-humanism/hsv-chaplaincy-challenge/. For the background to some of the challenges which have been mounted, but not judicially resolved, see Humanists Victoria, *Special Religious Instruction Campaign Chronology*. Retrieved from https://vichumanist.org.au/projects/religious-instruction/special-religious-instruction-chronology/.
60. Sehee, 'HSV Plays a Part in Successful Chaplaincy Challenge'.
61. Ibid.
62. *Grace Bible Church v. Reedman* (1984) 36 SASR 376.
63. James Spiegelman, *The Common Law Bill of Rights*, speech delivered at McPherson Lectures on Statutory Interpretation and Human Rights, University of Queensland, March 10, 2008.
64. *Church of the New Faith v. Commissioner for Pay-roll Tax (Vic)* (1983) 154 CLR 120, 130; *Re Bolton; Ex Parte Douglas Beane* (1987) 162 CLR 514, 523; Canterbury *Municipal Council v. Moslem Alawy Society Ltd* (1985) 1 NSWLR 525, 544.
65. *Minister for Immigration and Ethnics Affairs v. Teoh* (1995) 183 CLR 273, 287.
66. Fairness in Religions in School, *Who Is FIRIS?* Retrieved from www.religionsinschool.com.
67. Sehee, 'HSV Plays a Part in Successful Chaplaincy Challenge'.

2 Religion and the Public School Curriculum in Brazil

Nina Beatriz Stocco Ranieri

Introduction

Compulsory schooling, a phenomenon of rapid and widespread global implementation coordinated by the Nation States from the 19th century onwards, constituted a true revolution in the way children were educated. Until then, families decided what to teach their children, how to teach them, and who would do the teaching; this included religious education. However, starting in the 19th century, the tasks associated with educating children were delegated to strangers chosen neither by the students nor by their parents. The creation of secular schools, as opposed to religious schools, is one of the manifestations of this irreversible movement in education along with the nascent tensions that emerged between families and schools, between the church and national states (Meyer et al., 1992). The situation was, and remains, no different in Brazil.

Since the proclamation of the Brazilian Republic in 1889, legal debates on religion have included discussions on secularism, compulsory school enrollment, and public funding of confessional educational institutions under the strong influence of the Catholic Church. The adoption of Catholicism as the official religion of the ancient Brazilian Empire (1822–1889) and the consequent catechization promoted by the state apparatus, through public primary education, until the first Republican Constitution of 1891 are striking examples of the close relations between church and state.

In republican Brazil, the provision of religious education for optional enrollment in public schools was a constant element in the Federal Constitutions of 1931, 1946, 1967, and 1988. Along this route, from the end of the 19th century until the 21st century, attention is drawn to the fact that religious education was included in the curriculum of public schools due to pressure from groups outside the educational field, such as the Catholic Church, religious entities and conservative wings, or society based on political-ideological arguments (Cunha, 2007; Cury, 2004). On the other hand, during all of Brazil's Constituent Assemblies, from 1823 to 1988, in debates on freedom of education, the Catholic Church remained a traditional defender of the priority of families in the choice of education their children would receive.

In the most recent round of the struggles between the church and the laic state, the Supreme Court of Brazil – STF (Supremo Tribunal Federal – STF]), in the Direct Action of Unconstitutionality (Ação Direta de Inconstitucionalidade [ADI]) no. 4439, decided in 2017 that optional religious education in public schools could be confessional, meaning that classes are designed to teach the dogma of specific religions. As a result, families will be able to decide again which religion should be taught at public schools and by whom. In this case, what was at stake was the constitutionality of the teaching of a specific religion in light of the secularity of the state, the freedom of religion, the freedom to learn, and academic freedom (Federal Constitution of 1988, arts. 206, 207, 208).

Against this background, this chapter analyses the Supreme Court of Brazil's decision on religious education in public schools because the effects and impact of its order are not yet fully understood. More specifically, the chapter examines the legal foundation for education and religion in Brazil; the protection for freedom of religion or belief in education the nation affords, with a focus on religious education; and emerging issues in this regard. The chapter rounds out with a conclusion.

The Legal Foundation for Education and Religion

Brazil is a federal country whose public school system operates under a very complex set of state and local regulations and federal laws. At the federal level, the broad contours of the public educational systems and curricula are outlined in the Federal Constitution of 1988, the National Education Act of 1996 (NEA [BR]) (Law 9,396), and the National Education Plan of 2014 (NEP [BR]).

At the state and local levels, state constitutions along with state and municipal statutes regulate administrative, financial, and all other matters pertaining to the pedagogical activities of their respective schools, including regional and local curricula. As such, the federal government retains a broad legislative educational authority while the states and local governments are responsible for the direct execution of providing basic public education for children. Paradoxically, while Brazil's national education system is largely decentralized in its responsibilities, it remains very centralized when it comes to education policy.

Basic education in Brazil is compulsory and free, including early childhood, primary, and secondary school. Religious education is part of primary education, as set by the Federal Constitution, with optional enrollment during the normal school hours respecting the cultural and religious diversity of Brazil while prohibiting any forms of proselytizing as identified in the NEA of 1996.

The Federal Constitution of 1988 guarantees freedom of religion as a value to be preserved and protected, making freedom of belief and freedom of worship fundamental rights (art. 5, VI) in Brazil. Freedom of belief includes the choice of religion, the conversion to another religion, and the right to no religion at all. Freedom of worship includes the freedom to pray and practice liturgical rites at home or in public, as well as the protection of places of worship. Moreover, federal, state, and local governments are prohibited from hindering the exercise of religious worship services (art. 19, I). These provisions further guarantee not being deprived of other rights because of one's religious conviction, including the right to refuse to be subjected to specified impositions that contradict the religious or philosophical convictions of individuals or groups (art. 5, VIII).

Freedom of religion further guarantees other benefits on the part of the state, such as religious assistance in civil and military entities (art. 5°, VII). Thus, the secularity of the state is not to be confused with state indifference in terms of religion, as already decided by the STF in case no. 389/2010. The collaboration between the church and the state also takes place through the civil recognition of religious marriages (art. 226, § 3). In addition, the protection of religious denominations is guaranteed by tax immunity on patrimony, revenue, and services of temples (art. 150, VI, "b"). Finally, in education, the Constitution allows the allocation of public resources to nonprofit confessional schools.

The Protection for Freedom of Religion or Belief in Education

The protection of freedom of religion or belief in education is guaranteed by Article 210, § 1° of the Federal Constitution of 1988: "Religious education, with optional enrolment, will be the discipline of the normal hours of public elementary schools." The NEA of 1996 (art. 33) prohibits, according to the constitutional guideline of secularism, any form of proselytizing in the offering of religious education. This section also attributes to the state and municipal education systems the competence to definition of content as well as for identifying the qualification and admission of teachers: "Religious education, with optional enrolment, is an integral part of the basic education of the citizen and constitutes a discipline in regular school hours of public primary schools, guaranteeing respect for Brazil's religious diversity, rejecting any form of proselytizing."

The rule, therefore, is that of mandatory provision and optional enrollment, only for public schools and only in elementary education, a period when the development of children is driven by their psychological needs to achieve skills and autonomy for living as adults in a free society. At the same time, the constitutional and legal norms oblige teachers to respect religious differences, religious sentiments, freedom of conscience, belief, expression, and worship, recognizing equality and the dignity of every human person. The STF's decision in the case of religious education, addressed below, guarantees that the dogmas of faith are considered the core of the concept of religious education.

Judicial Analysis of the Freedom of Religion or Belief in Education

Prior to the ADI 4,439 of 2017, the STF examined two cases related to the secularity of the state that significantly reaffirmed the prevalence of secularity of the state in relation to religion neutrality. In the decriminalization of abortion of anencephalic fetuses in a claim of non-compliance with a fundamental precept ADPF 54–DF (Ação de Descumprimento de Preceito Fundamental [ADPF]), the Court ruled: "Brazil is a secular republic, appearing absolutely neutral as to religions."[1]

Next, in ADI 2,566–0 DF, a dispute over religious radio broadcasting, in which the scope of freedom of expression was examined in light of freedom of belief, the Court decided that the state must be indifferent to religious ideas that may eventually be preached by any confessional group because it is not lawful for the government to interdict or censor them.[2] As to religious education, ADI 4,439 was the first case the Court reviewed on this issue, representing a turning point in the role of the state from neutral to active. This was surprising because it was state officials who signed an agreement with the Catholic Church for religious education in public schools.

The Case of Religious Education – ADI 4,439: Secularity and Freedom of Education

The main point discussed in ADI 4,439 was the role of the state in the religious education of children who attended public schools. The action started with the Attorney General's (Procurador Geral da República – PGR) questioning the constitutionality of paragraph 1°, of art. 11 of Decree no. 7,107/2010. This paragraph expresses the ratification, by the National Congress, of the Concordat celebrated between Brazil and the Holy See in 2008, as follows: "§ 1°. Religious, Catholic and other religious denominations, with optional enrolment, constitute a discipline in the normal hours of public elementary schools, ensuring respect for the religious cultural diversity of Brazil, in accordance with the Constitution and other current laws, without any form of discrimination."

As an education specialist noted, this paragraph expresses what had never happened, not even during the Empire, when Catholicism was the official religion. Further, such a situation seemed impossible because in 1889, the Republican regime had abolished the state/church relationship: "the worldwide leadership of the Catholic Church managed for the Brazilian State to sign a treaty with it that guarantees it special privileges, in political, fiscal, labour, educational and other terms" (Cunha, 2014, 17).

According to the PGR, public schools are forbidden from becoming to become spaces for catechesis and religious proselytizing, whether of Catholicism or of any other denomination. Thus, secularism imposes on the state a neutral stance in relation to the different religious conceptions present in society, being forbidden to take sides in matters of faith, favor, or embracing of any belief or group of beliefs. For this reason, according to the PGR, the only way to make the state's secularity viable with regard to religious education in public schools would be through the adoption of a non-denominational model, which included doctrines and social dimensions of different religions. Of the 18 entities who submitted amici curiae – literally "friends of the court" who had an interest in the outcome but were not parties to the lawsuit – only seven spoke out against the PGR's request (STF, 2017).

Due to the possible repercussions of the issue, in June 2015, before the trial, a public hearing was held in which about 30 religious and civil society entities participated; of these, 23 spoke out against religious confessional education in the public school system and eight in favor (Brazilian Supreme Court, STF, Public Hearing, 2017b). In September 2017, the Court, by a majority of 6–5, ruled on the constitutionality of confessional religious education, finding that religious education in public schools could be denominational in nature despite Brazil's secular republican tradition.

The arguments for and against used by the members of the Court were based on the same articles of the Federal Constitution of 1988, namely: 5, VI and VIII; 19, I; and 210, paragraph 1, involving the harmonization of constitutional norms related to religious education, freedom of religion, and the principle of secularity of the state. Rather than engage in a lengthy discussion of the different approaches to these articles of the Constitution, suffice it to say that two major camps emerge in the Supreme Court: the secularists (5 dissent votes) and the confessionists (6 winning votes).

Secularists maintain that religious education in public establishments cannot avoid being confessional in light of Brazil's republican tradition. In support of this thesis, the secularists argued that in the Federal Constitution of 1988, the principles of equality, freedom of religion, and freedom of worship are guaranteed among fundamental rights (art. 5, VI and VIII).

According to the arguments raised by secularists, the request for rejecting the Concordat as unconstitutional should have prevailed because (1) in view of the secularity of the state, public spaces cannot be appropriated by religious entities; (2) the ideological link between religious teachers and religious institutions will establish illegal differences between lay and religious teachers in the public network; and (3) fostering tolerance and respect for differences requires plural religious training, in which the student has access not only to their own but also to the most diverse religious manifestations. Ergo, the secularists made it clear that religious education in public schools could only be of a non-denominational nature, cannot be attached to any religion, and cannot be designed to convey dogmas and beliefs of specific religions (STF, 2017).

On the other hand, confessionists maintain that the Constitution guarantees the compatibility of the secularity of the state with religious freedom for three main reasons. First, the Court explained that this is so because religious education is an individual subjective right, not a duty imposed by the state. Second, the Court pointed out that the constitutional text guarantees voluntary enrollment for religious education, which in turn ensures freedom of religion while preventing the government from creating its own religious education, with a specific content for the discipline. Third, the Court observed that it remains clear that the state is not only obliged to abstain and not interfere in the teaching of a certain belief, but also to guarantee the necessary means for religious education in public schools, in the broadest way, without discrimination, due to the freedom of all students to receive religious education if they wish.

Further, the majority of the Court stated that the principle of secularism in Brazil is related to the view of invoking God in the preamble to the Federal Constitution of 1988 ("God be praised") and in other constitu tional provisions such as art. 210, § 1°, which would effectively allow religious proselytizing; art. 226, § 2, which provides for religious marriage with civil effects; and art. 5, VII, which provides for religious assistance in official entities. Besides, neutrality in the provision of religious education is impossible because the dogmas of faith constitute its core, with their own structuring dogmas, postulates, methods, and conclusions. In other words, neutrality in religious education does not exist; what must exist is respect for differences in religious education. This core is fully protected by the freedom of belief of each one of the diverse religious denominations in Brazil. According to this perspective, then, in respect to the uniqueness of each religion, there is no way to confuse religious teaching with the study of history, philosophy, and/or science of religions (STF, 2017).

> It is in this context that the prediction of religious education must be understood: it is about taking advantage of the physical structure of public schools – as is widely available in the public space of hospitals and prisons, which are already used in partnerships – to ensure the free dissemination of beliefs and ideals of a religious nature to

those who profess the same faith and voluntarily adhere to the discipline, maintaining the neutrality of the State in this matter.[3]

In short, according to the winning arguments of the confessionists, (1) religious education in public schools as an elementary school subject for students aged 9 to 14 must be strictly optional and offered during normal school hours, and (2) the education systems may hire representatives of religions to teach the classes.

As a conclusion, one cannot fail to consider, as does Cunha (2014), that the use of public schools for the imposition of religious and political-ideological contents was a constant in Brazilian history, resulting from the weak autonomy of the educational field. This was also evident when the legislative decree that approved the Brazil–Vatican Concordat in 2010 was approved by the Chamber of Deputies with a 66% vote of its members, including evangelical deputies.

The fact that the Catholic Church was privileged was compensated by the future approval of the project of the General Law of Religions (Bill of the House No. 160/2009 [BR]), in which the mention of the Catholic Church was replaced by the expression "religious institutions." As a result of the tense correlation of forces, the Chamber of Deputies adopted a contradictory procedure: it approved the Concordat benefiting the Catholic Church and the General Law of Religions benefiting the evangelical churches. In so doing, the Chamber of Deputies approved confessional religious education and then permitted interfaith religious education. However, unlike the Concordat, which passed the legislative decree at an accelerated pace, the bill that would have granted evangelical churches the same political status as the Catholic Church was abandoned to the vicissitudes of ordinary procedure, being filed by the Senate, without appreciation, at the end of December 2018.

Emerging Issues

The STF's decision created practical problems for the implementation of religious confessional teaching in state and municipal educational systems. Until 2017, the year in which the National Education Council (Conselho Nacional de Educação [CNE]) approved the Common National Curriculum Base (Base Nacional Comum Curricular [BNCC])[4] in compliance with Article 26 of the NEA of 1996, religious education was regulated by the education systems (CNE Resolutions CEB n° 04/2010 and n° 07/2010).

With BNCC, religious education began to develop curricular requirements, initial and continuing training courses, and didactic-pedagogical materials contributing to the construction of the subject matter without confessional content. According to the Common National Curricular Base: Religious Education Area (CNE, 2018), "an intercultural and ethical change of theoretical and pedagogical foundations of religious education, because it favours or recognizes and respects the histories, memories, beliefs, convictions and values of different cultures, religious traditions and philosophies of life."[5] Evidently, a decision by the STF altered the view of a common national basis for the discipline of religion, given its confessional character. On the other hand, although it is not mandatory, religious education is a specific discipline of elementary education, being certain that there is no curricular component without defined content and without permission for teachers.

Experts have foreseen other problems such as how to avoid religious propaganda during classes; the secondary treatment minority religions, such as the Afro-Brazilian ones, receive; the growth of religious intolerance in schools; and the lack of affording teachers the ability to teach religion (Fischmann, 2012Caputo, 2012). Moreover, religious diversity can be compromised in a mostly Christian country such as Brazil, particularly by sectarianism.

On the other hand, the STF decision does not prohibit non-confessional religious education. As such, this raises a question about how equal conditions and access to religious education can be guaranteed for all. The organization of school hours and spaces need to offer different religious education orientations as well as activities for those who do not attend religious education classes. Even more serious is the intertwining of religious confessional teaching with other curricular content. In the area of science, for example, the attempts to impose creationism to the detriment of evolution, or the prohibition of sex education in basic education, are problematic.

Another important aspect is financing: the STF's decision does not indicate whether the funds will be public, shared, entirely private, or assumed by religious entities. Most Brazilian municipalities with up to 5,000 inhabitants (about 4,900 towns) are dependent financially on federal or state public funds, face scarcity of resources, have low administrative capacities, and encounter difficulties in formulating and implementing social programs, including education (FIRJAN, 2018). If religious education must be taught by members of students' own religious confession, one possible alternative would be the public call for public services, established by the Public Administration and Civil Society Organizations Voluntary Partnership Act of 2015 (Law 13.204) under a legal regime of mutual cooperation, and, preferably, without any costs to the federal government.

Conclusion

Confessional religious education is a controversial and recurring issue considering that the history of education in Brazil, from the Empire to the Republic, consisted of regular, habitual practices that were only restricted after the 1980s in different ways and for different reasons. Under the Federal Constitution of 1988 and NEA of 1996, the STF resolved whether considering confessional religious education can be offered in public schools without an affront to the secularity of the state (ADI 4,439).

The narrow winning margin standout of one vote in that case confirms its complexity. Another point to be emphasized is the use of the same articles of the Constitution to justify, in the defeated and winning votes, the unconstitutionality and constitutionality of religious confessional teaching, thereby demonstrating that the debate developed mainly on the ideological level. From this point of view, Brazil will face difficult cases in the form of litigation that cannot be subject to a clear rule of law and therefore allow greater discretion for judges to devise legal solutions for the social problems at hand.

The STF's jurisprudence on the right to education in Brazil took shape from the 2000s onwards. Until then, very few cases before the Court directly demanded protection for the individual or collective exercise of the right to education except in cases related to payment of enrollment fees.

After 2010, issues related to the financing and expansion of fundamental education by the states and municipalities (Judicial Appeal in Extraordinary Appeal 410,715–5) were litigated. Subsequently, the Court influenced the nature of federal legislation (The Federal Universities' Quotas Law [BR] Law 12,711/2012) governing the adoption of affirmative action by federal universities after the judgment of the ADPF no. 186/DF and Extraordinary Appeal (Recurso Extraordinário [RE]) no. 597.285 / RS.

As noted (Ranieri, 2008, 2009a, 2009b), some hypotheses may explain the phenomenon of this significant increase in legal actions relative to education in Brazil. Key aspects here were the strengthening of the protection of the right to education, with legal instruments appropriate to its implementation and characterization of elementary education as a public subjective right; the expansion of the activity of the Public Ministry by the Federal Constitution of 1988 (arts. 127 and 129), highlighting the defense of unavailable social and individual interests; and the consolidation of public civil action to defend collective interests in education.

The examples above are expressive. They demonstrate, in the first place, that the Supreme Court plays an important role in education in policing the boundaries of educational authority and obligation. Second, these examples reveal that the constitutional interpretations point to new ways of ensuring fundamental rights in addition to promoting their strengthening and influencing the legislature. Third, these examples reveal that after the year 2000, the participation of the STF in the realization of the right to education was more efficient than relying on legislature, a fact also borne out by thematic researches related to educational legislative production between 1995 and 2010.

Besides, until 2010 litigation before the STF related to the right to education prevailed, illustrating the importance of the material benefits to be guaranteed by and to the state, such as equal conditions for access and permanence in school, among others provided for in Brazilian legislation. The legal issues and circumstances associated with religious confessional teaching are entirely different, though. The litigation on religious schooling was about demands concerning rights in education basically involving controversies related to the scope and limits of the relationship between the state and individual freedom in education. With the decision of the STF, the limits of private autonomy vis-à-vis the state were expanded in the field of education and, as a result, Brazil adopted a new approach in education-related jurisprudence.

In the minefield of religion, though, it will not be easy for public educational systems to regulate the activities of public schools. Thus, the effects of the STF's decision are yet to be assessed and remain to be seen.

References

Brazilian Federal Constitution of 1891. Retrieved from www.planalto.gov.br/ccivil_03/constituicao/Constituicao91.htm

Brazilian Federal Constitution of 1988. Retrieved from www.stf.jus.br/arquivo/cms/legislacaoConstituicao/anexo/Brazil_federal_constitution.pdf

Brazilian Supreme Court. (2017a). *The ADI 4,439's Contests of Decision.* Retrieved from http://redir.stf.jus.br/paginadorpub/paginador.jsp?docTP=TP&docID=15085915redic.stf.jus.br

Brazilian Supreme Court. (2017b). *The Contents of the Public Hearing.* Retrieved from www.stf.jus.br/portal/cms/verNoticiaDetalhe.asp?idConteudo=293563

Brazil-Vatican Concordat of 2010. Decree no. 7,107/2010. Retrieved from www.planalto.gov.br/ccivil_03/_Ato2007-2010/2010/Decreto/D7107.htm

Caputo, Stela Guedes. (2012). *Educação nos terreiros e como a escola se relaciona com crianças de candomblé.* Rio de Janeiro: Pallas Editora.

Conselho Nacional De Educação – CNE. (2010). *Decisions CNE/CEB n° 04/2010 and 07/2010.* Brazilian Ministry of Education. Retrieved from http://portal.mec.gov.br/dmdocuments/rceb004_10.pdf

Conselho Nacional De Educação – CNE. (2018). *Common National Curricular Base: Religious Education Area.* Retrieved from http://basenacionalcomum.mec.gov.br/abase/#fundamental/a-area-de-ensino-religioso

Cunha, Luiz Antônio. (2007, Maio–Ago). Sintonia oscilante: Religião, moral e civismo no Brasil. 1931/1997. *Cadernos de Pesquisa,* 37(131). Retrieved from www.scielo.br/pdf/cp/v37n131/a0437131.pdf

Cunha, Luiz Antônio. (2014). A laicidade em disputa: Religião, moral e civismo na educação brasileira. *Revista Teias,* 15(36), 5–25. Estado, Educação Pública e Laicidade. Retrieved from www.e-publicacoes.uerj.br/index.php/revistateias/article/view/24381/17359

Cury, Carlos Roberto Jamil. (2004). Ensino religioso na escola pública: O retorno de uma polêmica recorrente. *Revista Brasileira de Educação Set /Out /Nov /Dez*, 27, 183–191. Retrieved from www.scielo.br/pdf/rbedu/n27/n27a12.pdf

FIRJAN – Federação das Indústrias do Rio de Janeiro. (2018). *Indice Firjan de Desenvolvimento Municipal. IFDM 2018. Ano base 2016.* Retrieved from http://publicacoes.firjan.org.br/ifdm2018/18/

Fischmann, Roseli. (2012, January–April). *Inconstitucional: O ensino religioso em escolas públicas em questão.* Notandum 28. CEMOrOC-Feusp/IJI-Universidade do Porto. Retrieved from www.hottopos.com/notand28/05-16Roseli.pdf

Meyer, John W., Francisco O. Ramirez and Yasemin Nuhoḡlu Soysal. (1992, April). World Expansion of Mass Education, 1870–1980. *Sociology of Education*, 65(2), 128–149. American Sociological Association. Retrieved from www.jstor.org/stable/2112679

National Education Act of 1996. Law 9,396. NEA. Brazil. Retrieved from www.planalto.gov.br/ccivil_03/Leis/L9394.htm

Public Administration and Civil Society Organizations Voluntary Partnership Act of 2015. Law 13.204. Retrieved from www.planalto.gov.br/ccivil_03/_Ato2015-2018/2015/Lei/L13204.htm

Ranieri, Nina. (2008). The States and the Right to Education in the Constitution of 1988: Comments on Jurisprudence in the Federal Supreme Court by Alexandre de Moraes. In: *Os 20 Anos da Constituição da República Federativa do Brasil.* São Paulo: Atlas, p. 183.

Ranieri, Nina. (2009a). *The Democratic State of Law and the Need to Prepare the Person for the Exercise of Citizenship, Though Education.* Habilitation presented at the Faculty of Law of the University of São Paulo, São Paulo.

Ranieri, Nina. (2009b). The Federal Supreme Court and International Education Law. In: Alberto do Amaral Junior e Liliana Jubilut (orgs.), *O STF e o Direito Internacional dos Direitos Humanos.* São Paulo: Quartier Latin.

Notes

1. http://redir.stf.jus.br/paginadorpub/paginador.jsp?docTP=TP&docID=3707334.
2. http://redir.stf.jus.br/paginadorpub/paginador.jsp?docTP=AC&docID=347623.
3. Brazilian Supreme Court. (2017a). www.stf.jus.br/arquivo/cms/noticiaNoticiaStf/anexo/ADI4439AM.pdf.
4. BNCC. Retrieved from http://basenacionalcomum.mec.gov.br/images/BNCC_EI_EF_110518_versaofinal_site.pdf.
5. Ibid., 435.

3 Education About Religion in Canada

Mark Anderson and Paul T. Clarke

Introduction

For millennia – long before Canadian Confederation in 1867 or the arrival of Christian influences to North America – Indigenous peoples have held a deep reverence for the spiritual; this has been integral to their entire way of being and knowing, and has included teaching their children about the Creator and the role of the sacred in all aspects of life.[1] However, by the late 18th and early 19th centuries the immigration of European settlers to North America was gathering momentum as was the influence of the colonial views of religion they brought with them. As a result, Judeo-Christian expressions of religion[2] quickly displaced Indigenous understandings of the spiritual realm, shaping Canada's nascency and development as a nation and significantly influencing public policy-making in critical arenas such as government, the courts, and education.[3] A century and a half after Confederation, this historically unquestioned marriage between institutionalized Judeo-Christianity and public[4] education has all but vanished, though notable exceptions do exist, such as Roman Catholic denominational schools in multiple provinces.

The advent of the *Canadian Charter of Rights and Freedoms*[5] made the divorce inevitable, as did profound social changes such as the gradual but ineluctable separation of church and state as well as the concomitant secularization[6] of Canadian society. Therefore, the responsibility for public K 12 education has shifted dramatically over the course of Canadian history, both pre-Confederation and since 1867, from families and church-affiliated institutions to provincial government-managed public schools:[7] "A striking characteristic of the practice of education in the present century [20th] is the extent to which the state has become involved in [public education's] funding and control."[8]

Not surprisingly then, the current relationship between education and religion in Canada is an inconsistent, complicated, and controversial one. As educational law scholars Dickinson and MacKay point out, ultimately "the field of education is so intricately related to other important walks of life, it often becomes the battleground for important debates on issues of social policy."[9] For example, publicly funded Roman Catholic schools in various provinces are legally permitted to display overtly Christian icons, offer particularly Christian ceremonies during school hours, and teach Christian curricula; yet, most other public education divisions have made a conscious effort to empty their schools of religious (most often Christian) expressions and influences.

There are many other seeming contradictions to be negotiated. Canadian policymakers are perpetually confronted by the spectre of having to discern between competing collective and individual rights, such as English and French linguistic and religious guarantees, when determining what and how children should be taught. Sifting through these divisive questions, including those about the role of religion in the country's public classrooms, tests the depth of Canadians' commitment to some of the most sacred principles undergirding Western liberal democracies, such as freedom of conscience and equality of opportunity.

This chapter illustrates that despite these challenges inherent to the Canadian context, jurisprudence has consistently upheld two conclusions regarding the teaching of religion in public classrooms. First, if the instruction does not indoctrinate[10] in a particular faith and does not exclude minority voices, it is legally permissible because it does not violate constitutional rights. Second, in their *ratio decidendi*, judges consistently suggest that teaching about religion is pedagogically invaluable in a multicultural democracy such as Canada because it is foundational to citizenship formation, and that some measure of cognitive dissonance is consistent with good teaching and necessary learning.

Context

The aforementioned legal and political complications regarding education about religion in Canada find their roots in the country's very inception in 1867. Confederation was seriously jeopardized until a political compromise – public funding of Protestant schools in Lower Canada (essentially Quebec) and Roman Catholic schools in Upper Canada (Ontario) – could be forged that legally secured the historically intimate union between religion and education (s. 93 of the *Constitution Act, 1867*).[11] This agreement, in practice, has mainly benefited Roman Catholic education systems in a handful of provinces to the exclusion of most, if not all, other forms of denominational education, especially given that public schools first established as Protestant institutions have been effectively secular for decades. While politically expedient and eminently practical at the time, the resultant *prima facie* unfairness[12] of the compromise precipitated an uneasy relationship between education and religion that persists today.

Exacerbating this unease is the fact that since 1867, Canada has relatively quickly morphed from a bicultural Christian outpost of the

Commonwealth[13] into a multicultural, putatively secular, G8 country: "Today, we are a pluralistic, multicultural . . . nation."[14] And yet, religious education rights in Alberta, Ontario, and Saskatchewan have remained immutably frozen by the *Constitution Act, 1867*, to the point that not even the *Charter* can alter them.[15]

The complications do not end there. For one, Canada does not have a federal education system or even a separate federal ministry of education. However, the separation of education from the national parliament has been neither clean nor complete:

> The federal government provides transfer payments to the provinces and territories and some of those funds are used to support education. In the absence of a federal voice on education, the Council of Ministers of Education (CMEC) was founded in 1967 with the purpose of providing a national voice for education.[16]

Additionally, various federal departments are concerned with "specialized" aspects of Canadian education, most notably funding of specified French education programs and some First Nations schooling.[17]

Further, even though each provincial government regulates its own education system, all policies and laws are subject to the *Constitution*,[18] including the *Charter*, as ultimately interpreted by the Supreme Court of Canada.[19] Khan illustrates the ironic tension: "On the one hand the rights and privileges of Protestant and Catholic denominational schools are constitutionally entrenched, and on the other hand, the *Constitution* prohibits discrimination on the grounds of conscience or religion."[20] Thus, due to the Confederation compromise and the realities of s. 93, Canadian public education today is as diverse as the provincial legislatures, histories, and cultures themselves.

Despite these provincial differences, a handful of consistencies can be found between the jurisdictions. For example, schooling typically is divided into three categories: elementary or primary covering kindergarten to the end of grade 8; secondary or high school, consisting of grades 9–12;[21] and post-secondary education at university or college. Education in each province is governed by an education minister who oversees a ministry or department. This provincial ministry then empowers board-governed school divisions to administrate and deliver educational programs. Almost without exception, classroom teachers in public schools are required to hold valid teacher certification, and all provincial curricula and course time requirements must be fulfilled. Education is com pulsory to the age of 16 in every province, except for Ontario, Manitoba, and New Brunswick, where that age is 18.[22]

While an exhaustive examination of how Canadian education is funded is beyond this chapter's scope, the following quick overview summarizes what is meant by "public funding of schools" in Canada. Beyond the aforementioned federal governmental transfer payments for specialized programs such as French, all other financial considerations fall to the provinces. In general,

> [P]rovincial funding for education is generated from personal and corporate income tax, consumption taxes (including sales and fuel), health and insurance levies, natural resource revenue, licenses and permits, return on investments, and general and special purpose transfer payments.[23]

In most instances, the largest sources of revenue for education are garnered through income tax and mill or tax rates levied on real property.

An important key point arises from this brief contextual overview. That is, denominational schools and religious education played key roles in the country's history and emerging polity. In fact, "public schools in Canada were never intended to be non-denominational,"[24] illustrating that religion was integral to education, both before and for many decades following Confederation. There has never been a time in Canadian history when public K–12 education in any province has been delivered through a monolithic, entirely secular system. Students have always had access to either publicly funded denominational schools and/or opportunities for some form of education about religion in public schools.

Pertinent Legislation

Naturally, this historical and contemporary nexus between Canadian public education and religion finds its legal authority in legislation. For example, any discussion regarding the relationship between education and the law in Canada begins with s. 52(1)[25] of the *Constitution Act, 1982*, which guarantees that the *Constitution Act, 1867* (including the provisions of s. 93) supersedes all federal and provincial legislation, which means that any law that violates it is of no force or effect.

Section 93 of the *Constitution Act, 1867* established that provincial legislatures are responsible for "laws in relation to education," with four restrictions that act much like a mini bill of rights limiting provincial plenary power over education in terms of denominational guarantees.[26] Notwithstanding these restrictions, s. 93 establishes that provincial governments enjoy considerable power over education, including the enshrinement of education acts[27] and the development and regulation of curricula.[28]

Complicating the now archaic compromise embedded in the *Constitution* was the enshrinement of the *Charter* in 1982. The primary tensions could be found in the pronounced differences between the community compromises of the *Constitution* and the individual liberties found in the *Charter*. The latter also impacts education about religion in public schools. This is hinted at in the wording of the *Charter*'s Preamble itself: "Canada is founded upon principles that recognize the supremacy of God."[29] While the Preamble has been legally impotent until a very recent case in Quebec, which is summarized later, it is more than a trivial matter to debate whether the remaining sections of the *Charter* should be interpreted through a theological lens or a secular one. Ontario Justice Brown articulates why: "Far from being a 'dead letter,' the Preamble poses fundamental questions of political philosophy, including the relationship between the transcendental and the political order."[30] At the very least, the Preamble insinuates that the religious cannot and should not be ignored by the courts and governments of the land.

Section 1 is also relevant to this discussion. It establishes the degree to which individual rights can be infringed upon by government action. Rights and freedoms are "subject only to such reasonable limits prescribed by law as can be demonstrably justified in a free and democratic society." The standard for determining what is meant by "reasonable limits" was established in the 1986 judgment in *R. v. Oakes.*[31]

The late Chief Justice Dickson wrote that the state must demonstrate that there is a pressing and substantial objective, that the means to achieve the objective are rationally connected to it, that the limitation of rights is as minimal as possible, and that there is a balance between the restriction and the objective. Put another way, s. 1 means rights are not absolute, but any potential infringement must neither impose exceptional burdens nor grant special privileges without due cause.[32] Thus, Canadian public schools must guard against creating "exceptional burdens or special privileges" for certain religious groups, all the while conceding the hypocrisy of the Confederation compromise, which already does precisely this for "public" Catholic schools.

Discussion of s. 1 and the Preamble leads directly to s. 2(a), which states: "Everyone has the following fundamental freedoms: (a) freedom of conscience and religion."[33] Some academics[34] argue the section theoretically defends parents' rights to educate their children in a manner consistent with their religious convictions.[35] Education professor Paul Clarke, by contrast, suggests that "giving parents exclusive control over whether or not their children will be exposed to explicit discussions about religion, sexuality, and sexual orientation is fraught with difficulty."[36] In sum, the section establishes that the state may not favour one religion over another and that religion alone "is not a legitimate policy consideration at all under the *Charter*."[37]

And yet, Section 29[38] protects existing constitutional rights and privileges for denominational, separate, and dissentient schools, reaffirming the legal and historical precedent that some forms of religious education cannot be challenged under the *Charter*, even if such privileges may seem grossly inequitable to other denominationally affiliated schools that have no access to public support. Section 29 simply limits the scope and impact of the *Charter* on pre-existing rights identified in s. 93 of the *Constitution Act* without denying provincial cabinets the legal latitude to offer education about religion in their public schools.

Summary of Pertinent Legislation

In short, nothing in the legislation either implicitly or explicitly prohibits teaching about religion in contemporary Canadian public high schools. Provincial regulations and statutes allow teaching about religion as long as no particular religious group(s) is either favoured or excluded. Legislation also established the premise that at least two publicly funded education systems could legally coexist in the same province. In Canada's early history, these systems were either Roman Catholic or Protestant, making Canadian public education a binary, exclusively Christian endeavor. Thus, s. 93 of the *Constitution* and provincial statutes carry the most weight when it comes to matters of education, because even though "[The *Charter*] has provided the greatest challenge to the historical collaboration between Church and State in education,"[39] it cannot be used to impugn the denominational rights enshrined at Confederation (s. 93). At the same time, the *Charter* protects those very same denominational rights under s. 29.

Pertinent Jurisprudence

There exists a substantial body of jurisprudence congruent with the preceding legislative framework that now recognizes that in public secular schools, teaching about religion and not indoctrinating students into a particular faith or religious perspective is both legal and constitutional. Further, private religious schools and denominational schools protected by the *Constitution* may continue to teach their faith-based perspective with the full protection of the law.

An illustrative case, *Keegstra v. Board of Education of Lacombe No. 14* (1983),[40] established that teachers may not use freedom of religion to justify indoctrination of students. A Board of Reference upheld the board of education's termination of a teacher's employment contract on the ground of insubordination. This case represents a blatant attempt by a public high school teacher to indoctrinate his grades 9 and 12 social studies students into anti-Semitic ways of thinking. Based on his religious beliefs, the teacher instructed his students about an international Jewish conspiracy, claiming that Jews were responsible for undermining Christianity and Western civilization.[41]

Following parental complaints, the superintendent of schools conducted an investigation of the instructor's teaching practices. As a result, he received oral and written warnings to change his approach by teaching the prescribed curriculum. When he did not conform to the superintendent's directives, the board of education held a hearing and decided to fire the teacher.

A Board of Reference affirmed the dismissal because the teacher's in-class racist opinions amounted to unjustifiable contractual violations. In addition, he used methods contrary to the provincial curriculum and refused to remedy his ways after numerous warnings. The Board of Reference noted that the teacher's approach precluded the teaching of social studies through critical inquiry:

> While the appellant may have prefaced his presentation of the material by a general statement that these were only theories, I am satisfied that the students did not have before them any contrary views or any contrary source material which may have led them to conclude that the theories being presented were in error.[42]

Freedom of religion was also at issue in *Zylberberg v. Sudbury Board of Education (Director)*.[43] A group of parents sought a declaration that a section of a provincial regulation governing education was unconstitutional for violating their freedom of religion as protected under Section 2(a) of the *Charter*. The regulation required that public schools be opened or closed each day with religious exercises consisting of the reading of the Scriptures and the repeating of the Lord's Prayer. None of the parents chose to use a provision under the regulation that would have allowed them to have their children exempted from participating in the religious exercises.

A majority of the Court of Appeal held that the section was antithetical to the *Charter*'s objective of promoting freedom of conscience and religion. It likewise rejected the contention that the requirement to seek an exemption did not constitute a form of constraint, compulsion, or coercion that served to undermine freedom of religion:

> While the majoritarian view may be that section 28 confers freedom of choice on the minority, the reality is that it imposes on religious minorities a compulsion to conform to the religious practices of the majority. The evidence in this case supports this view. The three appellants chose not to seek an exemption from religious exercises because of their concern about differentiating their children from other pupils. The peer pressure and the classroom norms to which children are acutely sensitive, in our opinion, are real and pervasive and operate to compel members of religious minorities to conform with majority religious practices.[44]

The court also ruled that the violation of Section 28 could not be justified under Section 1 of the *Charter*. The case demonstrates that one can teach students about morality without recourse to religious exercises and religious indoctrination.

In *Chamberlain v. Surrey School District No. 36*,[45] the Board of Trustees of the Surrey School District in British Columbia passed a resolution prohibiting the use of three books depicting children with same-sex parents as "Recommended Learning Resources." A primary school teacher and others applied for an order quashing the resolution, claiming it infringed on school legislation and the *Charter*. The facts revealed that the trustees who voted for the resolution had religious beliefs opposed to the morality of same-sex families.

A majority of the Supreme Court of Canada ruled that school legislation mandating that schools be conducted on "strictly secular principles" did not prevent religious concerns from influencing educational policy: "Religion is an integral aspect of people's lives, and cannot be left at the board room door."[46] Nonetheless, the majority agreed with the lower court's order quashing the resolution. The board had acted on the concern of specified parents about the morality of same-sex relationships, thereby violating the principles of secularism and tolerance in the school legislation. The school authorities failed to consider the interests of same-sex-parented families and their children in receiving equal recognition and respect in the school system. As the majority declared:

> A requirement of secularism implies that, although the board is indeed free to address the religious concerns of parents, it must be sure to do so in a manner that gives equal recognition and respect to other members of the community. Religious views that deny equal recognition and respect to the members of a minority group cannot be used to exclude the concerns of the minority group.[47]

In *Multani v. Commission scolaire Marguerite-Bourgeoys*,[48] the Supreme Court of Canada had to reconcile a minority student's constitutional right to freedom of religion with the state's interest in a safe school community for all students. Here, the principal of a French language school in Montreal told a Khalsa Sikh student that he could not wear his *kirpan* (a ceremonial dagger) at school. Yet, the student's religious beliefs and status as a baptized orthodox Sikh required him to wear the kirpan while at school.

The issue arose when the kirpan accidentally fell from the boy's outer clothing while in the schoolyard. The school board met with the family and agreed to allow the student to don the kirpan at school, provided specified safety conditions were met. The school governing board would not accept the compromise reached between the parties, alleging that the wearing of the kirpan violated the school's rules regarding dangerous and forbidden objects. The school board affirmed this decision. The student's parents took the matter to court, arguing that his right to wear the kirpan was protected under the *Charters* of both Canada and Québec on the grounds of religious freedom.

A majority of the Court concluded that interference with the student's freedom of religion was neither trivial nor insignificant. The Court added that prohibition against wearing the kirpan deprived the student of his right to attend a public school. The majority framed the school's obligation in these terms:

> Religious tolerance is a very important value of Canadian society. If some students consider it unfair that Gurbaj Singh may wear his *kirpan* to school while they are not allowed to have knives in their possession, it is incumbent on the schools to discharge their obligation to instil in their students this value that is . . . at the very foundation of our democracy.[49]

To be sure, the right to freedom of religion is not absolute. As the majority observed: "This Court has clearly recognized that freedom of religion can be limited when a person's freedom to act in accordance with his or her beliefs may cause harm to or interfere with the rights of others."[50] The student had to wear his blunted kirpan in a sheath, sewn inside his clothing, and had to submit to school authorities to ensure that he was following these dress requirements. Failure to do so meant losing his right to wear the kirpan. This reconciliation upholds the value of religious freedom yet does not forget the safety needs of those who attend our schools.

In *S.L. v. Commission scolaire des Chênes*,[51] and in the context of the public school system, the Supreme Court of Canada upheld the constitutional validity of Quebec's mandatory Ethics and Religious Culture (ERC) program, which obliges school curricula to address the beliefs and ethics of different world religions from a neutral[52] and objective viewpoint. The ERC program has two main objectives: the recognition of others and the pursuit of the common good. The first objective is rooted in the idea that all people possess equal value and dignity. The second aims to foster shared values of human rights and democracy.

Educational officials in Quebec seek to instill in all students openness to diversity and respect for others by mandating this program in their schools.[53] A group of parents argued that the program would confuse their children and interfere with their religious freedom under s. 2(a) of the *Charter* because it exposed them to information about various world religions from a secular perspective. The Court rejected the parents' argument, thereby affirming the constitutionality of the ERC Program. As Justice Deschamps explained:

> [P]arents are free to pass their personal beliefs on to their children if they so wish. However, the early exposure of children to realities

> that differ from those in their immediate family environment is a fact of life in society. The suggestion that exposing children to a variety of religious facts in itself infringes their religious freedom or that of their parents amounts to a rejection of the multicultural reality of Canadian society and ignores the Quebec government's obligations with regard to public education. Although such exposure can be a source of friction, it does not in itself constitute an infringement of s. 2(*a*) of the *Canadian Charter* and of s. 3 of the *Quebec Charter.*[54]

In *Loyola High School v. Quebec* (*Attorney General*),[55] the Supreme Court of Canada had to reconcile the state's interest in promoting the recognition of others and the pursuit of the common good, as championed by Quebec's mandatory ERC program for provincial schools, with a private Jesuit school's religious freedom as protected under both the Canadian and Quebec *Charters of Rights and Freedoms.* The minister of education could grant private schools exemptions from the ERC program if they could demonstrate that they would offer an alternative program the minister deemed to be equivalent. Loyola applied in writing for an exemption that the minister denied on the basis that the school's entire proposed program was to be taught from a Catholic perspective. Loyola sought judicial review of the minister's decision on the ground that it interfered with the school's freedom of religion.

A majority of the Court reasoned that Loyola could teach its own doctrine and ethical framework from a Catholic perspective, but it had to teach other religions' ethical frameworks from a neutral and objective perspective. As Justice Abella stated:

> My starting point is that in a religious high school, where students are learning about the precepts of one particular faith throughout their education, it is arguably even more important that they learn, in as objective a way as possible, about other belief systems and the reasons underlying those beliefs.[56]

Justice Abella held that this requirement for objectivity did not seriously undermine Loyola's religious freedom, claiming that to teach

> about the ethics of other religions is largely a factual exercise. It need not be a clash of values. . . . It is . . . a pedagogical tool utilized by good teachers for centuries – let the information, not the personal views of the teacher, guide the discussion.[57]

E.T. v. Hamilton-Wentworth District School Board[58] illustrates the struggle to balance the public education mandate to promote and uphold the values of equality and inclusion with an individual's right to freedom of religion. The applicant, E.T., was a father of two elementary school children and a member of the Greek Orthodox Church whose religious beliefs required him to protect his children from what he saw as "false teachings" in Ontario's public school curriculum. In his children's school, the father opposed the discussion or portrayal of homosexual or bisexual conduct in relationships and/or transgenderism as natural and healthy.

The father unsuccessfully sought an accommodation from the principal and the school board to stop his children from being exposed to the "false teachings." In court, and on the basis of his *Charter*-protected right to religious freedom, the father requested two orders from the board of education: information in advance as to specific curriculum areas being taught to his children, and permission to withdraw his children from classes, lessons, or activities that conflicted with his religious beliefs. A unanimous Court of Appeal rejected the father's arguments, concluding that there was no concrete evidence of interference with the father's right to religious freedom:

> E.T.'s claim rests upon his general and pervasive dissatisfaction with the nature of the Board's curriculum with respect to matters of equity, non-discrimination and inclusiveness. However, he has not proved a single instance where his children were coerced to do something that was contrary to his or their religious beliefs or where they were denied the right to manifest or observe their religion as they wished. Nor has he provided any evidence that his right to inculcate his children with his own religious views has been curtailed or infringed.[59]

In *Servatius v. Alberni School District No. 70*,[60] a Nuu-chah-nulth Elder visited an elementary school in British Columbia to demonstrate the practice of smudging. A few months later, an Indigenous dancer performed at an assembly and said a prayer. The purpose of these events was to acquaint students with Indigenous culture and to promote a sense of belonging in Indigenous children, 30% of whom make up the student population in the district. An evangelical Christian claimed that these events interfered with her religious freedoms and those of her children as guaranteed by the *Charter*. The mother also sought an order prohibiting future events of this nature. Evidence disclosed that the petitioner's children merely observed the Indigenous demonstrations – they were not smudged and were not engaged in the hoop dance or the prayer the dancer said.

The British Columbia Supreme Court rejected the mother's two main arguments that there were violations of state neutrality and compelled participation. On the first ground, the court stated: "The duty of state neutrality is fulfilled 'when the state neither favours nor hinders any particular religious belief.' "[61] The court found that neither the smudging nor the hoop dancing was – either by design or in their execution – an expression of the school district's beliefs or an expression of religious favouritism: "Rather, the organization of these events reflected a gathering momentum to incorporate the teaching of Indigenous worldviews and perspectives."[62] As for the second ground, the court ruled that, on an objective standard, being in a classroom containing smoke produced by an Elder burning sage, or being present when a dancer prayed, did not interfere with one's ability to act in accordance with religious beliefs, "even if this teaching results in some 'cognitive dissonance.' "[63]

In the fall of 2003, St. Theodore School in Saskatchewan opened as a publicly funded separate denominational school, in accordance with education legislation and the *Constitution.* The school had approximately the same enrolment and ratio of Catholic and non-Catholic students as the former public secular school, closed by its former school division (Good Spirit) for financial reasons. Good Spirit brought an action against the provincial government and the Christ the Teacher school board claiming the full funding of non-Catholic students to attend Catholic schools breached s. 2(a) (freedom of religion) and s. 15 (the right to equality) of the *Charter* and was, therefore, unconstitutional. The trial judge ruled in favour of Good Spirit, deciding that when Saskatchewan joined Canadian Confederation in 1905, the denominational protection afforded separate Roman Catholic schools was strictly limited to protecting Catholic doctrine, Catholic education, and Catholic students.

In *Saskatchewan v. Good Spirit School Division No. 204,*[64] a unanimous Court of Appeal overturned the trial judge's order, deciding that the relevant legislative scheme and the current funding regime were constitutional. Among its many holdings, the court noted the legislative framework protected two publicly funded education systems that parents could choose from: a *public* secular school division and a *separate* denominational school division (mainly Roman Catholic in Saskatchewan).

Good Spirit pleaded religious discrimination on the key fact that private religious schools receive partial per-pupil funding from the Saskatchewan government, and if they accept non-adherent students, those students would likewise be only funded partially. The court refuted this line of reasoning:

> This is not a proper application of the *Charter* right of religious freedom. There was no evidence presented to the trial judge or to this Court that private religious schools receive partial funding – for children of their faith *or* for the children of other faiths – because of discrimination, stereotyping or prejudice in breach of the *Charter* protection of freedom of religion.[65]

In 2019, the Quebec government passed into law *Bill 21, An Act Respecting the Laicity of the State,*[66] which forbids public servants, including public school teachers, from wearing religious symbols such as the hijab and kippah on the job. The purpose of the legislation is to uphold the public secular values that govern the public service and to ensure that the state acts and is seen to be acting in a neutral, non-religious manner. However, a number of individuals and groups have challenged the legislation on multiple fronts alleging, among other things, that it violates their religious freedom under both the Quebec and Canadian *Charters.* They likewise claim that it cannot be justified as a reasonable limit under s. 1 of the *Canadian Charter*. Given the significance of this issue, it is likely to be subject to litigation for many years and will most likely make its way to the Supreme Court of Canada for a ruling on the constitutionality of the new law.

Emerging Issues

Education is intricately entangled with all facets of Canadian daily life. Consideration of teaching about religion in publicly funded schools can complicate these entanglements, giving rise to innumerable potential legal implications. Although future cases may make forays into entirely new areas, it is more probable these cases will revisit familiar and ongoing tensions and jurisprudence in light of ever-morphing social, political, and legal contexts. These include but are not restricted to the increasing separation of church and state in Canada, the challenging logistics of ensuring inclusivity as Canadian society rapidly diversifies, and the adjudication of competing individual rights, collective needs, and state interests.

For example, in *Saskatchewan v. Good Spirit School Division No. 204,*[67] we noted that the Court of Appeal overturned a trial judge's order, ruling that public funding of denominationally affiliated schooling was constitutional because the Confederation compromise protected two publicly funded education systems that parents could choose from: a *public* secular (formerly Protestant in intent in most provinces) school division or a *separate* denominational school division, typically Roman Catholic. Even if the Supreme Court of Canada refuses to hear this appeal, we project that legal actions questioning this Roman Catholic exceptionalism will continue.

As the fabric of Canadian society continues to diversify, which we believe strengthens our liberal democracy, so too will competing notions of what it means to teach about religion. For example, there is the imperative to respond to the "94 Calls to Action" of the Truth and Reconciliation Commission of Canada,[68] which rightly assert the need for Indigenous control of Indigenous education, including all matters of language and culture that encompass spirituality and worldviews. Can Canadian classrooms make room for all such religious, non-religious, and spiritual perspectives? Who decides without merely advancing the tyranny of the majority? Will school calendars have to be amended to recognize and honour the high points of all major religions? Again, if that is not logistically possible, who decides which religions are to be recognized and which are to be excluded? What will the courts defend as they weigh both the constitutionally protected right to freedom of religion enshrined in the *Charter* and the need for reasonable limits on all rights claims encapsulated under its s. 1?

Finally, the constitutional amendments in Quebec and Newfoundland, which essentially ended the monopoly of denominationally affiliated school divisions, could eventually cause other provinces to re-examine not only the public funding of Roman Catholic school divisions, but also the symbolism and validity of using public tax money to fund any programs attempting to marry specific religious content and education in public schools. Unless we fund all bona fide religious schools such as Jewish and Muslim schools in Saskatchewan equally, how can we justify a narrow and privileging focus in a multicultural and multi-faith democracy guided by a *Charter* of rights and freedoms protecting freedom of religion?

Denominational schools present special challenges because three remaining provinces (Ontario, Saskatchewan, and Alberta) still grant privileged status to Christianity, and especially Roman Catholicism. Yet, this should not affect the continuing need to educate youth about religion in Canada's public secular schools for the pedagogical reasons advanced in this chapter.

Conclusion

As frequently alluded to in the preceding examinations of the legal realities regarding education and religion in Canada, case rulings have consistently endorsed the pedagogical merits of education about religion, especially in a multicultural democracy such as Canada.[69] In fact, numerous judges have been of the opinion that such education, if properly enacted and regulated, strengthens a free and diverse society.[70] That is, a vibrant, just, democratic state requires a literate citizenry, capable of discerning choices and critical thinking: "an education which takes as its central task the fostering of critical thinking is the education most suited for democratic life."[71]

Even more importantly, young citizens encouraged to act thoughtfully in weighing others' convictions and beliefs in accountable classroom environments might be better positioned to respect others' rights and differing viewpoints without feeling coerced into either unreflective approval of those ideas or abdication of their own. A truly democratic nation that values freedom of thought and speech should want to develop such a citizenry that can hold differences without rancor.[72] Further, the responsible teaching about religion honors the core values of the *Charter*, such as empathy, compassion, equality, and consensus-building, by moving Canadian students beyond the country's tricultural roots and history, and beyond the divisive tensions between the secular and the religious. The courts concur. We are reminded of Justice Deschamps's strong imperative in *Multani*:

> Religious tolerance is a very important value of Canadian society . . . it is incumbent on the schools to discharge their obligation to instil in their students this value that is at the very foundation of our democracy.[73]

If there is no legitimate attempt to include education about religion in the classroom, then public schools present only the secularist view already so prevalent in Canada.[74] Learning needs to include more truth claims in order to achieve the kind of diversity we aspire to in Canada. Campos agrees: the "secular creed . . . has within it the potential to become every bit as monistic, compulsory, and intolerant of any significant deviation from social verities as the traditional modes of belief it derided and displaced."[75] It is critical to our multicultural society that we avoid the pitfall of merely replacing one religious agenda with an equally monopolistic worldview.[76]

Education about religion is pedagogically critical in Canada because educators cannot in good conscience ignore or de-emphasize belief, human spirituality, or contemplation of the phenomenon we call "religious" and still claim to be offering the nation's students a grounded, holistic, and well-rounded education. For example, any ethical and authentic response by Canadians, including educators, to the "94 Calls to Action" of the Truth and Reconciliation Commission demands precisely this kind of inclusive education.[77]

While redressing the legacy of residential schools and advancing the process of Canadian reconciliation, one must acknowledge the central role spiritual leaders, spiritual practices (such as the Potlatch and Sun Dance), and spiritual values play in an Indigenous worldview. A better understanding of Indigenous history and spirituality is consistent with the goals of reconciliation in the context of a culturally, religiously, and spiritually diverse nation such as Canada. Recognizing what it means to be human often requires us to consider the role spirituality and religion play in the lives of all Canadians and is indispensable if we wish to provide students with a balanced, comprehensive education.

This approach to education is legally and constitutionally permissible provided one does not indoctrinate, coerce, or proselytize in public secular schools; within the limits prescribed by law, nobody should be expected to "bracket their beliefs when they enter the public square."[78] Journalist, politician, and Companion of the Order of Canada Claude Ryan is even more forceful: "But obliging some people to keep their opinions to themselves is in itself . . . [a] fundamentally undemocratic way of buying harmony among citizens of a free society."[79] Public policy governing education should not require individuals aiming to influence that policy to park their religious, secular, or other beliefs at the door; civility, rationality, evidence, and the demand for practical wisdom should be the parameters for a robust, organic, and constructive social dialogue.

Notes

1. See the Seven Sacred Teachings, which continue to serve as guiding spiritual and ethical principles for many Indigenous communities today in Canada: love, respect, courage, honesty, wisdom, humility, and truth. www.southernnetwork.org/site/seven-teachings.
2. Legal rulings have offered useful definitions of "religion." For example, the majority in *Syndicat Northcrest v. Amselem* (2004) broadly defined religion as both a particular and comprehensive system of faith and worship characterized by freely and deeply held personal convictions or beliefs that, in turn, inform an individual's spiritual or faith life and that are integral "to his or her self-definition and spiritual fulfillment" (para. 39). Therefore, in Canada, "religion" is commonly used as an umbrella term also encompassing concepts like "personal belief," "spirituality," and "faith."
3. Early in Canadian history, religious forces and the rule of law mutually informed each other in pseudo-theocratic fashion. Christian principles heavily influenced British law, which in turn formed the bedrock of subsequent legal and political systems in Commonwealth countries. Canada was no exception. Laws were imbued with Christian values and were enacted to preserve Christian social dominance and political will. More precisely, French Catholic and English Protestant theologies had profound impacts on our nation's founding legal systems and structures and, by extension, our education system.
4. Defined by Keith Walker and James Chomos as any school that is "entirely funded from government sources" (*A Guide to Saskatchewan School Law* (Saskatoon: University of Saskatchewan, 2003), 1.9).
5. Part I of the Constitution Act, 1982, being Schedule B to the Canada Act, 1982 (UK), 1982, c. 11 (hereinafter, Charter).
6. In this specific instance, we adopt Matthew Livingstone's view that "secularism" means the systematic attempt to remove all religious influences from state institutions and operations (*The Jesuits and Secularism.* A lecture presented at Campion College, Regina, SK, May, 2010). However, it should be noted that both the Supreme Court of Canada and the British Columbia Court of Appeal in their *Chamberlain* case judgements ruled that "secularism" in public policymaking must be inclusionary, including religious voices. Justice Mackenzie of the BC Court of Appeal (*Chamberlain v. Surrey School Board* (2000) 80 BCLR (3d) 181 (CA)) stated: "A religiously informed conscience should not be accorded any privilege, but neither should it be placed under a disability" (para. 28) at the table of public discourse.
7. Pre-Confederation, Upper and Lower Canada typically were populated by immigrants who sought to replicate the intimate relationship between church and state that characterized life in their countries of origin: "In the Old World from which Canada and its education systems sprang, the dominant vision of religion and the State was one of union and mutual support" (William F. Foster and William J. Smith, Religion and Education in Canada: Part I – The Traditional Framework, *Education and Law Journal,*

10(3) (2001), 393). Indeed, early Canadian education was heavily influenced by European socialtrends and educational models, Christian values, and classical philosophy (e.g., Socratic pedagogies). However, the education initially offered to children was very informal and extremely loosely structured. Early in Canada's history, "education was basically a local affair, and the responsibility for schooling largely a family matter" (Carolyn Gossage, *A Question of Privilege: Canada's Independent Schools* (Toronto: Peter Martin Associates Limited, 1977), 20). As families became more established and more solvent, independent, denominationally affiliated schools were formed in the 19th century. Thus, the formalization of education in the emerging colony was largely under the auspices of various denominations (e.g., Roman Catholic schools in New France). Not surprisingly, religious instruction was an integral part of education, or, more accurately, the daily curricula were infused with Christian values. J. D. Wilson, an educational historian at the University of British Columbia, illustrates this very point: "Fundamental to the creation of a system of free and universal education was the notion, common to the 19th century, that education and religion were inseparable" (as cited in Louis Sweet, *The Fourth 'R': Religion in Our Classrooms: A Special Report* (Toronto: Atkinson Fellowship in Public Policy, 1996, 10)).

8. Brian Crittenden, *Parents, the State and the Right to Educate* (Melbourne: Melbourne University Press, 1988), 158.
9. Greg M. Dickinson and A. Wayne MacKay (eds.), *Rights, Freedoms and the Education System in Canada: Cases and Materials* (Toronto: Emond-Montgomery, 1989), 39.
10. The ruling in an Ontario case (*Canadian Civil Liberties Assn. v. Ontario* (*Minister of Education*) (1990), also known in jurisprudence as *Elgin County*) is critical for establishing the difference between the proselytizing that characterized early public schooling in Canada and more contemporary education about religion that does not run afoul of the Charter and good pedagogy: (a) The school may sponsor the *study* of religion but may not sponsor the *practice* of religion. (b) The school may *expose* students to all religious views but may not *impose* any particular view. (c) The school's approach to religion is one of *instruction,* not one of *indoctrination.* (d) The function of the school is to *educate* about all religions, not to *convert* to any one religion. (e) The school's approach is *academic,* not *devotional.* (f) The school should *study* what all people believe but should not *teach* a student what to believe. (g) The school should strive for student *awareness* of all religions but should not press for student *acceptance* of any one religion. (h) The school should seek to *inform* the student about various beliefs but should not seek to *conform* him or her to any one belief (p. 28). Therefore, education about religion is different from indoctrination because it emphasizes student agency instead of suppressing individual critical thought for the uncontested promulgation of one view of truth.
11. Technically, the essential compromise was reached in the Scott Act, 1863, or earlier; however, the agreement became permanently binding when it was included in the Constitution Act, 1867, and later the Constitution Act, 1982. For this reason, it is frequently referred to as the Confederation compromise.
12. For example, the funding of Roman Catholic schools in Ontario is protected by the Constitution, whereas the *Adler v. Ontario* (*Minister of Education*) (1996) ruling established that provincial funding did not have to be extended to other denominationally affiliated schools, such as the Jewish school in question in the case.

13. First Nations people rightfully would object to Canadian history being characterized merely by its European influences; however, rightly or wrongly, the legal and political forces that came to bear on Confederation were informed by the predominantly Christian, bicultural society of 1867. As Farrow states, "Canada does indeed have its deepest roots in the Christian civilization of Europe" (D. Farrow (ed.), *Recognizing Religion in a Secular Society: Essays in Pluralism, Religion, and Public Policy* (Montreal and Kingston: McGill-Queen's University Press, 2004), p. 167). Therefore, by necessity, much of the ensuing discussion admittedly will have that focus, but that is not to negate or denude other vital voices in the history of this nation, especially the voices of those who lived on the land long before European settlers arrived.
14. Sweet, *The Fourth 'R'*, 7.
15. Section 29 states: "Nothing in this Charter abrogates or derogates from any rights or privileges guaranteed by or under the Constitution of Canada in respect of denominational, separate or dissentient schools." It should be noted that exceptions do exist, however: Newfoundland, after two controversial referenda, amended Term 17 of the Newfoundland Act, essentially eliminating a plethora of denominational school divisions and establishing a single-school system with opportunities for education about religion and religious observances, which all children, regardless of their religious affiliation, can attend; and in 1997, Quebec's Bill 180 reorganized its education system linguistically rather than denominationally. Whether Alberta, Ontario, and Saskatchewan, which are the only remaining provinces with constitutionally protected denominational rights, will follow the route of Newfoundland and Quebec remains to be seen.
16. Dawn Zinga, Ontario's Challenge: Denominational Rights in Public Education, *Canadian Journal of Educational Administration and Policy*, 80 (2008), 3.
17. "Indian education," as it was historically called, was one of the few educational jurisdictions that remained under the federal government's purview in 1867, as mandated in s. 91(24) of the Constitution Act. The education of all registered Indians is regulated by the Indian Act (ss. 114–122). From 1876 on, "the federal government enlist[ed] the services of the churches to operate schools among Indian communities" (Jonathan C. Young and Benjamin R. Levin (eds.), *Understanding Canadian Schools: An Introduction to Educational Administration,* 3rd ed. (Scarborough: Thomson & Nelson, 2002), 52). Not surprisingly, the church-run schools had the dual aim of both educating and "Christianizing" First Nations children. Any educational good that might have been achieved on occasion was far outstripped by the human cost, as students were much too often subjected to everything from indoctrination to sexual abuse because accountability guidelines for and supervision of the schools were nominal. Thus, by the 1950s, the federal government began to exert more control over residential schools (p. 52) until the last residential school directly under the auspices of a Christian denomination closed its doors by the mid-1970s. During the years leading up to the formation of the Assembly of First Nations in 1988, aboriginal parents and authorities made a concerted effort to rectify the situation by gaining control over their children's education. This tragic history of residential schools provides significant lessons regarding the dangers of proselytizing rather than teaching about religion. Notably, First Nations schools tend to allow and even promote spiritual education.
18. As Hogg (2007) explains in his work *Constitutional Law of Canada*, 5th ed. (Toronto: Carswell), there are three branches or levels of the Canadian government: the legislative, which initiates and enacts laws; the executive, which

implements and administers them; and the judicial, which interprets them. The judiciary can and does make decisions independent of the prime minister or Cabinet. While some scholars (like Farrow in Douglas Farrow (ed.), *Recognizing Religion in a Secular Society: Essays in Pluralism, Religion, and Public Policy* (Montreal: McGill-Queen's University Press, 2004)) would contend that the Supreme Court of Canada is merely a manifestation of the federal government's political agenda, others (like Hogg) maintain that the judiciary operates as an independent branch of the Canadian government.

19. Judicial rulings have tended to comment on whether legislation or policies are unconstitutional or unlawful rather than advocate for a specific educational agenda: as MacKay accurately surmised, "it is safe to predict that the judges will not revolutionize the education system" (A. Wayne MacKay, The Equality Provisions of the Charter and Education: A Structural Analysis, *Canadian Journal of Education,* 11(3) (1986), 309.
20. Anwar Khan, Canadian Education: The Legal Position of Religion, *Liverpool Law Review,* 20 (1998), 138.
21. Some provinces, like Alberta, have a distinct junior high program (grades 7–9), while other provinces (like Prince Edward Island) refer to these same grades as intermediate school or middle school. Again, the provinces can vary greatly in their K–12 organization.
22. Even into the 1950s, most Canadians "finished school after eight or ten years, and the rate of high-school completion was still low" (Jonathan C. Young, Benjamin R. Levin, & Dawn C. Wallin (eds.), *Understanding Canadian Schools: An Introduction to Educational Administration,* 4th ed. (Toronto: Thomson & Nelson, 2007), 303).
23. V. J. Hajnal, *Public School Finance in Saskatchewan: An Introspection* (Saskatoon: University of Saskatchewan, SSTA Research Centre Report #95–01, 1995), 2–3.
24. W. Rod Dolmage, Public Funding of Parochial Schools: The Legal Arguments, *The Saskatchewan Educational Administrator,* 20 (1988), 11.
25. According to this section: "The *Constitution of Canada* is the supreme law of Canada, and any law that is inconsistent with the provisions of the *Constitution* is, to the extent of the inconsistency, of no force and effect."
26. According to Section 93: "In and for each Province the Legislature may exclusively make Laws in relation to Education, subject and according to the following Provisions: (1) Nothing in any such Law shall prejudicially affect any Right or Privilege with respect to Denominational Schools which any Class of Persons have by Law in the Province at the Union: (2) All the Powers, Privileges, and Duties at the Union by Law conferred and imposed in Upper Canada on the Separate Schools and School Trustees of the Queen's Roman Catholic Subjects shall be and the same are hereby extended to the Dissentient Schools of the Queen's Protestant and Roman Catholic Subjects in Quebec: (3) Where in any Province a System of Separate or Dissentient Schools exists by Law at the Union or is thereafter established by the Legislature of the Province, an Appeal shall lie to the Governor General in Council from any Act or Decision of any Provincial Authority affecting any Right or Privilege of the Protestant or Roman Catholic Minority of the Queen's Subjects in relation to Education: (4) In case any such Provincial Law as from Time to Time seems to the Governor General in Council requisite for the Execution of the Provisions of this Section is not made, or in case any Decision of the Governor General in Council on any Appeal under this Section is not duly executed by the proper Provincial Authority in that Behalf, then and in every such Case, and as far as the Circumstances of each Case require,

the Parliament of Canada may make remedial Laws for the due Execution of the Provisions of this Section and of any Decision of the Governor General in Council under this Section. (50) Section 93A: Paragraphs (1) to (4) of section 93 do not apply to Quebec (50.1); paragraph (1) does not strictly apply to Saskatchewan and Alberta."

27. Provincial regulations and statutes, such as education acts, also typically allow for properly regulated teaching about religion, and in some provinces (e.g., Ontario) protect publicly funded denominational schools; however, they are too diverse and numerous to explore in any detail here.
28. William F. Foster and William J. Smith, Religion and Education in Canada: Part I – The Traditional Framework, *Education & Law Journal*, 10(3) (2001), 447. Truthfully, the four restrictions have only benefited rights claims for Roman Catholics and Protestants at the time of Confederation and a handful of provinces once they entered the Dominion (like Saskatchewan). Section 93 does not accurately reflect contemporary Canadian diversity. Thus, it is a good example of how the law does not always evolve at the same pace as our society. As Walker argues, "legislation that satisfied past generations is obviously archaic for the heterogeneity of today" (Keith Walker, The Private School Debate, *Saskatchewan Educational Administrator*, 21(2) (1989), 21).
29. Some critics (like Constitutional expert Hogg (see note 18) contend the statement's intention and ideology is patently contradictory to the nature of the rest of the Charter. However, referencing the divine obviously was important to enough politicians at the time to be given such a prominent position in the Charter, almost as if it were placed there to provide the overall context within which one theoretically should read and interpret the rest of the document. By contrast, in *R. v. Sharpe* (1999) BCCA 416, the BC Court of Appeal referred to the phrasing as a "dead letter."
30. David M. Brown, Freedom from or Freedom For? Religion as a Case Study in Defining the Content of *Charter* Rights, *University of British Columbia Law Review*, 33 (2000), 615.
31. In *R. v. Oakes*, 1986 1 S.C.R. 103 (S.C.C.), the Court first articulated the test under Section 1: "To establish that a limit is reasonable and demonstrably justified in a free and democratic society, two central criteria must be satisfied. First, the objective, which the measures responsible for a limit on a *Charter* right or freedom are designed to serve, must be 'of sufficient importance to warrant overriding a constitutionally protected right or freedom': . . . The standard must be high in order to ensure that objectives which are trivial or discordant with the principles integral to a free and democratic society do not gain s. 1 protection. It is necessary, at a minimum, that an objective relate to concerns which are pressing and substantial in a free and democratic society before it can be characterized as sufficiently important. Second, once a sufficiently significant objective is recognized, then the party invoking s. 1 must show that the means chosen are reasonable and demonstrably justified. This involves 'a form of proportionality test': . . . Although the nature of the proportionality test will vary depending on the circumstances, in each case courts will be required to balance the interests of society with those of individuals and groups. There are . . . three important components of a proportionality test. First, the measures adopted must be carefully designed to achieve the objective in question. They must not be arbitrary, unfair or based on irrational considerations. In short, they must be rationally connected to the objective. Second, the means, even if rationally connected to the objective in this first sense, should impair 'as little as possible' the right or freedom in question: . . . Third, there must be a proportionality between the effects of

the measures which are responsible for limiting the *Charter* right or freedom, and the objective which has been identified as of 'sufficient importance' " (at para. 69–70).

32. *R. v. Oakes*, 1986 1 S.C.R. 103 (S.C.C.), para. 69–71.
33. Section 2(a) is the successor to s. 1(c) of the 1960 *Bill of Rights* regarding freedom of religion and conscience, which states: "1. It is hereby recognized and declared that in Canada there have existed and shall continue to exist without discrimination by reason of race, national origin, colour, religion or sex, the following human rights and fundamental freedoms, namely. . . (c) freedom of religion."
34. For example, John C. Long and Romulo Magsino, In Legal Issues in Religion and Education, *Education and Law Journal*, 4(2) (1992).
35. Specific cases exploring this contention can be found in the next section and will demonstrate that the Supreme Court has not accepted such logic.
36. Paul Clarke, Parental Rights, the Charter and Education: The Evolving Story, *Education Law Journal*, 19(3) (2010), 238.
37. Dickinson and MacKay, *Rights, Freedoms and the Education System in Canada*, 81.
38. According to s. 29, "Nothing in this *Charter* abrogates or derogates from any rights or privileges guaranteed by or under the Constitution of Canada in respect of denominational, separate or dissentient schools."
39. Yvonne M. Martin, Religion in Schools: Legally Speaking, *Education Canada*, 36(4) (1996), 43.
40. *Keegstra v. Board of Education of Lacombe No. 14* (1983), 25 Alta. L.R. (2d) 270 (Bd. Of Ref.).
41. In *R. v. Keegstra* (1990) 3 S.C.R. 697, the Supreme Court of Canada upheld the teacher's conviction of wilfully promoting hatred against an identifiable group under the *Criminal Code of Canada*. The Court stated: "Mr. Keegstra's teachings attributed various evil qualities to Jews. He thus described Jews to his pupils as 'treacherous,' 'subversive,' 'sadistic,' 'money loving,' 'power hungry' and 'child killers' " (p. 714).
42. See note 1 at p. 280.
43. (1988), 52 DLR (4th) 577 (Ontario Court of Appeal).
44. Ibid., 591.
45. *Chamberlain v. Surrey School District No. 36* (2002), S.C.J. No. 87.
46. Para. 99.
47. Ibid.
48. 2006 SCC 6.
49. Para. 76.
50. Para. 26.
51. 2012 SCC 7.
52. Even though the authors are skeptical of claims that any teaching can be conducted in an entirely neutral and objective fashion, the terms "neutral" and "objective" nonetheless were used by the Court in its decision. See note 56.
53. Para. 11.
54. Para. 40. For a detailed review of this case, see P. T. Clarke, Religion and Public Schools in Quebec: The Supreme Court of Canada Has Spoken . . . At Least for Now, *Education and Law Journal*, 21(2) (2012), 167–183.
55. 2015 SCC 12.
56. Para. 72.
57. Para. 75.
58. *E.T. v. Hamilton-Wentworth District School Board*, 2017, ONCA 893.
59. Para. 27.
60. 2020 BCSC 15.

61. Para. 70.
62. Para. 94.
63. Para. 108.
64. 2020 SKCA 34.
65. Para. 8.
66. SQ 2019 c. 12.
67. 2020 SKCA 34.
68. http://trc.ca/assets/pdf/Calls_to_Action_English2.pdf.
69. As Lacourciere J.A. concluded in an Ontario case ruling (*Zylberberg* (1988)), "the removal of all religion from the school environment would be more consistent with the encouragement of a homogeneous society than with the preservation or enhancement of a multicultural one" (p. 27).
70. Admittedly, there are risks teaching about religion (like the indoctrination that occurred in residential schools), just as there are in any classroom (like Keegstra's denial of the Holocaust in his social studies lessons). However, Clarke is confident that the Charter does provide a "reliable bulwark against harmful and unjustifiable manifestations of religion in our public schools" (Paul Clarke, Religion, Public Education and the Charter: Where Do We Go Now? *McGill Journal of Education*, 40(3) (2005), 352). The courts support the notion that modelling for students how to rationally sort through all manner of controversial topics and questions is sound pedagogy in a diverse and free nation. Teaching about religion is only as problematic as the teacher's abilities and motivations, just as it is with all other potentially sensitive subject areas, like sex and the Holocaust. Essentially, the potential risks can be mitigated if all schools meet provincial accountability guidelines (most notably curriculum requirements and the hiring of certified teachers), if the education focuses on the value of the search rather than on proselytizing, and if the fundamental principles of freedom and equality enshrined in the Charter are upheld. The best teachers strive to include many viewpoints, not to disenfranchise some; to promote discernment, critical thought, and understanding, not to indoctrinate; and to expose students to the rich secular-religious diversity found in Canadian society, not to inculcate personal agendas. The Quebec Ministry summarizes this imperative well in this translation of its *Ethics, Religion and Culture* curriculum: "As these disciplines relate to personal and family dynamics which are complex and often delicate, an additional duty and reserve is expected from the teacher to not assert his beliefs or his views. However, when an opinion issued undermines the dignity of the person or proposed actions that undermine the common good, the teacher intervenes by referring to the . . . goals of the program. He must also cultivate the art of questioning by promoting values such as openness to diversity, respect for beliefs, recognition of self and others and the common good" (*L. (S.). v. Commission scolaire des Chênes* (2010), QCCA. 346, at para 21).
71. Harvey Siegel, *Educating Reason: Rationality, Critical Thinking, and Education* (London: Routledge, 1988), 61.
72. In the *Chamberlain v. Surrey School District* ruling, Chief Justice McLachlin notes that embracing the process of respectful debate is vital in a free and diverse society. She calls it learning to engage in "cognitive dissonance."
73. Para. 76, 99.
74. Secularist viewpoints often claim social neutrality, which sounds like a laudable goal but is a fictitious condition: "There is no such thing as a point of view – certainly not one sufficiently comprehensive to survey or to organize a society – that is either philosophically or theologically neutral" (Farrow, *Recognizing Religion in a Secular Society*, 165). In fact, it would be academically

irresponsible to suggest that any education is not at least somewhat indoctrinating. Therefore, arguably, it is impossible to offer Canadian students any kind of education that is entirely "religiously" neutral. All we can hope to do to maintain academic integrity and balance is to champion equality and inclusivity and not pretend that modern education is somehow a "religiously" neutral or morally benign endeavor.

75. Paul F. Campos, Secular Fundamentalism, *Columbia Law Review*, 94 (1994), 1825.
76. We are reminded here of earlier definitions of "secular," as offered in the *Chamberlain* (2002) ruling, in which the Supreme Court of Canada found that "secular" should mean inclusion of diverse voices, including the religious.
77. The Truth and Reconciliation Commission of Canada (TRC) was established in 2008 to document the too often abusive history and tragic consequences of church-administrated (residential) schools. In 2015, the TRC released a summary report called *94 Calls to Action*, including seven regarding education. See http://trc.ca/assets/pdf/Calls_to_Action_English2.pdf.
78. Jean Elshtain, Persons, Politics, and a Catholic Understanding of Human Rights, in Douglas Farrow (ed.), *Recognizing Religion in a Secular Society: Essays in Pluralism, Religion, and Public Policy* (Montreal and Kingston: McGill-Queen's University Press, 2004), 38.
79. Claude Ryan, Foreword, in D. Farrow (ed.), *Recognizing Religion in a Secular Society* (Montreal and Kingston: McGill-Queen's University Press, 2004), x.

4 Law, Education, and the Place of Religion in Public Schools in England

Javier García Oliva and Helen Hall

Introduction

In many respects, England[1] is an idiosyncratic nation, a trait that certainly applies where the legal treatment of religion is concerned.[2] The overarching relationship between faith and the state in England is unusual and, as might be anticipated, this filters through into the place of spirituality in schools. As is often the case, there is some distance between the law as articulated in theory and applied in practice, both where constitutional precepts and statutory law on education are concerned.[3]

Like the plot of a long-running television drama, it can be difficult for those immersed within it to guide newcomers through the twists and turns. Consequently, within this opening assessment of the legal foundation for education and religion, we start our tour with some preliminary words about the character of the Constitution and legal framework. This backdrop provides the stage on which the regulation of education is played out; without this context, the picture would appear either bewildering or distorted.

As a reader by now may expect, the fundamental structure of this chapter is isomorphic to the other assessments of national paradigms within this book, so it follows the same steps. However, we note that in our exploration of religion and ideological freedom in state schools in England,[4] a variety of identifiable themes recur in different guises. Some of the refrains are common to the discourse in almost all jurisdictions such as questions relating to the mechanisms for protecting the liberties of parents, pupils, and staff, or the wearing and displaying of symbols relating to faith. In contrast, others arise out of the particular character of the English setting: the concept of religious ethos, the requirement for collective worship, and the relationship religion has with the wider curriculum.

This chapter considers all of these themes within the course of this discussion as different issues naturally arise in the unfolding dialogue. We then draw together our thoughts for some closing reflections in the concluding paragraphs. We hope at this stage to offer some insight both into English responses to universal challenges in this arena and to conundrums that emerge about of the very particular legal and societal backdrop being addressed.

The Legal Foundation for Education and Religion

Constitutional Treatment of Religion

As is well-known for those interested in law, religion, and education, England has an established church, forged in the turbulence of the Age of Reformation and successive Tudor monarchs.[5] Yet, this national church was encased within constitutional arrangements forged in the fires of civil war: the trial and execution of Charles I as the culmination of a conflict sparked in large part by religion and the forcible dispossession of his younger son, James II, for his Catholic faith. Although the church of the Henrician Reformation might have been envisioned by its royal architect as a creature of the Crown, it rapidly became the church of the social and political elite, while at the same time Parliament gradually drained power from the monarchy, absorbing it for itself.

This meant that those governing English society effectively formed a closed shop in terms of faith from the so-called Glorious Revolution through to the early 19th century. Fortunately, this ideological hegemony became increasingly untenable by the 1800s, but the manner in which it was dismantled was unusual such that it shapes the legal landscape in the 21st century. This is a topic on which we have written extensively, but for present purposes we wish to draw out three points which are essential for understanding the contemporary context.[6]

First, no revolution, either violent or political, ever toppled the position of the Church of England. This meant that reforms happened on a piecemeal, ad hoc basis as inconsistencies were identified and addressed. The lack of systematic root and branch reform left some lumps in the legal lawn, signifying that more by chance than design, some elements of Anglican privilege were to remain. It is also fair to observe that some social questions were more contentious than others. Education was always a political hot potato, and in historical times it was generally other Christian groups demanding a stake in the regime.[7] The resulting tussles have left behind some benefits specific to the Church of England, yet other provisions refer expressly to Christianity in general terms instead of "faith" more widely defined.[8]

Second, generally speaking, Anglican privilege was not removed from the Church of England but was widened to include other faith groups within its remit. The levelling tendencies of this legal evolution therefore gradually created an environment in which religion was regarded as a positive phenomenon and supported by the law. It had always been axiomatic that the faith of the Church of England was to be facilitated and supported, such that parity of treatment demanded that other religious traditions, and indeed conscientious positions, receive similar respect.

Third, the constitutional model of Establishment can be seen as a set of Russian nesting dolls. The smallest, inner doll represents the ties between the state and the Church of England; the middle doll signifies systemic support for Christianity more widely, which arose from the historical context; and the largest, outer doll, encasing the others, can be understood as the generally positive and supportive stance towards faith and conscience. All three layers of Establishment can be discerned in the structure of the law around religion in state schools.

The Religious Ethos of Schools

Entirely separate from the division between privately financed and publicly funded schools[9] is the distinction between schools with a specially defined religious ethos, or, in common parlance, "faith schools,"[10] and schools without a specially defined religious ethos.[11] Understanding the significance of this categorization is crucial in two respects.

First, all faith schools, whether privately financed or state funded, enjoy exceptions from the otherwise all-prevailing Equality Law, which prohibits discrimination on grounds of religion or belief.[12] This means that within the parameters allowed, authorities in these schools may select both pupils and teaching staff on the basis of their religious convictions.

Second, non-faith schools are not secular in nature, at least if they are funded by taxpayers. As Rivers justifiably argues, the operation of Establishment means that all state schools are in some sense "faith schools."[13] In light of the requirements discussed below, both for a daily act of worship and the involvement of the Church of England in setting Religious Education curricula, it would be difficult to deny that "Anglican" is the default religious character. Having noted this, it is important to emphasise that 4,644 Church of England "faith schools" enjoy the special status in terms of the Equality Law that comes with this designation.[14]

Daily Act of Worship

Officials in publicly funded schools without specially defined religious characters are required by statute to conduct a daily act of worship,[15] which is "wholly or mainly of a broadly Christian character."[16] Government guidance on this, published in 1994, which remains in force, states the aim of this activity:

> Collective worship in schools should aim to provide the opportunity for pupils to worship God, to consider spiritual and moral

> issues and to explore their own beliefs; to encourage participation and response, whether through active involvement in the presentation of worship or through listening to and joining in the worship offered; and to develop community spirit, promote a common ethos and shared values, and reinforce positive attitudes.[17]

There are no requirements about the time of day or the size of the group in which this must take place. The guidance does not require the whole school community to gather in an assembly hall, nor must it take any prescribed form. It should be observed that the mandate is for the worship to be of Christian, rather than Anglican, character. Further, the caveat "wholly or mainly of a broadly Christian character" gives ample scope for the accommodation of other faith perspectives, encompassing themes such as compassion and respect for fellow human beings, animals, and the environment.

It is possible, then, to satisfy the requirement of the legislation and formulate worship which will be acceptable to many people across a spectrum of faith traditions. Nonetheless, there is a stated aim that it should involve God, meaning that an exclusively humanist or atheist interpretation of the statute is not compatible with the guidance. While it might be possible to devise a formula that is secular but in harmony with Christian values, if no concept of the Divine ever featured during the course of the school year, the rules would be clearly transgressed. The qualification "mainly" allows for some atheist or humanist elements to be woven into the programme, but these may not lawfully evict religious-based actions altogether.

As might be assumed, there is provision that faith schools will provide worship in conformity with the character of the institution.[18] What this means and how it is interpreted depends on the school's trust deeds and other foundational documents.

Religious Education and the Standing Advisory Council on Religious Education

Every local authority is obliged to set up a Standing Advisory Council on Religious Education (SACRE),[19] a subject that all state-funded schools are tasked with delivering.[20] Church of England representation on each SACRE is mandatory, but there is scope for other religious, and indeed humanist, representatives to be incorporated. Non-statutory governmental guidance strongly encourages multiple religious perspectives to be incorporated into the SACRE, and in practice this is the case in the overwhelming majority of contexts.[21]

Nevertheless, in granting the Church of England a seat at the table as of right, and not extending this automatic invitation to other faith groups, there is an undeniable favouring of the established church. One possible explanation for the lack of reform may lie in pragmatism, in that the Church of England has a parochial structure that covers every community, while the density of other faith groups varies dramatically from region to region and even between districts in the same urban area.[22]

For instance, in a location with a majority Muslim population, it would make no sense to fail to have Muslim representation, but in other parts of the country it might be difficult to find a Muslim representative. Equally, not all faith groups have a single, cohesive hierarchical structure or identity that would make it a challenge were there a blanket requirement to select a delegate, and might even result in the local members of that community disputing the stance or appropriateness of any appointee. This is not intended as a plea in mitigation for the current system but a reflection that were reforms to be undertaken, it might make more practical sense to demolish the existing structure and begin again. Trying to repurpose a model which was built around a Church of England template to fit the diverse shapes and sizes of religious groups in contemporary Britain may be doomed to frustration and, worse, inadvertent exclusion.

Setting aside the membership of the steering group on the curriculum, it must be stressed that the teaching of Religious Education must be religiously neutral; this has been the norm since the 19th century.[23] The purpose of Religious Education is academic study rather than the practice of devotion. Nevertheless, the impossibility for achieving neutral or uncontroversial interpretations of complex material involving human culture means that even the scholarly examination of religion is a sensitive area. It is thus unsurprising that the study of religion is included in the formal statutory structures for the protection of ideological freedom to which the chapter now turns.

The Protection for Freedom of Religion or Belief in Education

Overarching Provisions

The British government signed the European Convention on Human Rights (ECHR) in the early 1950s, yet the ECHR was not incorporated into domestic law until the close of the 20th century.[24] "Bringing the Convention home" means that the following rights are enforceable in English courts: the freedom of conscience and belief,[25] private and family life,[26] and education in conformity with parental philosophical and religious teachings.[27] Further, as public bodies, state-maintained schools are required to act in conformity with the ECHR. The significance of this high level of protection and challenge should not be underestimated, but other features of the Constitutional Culture of England that are relevant.

One point that deserves mention is the unquestionable profile of the United Nations Convention on the Rights of the Child (UNCRC)[28] within educational circles. This document and its importance have been strongly promoted by the Children's Commissioners[29] in each of the component nations, including England.[30] However, even though it has been ratified by the United Kingdom (UK), it has not been incorporated into the domestic legal framework, meaning that it has only persuasive force in British courts as a result.

Nevertheless, the ongoing drive to make young people aware of their rights in the international law arena, and confident in asserting them, is worth noting in this context. If pupils have posters on the walls of their classrooms and/or lessons reminding them that they possess, among other things, a right to freedom of religion, this can only help to empower them in demanding respect for that right.[31]

We can attest that in our work, regularly visiting schools to talk about human rights as part of the outreach programs of our respective universities, we are invariably struck with how well-informed and articulate pupils are about their freedoms from primary age right through to 18-year-olds. Consequently, this treaty guarantee of religious liberty for young people is not without direct influence at the grassroots level, despite its weakness in juridical terms.

It should also be noted that in addition to these human rights instruments, both international and domestic, there is the wider legal environment to consider. This is arguably a double-edged sword in this context. On the one hand, from at least the 19th century, there has been a strong common law trope of respecting individual liberty when it comes to freedom of belief,[32] but balanced against this there is also, as we have discussed at length above, firm support for facilitating collective religious practice.

The judicial approach tends to mirror the statutory one that we are about to address, in essence demanding that individuals be excused participation in matters that offend their beliefs, unless there is some countervailing need for compliance, but protecting the right of groups to continue with their practices.[33] In other words, individuals cannot usually be compelled to join in practices or ceremonies that they find objectionable, but will not be permitted to demand that organizations with which they are associated cease the activity in question.

In examining the English context, it is important to keep front and centre the idea that there is no concept of a right to religiously neutral space in general terms or in the specific context of education. Neither is there any guarantee that faith will be kept safely contained in a designated area, like dangerous substances in the school chemistry laboratory. That is simply not the norm that English law or English schools are seeking to achieve. In fact, such a project would undermine the entire purpose and project of facilitating faith schools supported by taxpayers.

It would also be out of step with at least the juridical position of schools within a specially defined religious ethos, given their default Anglican character. This being so, how are the human rights guarantees set out above ensured in practice?

Daily Worship

Parents have a right to withdraw their children from daily worship, and young people of sixth form ages 16 and over have the right to withdraw themselves should they wish to do so.[34] Because the law does not specify what withdrawal means, there is scope for negotiation and flexibility. Therefore, some families might be content if it is agreed that pupils are permitted to sit quietly during prayers but are not expected to verbally join in or adopt a physical posture of prayer. Still others might consider it more appropriate for pupils to be physically removed from the rooms where the religious worship takes place.

It is difficult to defend the current regime in respect of children's rights and autonomy, given the failure to provide any mechanism to honour the choices of young people to attend or not attend worship, independently of parental preferences. As Lundy argues, this position is not reconcilable with the UNCRC[35] and it is out of step with child law in England more generally. Parental decision-making capacity is very deliberately labelled "parental responsibility," not a form of parental right[36] that has been interpreted to exist for the benefit for the *child*, not the adult holder,[37] and is a tapering right.[38] In other words, once a child achieves capacity to make an informed choice about a particular issue, parental responsibility for that issue terminates. So, for instance, a 14-year-old child might be capable of deciding whether to have an ear-lobe pierced but not to choose whether to cease taking medicine controlling her epilepsy.

A blanket legislative policy that only young people aged 16 and above can determine their involvement in worship, an action unlikely in most cases to have dramatic or irreversible consequences, drives a coach and horses through these well-established principles of English law. Commentators may have differing opinions on the English legal regime in respect of child autonomy. Regardless, it is undeniable that the policy on daily worship is anomalous.

The rights accorded to parents, combined with an institutional option for school authorities to apply for a determination from their SACRE that the worship provided for some or all of their pupils should be excused from the "broadly Christian" requirement,[39] means that the ideological freedoms of adults receive extensive consideration and protection. There are also, quite rightly, provisions that prevent staff members from experiencing discriminatory treatment on the basis of their choice to attend or not to attend worship.[40] Yet, the young people who are intended to be the primary recipients and beneficiaries of this worship are much less well provided for in terms of protecting their rights.

Religious Education

In terms of a right to withdrawal from religious education, the position effectively mirrors that of daily worship, meaning that children's rights are assumed to be coterminous with parental ideological liberty, at least until the age of 16.[41] There is also provision for parents to withdraw their children from school during Religious Education classes in order to enable them to receive alternative instruction. This, in practice, is rarely used, as in pragmatic terms it is going to be a logistical challenge for most families and schools to achieve this for a single lesson in the course of a school day. Further, the academic, as opposed to devotional, nature of the study makes withdrawal a less pressing issue in the eyes of many parents, especially because a syllabus must reflect the religious landscape of the UK and including humanist and other nonreligious worldviews.[42]

Relationships and Sex Education

Because the statutory framework in relation sex education is changing in England, it is a matter of concern for some faith communities.[43] The currently existing right to withdraw pupils from sex education will be retained and will continue to be vested in parents. Yet, it is clear that there will be no wider option to remove pupils from teaching in this subject. The assurance that there will be no sex education element in the phrase has the double-edged sword for some parents of a lack of optional withdrawal for younger pupils. It also means that parents cannot prevent their children from learning about the diversity of families and relationships in contemporary England. Because this has already been the subject of considerable controversy, it therefore seems an appropriate juncture at which to move on to our assessment of the judicial analysis of these debates.

Judicial Analysis of the Freedom of Religion or Belief in Education

Traditional Concerns: Collective Worship, Religious Education, and School Uniforms

It is undeniable that some elements of English society are discontented about the current legislative framework in relation to both Collective Worship and Religious Education and are actively campaigning for change. Of these, Humanists UK[44] and the National Secular Society[45] are the largest and most high-profile examples. Nevertheless, it is accurate to observe that in political terms, reform is not high on the agenda for any of the main parties, partly perhaps because it is a Pandora's box that neither side wishes to open. It is also the case that both Labour and Conservative governments have been consistently supportive of schools with a religious ethos. Perhaps for a combination of all of these reasons, although these issues have come before the courts on occasion,[46] there has not been either a plethora of litigation or a great volume of political discussion, at least in comparison to some other jurisdictions covered in this book.

We argue that this may relate in part to the way in which the rules of engagement have been drawn up, as there was never any promise of achieving a religiously neutral space in state funded education and, therefore, there is no scope for action on the basis that this guarantee has been dishonoured. Neither is there a strong political tradition, or anticlericalism or secularism, of the sort witnessed in countries such as Spain because faith itself does not tend to be a political issue.

It is also important for us to stress the significance of acknowledging the distinction between the letter of the law on the page and the way in which rules are interpreted and applied. For example, most school authorities are at pains to interpret the "broadly Christian character" in a way that is inclusive and to de facto provide multi-faith, humanist-respecting acts of worship or reflection in a manner that is broadly legally compliant but also socially sensitive. We are not suggesting that England is any sort of paragon of perfection, but there is a strong commitment across much of the educational sector towards fostering respect, inclusion, and understanding of diversity.[47] Reading the law in the abstract, without an awareness of its embodied context, would create a very misleading impression.

Ironically, or perhaps indicatively, courts at one stage witnessed more litigation over religious dress and symbols than assemblies or Religious Education.[48] Anyone who has experience of having passed through the English school system is aware of the curious cultural obsession with the minutiae of uniform requirements and the glee with which at least a certain kind of teaching professional enforces them. This is comically immortalized by the novelist Sue Townsend in *The Secret Diary of Adrian Mole, Aged 13¾*,[49] which features the ordinarily conformist Adrian getting into conflict with school authorities for wearing red socks under his black school trousers.

The stream of litigation has now established some clear principles but, unsurprisingly, has begun to dry up in recent years. The leading case in many respects remains the 2006 *Begum* case, which sheds useful light on the underlying principles.[50] An action was brought by Shabina Begum on the basis that her school uniform did not permit her to wear a jilbab – a form of Islamic dress which she considered to be appropriate for her post-puberty. The House of Lords found that the policy did interfere with her Article 9(2) right to manifest her religious beliefs, very robustly rejecting any suggestion that there was no interference on the basis that the pupil could seek an alternative education in a setting more conducive to her religious needs.

In its rationale, the House of Lords went on to stress that Article 9(2) of the ECHR is a qualified right, and that in this instance the limitation on religious freedom was justified. School authorities had developed their policy in consultation with the community and had drawn up clothing requirements that respected the religious needs expressed by the Islamic voices and at the same time were safe and practical for a school environment. Further, the House of Lords stressed that some sections of the Muslim community were uncomfortable with the wearing of more conservative dress in school, on the basis that it might generate unwelcome pressure for other young women to conform.

In summary, pupils have a right to manifest their religious beliefs in the form of dress and symbols, but this may be limited to such as extent as is necessary to satisfy legitimate aims of the schools. So, a garment such as a jilbab is more likely to be found problematic than a Sikh bangle, in light of the different practical implications, but the outcome of individual cases will always depend on the facts at issue.

The other dimension of *Begum* that is worthy of mention was that no discussion was undertaken about the operation of Article 9 ECHR in relation to minors. In other words, did the child in whose name the litigation was being brought forward genuinely hold the requisite belief? The issue is pertinent in *Begum*, because there were some doubts about the independence of choice being made by the litigant and suspicions of family pressure. It is true that commentators such as Fernández have dismissed this as "anti-Muslim prejudice," but from our perspective this is a misplaced concern because the independence of belief for minor applicants should always be addressed seriously by courts in Article 9 cases.[51]

Because parents or other appropriate adults may properly assert their own Article 8, 9, and Protocol 2 Article 1 rights in respect of the education of their children, it is neither necessary nor desirable to give them a second bite of the cherry by appropriating the legal identities of their children. This holds good whether the case involves Muslim, atheist, pagan, or vegetarian minors because the children in question are independent legal persons and not parental satellites.

Aside from this specific concern, the picture in respect of religious dress and symbols is now relatively settled. It may also be that there was a growth of cultural understanding and sensitivity in the course of the 20th century, and that human rights and modern equality law[52] have become more embedded in the praxis of schools and other public institutions. We therefore turn our attention to more recent areas of controversy, in particular around sexuality and gender identity.

Sexuality, and Gender Identity

As outlined above, the legal framework around teaching children about human relationships and sexuality is changing. It must be understood that this is taking place in the context of controversies that have arisen under the existing regime, in which community representatives, in particular Muslim and conservative Christian, have objection to teaching in schools around LGBT issues. The dissent has escalated to the point of protest in some instances that is so serious as to necessitate court action to prevent intimidating demonstrations on a repeated basis, making both staff and pupils afraid to enter schools.[53]

The response of the courts to date has been to protect the right of schools to educate children in compliance with statutory frameworks, and the need to do this has justified the undeniable restriction of the Articles 9 and 10[54] rights of parents and other protestors. However, it raises questions about the judicial approach were a case to be brought on the basis that the lack of a right to withdraw pupils from wider relationships teaching was in breach of Articles 8, 9, and Protocol 2 Article 1 of the ECHR. If challenges are put forward on this basis following the coming into force of the new rules, what does current case law suggest about the outcome?

As a starting point, we should emphasize, of course, the consistent position of the Strasbourg and domestic courts in asserting that there is no hierarchy of Convention rights. Thus, where a clash occurs, the prioritization in a particular factual paradigm does not indicate that one fundamental freedom has been favoured over another and could similarly expect to triumph in future litigation.[55]

It is perhaps not entirely helpful to view this debate solely through the prism of state action versus individual religious or ideological freedoms. Indeed, this could equally as well be seen as a contest between the rights of parents and children, because both dimensions are important in terms of the legal balancing exercise to be undertaken. This is not simply a matter of individuals or communities versus the power of the state; it is also a question of adults entrusted with legal responsibilities and powers being considered in relation to the children who are the subjects of the same. There is the perennial, thorny problem of safeguarding the family unit from undue intrusion, on the one hand, and giving appropriate recognition to the rights of children as vulnerable and systemically disempowered human beings on the other.[56]

Beginning with the keystone case of *Gillick*,[57] we are confronted with the principle, previously outlined, that parental responsibility is a child-centred concept. Accordingly, this responsibility only confers on adults authority for the benefit of children. As a result, then, this authority is naturally and gradually shed as capacity of minors grows, just as milk-teeth are shed one by one from the mouth as adult dentition emerges.

As a corollary, we also face the basic principle that parents do not enjoy the right to control the information that third parties may supply to their children, provided that such parties are acting lawfully.

Gillick concerned a mother who sought assurance in the abstract that her daughters would not receive contraceptive advice or medical treatment without her knowledge. The claim, of course, spectacularly backfired when the court drew the opposite conclusion and she inadvertently succeeded in making her name synonymous with children's rights for evermore. This means that while those with parental responsibility can limit the flow of information to their children by controlling their young, for instance, in relation to access to the internet, television, or books, they have no legal right to prevent third parties from furnishing the children with information should the opportunity arise. For example, a zookeeper giving a talk about lions does not have to obtain parental permission before revealing knowledge to children about mammalian reproduction. If the zookeeper happens to be discussing mating and cubs, then that is entirely legitimate, regardless of the age of the audience.

Nor it is not suggested that there is no distinction between visiting a zoo and sending a child to a state school. Still, the basic principle that there is no right to regulate lawful communications from third parties is a key one that should not be lost in the mist. The Protocol 2 Article 1 provision of the ECHR was designed to protect children against the evils of state indoctrination.[58] It is not intended to give families a right to demand à la carte education in state schools, cherry-picking aspects of the curriculum that they find acceptable to their worldview. As such, we argue that this is apparent from first principles, given that such an interpretation would effectively undermine the entire project of publicly provided education. If every parent could veto choices of books in English literature, for instance, excluding all references to witchcraft or feminism, or topics in history, it would be impossible for schools to cope in terms of administration and resources.

Aside from this, though, we argue that it is also apparent in the response that the UK legal framework has made to the teaching of creationism in publicly funded schools. The parameters within which academies, the most autonomous form of state school in respect of governance, must operate no longer allow for creationism to be presented as a scientific theory.[59] Consequently, if such a restraint on collective intellectual freedom is permitted and desirable as a sine qua non for publicly funded education, we argue that a fortiori individual religious freedom must be subject to restraints.

The creationism case also highlights that the reasoning behind this is not simply a question of resources, because there are also collective concerns about the quality of education in terms of content as well as systemic acceptance of the need to draw lines around what is acceptable in academic and ideological terms. At the most extreme end of the spectrum, very few people would advocate for racist, right-wing extremists to prevent their children from being exposed to a different way of viewing the world and avoid having their children participate in Black History Month. Therefore, the mere fact that some parents find the content of relationships education unpalatable on ideological grounds does not render it unlawful because there can be no overarching right of ideological veto.

Having acknowledged these arguments about parental rights, it is unquestionable that tensions around ideology and identity continue to simmer within British society. Moreover, these tensions lurk in the background of legal and social clashes around religious freedoms and schools. From 2014, schools have had a duty to promote "British Values,"[60] which explicitly include recognition of living in a religiously plural society and rejecting all forms of discrimination.[61] The link between this initiative and the much-criticized antiterrorist "Prevent Strategy," which many citizens felt was unfairly angled towards Islam, understandably increased disquiet in some quarters.[62] Some, at least, of the anger expressed about elements of the curriculum in state schools being opposed to religious teaching relates to a sense in some communities of living in a hostile environment in which their culture and worldview are no longer welcome.[63]

The evil of Islamophobia and the urgency of tackling it more effectively should not be downplayed, but at the same time other faith communities feel out of step with the values now enshrined in the legal framework, specifically the teaching on relationships in state schools.[64] It cannot be denied that one of the reasons why Religious Education is apt to be controversial is that it has always included a "moral" dimension, such that if the teaching of social ethics is to exported from Religious Education to Relationships Education, then the same issues will arise. It is not possible to escape Groundhog Day with a relabelling exercise.

Equally, a liberal democratic state does have an obligation to ensure that the freedoms and dignity guaranteed by its constitution are enhanced and religious minorities are not the only minorities whose needs must be considered. If merely teaching about the existence of same-sex relationships and the need for respect for different kinds of people is sufficient to rouse public demonstration in some school communities, what must it feel like to be a child of gay parents in such a setting? In any future litigation around the new framework, judges will have to tread their way through a minefield of intersecting needs and vulnerabilities.

Emerging Issues

A separate but related delicate area is also to be observed in the rapidly evolving debate around religion, belief, and gender identity. On the one hand, there has been a dramatic growth in the number of children in state schools who are transgender, identify as nonbinary,[65] or feel able to be open about a physical intersex condition in a way that would have been challenging in previous generations, sometimes choosing not to identify as male or female.[66]

Questions around transgender rights in particular continue to be a battleground, with both conservative religious voices and some sections of the feminist movement making a somewhat unexpected alliance. In a recent ruling, *Forstater v. CGD*,[67] an employment tribunal found that the opinion that transwomen were not women failed to meet the threshold to qualify as a viewpoint deserving protection in a democratic society. This sent a powerful message that the courts will uphold the provisions of equality law in respect of gender identity, and it is highly likely to have serious implications for ongoing debates in educational contexts.

In recent times there have been threats of employment proceedings from an Oxford teacher dismissed after "misgendering" a transgender pupil. He claimed that this was accidental, but openly admitted to deliberately avoiding use of the masculine pronouns which the student elected to use.[68]

Further, parents in an Isle of Wight primary school complained that they had not been consulted about a pupil in the class transitioning, arguing that this would have a negative impact on their son, who would be confused and at risk of punishment for asking questions.[69] Interestingly, the school in this case was a Church of England faith school, which affirmed its commitment to supporting the pupil and equality law. At the same time, there was no evidence whatsoever that fellow students asking questions would in any way be disciplined as opposed to receiving age-appropriate answers as they processed the change in their friend. In light of this, it is hard to imagine what cause of action the parents could have hoped to bring in English law. Given that this is clearly another arena in which some religious communities regard government policy and equality law on gender identity to be at odds with their faith, it is likely that it will generate further conflict in educational contexts.

Conclusion

We have seen that, paradoxically, although the stance of the legal framework towards religion is extremely accommodating, the bulk of litigation being brought forward is from families with religious convictions as opposed to those defending secularist ideology. Moreover, the key concern does not relate to the residual privilege enjoyed by both Anglicanism and Christianity because the practical application and interpretation of the legal paradigm is by and large flexible, inclusive, and accommodating.

The present locus of tension is far more around the teaching about relationships, sexuality, and gender, which altogether is ethical in nature and is found outside of Religious Education and provisions on conscientious objection. Given that the clash reflects a wider social and political struggle at present, it is doubtful that there will be any clear or definite resolution in law for the foreseeable future.

Notes

1. This discussion specifically relates to England, rather than the UK as a whole, because devolution arrangements in place, combined with differing relations between church and state in Wales, Scotland, and Northern Ireland, mean that the legal, social, and political arrangements around religion in schools are radically different within each of the component nations of the state.
2. J García Oliva, Church, State and Establishment in the United Kingdom in the 21st Century: Anachronism or Idiosyncrasy? *Public Law* (2010), 482.
3. D. Feldman, One, None or Several? Perspectives of the UK's Constitution(s), *Cambridge Law Journal*, 64(2) (2005), 329, 335.
4. In European English, the term "public schools" ordinarily signifies "private schools," so for the sake of clarity, we have opted to consistently use the term "state schools."
5. For a detailed discussion of the sociocultural impact of this upheaval, see E. Duffy, *The Voices of Morebath: Reformation and Rebellion in an English Village* (London: Yale University Press, 2003).
6. J. García Oliva and H. Hall, *Law, Religion and the Constitution: Balancing Beliefs in Britain* (Abingdon: Routledge, 2018).
7. See, for example, the controversy over the Elementary Education Act 1870, discussed by F. Cordasco, *A Brief History of Education* (Totowa, NJ: Littlefield, 1987), 92–100.
8. Education Act 1996, s 390: This requires that the statutory daily act of worship in state schools be "wholly or mainly of a broadly Christian character."
9. R. Sandberg, *Law and Religion* (Cambridge: Cambridge University Press, 2012), 152.
10. It should also be noted that there are a variety of possible governance arrangements for state funded faith schools, and indeed non-faith schools. A detailed survey of them is out of the scope of this study, but for some more detailed consideration of the different arrangements and that implications of this specifically relating to faith, see J. García Oliva and D. Ginn, The Religious and Ideological Freedom of Teachers in the English Legal Framework, *Oxford Journal of Law and Religion*, 7(2) (2018), 1.
11. School Standards and Framework Act 1998, ss 58–69 (as amended).
12. Equality Act 2010 s4.
13. J. Rivers, *The Law of Organized Religions* (Oxford: Oxford University Press, 2010), 234.
14. Church Schools and Academies, Church of England, n.d. Retrieved from www.churchofengland. org/about/education-and-schools/church-schools-and-academies.
15. Education Act 1996, s390.
16. Ibid., sch20.

17. HM Government, "Collective Worship in Schools" Guidance Document (31/1/94) para. 50. Retrieved June 20, 2020, from www.gov.uk/government/publications/collective-worship-in-schools.
18. School Standards and Framework Act 1998, s63.
19. Education Act 1996, s390.
20. Education Act 2002, s80.
21. HM Government, *Religious Education in English Schools: Non-Statutory Guidance*, 2010. See especially pp. 19–25.
22. Church of England, *Research and Statistics*. Retrieved June 20, 2020, from www.churchofengland.org/researchandstats.
23. Education Act 1870, s14.
24. Human Rights Act 1998.
25. However, it should be noted that the drafting of Article 9 refers expressly to a right to manifest a belief on a profound and serious matter. Regrettably, neither the UK nor Strasbourg courts have discussed in depth how this might relate to religious freedom for children too young to form independent beliefs. See further García Oliva and H. Hall, Religious Decision-Making and the Capacity of Children in the United Kingdom, *Laicidad y Libertades* (2013), 137–170.
26. European Convention on Human Rights Article 8.
27. European Convention on Human Rights Article 9 and Protocol 2 Article 1.
28. United Nations Convention on the Rights of the Child 1989. Retrieved from www.unicef.org/child-rights-convention.
29. HM Government, *The Office of Children's Commissioner*. Retrieved June 6, 2020, from www.gov.uk/government/organisations/office-of-the-children-s-commissioner#:~:text=The%20Office%20of%20the%20Children's%20Commissioner%20promotes%20the%20rights%2C%20views,or%20decisions%20affecting%20their%20lives.&text=Office%20of%20the%20Children's%20Commissioner%20is%20an%20executive%20non%2Ddepartmental,by%20the%20Department%20for%20Education: "The Office of the Children's Commissioner promotes the rights, views and interests of children in policies or decisions affecting their lives. They particularly represent children who are vulnerable or who find it hard to make their views known. The Children's Commissioner is an executive, non-departmental public body, sponsored by the Department for Education."
30. The Children's Commissioner, *Guide to the UNCRC*, October 1, 2014. Retrieved June 20, 2020, from www.childrenscommissioner.gov.uk/publication/guide-to-the-uncrc/.
31. UNCRC, Article 14.
32. See, for example, *R (Jenkins) v. H M Coroner for Portsmouth and South East Hampshire* (2008) EWHC 3229.
33. For instance, bids to replace the current regime of allowing witnesses in court a choice of forming of oath in favour of a single secular oath have been rejected. See National Secular Society, *Magistrates Reject Proposal for Single Secular Oath*, October 21, 2013. Retrieved June 20, 2020, from www.secularism.org.uk/news/2013/10/oath-taking-debated-in-england-wales-and-ireland.
34. See School Standards and Framework Act 1998 s71; and Education and Inspections Act 2006 s55.
35. L. Lundy, Voice Is Not Enough: Conceptualizing Article 12 of the United Nations Convention on the Rights of the Child, *British Educational Research Journal*, 33 (2013), 297.
36. Children Act 1989, s3.

37. The holder of parental responsibility may be a parent, either legally or biologically; see Children Act 1989, s2.
38. *Gillick v. West Norfolk and Wisbech Area Health Authority* [1986] AC 112.
39. *School Standards and Framework Act 1998*, s20.
40. Ibid., s59(2).
41. Ibid., s71.
42. *R (Fox) v. Secretary of State for Education* (2015) EWHC 3404 (Admin).
43. Children and Social Work Act 2017, s34 provides for relationships and sex education to be taught in all English schools. From September 2020, the Relationships Education, Relationships and Sex Education and Health Education (England) Regulations 2019 will come into force. The Department for Education has also produced a briefing note on the same: HM Government, *Relationships Education, Relationships and Sex Education and Health Education FAQs*, April 5, 2019. Retrieved June 20, 2020, from www.gov.uk/government/news/relationships-education-relationships-and-sex-education-rse-and-health-education-faqs.
44. Humanists UK, *Campaigns.* Retrieved June 20, 2020, from https://humanism.org.uk/education/assemblies-for-all/.
45. National Secular Society, *Right to Education.* Retrieved June 20, 2020, from www.secularism.org.uk/faith-schools/right-to-education.html.
46. *R (Fox) v. Secretary of State for Education* (2015) EWHC 3404 (Admin).
47. See, for example, Nottingham Primary Academy. Retrieved June 20, 2020, from http://primary.nottinghamacademy.org/page/?title=British+Values&pid=139.
48. *R (Playfoot) v. Millais School Governing Body EWHC* 1698 (Admin); *R v. Headteacher and Governors of Denbigh High School*, ex p Begum UKHL 15, (2007) 1 AC 100; *R (Watkins-Singh) v. The Governing Body of Aberdare Girls' High School and Another* (2008) EWHC 1865 (Admin).
49. S. Townsend, *The Secret Diary of Adrian Mole, Aged 13¾* (London: Methuen, 1982).
50. *R v. Headteacher and Governors of Denbigh High School*, ex p Begum UKHL 15.
51. S. Fernandez, The Crusade Over the Bodies of Women, in M. Malik (ed.), *Anti-Muslim Prejudice Past and Present* (Abingdon: Routledge, 2010), 61–78, 65.
52. See, for instance, the consolidating statute Equality Act 2010.
53. High Court Bans Birmingham School Protests Against LGBT Lessons, *The Guardian*, May 31, 2019. Retrieved June 20, 2020, from www.theguardian.com/education/2019/may/31/high-court-bans-birmingham-school-protests-against-lgbt-lessons; LGBT Teaching Row: Birmingham Primary School Protests Permanently Banned, *BBC News*, November 26, 2019. Retrieved June 20, 2020, from www.bbc.co.uk/news/uk-england-birmingham-50557227.
54. ECHR Right to Freedom of Expression.
55. *Eweida v. United Kingdom* (2013) ECHR 37.
56. See further A. Bainham and S. Gilmore, *Children the Modern Law* (Bristol: Jordon, 2013).
57. *Gillick v. West Norfolk and Wisbech Area Health Authority* (1986) AC 112.
58. P. Taylor, *Freedom of Religion* (Cambridge: Cambridge University Press, 2005), 166.
59. HM Government, *Church Academies: Model Documents* (Current guidance, February 15, 2019). Retrieved June 20, 2020, from www.gov.uk/government/publications/church-academies-model-documents.
60. Department for Education, Promoting Fundamental British Values as Part of SMSC in Schools: Departmental Advice for Maintained Schools, November 2014. See also Education Act 2002 s78.
61. Ibid., 5.

62. M. Elshimi, *De-Radicalisation and the Prevent Strategy* (Abingdon: Routledge, 2017), 127.
63. I. Zempi and I. Awan, *Islamophobia: Lived Experiences of Online and Offline Victimisation* (Bristol: Policy Press, 2016).
64. A. Hatcher, *Political and Religious Identities of British Evangelicals* (London: Palgrave Macmillan, 2017), 60–62.
65. Rise in Trans Children Puts British Schools to the Test, *The Guardian*, July 17, 2016. Retrieved from www.theguardian.com/society/2016/jul/12/rise-in-trans-children-puts-british-schools-to-the-test.
66. S. Colligan, Why the Intersexed Shouldn't Be Fixed: Insights from Queer Theory and Disability Studies, in B. Smith and B. Hutchinson (eds.), *Gendering Disability* (New Brunswick: Rutgers University Press, 2004), 45–60.
67. *Maya Forstater v. CGD Europe and others:* 2200909/2019 (2019).
68. Oxford Teacher Investigated for Misgendering Pupil to Sue School, *BBC News*, December 11, 2017. Retrieved June 20, 2020, from www.bbc.co.uk/news/uk-england-oxfordshire-42312342.
69. Parents Removed Son From School in Pupil Gender Row, *BBC News*, August 11, 2017. Retrieved from www.bbc.co.uk/news/uk-england-hampshire-41224146.

5 Religion in the Hungarian Education System

Balázs Szabolcs Gerencsér and Nóra Zsuzsanna Csekő-Lengyel

Introduction

School is the place where most people spend years of the most determinative periods of their lives. Because the knowledge acquired in schools and educational systems has a large impact on the lives of students, especially as they grow older, who are allowed to serve as teachers and what is permitted to be taught in schools are of utmost importance to individuals and society.

In Hungary, as in every European country, religious denominations had a leading role in the formation of the education system: monasteries and local religious communities ensured the knowledge transfer between generations without any state intervention. After the Reformation and due to the impact of the ideas of the French Revolution, new acts were adopted in the field of education almost everywhere.

The Ratio Educationis, adopted in 1777 (followed by Ratio Educationis II in 1806),[1] was the first Act enacted in Hungary regulating the educational system, as it laid down the foundations of the public education system. This move toward regulation occurred as the state became active in the field of education and newly established public schools were spreading rapidly. Still, the rate of church-run schools in Hungary was higher, while compulsory religious education in public schools remained until the end of World War II (Mészáros, 2000, 275).

Hungary fell under the influence of the Soviet Union after World War II. This loss of freedom concerned not only Hungary's economy and political organization but also its educational system and the churches. After 1948, the Soviet-oriented regime considered the churches enemies, such that the Hungarian Communist Party started to persecute religious institutions. All religious activities were banned, most of the monasteries were disbanded, and the right to freedom of religion was restricted. The formerly installed categories among the churches – established, acknowledged, and tolerated denominations – were abolished, after which only one category remained: acknowledged denominations, which enjoyed legal equality. The legal personality of acknowledged denominations was acknowledged by the state, and multilateral contracts were concluded between the religious bodies – namely the Reformed, Lutheran, Unitarian, and Catholic Churches and the Alliance of Jewish Communities – and the government between 1948 and 1950 (Köbel 2016, 91).

In the field of education, regarding the relationship of the churches and the state, three issues must be mentioned. First, the situation of the church-run schools; during the post-war period, two-thirds of the elementary schools and one-third of the secondary schools were church-run schools. Second, religious education was a concern. Third, ecclesiastical higher education was at issue. According to an act adopted in 1948,[2] the property of the churches connected to education, such as school buildings and their equipment, were nationalized without compensation, and teachers of the church-run schools become public servants. Following that, only ten church-run schools were operated under strict state control.

The Constitution that was adopted in 1949 formally ensured freedom of religion and conscience. However, in reality, it was difficult to enforce this right. After 1949 compulsory religious education in public schools was abolished as a consequence of the separation of state and church and was available only in primary schools and in secondary school as an optional subject. Consequently, the majority of young generations who attended other types of schools, such as vocational schools, were left without religious education.

As far as optional religious education in public schools was concerned, no regulations were adopted to guarantee its enforcement. In addition, abuse of those enrolled in religious education was a common phenomenon, as administrators in public schools refused to make free rooms available in their schools, or they tried to convince parents not to apply for the subject, or they used administrative means to prevent students from applying to take the class. Thus the number of children who applied for the optional religious education decreased radically, such that in 1951, 43.2% of children applied for religious education, but in 1953, only 13% did so (Köbel 2016, 113).

The optional religious education was available only in school buildings after the obligatory subjects were completed, and their curricula and books had to be sent to and approved by the competent ministry. Due to the persecution of priests and monks combined with the decreasing numbers of the students in the theological faculties at the universities, the number of teachers of religion decreased. The upshot was that only members of the clergy were allowed to teach in the schools.

As the regulations at issue changed slowly, the system softened. By 1975, religious education was permitted not only in public schools and in the ten still existing church-run schools, but also in the buildings of the local churches. After 1983, laypeople were allowed to teach religious education in schools.

The Legal Foundation for Education and Religion

Constitutional Background in the First Period: 1989–2010

Following the collapse of the Soviet Union, Hungary began her journey of becoming an independent democratic State again. The democratic amendment text of Act XX of 1949 on the Constitution of the Republic of Hungary (hereinafter, 1989 Constitution) added multiple fundamental rights and freedoms for its people.

The 1989 Constitution did not contain any explicit provisions with regard to religious education. Still, three provisions of the 1989 Constitution need to be highlighted. The first noteworthy provision is Article 60, which declared the freedom of religion. According to this Article, in the Republic of Hungary everyone has the right to freedom of thought, freedom of conscience, and freedom of religion. This right includes the free choice or acceptance of a religion or belief and the freedom to express or decline to profess it publicly or privately, to exercise and teach such religions and beliefs by way of religious actions, rites, or in any other way, either individually or in a group. The freedom of religion and the freedom from religion are equally protected, whereas freedom of religion is not limited except in specified instances as they arises. The 1989 Constitution also mandates the separation of church and state in the Republic of Hungary but also that some cooperation between them is possible (Horváth, 2009, 2595).

The second important provision, Article 70/J, declared the parents and guardians were obligated to ensure the education of their young children. The third significant provision, Article 67, recognized the right of parents to choose the form of education they provide for their children. Together, these provisions created the possibility of freedom of religion, the free operation of the churches, and the constitutional basis for religious education in schools. In addition to above mentioned rights, it is important to acknowledge that Article 70/A prohibits discrimination, especially in the field of religious belief.

There is no universal model for the relationship between state and church because national traditions differ in every country (Schanda, 1995, 35–43). Despite tendencies making societies more secular, religion remains a determinative factor of the identity of individuals and communities (Schanda, 2019, 813–821). In Hungary, after 1990 the principle of neutrality was declared, which meant that there were no privileged or preferred religions or confessions. This also meant that the state should remain neutral in matters concerning ideology, there should be no official ideology (be it religious or secular), and the state should not identify with any ideology. In this way, then, the state must not be institutionally attached to a number of churches or to any single church (Schanda, 2013, 140).

The separation of state and churches with the neutrality and equality of the churches results in the fulfilment of freedom of religion and conscience and its guarantees (Köbel, 2016, 43). The state was not allowed to found any institution or state organization to control or supervise the activity of the churches and was not allowed to keep a record of religious affiliation. Moreover, the state had no competence to examine the organizational and operational rules of the churches. Religious communities were not allowed to make use of state power, and in the relationship between the individuals and their church, the state played no role (Schanda, 2013, 140).

According to the landmark decision of the Constitutional Court (Decision nr. 4/1993. [II. 12, on the review of the Act XXXII of 1991 on the Settlement of Property Status of the Former Real Estate of Churches], the state had to remain neutral in cases concerning the right to freedom of religion and conscience. Further, the Court made it clear that the state had to protect the freedom of conscience and religion without considering its value or its content and that the state could not to favor any church or influence its internal worship. However, the separation did not mean that the state ought to ignore the characteristics of religion and church in its legislation. Instead, the Court explained that the state had to take into account the place of churches in light of their historical and social roles, especially in the fields of education, health care, and social matters.

Concerning education, the Constitutional Court ruled that public schools could not be bound to any religion or ideology, but they had to provide students with a broad, balanced, and objective education with respect to ideological ideas, offering them the possibility of free and well-founded choices. In exercising their freedom of religion, the Court indicated that parents had the right to send their children to church-run schools. The Court also observed that while the state had to ensure the legal possibility for establishing church-run schools, it was not obliged to establish such schools. However, where church-run schools already exist or were established, the state was required to support them to the extent that they undertook the teaching of the state's educational programs.

After the political transition in 1989–1990, the free operation of the churches resumed. Moreover, new churches were established and the number of church-run schools increased slowly due to the newly adopted Act IV of 1990 on the Freedom of Conscience and Religion and on Churches (hereinafter, 1990 Church Act) (Durham et al., 2004, 153).[3] As far as religious education in public schools was concerned, a heated debate began not only in the Parliament but also in the wider society. The major question at issue was the possibility of religious education in public schools. Some argued that religious education was to be part of the curriculum, while others did not want it allowed in public schools at all. Those who opposed religious instruction were mostly concerned that if such classes were organized after compulsory school activities, and the parents had to apply for it, that would have resulted in them having to declare their religious affiliation.

Pursuant to Section 5 of the 1990 Church Act, parents have the right to decide about the religious education of their children, and the churches, as legal entities, had the right to freely organize religious education in public schools. Finally, supporters and opponents of the 1990 Church Act reached a compromise such that there was a free choice, based on the right to freedom of religion, to take part in or not attend religious education classes in public schools. Still, under Paragraph 2, Section 17 of the 1990 Church Act, churches (again as legal entities) were allowed to organize religious education in public schools as long as it was not mandatory.

Religious Education in Schools Between 1990 and 2010

After 1990, the number of church-run schools slowly increased because the state returned the formerly socialized schools to the churches, which had the option of choosing between the return of their property or financial compensation, parental wishes for their children, and state support. The Act LXXIX of 1993 on public education (hereinafter, 1993 Education Act) declared that the state has the responsibility to establish and maintain kindergartens for children between age 3 and 6 and schools at the primary and secondary levels for students between the ages of 7 and 18.

According to the 1993 Education Act,[4] schools could be operated by the state or other non-state-run legal entities. Consequently, under Paragraph 2, Section 3 of the 1993 Education Act, once organizers met the legal and administrative criteria, schools could be established not only by the state but also by local communities, churches, minority communities, enterprises, foundations, associations, and private individuals. Public schools were founded at every school level: churches mainly focused on the secondary level of education, while other schools founded by foundations or associations (hereinafter, private schools) were dedicated to specific identified methodologies or offered special pedagogic programs.

Although official data on religious affiliation had not been collected, the need for church-run schools and religious education in public schools was perceptible after the anti-religious decades. Religious education is not only about dissemination of information about religious communities and of religious regulations. Rather, the aim of religious education is to impact individuals' entire personalities and to educate students to become religious adults capable of being members of the religious community who live their lives based on the teachings of their religions. After the decades when the right to freedom of religion was restricted and religious education in schools was strictly controlled, it was an understandable demand not only from the churches but also from society for everyone to have the right to access religious education in schools.

Educational institutions founded by public entities are bound by the principle of neutrality with regard to religion, while church-run schools are not. Paragraph 1, Section 4 of the 1993 Education Act declared that state and local municipalities had to respect the rights of parents and legal guardians in light of their obligations to ensure the education of their children regarding their religion or religious conviction. Under Paragraph 2, Section 4 of the 1993 Education Act, public schools were not to be committed to any religions or ideologies, and that instruction had to be based on neutral and pluralistic information. The Act prescribed that in public schools, optional religious education must be ensured.

As established in Paragraph 4, Section 4 of the 1993 Education Act, determining curricula in church-run schools, the selection and the control of teacher of religions, the organization of administrative procedure (such as making an application for a course of study or the issuance of certificates to this effect) were up to the competence of church officials. Even so, the state had to provide the classroom for the course and the technical and administrative conditions for the application and operation This part of the law also specified that teachers of the religion were not members of the school staff but were employed by their churches directly. Further, grades for religion classes were not included in school reports, and churches could decide freely about the content of the classes without any state control.

To summarize, there were two possible ways students could receive religious education in schools.[5] Students who attended attend church-run schools had a compulsory class in religious education while their peers in public schools had the option of applying for and enrolling in such classes. Both the 1989 Constitution and Paragraphs 2–3, Section 41 of the 1993 Education Act ensured the rights of the parents and legal guardians – not their children – to choose the schools they attended and whether to participate in religious education. At the same time, Paragraph 3, Section 13 ensured the right of parents or guardians to request that officials in public school facilitate the religious education for their children and to respect their beliefs and requests by doing as they were asked. Presently, nearly 1,500,000 children attend K–12 education in Hungary, of which nearly 220,000 are enrolled in church-run schools; as of 2020, it is worth noting that Hungary's total population in about 9.8 million.[6]

State Control and Financial Support

The state had the obligation to carry out the dictates of the acts but could not control the activities of the churches in doing so. As described above, this means that the curricula of the religious education could not be approved by the state, and there was no state organ established to control the religious education that the churches provided. The state only reached agreements with some churches, the first being the Concordat between the Holy See and Hungary in 1998,[7] which mainly focused on financial and property issues (Erdő, 1997, 349–355). Following these agreements, the state acknowledged that churches had started to operate educational, cultural, and social institutions, and through the activities of these institutions they took part in carrying out public service tasks in order to promote the common good (Köbel, 2016, 259).

Public education was financed by the central budget. At the same time, church-run schools were entitled to the national average of public spending on schools (Gerencsér, 2017a, 104–106). Consequently, as churches performed public functions when operating schools, Paragraph 6, Section 4 of the 1993 Education Act dictated that the state had to provide financial support in such a proportion as they performed the public function of educating students. These schools enjoyed significantly more favorable financial conditions than private schools, which had the option of not providing religious education; still, while these schools continued to be entitled to specified public subsidies, they did not receive full funding from the state budget (Schanda, 2011, 219–220).

The Protection for Freedom of Religion or Belief in Education

The Second Period: Constitutional Basis and New Acts, 2010 and Beyond

In 2011, the Parliament adopted a new Constitution, and the Fundamental Law of Hungary was adopted.[8] The new Constitution contains provisions similar to those in the 1989 Constitution but made some relevant changes. For example, Article VII of the Fundamental Law ensures the right to freedom of thought, conscience, and religion. The content of this right is the same as before, but provisions regarding the establishment and the categories of the churches were changed,[9] which had an obvious influence on who can provide religious education in schools.

Another noteworthy change in the Fundamental Law is found in Article XVI. This new provision ensures the right of parents to direct the upbringing of their children, which not only obliges them to care for their minor children but also to ensure that the receive schooling for them. This article also adds a new element, namely that every Hungarian citizen has the right to an education (Ádány et al., 2015, 104). This right is ensured by extending and generalizing public education; by providing free and compulsory primary education and free and generally accessible secondary education; making higher education accessible to everyone according to their abilities; and providing financial support as provided for by an Act to those receiving education (art. XI).

After the Fundamental Law came into effect and the adoption of the law on national education was on the agenda, the discussion about religious education in schools resurfaced. At the heart of the changes was that the proposed Act on National Education introduced compulsory ethics classes in public schools that could be substituted with religious and moral education classes (hereinafter, religious education).

It first appeared that this provision in the Act mandated compulsory religious education in public schools, but it did not: only ethics classes became part of the compulsory curriculum, which, based on the choice of the parents and at their request, can be substituted with religious education classes. However, the new regulation raised multiple questions regarding the level of the education system to which it applied, who would organize the religious education classes, who would determine the curriculum, who would pay the salary of teachers of religion, and who decided the eligibility of individuals who would serve as the teachers. Finally, Act CCVI of 2011 (hereinafter, 2011 Church Act) on the right to freedom of conscience and religion and on the legal status of churches, denominations, and religious communities, was adopted along with Act CXC of 2011 on National Public Education (hereinafter, 2011 Education Act). Both acts contain detailed rules about these issues.

Another important change has taken place: after 2011, the operation of the majority of public schools was transferred from municipalities to the state. This change also impacted church-run schools and private schools because some municipalities assigned their schools to the churches instead of the state. This resulted that the number of church-run schools increased significantly, and in some small towns church-run schools had a monopoly, thereby raising questions.

After 1990, the number of church-run schools slowly increased, in spite of the fact that the number of children decreased, due to favorable financial conditions such as state support for these church-run schools (Imre, 2005, 475–491). Until 2000, the number of church-run schools was on the low side, on average between 5%–6% of the total number of schools in Hungary. Between 2001 and 2009 the percentage of church-run schools rose only slowly. Then, between 2010 and 2014, the number of church-run schools increased rapidly, by 68% (Hermann and Varga, 2016, 311–333, 3013). At the same time, the number of private schools decreased to 20%, so that in 2014, there were 268 private schools and 436 church-run schools in Hungary (Hermann and Varga, 2016, 11–26).

Religious Education in Schools – Special Rules

According to Paragraph 1, Section 19/A of the 2011 Church Act, an ecclesiastical legal person may organize faith-based education in educational institutions maintained by the state, a local government, or a national minority self-government, or in institutions of higher education maintained by the state or a self-government of a national minority. The material conditions required for faith-based education and the time slots for it (which do not clash with other school activities) must be ensured by officials in the educational institutions and the institutions of higher education. Even so, the persons contributing to the faith-based education must be delegated by the ecclesiastical legal persons (Para. 2 Sec. 19/A.). The costs of faith-based education are borne by the state.

The 2011 Education Act further dictates that in the educational institutions of the state and local governments, knowledge and religious and ideological information shall be communicated comprehensively and in an objective manner. In other words, teachers of religious education must respect the religious and ideological belief of their students, their parents, and other teachers throughout the educational process, while simultaneously allowing the students to attend the religious education courses.

Pursuant to the 2011 Education Act, the state and municipalities along with non-state operators – namely, ecclesiastical legal persons, national minority self-government, organization performing religious activities, and other person or organization – have the right to form or open public education institutions. Institutions, such as schools founded by non-state actors, have the right to deviate from the general rules subject to the exceptions reviewed below. Officials in these institutions are acknowledged as being committed to various religions or ideologies; the acceptance of specific religions or ideologies may be stipulated as a precondition for the admission of students, and it may be tested in the context of an admission examination procedure.

Provisions on compulsory admission and setting the numbers of students in classes and groups shall not apply, except to provisions addressing maximum head counts of pupils enrolled. Admissions criteria must also describe the payment obligations of parents or guardians. Educational institutions operated by churches, referred to as school-running churches, and their officials may apply ideological and religious criteria and prescribe them as preconditions for the employment of teachers and other employees. As to the appointment of deputy heads of institutions, those operating school shall have the right to hire as they see fit.

As to what is taught, officials at school-running churches may prescribe the selection of specific general curricula for instruction chosen from a list provided by the minister responsible for education and may determine which textbooks and teaching materials should be used in classes. Officials of school-running churches may incorporate knowledge corresponding to their religious or ideological conviction into their pedagogical courses of study along with religious education programs corresponding to the teachings of their sponsoring church.

As part of their Organizational and Operational Rules, authorities in school-running churches may prescribe rules and standards of behavior and appearance as well as rights and obligations relating to religious activities corresponding to the teachings of their sponsoring churches. If religious education is included in school curricula as a subject, the teachers of religion, who are not counted in the number or regular teaching staff required in state institutions, must have the necessary religious qualifications obtained in institutions of higher education and be appointed by the competent church authorities. Finally, the Organizational and Operational Rules of educational institutions and their pedagogical program go into effect at the direction of the operator once schools are open and ready to serve children.

Analysis of the Freedom of Religion or Belief in Education

Children typically receive religious education first in their families and then in the religious communities to which they belong. Parents have the constitutional right to decide on the education of their children and to choose the schools they will attend. On its part, the state ensures that parents have the right to choose whether to send their children to public schools, church-run schools, or private schools.

This leads to a question about the task of the schools and the aim of religious education. Presently, economic interest in the field of education is intense: the role of schools and educators is often viewed as being designed to produce a competent labor force while not developing students' free personalities. Schools today face a number of new challenges: society expects them to solve problems that fall outside of the realm of education, such as developing eco-conscious thinking and developing new skills (Pusztai and Török, 2017, 346–347). In this context, religious education not only serves the dissemination of information on religion, but it also introduces students into the faiths of their chosen religions. In church-run schools, while it should be obvious that religious education is part of the compulsory curriculum, the situation in public schools remains to be seen.

Based on the present applicable law, religious education may be realized in three ways. First, compulsory religious education exists in church-run schools, based on the faith of the church operating the schools. The rules applicable to these schools were discussed above. These schools can identify themselves with particular religions and are allowed to display religious symbols on the buildings and in their classrooms, and the grades students earn in these classes can be included on students' school reports (Schanda, 2015, 97). Second, optional religious education is available in secondary schools, in church-run schools for different religious communities other than the school-running churches, and in private institutions, thereby ensuring the exercise of freedom of religion for all of their students.

Third, there is the so-called compulsorily chosen religious education subject in public schools, which is the optional equivalent of the compulsory ethics classes. Public schools are neutral. There are no religious symbols in public institutions, nor are there celebrations of religious feasts that have not been incorporated into the public culture.

In line with Paragraph 3, Section 3 of the 2011 Education Act,[10] officials in these schools must provide objective and multi-sided information about religious and philosophical convictions with respect to the religions and convictions of their students, their parents, and teachers.

Paragraph (d), Section 63 of the 2011 Education Act specifies that teachers in these schools have the right to express or refrain from stating their opinion or beliefs and cannot be subjected to discrimination based on how they choose to act in this regard; it also mandates that teachers must teach on neutral bases so as not to influence the students or spread their conviction. However, parents and their children have the right to freedom of religion, which must be ensured in these and all public schools.

Ethics classes are part of the compulsory curriculum. This allows legal church entities to organize religious education classes on the request of parents who, consistent with Paragraph 1, Section 35 of the 2011 Education Act, must take the opinions of their children into account when applying for such courses. Insofar as religious education is part of school programs and must be organized in conformity with the order of compulsory curricular activities, students taking part in the religious classes have no free time during the day.

As to religious education, officials in schools and church legal entities are bound to cooperate. Authorities in public schools must provide the appropriate conditions, such as classroom space. The task of church officials is to employ and supervise the teachers of religion while defining the content of the classes in addition to administering the schools, establishing application procedures, supervising the classes, and issuing certificates for completion of the classes. Even though the teachers of religion are employed by the church and their salaries are paid by the church, the state must provide financial subsidies to the church.

Emerging Issues

The fact that pupils in public schools have direct access to the teaching of religion creates a particular tension with regard to the churches. Because religious education is organized in the same way in the churches, there are those who, despite being religious, do not choose the religious education in the church. This is understandably of concern to churches, that the teaching of religious matters in schools may lead to the weakening of church communities because those children who attends religious education in their schools will not be a part of the communities where their families worship. At the same time, students have the opportunity to select a moral education as an option, an option that is not without precedent because since 1999, the curricula in some grades has included Human and Social Knowledge and Ethics as individual subjects.

The question, then, is whether religious education is an alternative to moral studies. Another concern is whether children who choose moral studies might be deprived of exposure to some important knowledge. Another concern emerges because this issue cannot be examined from a legal point of view due to separation of religion and the state. On the other hand, it is an important legal question addressing whether the state, through various officials, has the right to form an opinion on the curricula in the religious education the churches provide in public schools. In such instances, the interest in public control and quality assurance, which is ultimately an element of the right to education, may conflict with religious freedom and the autonomy of churches.

The dramatic increase in the number of church-run schools over the past decade or so has brought about new challenges (Gerencsér, 2012, 113). One example was that because the instructors teaching religion and faith did so both in schools and in churches, they had to be employed by both institutions. Moreover, it was difficult to prepare so many specialized teachers. Another problem occurred at the sociological periphery, where the state was happy to hand over the task to the church-run schools, but families and children living in poorer, more difficult-to-manage areas are largely overlooked and so deprived of such instruction. In such situations, churches must provide the service for which they are contractually obligated, even if it imposes a heavy burden on them. However, this challenge leads to church officials having to outsource the provision of some instruction, a topic addressed in our conclusions.

Conclusions

In the hundreds of years of history of Hungarian education, there had been a significant tradition of involving churches. In the Middle Ages, education provided by the church was dominant, whereas from the 18th century the role of public education grew. During the years under communist rule, 1948 to 1989, the state became the exclusive actor in all public services, including education. This monopolized system was replaced by postcommunist changes in the political system during 1989–1990, which brought back the possibility of non-state actors participating in education.

This chapter highlighted the significant reforms that have taken place in education during the 30-year process of transformation. Examining these reforms from the perspective of church actors illustrates how the process strengthened non-state actors. This also means that there was more of a public-private balance in education once the communist dictatorship ended. Recently, though, the state has pursued a process of centralization in the education as well as in the human public services sector, such as in health care, as it has removed the competencies from local self-governments into centralized governmental agencies in order to ensure quality management and cost controls. Moreover, because the state, rather than local self-governments, became the main actor in public education, the involvement of local communities has diminished.

By strengthening the state, the diminishment of the role of local actors results in a kind of outsourcing of public services (Gerencsér, 2017b, 249). In so doing, the state acknowledges that it is unable to provide some of the public services on its own while making non-state actors such as churches indispensable, thereby placing them in a stronger position. Church schools have also gained high levels of social recognition both for the quality of education they provide and for the organization of educational and community life for their members.

The final question for Hungarian church-run schools to consider is how dependent they are on current political interests. In other words, separation of state and church does not in any way preclude the possibility of cooperation between the state and the churches in Hungary (Szuromi, 2014, 156). This is particularly relevant in such public services as education, where the church has a great amount of significant experience and the infrastructure needed to operate schools effectively. Within this system of cooperation, the interests of both parties are important: the church receives support from the Ministry of Education and the state ensures that outsourced public functions are well-controlled and operated.

According to the rules regarding church-run schools, it is clear that the control mechanisms of the state cannot intervene in the church's internal affairs. Instead, state officials should focus only on educational activity (Schanda and Csiziné Schlosser, 2009, 80–81).[11] This process confers lawfulness on the schools, when state authorities set the conditions under which church schools must operate because the state must consider, or at least tolerate, the internal structural peculiarities of the churches to some extent when their officials operate educational institutions.

For the purposes of legal certainty, processes regulating the conduct of educational officials must address the constitutional basis, international legal background, and contractual foundations of the schools. Still, as important as they are, one must be aware of the reality that that the clearly established legal rules are subject to the variability of daily political processes. Even so, such multi-dimensional legal protections help to ensure stable and predictable operations in church (and other) schools in Hungary.

References

Ádány, T., N. Balogh-Békesi, Z. Balogh and B. Hajas. (2015). Rights and Freedoms. In: A. Varga, A. Patyi and B. Schanda (eds.), *The Basic (Fundamental) Law of Hungary – a Commentary of the New Hungarian Constitution*. Dublin: Clarus.

Cole Durham, W. Jr. and Ferrari Silvio (eds.). (2004). *Laws on Religion and the State in Post-Communist Europe*. Leuven: Peeters.

Erdő, Péter. (1997). Megállapodás az Apostoli Szentszék és a Magyar Köztársaság között. *Távlatok*, 35–36.

Gerencsér, Balázs Szabolcs. (2012). Safe Educational Environment in Hungary. *European Journal for Education Law and Policy: Journal of the European Association for Education Law and Policy*, 8.

Gerencsér, Balázs Szabolcs. (2017a). State and Church – Education in Hungary: The Content of a Human Right and the Role of External Instruments. In: De Groof Jan, du Plessis Georgia and Smirnova Maria (eds.), *Religion, Law and Education: Tensions and Perspectives*. Oisterwijk: Wolf Legal.

Gerencsér, Balázs Szabolcs. (2017b). Education in Hungary. In: J. Russo Charles (szerk.), *The Yearbook of Education Law 2017*. Cleveland, OH: Education Law Association.

Hermann, Zoltán and Júlia Varga. (2016). Állami, önkormányzati, egyházi és alapítványi iskolák. In: *Társadalmi Riport*. Budapest: Tárki.

Horváth, Enikő. (2009). The Right to Education [A művelődéshez való jog]. In: A. Jakab (ed.), *Commentary on the Hungarian Constitution* [Az alkotmány kommentárja]. Budapest: Századvég, 2nd ed.

Imre, Anna. (2005). A felekezeti középiskolák jellemzői a statisztikai adatok tükrében. *Education*, 3.

Köbel, Szilvia (ed.). (2016). *Az állami és a felekezeti Egyházjog alapja*. Budapest: Patrocinium.

Mészáros, István. (2000). *A katolikus iskola ezeréves története Magyarországon*. Budapest: Szent István Társulat, Bp.

Pusztai, Gabriella. (2017). Török, Balázs: Egyházi fenntartású iskolák. *Vigilia*, 5.

Schanda, Balázs. (1995). Az állam és az egyház viszonyának lehetséges modelljei. *Társadalmi Szemle*, 5.

Schanda, Balázs. (2011). Religion in Public Education in Hungary. In: Gerhard Robbers (ed.), *Religion in Public Education, European Consortium for Church and State Research*. Retrieved from https://ubt.opus.hbz-nrw.de/opus45-ubtr/frontdoor/deliver/index/docId/502/file/Robbersed_Religion_in_Public_Education.pdf

Schanda, Balázs. (2013). *Religious Education in Hungary*. The Routledge International Handbook of Religious Education. London: Routledge.

Schanda, Balázs. (2015). *Religion and Law in Hungary*. Alphen an den Rijn: Wolters Kluwer.

Schanda, Balázs. (2019). Állami egyházjogi modellek Európában – konvergencia és különbözőségek. *Magyar Tudomány*, 6.

Schanda, Balázs and Annamária Csiziné Schlosser. (2009). New Developments in the Practice of the European Court of Human Rights Regarding Religious Freedom [Újabb fejlemények az Európai Emberi Jogi Bíróság vallásszabadsággal kapcsolatos gyakorlatában]. *Iustum Aequum Salutare*, 2.

Szuromi, Szabolcs. (2014). Spanyol állami egyházjog – új hangsúlyok. *Iustum Aequum Salutare*, 2.

Notes

1. Ratio educationis publicae, 1806. István Mészáros: A Ratio educationis 1777-i és 1806-i kiadásának Magyar nyelvű fordításai. Akadémiai Kiadó, Budapest, 1981.
2. Act XXXIII of 1948 on nationalization of church-run schools and their property
3. For an English translation of the 1990 Hungarian law in W. Cole Durham, Jr. and Silvio Ferrari (eds.), Laws on Religion and the State in Post-Communist Europe 153 et seq. (2004).
4. For an English version of this Act, see retrieved from www.unesco.org/education/edurights/media/docs/c0d134c642af51adbb9a5d929a8a65d-5c7c510c8.pdf.
5. In this case, school means kindergarten, primary school, secondary school, and dormitory.
6. See data from Hungarian Official Statistics, ksh.hu.
7. Text retrieved from www.concordatwatch.eu/topic-753.834
8. Text retrieved from www.kormany.hu/download/e/02/00000/The%20New%20Fundamental%20Law%20of%20Hungary.pdf.
9. The regulations regarding the establishment and the categories of the churches have been changed several times since 2012, and this was in the subject of the examination of the European Court of Human Rights, as several churches lost their former status. See *Magyar Keresztény Mennonita Egyház and Others v. Hungary*, Application nos. 70945/11, 23611/12, 26998/12, 41150/12, 41155/12, 41553/12, 54977/12 and 56581/12, August 28, 2016.
10. The original 2011 Education Act is available in English. Retrieved from www.ilo.org/dyn/natlex/docs/ELECTRONIC/106832/131356/F-1702001629/act_national_education.pdf. The official version currently in force is retrieved from http://njt.hu/cgi_bin/njt_doc.cgi?docid=139880.370725.
11. We can find an indirect hint on this in the judgments of the European Court of Human Rights.

6 Law, Education, and the Place of Religion in Public Schools in Italy

Giovanni Patriarca

Introduction

Since the second half of the 19th century, Italy has witnessed great historical changes and important social movements in conjunction with their political consequences on its population. Moreover, due to its geographical position, Italy has long served as a kind of bridge between East and West as its coasts have seen empires and trade, migrants leaving for distant lands, and more recently, immigrants arriving from other countries.

Strongly impacted by its European dimension, Italy's contemporary political and social history is reflected in educational decisions impacting its schools. Further, in the time span from national unification in 1861 until democratic rule after World War II, from the "Italian economic miracle" in the 1960s to the most recent reforms, the relationship between education and religion has been consistently at the centre of the country's agenda. Against this background, the remainder of this chapter examines the key issues associated with teaching religion in Italy's state (or public) schools.

Historical Background

A history of the Italian school system must include a review of the significant connection between religion and politics. The physical presence of the centre of Christianity in Rome as well as the strong moral and political influence of the papacy make the legislative process regarding educational policies and religious education completely peculiar in Italy.

In the already complicated relationship between state and church in its modern evolution, positions become conflicted when public school officials begin to claim greater autonomy. In the history of educational policies, the reference points are the Albertine Statute of March 4, 1848 – applied primarily to the Kingdom of Sardinia and, subsequently, with the national unity to all of the Kingdom of Italy – and the Casati Law (n. 3725 of November 13, 1859).

Article 1 of the Albertine Statute declares: "The Catholic Apostolic Roman Religion is the only State Religion. The other cults now in existence are tolerated in accordance with the law." It is clear the liberal principle of tolerance of other faiths based mainly on their historical presence in Piedmont of the Jewish and Waldensian communities was not observed.[1]

The application of the Casati Law to the whole of the peninsula makes it "the first national law of the Italian public school."[2] The objective of the law was to promote the autonomy of public education by seeking to distance itself from ecclesiastical hegemony. It also indicated the modalities of Catholic religious education because in primary schools, a single teacher teaches compulsory religious education for only the first two years. In secondary schools, though, the law allowed a spiritual director to be present.

According to the Regulations for Normal and Magistral Schools of Aspiring Teachers in Royal Decree no. 4151 of June 24, 1860, religious education was compulsory in the magisterial schools, which had the task of training future teachers. This approach was also extended to the *Regulation for Normal and Magistral Schools and Examinations of License of Masters and Teachers of Primary Schools* in Royal Decree n. 315 of November 9, 1861, where both "religion and morals" and "catechism and sacred history" were key subjects for obtaining the teaching licence.

Even after the Capture of Rome, on September 20, 1870, with the consequent defeat of the state of the church by the Piedmontese troops, the so-called Roman question is at the heart of the political disputes and has a considerable influence on the educational decisions of the then recently unified Italy. The Circular Letter of September 29, 1870, signed by Minister of Public Education Cesare Correnti, stipulated that school religious instruction should be given only at the request of the parents of pupils. In the same context, on January 26, 1873, theological faculties in the state universities were abolished. Even today in Italy, it is not possible to study theology in public and private Italian universities, unlike in other countries, because this can be done only in pontifical universities.

Compulsory primary education was implemented through the Coppino Law of July 15, 1877, and the first national educational programs came about in the Royal Decree of October 10, 1877. Under this approach, educators paid greater attention to language and scientific subjects and to ethical notions about "the duties of man and of the citizen." However, there were no provisions for religious education. At the same time, Law no. 3918 of June 23, 1877, abolished the figure of the "spiritual director" in high schools and technical schools.

The vision of the Risorgimento was applied by the Royal Decree no. 5292 of February 16, 1888, Regulation for Elementary Education, to elementary school programmes. Under this approach, the teaching of the Catholic religion was completely suppressed and replaced by "the first notions of the duties of man and of the citizen." This approach was confirmed over the years in an endless series of disputes between and among the Catholic, socialist, and liberal factions.

The place of religion in public schools was a central theme in parliamentary politics, even in the early years of the 20th century. Even as extreme ideological disputes raged on, Law no. 407 of July 8, 1904, introduced a new dimension in schooling by increasing compulsory attendance to 12 years. According to Article 10, educators could provide instruction about public morality while leaving religious education in the background. The Royal Decree n. 150 of February 6, 1908 (the so-called Rava Regulation) confirmed that teaching religion was optional. In addition, it required officials in municipalities, many of which faced great economic difficulty, to ensure that children received religious education at the request of their parents and with the agreement of their teachers.

From the Gentile Reform to the Concordats

Religious education was at the centre of tensions in Italian education and politics for decades. During the fascist dictatorship, the Royal Decree no. 2185 of October 1, 1923, promulgated the Gentile Reform. According to this decree, the teaching of the Catholic religion was compulsory in elementary schools. However, Circular Letter no. 2 of January 5, 1924, issued by the Ministry of National Education, allowed pupils who professed other faiths to abstain from receiving instruction about Catholicism.

The 1929 agreements between the state and the church, known as the Lateran Treaty or Lateran Pacts, consisted of three separate instruments: the Conciliation Treaty, the Financial Convention, and the Concordat, which recognized Vatican City as a separate nation while the papacy acknowledged Italy as a sovereign country with Rome as its capital.[3] Further, Article 36 of the Concordat introduced the obligation that the "hour of religion," namely teaching about Catholicism in public elementary schools, would be introduced in high schools. Also, this Article granted bishops the authority to appoint or dismiss teachers who delivered the instruction and approving the textbooks they used.

A year later, Law no. 824 of June 5, 1930, stipulated that the teaching of religion is compulsory and

> is conferred by annual commission, from October 1 each year to September 30 of the following year, by the head of the institute, in accordance with the diocesan Bishop. The task is entrusted to priests and religious approved by the ecclesiastical authority; in a subsidiary way, to lay persons recognized as suitable by the diocesan Bishop.[4]

During the initial postwar years, the preceding arrangement remained unchanged. However, social changes and the Second Vatican Council returned the question of religion in public schools to the centre of debate. The movement culminated in 1984 with the revision of the 1929 agreement that included a new formula for *pedagogical cooperation* between the Catholic Church and the state for a cultural accompaniment and intellectual maturation of students. Still, the freedom of conscience and the responsibility of parents in choosing this discipline remains central, namely religious education, consistent with what would be included in Article 14 of the United Nations Convention on the Rights of the Child.[5] In this context, the teaching of the Catholic religion is characterized as an open proposal of religious culture (Law no. 121 of March 25, 1985) rather than as catechesis.[6]

The New Concordat of 1985[7] became effective after the 1984 Villa Madama Agreement, named after a Renaissance villa that serves as an institutional residence of the Italian government and is where many diplomatic meetings occur. The Villa Madama Agreement[8] between Italy and the Holy See partially revisited the Lateran Pacts of 1929 with the upshot that the national government no longer recognizes Roman Catholicism as the state religion.[9] Consequently, compulsory religious education is no longer mandated in public schools; now, whether students receive such instruction is up to their parents. Even so, the New Concordat does guarantee the Catholic Church the right to establish its own schools.

Subsequently, the Memorandum of Understanding Between the Italian Government and the Italian Bishops Conference (Decree of the President of the Republic no. 751 of December 16, 1985) recognized Catholic religious education as being "formative and [of] cultural dignity equal to that of other disciplines" (Article 4, Paragraph 1).[10]

Toward a Pluralistic Approach

In a context of increasing pluralism such as Italy, the possibility of cultural and religious formation was extended to members of other faiths and denominations as witnessed by the Agreement With the Waldensian Round Table of 1984 (Art. 10 of the Law no. 449 of August 11, 1984).[11] It is also present in Paragraph 1 of Article 12 of Law no. 516 of November 22, 1988, Norms for the Regulation of Relations Between the State and the Italian Union of Adventist Christian Churches of the Seventh Day, then taken up by other agreements reached in the following years. Although the religious educations of non-Catholic confessions were left the opportunity of free curricular initiatives, in the course of time they were articulated on the false line of Catholic religious education, which has gradually been structured according to the agreements between the Ministry of Education and the Italian Bishops Conference.

Currently, the legislation provides that religious education in Italian schools is optional. It is weekly structured in this way: an hour and a half per kindergarten/nursery school, two hours per primary school, and one hour per secondary school of first and second grades. Alternative teaching must be provided to those whose do not want their children to attend religious education classes. Such a choice must be communicated at the beginning of the course and can be freely modified. This hourly rule also extends to all religious denominations.

With the collapse of the Soviet Union and the consequent geopolitical reorganization of the Warsaw Pact countries, now partially integrated into the European Union, which has expanded to the East, Italy has seen the growth of the Orthodox presence. Law no. 126 of July 30, 2012, on relations between Italy and the Sacred Orthodox Archdiocese of Italy and Malta is responsible mainly for the Greek- and Romanian-speaking faithful. As such, the door for Orthodox religious education in Italian public schools has been opened (Art. 11, Sub. 4).[12]

In recent decades migration from Muslim-majority countries has, not surprisingly, diverted attention to the demands of these communities.[13] The Islamic presence in Italy amounts to about 3.1% of the population and is growing.[14] At the moment there are no agreements with the Italian state on educational matters even if contacts are ongoing.[15] A theme of debate, also common to other confessions or religious bodies, is about religious habits, alimentary traditions, and norms, especially in the canteens (cafeterias) in public schools.[16]

Church, Religious Education, and Teachers: An Overview of the Legislation

Teachers who possess professional qualifications for Catholic religious education are trained and initiated by their diocesan religious authorities but paid by the state. Until 2003, all teachers in Catholic religious education were appointed by the Office for Schools of the Diocesan Curia on annual contracts that were renewed at the discretion of the ecclesiastical authorities. Law no. 186 of July 18, 2003, provided for a national competition (*Concorso nazionale*) with the possibility of permanent contracts. However, diocesan authorities are responsible for the revocation of permanent contracts for the teachers of Catholic religious education for reasons such as didactic incapacity and moral (mis)conduct.

The Decree of the President of the Republic no. 75 of December 16, 1985, and the Decree of the President of the Republic no. 175 of August 20, 2012, set the professional qualifications for secondary school religious education teachers. Educators are required to have earned an academic degree that is a baccalaureate, licentiate, or doctoral degree in theology or other ecclesiastical discipline. Further, the degree must be conferred by a faculty approved by the Holy See or the academic

Diploma in Religious Sciences and be granted by the Higher Institute of Religious Sciences approved by the Holy See.

According to the reform promulgated by the Congregation for Catholic Education (that is, the Holy See) in 2008, the study and teaching of religious studies offer the necessary elements to create a synthesis between faith and culture in the particular locales in which the church exists. The Higher Institute of Religious Sciences addresses the requirements of service to the church specific to the particular demands of given times and places. The manner of study, the pedagogical methods, and the investment of energy needed at the core of these institutes differ from that required in the faculties of theology.[17]

The enabling character of the pontifical academic restores the historical *querelle* or their recognition by the Italian State. Such a situation has seen a series of stages still in progress. After the Concordat, a very slow process was initiated in accordance with Article 10 Sub. 2 of Law no. 121 of March 25, 1985, and the Decree of the President of the Republic no. 175 of February 2, 1995. The adoption of the agreement between Italy and the Holy See of February 13, 2019 – which deals with the recognition of degrees obtained in ecclesiastical faculties and universities and was later converted into the Decree of the President of the Republic no. 63 of May 27, 2019 – was a further step forward, thereby demonstrating the timeliness of this process from a diplomatic and legal point of view.

The suitability of the ecclesiastical authority and the professional training approved only in pontifical institutions have resulted in criticisms by secularist associations and liberal/radical parties over the years, which propose either a more general "hour of ethics" or "history of religions,"[18] considering the extreme need to know other religious expressions or *Weltanschauung* in a multidenominational and pluralistic society.[19]

Despite social and cultural changes and a significant process of secularization, about 90% of pupils in kindergartens and primary schools and 80% in secondary schools attend religious education classes.[20] Yet, there has been a sharp decline in recent years, especially in vocational institutes, in large urban conglomerates as well as in the centre-north of the country, specifically Tuscany, Emilia-Romagna, and Piedmont.[21]

The curriculum in religious education is based on the *Memorandum Between the Italian Ministry of Education and the Italian Bishops Conference on the Specific Objectives of Learning Catholic Religion* (2003).[22] Pursuant to the agreement, the program "helps to promote the acquisition of religious culture for the formation of man and citizen and the knowledge of the principles of Catholicism that are part of the historical heritage of the country" (Art. 1). The teaching also offers

> specific content and tools for a reading of the historical-cultural reality in which they live; it meets the needs of truth and the search for the meaning of life, contributes to the formation of the moral

conscience, and offers elements for conscious and responsible choices in the face of the religious problem.

(Art. 1)[23]

Curriculum and Didactics in Catholic Religious Education

In the national curriculum for Catholic religious teaching, the need for a more dynamic approach is evident: religious experience must be presented with the specificity of the Christian salvation proposal and with the church as clearly identified with the community of those who believe in Jesus Christ and are committed to putting into practice his teachings. The figure of Jesus Christ is at the centre of the didactics with his historical event, message and testimony, sacrifice, and mystery. Consequently, students should grasp the meaning of the sacraments and their value in the life of Christians. In this frame, the study of the Bible (the New and Old Testaments) is fundamental not only as the sacred books for Jews and Christians but also as a point of reference of European culture, distinguishing it from other types of texts, including those of other religions.[24]

The subject matter calls on pupils at the primary school level to reflect on God the Creator and Father, on the fundamental facts of the life of Jesus, and to learn to connect the main contents of his teaching to the traditions of the environment in which they live, recognizing the profound meaning of Christian celebrations, feasts, and the liturgy. This allows teachers to introduce the centrality of a specific religious language, identifying the significant expressions of art, starting with those present in their own geographic areas, to detect how it has been interpreted and communicated by artists over the centuries.[25]

At the secondary level, students will have the opportunity to undertake a philosophical and theological educational path designed to lead them to inquiry into the deepest questions on the meaning of life from a religious perspective. The students engage on the same path about the many and various manifestations of religious experiences, the elements that qualify them, and the importance of the Catholic religion in the history of Italian society and culture. In this way, the teaching of religion offers its specific contribution to the full development of the pupils' personality and anthropological vision.[26]

It is also highlighted that, like in any other educational process, a shared co-responsibility is necessary. Thus, also the teaching of Catholic religion "requires a convergence of attention and responsible collaboration on the part of all the interested parties: families, young people, the Christian community and civil society."[27]

In this context, religion teachers become the focus of long-term educational perspectives. As a point of reference, religion teachers are persons of synthesis, first of all on the level of cultural mediation, proper to their educational service. The teachers must foster the synthesis between faith and culture, between the gospel and history, and between the needs of the students and their profound aspirations. Those teaching, therefore, must have the continuous ability to verify and harmonize the different and complementary levels: theological, cultural, pedagogical, and didactic. The educational work of religion teachers should tend, in fact, to make young people acquire the ability to accept critically the religious, moral, and cultural messages that reality offers, helping them to grasp their meanings for life.[28]

This educational approach is even more essential in a migratory and pluri-religious context. Both from a purely sociological standpoint and from a demographic perspective, the statistical data confirm a migratory trend that is now consolidated in an important presence of second generations, focusing on education as the primary source of economic mobility despite some persistent social problems.[29] Without a doubt, one of the main factors of integration is a good knowledge of the Italian language and culture as a vehicle for inclusion.[30] In this framework, the integrated and historical system of the Oratorio or Parish Youth Clubs,[31] which has always been in dialogue with local schools and educational institutions, is also a point of reference for the so-called new Italians, not just because of Christian confessions,[32] with its innovative and cutting-edge methods of informal education, defined through sport, music, theatre, and a long series of cultural activities.[33]

In the vortex of the rapid societal transformations generating many conflicts on a global and regional level, Italian society finds itself facing a series of emerging challenges to which no answers can be found by erasing religious history and the vital contribution of Christianity: "The history from which we come is an unchangeable fact and the traces – that the Church has left and continues to offer in it – constitute an evident and effective contribution to the growth of everyone's society."[34] This aspect is crucial, because "education cannot be neutral."[35] The main mission of Catholic religious education, then, "is to develop the sense of the true, the sense of the good and the sense of the beautiful. . . . Because development is the result of various elements which interact and stimulate the mind, the conscience, the affections, the body."[36] Through this journey, Catholic religious teaching is designed to help integrate

> the language of the mind, the language of the heart and the language of the hands. Harmoniously though, that is, to think what you feel and what you do; to feel deeply what you think and what you do; and to do well what you think and what you feel."[37]

The widespread impact of the coronavirus and its dramatic consequences created new challenges to the teaching of religious education, too. As stated in the Circular Letter to Schools, Universities and Educational Institutions, published by the Congregation for Catholic Education of the Holy See on September 10, 2020:

> distance learning – albeit necessary in this extremely critical moment – has shown how the educational environment is made up of people who meet and interact directly and "face-to-face"; this is not a mere secondary context to educational activity, but is the very essence of the relationship of exchange and dialogue (between teachers and learners) that is indispensable for the formation of the human person and for a critical understanding of reality.[38]

The Letter continued to note that because they are closely interrelated,

> Real human persons are the heart and soul of formal and informal educational processes, as well as an inexhaustible source of life by virtue of their essentially relational and communal nature, which always implies a twofold dimension: vertical (open to communion with God) and horizontal (communion among human beings). Catholic education – inspired by the Christian vision of reality in all its expressions – aims at the integral formation of human persons who are called to live a specific vocation responsibly in solidarity with other people.[39]

Brief History of a Controversy

The public display of the crucifix in Italian state schools is a matter of controversy. For some, it expresses Christian mercy and the values of forgiveness and compassion; for others, it represents the sign of the imposition of Christian culture and, in particular, of the Catholic religion. Italian legislation is also cumbersome and imprecise on this issue. The presence of the crucifix, though, appears to be a tradition linked to Italy's own history. In recent years, the contrast has been sharpened by the cases of *Abano Terme* of 2002,[40] the *Ofena Case* of 2003,[41] and the appeal of the Union of Atheists and Rationalist Agnostics (*Unione degli Atei e degli Agnostici Razionalisti* [UAAR]),[42] to which the Opinion no. 556/2006 of the Italian Council of State (*Consiglio di Stato*) has responded.

The opinion says that, in essence, at the present, while there are no positive elements of concrete discrimination against non-Catholic believers, the class crucifix presents, for its part, a formative value of no qualifying weight for the purposes of freedom. The court continued, observing that on the contrary, the crucifix must be understood as one of the symbols of the principles of freedom, equality, and tolerance, and finally of the laicity of the state itself, founding the nation's coexistence and now acquired the legal, social, and cultural heritage of Italy.[43]

The court added that in Italy, the crucifix is apt to express, precisely in a symbolic but adequate way, the religious origin of the values of tolerance, mutual respect, the valorization of the person, the affirmation of her rights, with regard to her freedom, of autonomy of moral conscience towards authority, of human solidarity, of refusal of all discrimination, which characterize Italian civilization. The court pointed out that these values, which have imbued themselves with the traditions, way of life, and culture of the Italian people, underlie and emerge from the fundamental norms of the nation's Constitutional Charter, as accepted in the Fundamental Principles and Part I thereof, and specifically to those referred to by the Constitutional Court, outlining the secular character of the Italian state.[44]

Because the previous opinion was not enough to calm the mood, Soile Lautsi, a Finnish-born Italian national, turned to the European Court of Human Rights. She claimed that the presence of the crucifix

> was incompatible with the obligation on the State, in the exercise of the functions which it assumed in relation to education and to teaching, to respect the right of parents to ensure such education and teaching in accordance with their own religious and philosophical convictions.[45]

In the first instance, on November 3, 2009, the European Court of Human Rights ordered Italy to compensate the claimant 5,000 euros for moral damages, because in not mandating the removal of the crucifixes from the Italian schools, their presence in the classrooms was a violation of the right of parents to educate their children according to their beliefs and the right of pupils to freedom of religion based on the fact that states

> must observe the strictest denominational neutrality. This is not limited to the school curriculum, but also extends to "the school environment." As primary and secondary schooling are compulsory, the State should not impose on pupils, against their will and without their being able to extract themselves, the symbol of a religion with which they do not identify.[46]

The Grand Chamber of the European Court of Human Rights subsequently overturned its own initial order on March 18, 2011. The Court reasoned, by a majority of 15 votes to 2, that the presence of the crucifixes did not violate Article 2 of Protocol No. 1 (right to education). The Court thus allowed the crucifixes to remain in Italian state schools, absent evidence that they had a negative influence on the pupils.[47]

Emerging Issues

Cultural diversity is the leitmotif of contemporary Italian society and the basis of its educational policies. As in all developed countries, despite a certain rebirth of religious sensitivity in a post-secular era,[48] the phenomenon of "believing without belonging" has spread in stark contrast to any institutionalized procedure[49] as well as individualistic formulas of "belonging without believing."[50] These attitudes confirm an unprecedented freedom of choice in a context of the great amount digital information available so as to produce a situation of religiousness à la carte with an infinite series of hermeneutic and antidogmatic interpretations, some of which are often contradictory.[51] This anthropological situation radically affects schools, their pedagogical languages, and didactic curricula.

At the explicit request of many states, in 2007 the Organization for Security and Co-operation in Europe (OSCE) published the *Toledo Guiding Principles on Teaching About Religions and Beliefs in Public Schools.*[52] The report was named after the famous medieval School of Translators, a symbol of the encounter between the three monotheistic religions, according to which "teaching about religions and beliefs must be fair, accurate and based on sound scholarship; students should learn in an environment that is respectful of human rights, freedoms and civic values."[53]

The *Toledo Guiding Principles* were followed by the 2008 *White Paper on Intercultural Dialogue*[54] and the 2014 *Signposts. Policy and Practice for Teaching About Religions and Non-religious World Views in Intercultural Education.*[55] Both of these documents, which were published by the Council of Europe, promote mutual understanding through intercultural and interreligious education. From the perspective of continental integration policies and in the face of a pressing request from families, Italy has also adapted these documents in its own way through a more far-reaching set of educational offerings, including an alternative to the "hour of religion."

These themes have influenced not only the general educational enterprise[56] but also the teaching of the Catholic religion, which developed in the framework of Christian humanism[57] tools for educating to citizenship, tolerance, peace, democracy, and inclusion.[58] These themes also impact civic responsibility and fraternity,[59] which declined through "pedagogies of encounter, such as service-learning and character education, whereby students apply academic learning to enact positive solutions to issues of injustice, inequality, and social strife in communities."[60]

Conclusion

Apart from the administrative and ideological controversies described in this chapter, religious education, in all of its different expressions, is an integral part of the Italian historical, cultural, and artistic patrimony. Further, it is necessary for educational and other leaders in Italy to gain a greater knowledge of the "new religions" in the nation such as Islam, Sikhism, Buddhism, and Hinduism in a context of increasing secularism and consequent religious illiteracy.[61]

In the last years of the so-called Second Republic – after 1994 – Italy faced a series of partially implemented and partially aborted educational reforms and counter-reforms led by Moratti during 2003–2005, Gelmini during 2008–2011, and Renzi-Giannini during 2015–2017.[62] In addition, developments in the wake of a greater focus on pluralism, intercultural dialogue, and inclusive policies,[63] and religious education based on freedom, mutual respect, and recognition of human rights according to the dictates of the Republic of Italy's Constitution[64] can still play a major role on the shape of education in the nation.

For these reasons, educational leaders have directed their efforts towards a reformulation of the curriculum, especially in Catholic religious education.[65] These efforts are more attention to personalized didactics,[66] the development of new learning models,[67] and the accompaniment of students in the light of pedagogical discernment,[68] which "is a path of freedom that brings to full fruit what is unique in each person, something so personal that only God knows it. Others cannot fully understand or predict from the outside how it will develop."[69]

Notes

1. See E. Genre, L'insegnamento della religione. *Enciclopedia Treccani.* Retrieved February 25, 2020, from www.treccani.it/enciclopedia/l-insegnamento-della-religione_%28Cristiani-d%27Italia%29/.
2. N. Pagano, *Religione e libertà nella scuola: l'insegnamento della religione cattolica dallo Statuto albertino ai giorni nostri* (Rome: Claudiana, 1990), 18.
3. See the Lateran Treaty, February 11, 1929. Retrieved from www.whitehorsemedia.com/docs/the_lateran_treaty.pdf.
4. Law no. 824 of June 5, 1930 (author's translation).
5. G. Dalla Torre, *Lezioni di diritto ecclesiastico* (Turin: Giappicchelli, 2019), 237. The Convention is retrieved from www.ohchr.org/en/professionalinterest/pages/crc.aspx.
6. Cfr. F. Costa, L'insegnamento della religione nelle scuole, in: *I nuovi accordi concordatari tra Chiesa e Stato in Italia* (Rome: Urbaniana University Press, 1985), 232–247.
7. Retrieved in Italian from www.vatican.va/roman_curia/secretariat_state/archivio/documents/rc_seg-st_19850603_santa-sede-italia_it.html.
8. For a good discussion of the underlying issues, see Elena Ervas, The Agreements Between Church and State: The Italian Perspective, *Brigham Young University Law Review* (2017), 869–893.
9. See E. J. Dionne, Jr., Italy and Pope Ratify a New Concordat, *New York Times,* June 4, 1985. Retrieved from www.nytimes.com/1985/06/04/world/italy-and-pope-ratify-a-new-concordat.html.
10. Author's translation.

11. See also E. Genre, *Diaconia e solidarietà: I valdesi dalla borsa dei poveri all'Otto per mille* (Rome: Claudiana, 2017).
12. Cf. V. Parlato, La legge n. 126 del 2012 relativa ai rapporti tra Italia e Sacra Arcidiocesi Ortodossa d'Italia e Malta, *Stato, Chiese e pluralismo confessionale. Rivista telematica*, 36 (2012), 1–19. Retrieved from www.statoechiese.it.
13. Cf. R. Guolo, Islam e scuola pubblica: orientamenti di genitori di religione islamica in Piemonte, *Ricerche di Pedagogia e Didattica – I saperi pubblici della/sulla religione*, 4(2) (2009), 1–16.
14. B. E. Sawe, The Religious Demographics of Italy, *World Atlas*, July 29, 2019. Retrieved from www.worldatlas.com/articles/the-religious-demographics-of-italy.html.
15. See S. Coglievina, Religious Education in Italian Public Schools: What Room for Islam, *Stato, Chiese e pluralismo confessionale: Rivista telematica*, 29 (2017), 1–15. Retrieved from www.statoechiese.it.
16. See M. C. Giorda and M. Bossi, Mense scolastiche e diversità religiosa: Il caso di Milano, *Stato, Chiese e pluralismo confessionale: Rivista telematica*, 24 (2016), 1–40. Retrieved from www.statoechiese.it.
17. Congregation for Catholic Education, *Reform for the Higher Institute of Religious Sciences* (Vatican City: Congregation for Catholic Education, 2008), 4.
18. Cf. G. Arrigoni, C. Consonni and A. Però (eds.), *Proposte per l'insegnamento della storia delle religioni nelle scuole italiane* (Bergamo: Sestante, 2014).
19. See E. Pace (ed.), *Le religioni nell'Italia che cambia: Mappe e bussole* (Rome: Carocci Editore, 2013).
20. S. Intravaia, Scuola, alle superiori sempre più studenti disertano l'ora di religione, *La Repubblica*, December 3, 2018. Retrieved March 9, 2020, from www.repubblica.it/scuola/2018/12/03/news/scuola_alle_superiori_sempre_piu_studenti_disertano_l_ora_di_religione-213283008/?ref=fbpr&fbclid=IwAR10rXLC1Y w2QmRd8lp_WXpIHoRGn8ByggJ7FSSuMfFYqq_9TfOtYW0H4iM.
21. Ibid.
22. Intesa tra Ministero dell'Istruzione e Conferenza Episcopale Italiana circa gli Obiettivi specifici di apprendimento dell'IRC (2003). Retrieved from https://www.chiesacattolica.it/wp-content/uploads/sites/31/2017/02/IntesMinIstr_CEI03.pdf, unavailable in English.
23. Author's translation.
24. See www.chiesacattolica.it/wp-content/uploads/sites/31/2017/02/Intesa_programmi_IRC_15.07.87.pdf.
25. See www.chiesadimilano.it/servizioperlapastoralescolastica/files/2017/05/INDICAZION_NAZIONALI_IRC_PRIMO_SECONDO_CICLO.pdf, unavailable in English.
26. Italian Catholic Bishops' Conference, *Insegnare religione cattolica oggi: Nota pastorale sull'insegnamento della religione cattolica nelle scuole pubbliche* (Rome: Italian Catholic Bishops' Conference, 1991), 6. Unavailable in English.
27. www.chiesadimilano.it/servizioperlapastoralescolastica/files/2017/05/INDICAZION_NAZIONALI_IRC_PRIMO_SECONDO_CICLO.pdf.
28. Ibid.
29. M. Colombo, I giovani migranti nelle scuole italiane. Percorsi educativi, diseguaglianze, risorse, *REMHU – Revista Interdisciplinar da Mobilidade Humana*, 22(42) (2014), 159–170. Unavailable in English.
30. A. Mochi, *L'integrazione degli alunni immigrati in Italia e in altri paesi a confronto per un futuro studio europeo.* Retrieved February 27, 2017, from http://eurydice.indire.it/lintegrazione-degli-alunni-immigrati-nelle-scuole-deuropa/. Unavailable in English.

31. V. Premazzi, *Il meticciato dell'Oratorio.* Retrieved November 5, 2018, from www.oasiscenter.eu/it/il-meticciato-all-oratorio. Unavailable in English.
32. S. Pasta, Mio padre è iraniano, ma io vado all'oratorio. Con altri centomila bimbi "stranieri," *Corriere della Sera,* July 3, 2014. Retrieved from http://lacittanuova.milano.corriere.it/2014/07/03/mio-padre-e-iraniano-ma-io-vado-alloratorio-con-altri-centomila-bimbi-stranieri/. Unavailable in English.
33. See Caritas Ambrosiana et al., *Educare generando futuro: I minori di origine straniera in Oratorio: dall'integrazione alla condivisione* (Milan: Caritas, 2014). Unavailable in English.
34. Italian Catholic Bishops' Conference, *Messaggio della Presidenza della Conferenza Episcopale Italiana in vista della scelta di avvalersi dell'insegnamento della religione cattolica nell'anno scolastico 2015–2016* (Rome: Italian Catholic Bishops' Conference, 2015). Unavailable in English.
35. Pope Francis, *Address to Students and Teachers from Schools Across Italy,* May 10, 2014. Retrieved from www.vatican.va/content/francesco/en/speeches/2014/may/documents/papa-francesco_20140510_mondo-della-scuola.html.
36. Ibid.
37. Ibid.
38. Congregation for Catholic Education, *Circular Letter to Schools, Universities and Educational Institutions* (Vatican City, September 10, 2020). Retrieved from www.educatio.va/content/ dam/cec/Documenti/2020-09/EN-CONGREGATIO-LETTERA-COVID.pdf.
39. Ibid.
40. Opinion no. 56/04 (Appeal no. 2007/02) of the Regional Administrative Court (TAR) for Veneto.
41. V Decree, October 23, 2003 of the Court of L'Aquila.
42. Decree no. 389, December 15, 2004, of the Constitutional Court.
43. Opinion no. 556/2006 of the Italian Council of State (author's translation).
44. Ibid.
45. *Case of Lautsi and Others v. Italy* (Application no. 30814/06), European Court of Human Rights, press release of November 3, 2009.
46. Ibid.
47. Ibid., Grand Chamber, March 18, 2011. See also Benjamin Mann, European Court Says Crucifixes Can Remain in Italian Schools, Catholic News Agency, March 18, 2011. Retrieved from www.catholicnewsagency.com/news/european-court-says-crucifixes-can-remain-in-italian-schools.
48. M. Staudigl and J. W. Alvis, Phenomenology and the Post-Secular Turn: Reconsidering the 'Return of the Religious', *International Journal of Philosophical Studies,* 24(5) (2016), 589–599.
49. P. Tromp, A. Pless and D. Houtman, *Believing Without Belonging* in Twenty European Countries (1981–2008): De-Institutionalization of Christianity or Spiritualization of Religion? *Review of Religious Research,* September 19, 2020. https://doi.org/10.1007/s13644-020-00432-z.
50. B. Mountford, *Christian Atheist: Belonging Without Believing* (Park Lane Ropley Hampshire: John Hunt Publishing, 2001).
51. G. Patriarca, Against Apathy: Reconstruction of a Cultural Identity, *Journal of Markets and Morality,* 16(2) (2014), 543–568.
52. www.osce.org/odihr/29154.
53. J. Miller, *So, What Do the Toledo Guiding Principles Have to Do with Me?* Retrieved from www.religiouseducationcouncil.org.uk/wp-content/uploads/2018/02/toledo-article.pdf.

54. www.coe.int/t/dg4/intercultural/source/white%20paper_final_revised_en.pdf.
55. https://rm.coe.int/CoERMPublicCommonSearchServices/DisplayDCTMContent?documentId=09000016806cd2f5.
56. See A. Bernardo and A. Saggioro (eds.), *I Princìpi di Toledo e le religioni a scuola, traduzione, presentazione e discussione dei Toledo, Guiding Principles on Teaching About Religions and Beliefs in Public Schools* (*OCES/ODIHR*) (Rome: Aracne, 2015).
57. Congregation for Catholic Education, *Educating to Fraternal Humanism: Building a "Civilization of Love" 50 Years After Populorum Progressio* (Vatican City: Congregation for Catholic Education, 2017).
58. See Italian Catholic Bishops Conference, *Educare: Infinito presente. La pastorale della Chiesa per la Scuola* (Rome: CEI-Conferenza Episcopale Italiana, 2020).
59. "What happens when fraternity is not consciously cultivated, when there is a lack of political will to promote it through education in fraternity, through dialogue and through the recognition of the values of reciprocity and mutual enrichment? Liberty becomes nothing more than a condition for living as we will, completely free to choose to whom or what we will belong, or simply to possess or exploit. This shallow understanding has little to do with the richness of a liberty directed above all to love." Pope Francis, *Encyclical Letter Fratelli Tutti*, October 3, 2020, 103.
60. A. Furco, Learning to Be Brothers and Sisters: *Fratelli Tutti* and Education, in Scholas Occurrentes (ed.), *Aprender a ser hermanos y hermanas: Fratelli Tutti y la educación* (Vatican City: Pontifical Foundation Scholas Occurrentes, 2020), 15.
61. A. Melloni (ed.), *Rapporto sull'analfabetismo religioso in Italia* (Bologna: Il Mulino, 2014).
62. See Invictus Editore, *Codice della Scuola: dalla Riforma Moratti alla Riforma Gelmini e il progetto di Riforma Renzi – Giannini* (Cesena: Invictus Editore, 2019).
63. See R. Di Massa, *Percorso legislativo dell'inclusione scolastica: Dalla Costituzione alla legge 107/2015 e decreti attuativi* (Naples: Pasquale D'Arco Editore, 2019).
64. Cf. C. Cardia, Novanta anni dai Patti Lateranensi, *Ephemerides Iuris Canonici*, A. 59(2) (2019), 421–444.
65. L. Raspi, *Legislazione scolastica e insegnamento della religione cattolica* (Milan: Glossa, 2020).
66. S. Cicatelli, *Guida all'insegnamento della religione cattolica. Secondo le nuove indicazioni* (Brescia: Editrice La Scuola, 2015).
67. F. Pajer, *Scuola e religione in Italia: Quarant'anni di ricerche e dibattiti* (Rome: Aracne, 2019).
68. See Centro Studi per la Scuola Cattolica-CSSC, *Personalizzazione e Curriculo: Scuola Cattolica in Italia. XXI Rapporto-2019* (Brescia: Scholé, 2019).
69. Pope Francis, Post-Synodal Apostolic Exhortation, *Christus Vivit*, March 25, 2019, para. 295. Retrieved from www.vatican.va/content/francesco/en/apost_exhortations/documents/papa-francesco_esortazione-ap_20190325_christus-vivit.html.

7 Law, Education, and the Place of Religion in Public Schools in Malaysia

Fatt Hee Tie

Introduction

The three domains of law, education, and religion in public schools in Malaysia are associated closely with each other. The interrelatedness between the three is the result of the government's due recognition of a specific religion as the official religion of the country. Consequently, teaching the official religion in public schools to pupils from one faith is a peculiar feature in the Malaysian education system. In all circumstances, the law is used to protect and mandate the teaching of this particular religion in public schools. Affording this protected status to the one religion is attributed to the fact that the country seeks to propagate the religion of the majority population that shares one common belief in the school system while allowing other religions to be practiced in the public domain.

In 2019, the Malaysian Statistics Department reported that the country's population is estimated to be about 29.4 million. Almost 69.3% of the population consists of the *Bumiputra*, a term used to describe the Malay race and other Indigenous peoples; 22.8% Chinese; 6.9% Indian; and 1% of other races.

The official religion of the country is Islam. Almost 69% of the population professes the Islamic faith. Individuals born as Malays automatically become Muslim and are not allowed to change their religion. Thus, one must be cognizant of the fact that a discussion on the teaching of religion in public schools in the Malaysian context means an intellectual discourse that centers primarily on the religion of Islam. Although non-Muslim pupils are free to practice their religion, the government provides complete support to the teaching of the religion of Islam in public schools. Besides the federal government, the states in Malaysia also play active roles in promoting the teaching of Islam in schools. At the same time, it is pertinent to note that the teaching of other religions such as Buddhism, Christianity, and Hinduism in public schools is allowed. However, in reality, such religious classes are almost nonexistent.

The Teaching of Islam in Malaysian Schools

Islam is taught at all levels of the school system in Malaysia. Generally, schools in Malaysia are categorized as public and private. Because the federal government provides full financial support to the public schools, it has absolute authority to set the direction and policies about teaching Islam in these public schools. In fact, it is mandatory for public schools to implement policies adhering to the national philosophy of education, the national curriculum, and the preparation of pupils to sit for the common national examination system. Public school officials must also comply with the federal government's directives with respect to the teaching of Islam.

The Malaysian school system consists of public and private preschools, primary schools, and secondary schools. There are two types of preschools. The first type are the public preschools set up by the Ministry of Education. The second type are established by other agencies including both the private sector and Islamic organizations. In addition, these organizations, such as the Muslim Youth Movement, are allowed to establish Islamic primary schools.

There are six types of public primary schools. These are government schools, which consist of publicly funded national schools; government-aided schools known as publicly funded national-type schools, including Chinese national-type schools and Tamil national-type schools; special education primary schools catering to pupils with special needs; special mode primary schools; and government-aided religious schools. In addition, other government agencies are allowed to establish the People's Religious Primary School and State Religious Primary School.

There are 11 types of public secondary schools: regular secondary schools, fully residential schools, religious schools, technical vocational colleges, special education schools, special model schools, sports schools, arts schools, government-aided religious schools, care and guidance network schools, and Form Six colleges. Other government agencies also establish the People's Religious Secondary School and the State Religious Secondary School.

The People's Religious Primary and Secondary Schools started as a "cottage" or "community" institution. The teachers managed these schools with the help of their local communities and have increased in number as parental demands to enroll their children in this type of religious school have gradually increased. Muslim parents are becoming more aware of the need to further develop the spiritual and personal development of their children.

State governments established both state religious primary and secondary schools that are administered by state religious agencies to teach the national curriculum and the state's own religious curriculum. The state government provides the financial support, teachers, and infrastructural assistance. Because the Ministry of Education does not administer these schools, they are free from the control of the federal government. The independent and autonomous nature of these state religious schools tends to pose a challenge to the Ministry of Education.

The two categories of public schools and religious schools set up by the other government agencies focus on teaching of Islam. Further, the Ministry of Education has established national religious secondary schools that teach Islamic religious education and Arabic studies.

In sum, the teaching of Islam as a subject can be found at all the different levels of the Malaysian school system because educators teach the Islamic faith to students who are Muslims. Moreover, it is compulsory for Muslim pupils to attend these religious classes that start in preschool and last until the end of secondary – a duration of 12 years. Non-Muslim students attend a subject called Moral Education while their Muslim classmates attend the religious class. Both of these subjects are taught in school during regular school hours.

The Legal Foundation for Education and Religion

Malaysia's Federal Constitution[1] and the Education Act of 1996[2] are the two primary pieces of legislations governing the teaching of Islamic in public schools. Both of these instruments set out the legal framework regulating the educational system as a whole and, specifically, the place of religion in public schools. In addition, the Ministry of Education implements the policies that the federal government adopts through its administrative letters. These letters contain regulations such as teaching hours for each subject, school discipline, school uniforms, and school attendance.

The Federal Constitution represents the supreme law of the federation.[3] The judiciary and legislators recognized that the laws that were passed after the country's independence but are inconsistent with the Federal Constitution must be deemed void. While the Federal Constitution expressly states that Islam is the religion of the federation, it allows other religions to be practiced freely in the country.[4] The ruler of the states is automatically the head of the religion of Islam. In the case where some states do not have a ruler, the constitution of the state confers on the king the position of head of the religion of Islam in that particular state.[5]

As noted, the Federal Constitution provides all citizens the right to freedom of religion.[6] Put another way, individuals have the right to profess and practice their religions. Religious groups also have the right to manage their own affairs and to establish and maintain institutions for religious purposes.[7] However, there is one important exception to freedom of religion: both federal and state law prohibits the propagation of any religious doctrine or belief to individuals who profess the religion of Islam.[8]

The Federal Constitution also sets out the rights of the citizens in respect of education.[9] It states that there shall not be any discrimination against any citizen on the grounds of religion, race, descent, or place of birth (a) in the administration of any educational institution maintained by a public authority and, in particular, the admission of pupils or the payment of fees; or (b) in providing out of the funds of a public authority financial aid for the maintenance or education of pupils or students in any educational institution, regardless of whether it is maintained by a public authority and whether within or outside the federation.

All religious groups have the constitutional right to establish and maintain institutions for the education of children in their own religions.[10] The Federal Constitution bans all forms of discrimination on the ground of religion in any law relating to such institutions or in the administration of any such law.[11] Even so, it is lawful for the federal and state governments to establish, maintain, or assist in establishing or maintaining Islamic institutions or providing or assisting in providing instruction in the religion of Islam while incurring such expenditure as may be necessary for the purpose. Further, the states are vested with the authority over all matters that are related to religion.

The jurisdiction over Islamic religious education tends to occupy a grey area between the federal government and the nine state governments since Malaysia achieved independence in 1957. The Malay rulers act as the heads of the Islamic faith in their respective states. The Federal Constitution sets forth the authority of both the federal and state governments' authority over Islam.[12] As noted, both the position of Islam as the religion of the federation and the position of the king, who is a constitutionally appointed monarch, are stated clearly in the Federal Constitution. The position of the king is rotated every five years among the nine state rulers. His Majesty the King also acts as the head of the Islamic faith in the four states not having hereditary rulers.[13]

The Federal Constitution also reiterates that no persons shall be required to receive instruction in or to take part in any ceremony or act of worship of a religion other than their own.[14] Parents or guardians decide the religion of their children under the age of 18 years.[15] To a certain extent, this provision vests responsibility on parents or guardians to bring up a child according to their wishes.

Teaching Religion and the Education Act of 1996

The purpose of the Education Act 1996 (hereinafter, the 1996 Act), as stated in its Preamble, is to provide in a general manner for education and for all other matters related to education in Malaysia.[16] At the same time, the National Education Policy is based on the National Education Philosophy that is expressed more specifically in the 1996 Act. According to its provisions, the Education Act of 1996 declares that Malaysia's educational system strives to develop the potential of students in a holistic and integrated manner. At the same time, the purpose of the 1996 Act is to produce students that are intellectually, spiritually, emotionally, and physically balanced and harmonious. Students are taught to have a firm belief in and devotion to God. Generally, at both the primary and secondary school levels, teaching the spiritual domain tends to focus mainly on instruction about one religion, namely Islamic.

The 1996 Act vests the minister of education with the power to issue general directions to the education officers.[17] The minister may give officers appointed under the administration. Part II of the 1996 Act affords that directions of a general character are related to the exercise of the powers and discretion conferred on the officers. The general directions also cover the duties the minister of education assigns to officers. In addition, the minister of education has the power to issue special directions such as to governors of public educational institutions, newly appointed board members, employees or head teachers of educational institutions, and/or members of the Central Board.[18]

Malaysia's 1996 Act mandates that educators in all schools, including religious schools, must teach the national curriculum. Private schools can satisfy this condition if they teach the core subjects in the national curriculum.[19] The core subjects in the national curriculum at the primary school consist of the national language; the English language; the Chinese language, for pupils in national-type schools (Chinese); the Tamil language, for pupils in national-type schools (Tamil); mathematics; science; local studies; Islamic education, for pupils professing the religion of Islam; and Moral Education, for pupils not professing the religion of Islam.[20]

The core subjects at the secondary school comprises the following subjects: the national language; English language; mathematics; science; history; Islamic education, for pupils professing the religion of Islam; and Moral Education, for pupils not professing the religion of Islam.[21]

Pursuant to the National Curriculum, both Islamic Education and Moral Education are aimed at developing respect for individuals that allows, to a certain extent, some freedom to embrace religion in a diverse and multireligious society. In fact, schools have taught Moral Education since 1988. The subject is taught to non-Muslim students who profess different religions such as Buddhism, Christianity, Hinduism, Taoism, Sikh, Baha'i, and other faiths.[22] This class teaches pupils common values that exist in different religions, namely those related to self-development, family, the environment, patriotism, human rights, democracy, and peace and harmony. The values in the self-development section are belief in God, trustworthiness, self-esteem, responsibility, humility, tolerance, self-reliance, diligence, love, justice, rationality, and moderation.

Moral Education also focuses on moral reasoning, moral feeling, and moral action. Additionally, moral education is an examination subject in the uniform public examination system. Unfortunately, pupils studying Moral Education tend to resort to memorization and rote learning of these values because their sole purposes are often to obtain good grades on the public examinations.

The 1996 Act does not have a specific provision for the establishment of religious schools. Nevertheless, it vests wide powers to the minister to establish educational institutions not provided for under the terms of the Education Act of 1996. This also includes the setting up of Islamic religious schools.[23]

As noted, the three categories of Islamic religious schools are found at all levels of Malaysia's educational system. The first category consists of schools established by the federal government, known as government religious schools; these schools teach the national curriculum and the Islamic faith. The second category consists of state religious schools wherein states have constitutional jurisdiction over Islam; these schools are under the jurisdiction of the state religious authorities. The third category of religious schools consists of government-aided religious schools; both the Ministry of Education and state religious authorities control these schools. The latter two categories teach both the national and religious curricula. Finally, private Islamic religious schools establish People's Religious Schools and Private Religious Schools. The pupils enrolled in these schools, which are generally small in number, are situated mainly in rural areas.

Teaching of the Islamic Faith

Schools are allowed to teach the Islamic faith where five or more pupils profess Islam.[24] The state authority is responsible to employ and support teachers in the state religious schools. The subject is taught for a period of at least two hours a week within normal teaching hours. In public schools, the teaching period is not rigid, as the minister of education can also decide the teaching period for particular schools.[25] The governors or other persons responsible for the management of the private schools must make the arrangements to provide for the teaching of Islam.[26] Where the governors or other persons are responsible for the management of two or more educational institutions, special arrangements can be made for the teaching of the Islamic faith jointly with the approval of the registrar of schools.[27]

Schools are allowed to teach religion classes to pupils that profess other faiths. Although such classes are very small in number and in most cases nonexistent, the statute does provide a form of freedom for the teaching of other religion in school.[28] The governors of government-aided schools may provide for religious teaching in faiths other than Islam subject to two conditions: "(a) no such provision shall be defrayed from monies provided by Parliament; and, (b) no pupils shall attend classes in religions other than those which they professes except with the written consent of their parents."[29] These classes do not receive any form of financial assistance from the government. Parental consent is important to avoid potential misunderstanding and minimize future conflict among parents from different faith.

On the other hand, Islamic educational institutions or schools that are not established or maintained by the minister or state government are eligible to receive financial assistance in the form of a grant.[30] Parliament may provide the monies to these Islamic schools. The state government also provides financial assistance to these educational institutions and other schools that confine their teaching exclusively to Islam.

The Protection of Freedom of Religion or Belief in the Area of Education

The protection of freedom of religion tends to place more emphasis on protecting the teaching of Islam in Malaysian public and private schools. The ethos of schools has gradually succeeded in increasing awareness among Muslim pupils of their calling. The national education system's overemphasis on religious practices has resulted in public schools setting aside a special hall or room for Muslim pupils to pray that is now a permanent fixture of public primary and secondary schools. Educators in public school premises also conduct Islamic prayers and activities that include having Muslim pupils recite supplications during school assemblies or even before classes commence, and mandatorily requiring Muslim girls to wear Islamic dress.

Changes to the curriculum have led to an increase in the number of periods in the teaching of Islamic. These changes strive to allow Muslim pupils to acquire a greater understanding of the Koran. The reforms in the national schools have also affected the People's Religious Schools as they began to change their curricula following the implementation of the Secondary School New Curriculum. However, the People's Religious Schools lack the financial resources to employ qualified teachers and establish school facilities such as science and computer laboratories. As a result, the standard and quality of the People's Religious School is low, as reflected by the poor academic performance of their pupils. For example, in 2010, only 29.6% of secondary students in the People's Religious Schools met the minimum competency level for the Lower Secondary Assessment, compared to 63.3% for the State Religious Secondary Schools. The national average is 67.4%.[31]

Judicial Analysis of the Freedom of Religion or Belief in Education

In most countries, freedom of religion is often closely associated with the freedom granted to individuals to observe a set of rituals, practices, and customs according to their faiths. For instance, these practices include wearing such religious attire or items as an Islamic headscarf, a Sikh kirpan, or a cross or crucifix.

In some countries, their constitutions or statutes identify and guarantee the rights of individuals to profess their religions. While such constitutional guarantees of freedom of religion are absolute in nature, it may be implied that individuals have the liberty to wear attire based on their beliefs. Conversely, the constitutional right to freedom of religion is presumed to be violated in circumstances when authorities impose restrictions to control individuals' liberty to wear attire based on their faiths or beliefs. Any form of restrictions or regulations to prohibit individuals from wear their religious attire is deemed to be ultra vires of national constitutions or statutes.

Generally, there is reported litigation related to the freedom of religion in public schools addressing the rights of pupils to wear religious attire to school. Not surprisingly, the question arose in Malaysia over whether the public interest should be accorded greater protection as against private individual interest.

In *Meor Atiqulrahman bin Ishak and others v. Fatimah bin Sihi and Others*, three primary school pupils wore a religious headgear, also referred to as a *serban* or a turban, to school as a manifestation of their faith in Islam.[32] However, before the incident, school officials had introduced their own regulations on school uniforms stipulating specifically the type of uniforms that pupils could wear to school. Because the regulation prohibited pupils from wearing religious headgear to school, the headmistress had advised the students in question to refrain from wearing the headgear to school on multiple occasions.

When the pupils refused to comply with the rule, school officials expelled them for violating the rule, and their parents filed suit claiming that the Federal Constitution provides freedom of religion that includes the freedom to wear one's religious attire. The parents further alleged that the headmistress acted ultra vires in light of protections the Federal Constitution provides. Consequently, they parents sought a judicial order declaring the expulsions to be null and void.

The High Court ruled in favor of the plaintiffs. It held that the headmistress's decision to expel the pupils was ultra vires. The headmistress did not have the jurisdiction to prevent the pupils from wearing the serban. The Federal Constitution had vested in the pupils a fundamental constitutional right to practice their religion while pointing out that Islam did not prohibit the practice of wearing a headgear. The headmistress then appealed to the Court of Appeal.

The Court of Appeal decided in favor of the headmistress, holding that the parents had to bear the burden of proof to show that the wearing of the headgear was mandatory in Islam.[33] The court found that the parents failed to adduce sufficient relevant and admissible evidence to prove that the practice of wearing the type of religious attire was compulsory. The evidence did not show that the practice of wearing a headgear represents an integral part of the Islamic faith. The court also acknowledged that school officials have the authority to prescribe appropriate dress code for the pupils and that they may adopt regulations related to school uniforms. The court refused to interfere with the authority of school officials to manage their own daily affairs. The court would only do so if school authorities failed to exercise their duty to act bona fide. The parents then appealed to the Federal Court.

The Federal Court affirmed the judgment of the Court of Appeal, agreeing that the school regulations did not impose a complete ban on the pupils. The court thus observed that the pupils were allowed to wear the headgear when they enter the school's prayer room.[34] In addition, the court reiterated that because school leaders and teachers possess vast experience in maintaining school discipline, they are allowed to introduce their own regulations on school uniforms for the general good of all the pupils In so noting, the court recognized that school regulations play an important role in creating safe and conducive learning environments.

Generally, the case illustrates the trust and recognition by the judiciary on the authority of school officials to establish their own regulations. In its rationale, the court sought to strike a balance between protecting the rights of individual to freedom of religion and at the same time safeguarding public interests. It must be recalled that in Malaysian public schools, religion is not left outside the school gate; the teaching of Islam to Muslim pupils has been an integral part of the school curriculum for the past 60 years. The present status quo would remain in future, particularly when there is minimal separation between the education system and politics. Thus, it is impossible to place religion outside the school gate because religion has been deeply entrenched in the educational system since the country obtained independence in 1957.

Emerging Issues

Three emerging issues are related to the teaching of Islam in Malaysian public or state-funded schools. These issues address federal versus state jurisdiction over Islamic religious schools, overemphasis on the teaching of Islam in public schools, and the lack of opportunities for pupils from different religions to learn about the faiths of their peers.

First, the federal government exercises rigid and absolute control over all aspects of public religious schools including such matters as policy, finance, management, and the intake of teachers. On the other hand, state governments have the authority to establish their own independent state schools such as the *tahfiz* schools. Of course, the state governments control the management of these religious schools because they do not come under the jurisdiction of the federal government or the Ministry of Education. Further, it is not compulsory for these state religious schools to be registered with the Ministry of Education. In 2019, when proposals were made to place the state religious schools under the jurisdiction of the federal government, a number of incidents occurred including deaths resulting from fire in the state religious schools, allegations of pupil abuse by teachers, and the use of excessive punishment.

In 2019, a state religious school planned to introduce a form of punishment that was harsh and abusive in nature. The proposed new disciplinary regulations stated that pupils who misbehaved would receive 60 strokes of the cane and be forced to stand under the sun for more than three hours. Pupils who violated school regulations would also have their heads shaved bald. When school authorities asked the parents to sign the consent form, many objected to the proposal to implement the inhumane punishments, with some seeking the help of the Ministry of Education. Others argued that the Ministry of Education should not interfere in the affairs of the state religious schools because they believed that such interference would have infringed on the state's jurisdiction over Islam.[35] Further, due to the provisions in the state's legislation, the federal government did not have a voice in the affairs of the state religious school. As such, it is likely that the federal government will allow the state religious schools to maintain their status quo by remaining noncommittal in the affairs of the state religious schools.

The second emerging issue relates to the growing concern among some Muslim parents over the teaching of Islam in public schools. Unlike other subjects in school curricula, the federal government has placed a great deal of emphasis on the teaching of Islam in public schools. Some Muslim parents claimed that the government residential schools, in particular, tend to overemphasize the observance religious rituals, practices, and activities.[36] As a result, these activities had taken up a great deal of the time and energy of their children away from their studies. These public religious schools frequently asked the Muslim pupils to attend compulsory sessions to perform congregational prayers, special prayers, and non-obligatory rituals; the upshot is that the activities have negatively affected the academic performance of some of the students.

Both the residential and public schools in Malaysia have become overwhelming religious in nature. Further, during the past 20 years, religious overtones and symbols have increased in public schools with an increased religious polarization of the educational system. As a result, many non-Muslim parents from other races, ethnic groups, and religions prefer to send their children to the vernacular Chinese and Tamil primary schools rather than the national public schools.

In public schools, the time allocated for teaching religion sometimes exceeded that set aside for instruction on other subjects, as critics claimed that the Ministry of Education needed to consider revamping the curriculum and content of Islamic Education as a subject in public schools. An activist, Siti Kassim, suggested that the Ministry of Education has to play a more serious and active role in finding a place outside the public school system where parents can opt to indoctrinate their children in any religion, and vetting, monitoring, and regulating all religious centers, classes, and textbooks to ensure that schools do not teach and indoctrinate students with extreme and radical ideology. She strongly advocated that the present system should be reformed as follows:

> We need to set our education priority right. Religion is not education. Religion is personal beliefs. With that, all mandatory religious exams in public schools must be abolished. Religion is not something to be made into exams within a public education system. The right place for theocratic studies is not in public schools but in specialized religious seminaries and tertiary institutions. If Malaysia is ever to be a developed nation, its mindset must mirror that of a developed civilization. And that starts with education where critical thinking, science and an irreligious curriculum builds a peaceful, forward looking mindset.[37]

Kassim strongly believed that critical thinking and the field of science should be accorded utmost priority. The author of this chapter is of the opinion that the authorities are likely to ignore Kassim's constructive proposal. The author reaches this conclusion because in the 63 years since independence, the officials in the educational system have placed a great amount of emphasis on the teaching of Islam in public school.

In fact, it is currently compulsory for Muslim pupils to attend Islamic education classes in public schools. Consequently, it appears that policies intended to change such fossilized thinking would indeed be a futile, impossible task. Under the current system there is, to a certain extent, a certain form of compulsion in religion because it is mandatory for Muslim pupils to attend the Islamic education class such that their failure to do so would result in severe punishments.

Additionally, there is a close relationship between politics and religion in Malaysia. If a change were to occur, certain politicians would lose votes if what is perceived as a radical reform grants Muslim pupils the freedom to choose whether to attend these classes. Moreover, the suggestion to remove religion from the school system would likely meet with hostile reactions and even threats to national security. Accordingly, religion will continue to remain an integral part of the public schools' curriculum, and religious indoctrination would remain as institutionalized because Islamization is a permanent feature, deeply embedded in the Malaysian school system.

The third issue is the lack of opportunities for pupils from different religions to learn about each other's religion. In a multiracial and multicultural country, the opportunity to learn about another person's religion can promote a better understanding of each other and as a result, foster national unity. In an open letter to the prime minister, an Islamic scholar and leader, Mohd Asri Zainal Abidin, suggested that the teaching of Islam in schools should be reformed in several ways.[38] First, he stated that Islamic education as a subject must be taken out of the regular school curriculum and be taught in the afternoon session so that it can be separated from the national curriculum. Earlier, some expressed concern over the nature and changing character of public schools that has become more Islamic in nature as these public national schools have gradually evolved into public religious schools. However, the politicians rejected the suggestion because the subject had been long entrenched in the national education system.[39] If politicians allowed such a change, some fear that they would certainly lose the support of the majority race in the country's next general election.

Second, Mohd Asri Zainal Abidin was of the opinion that *zakat* collection should be used to pay for the salary of Islamic subject teachers. Under Islamic law, zakat is an annual payment used for charitable and religious purposes. He thought that allowing the payment of this form of salary would allow the state religious institutions, rather than the federal government, to have better control over syllabi and the intake of teachers. At present, public schools are focused on teaching only one religion due to the racial composition of pupils in public schools because almost 70% of pupils in public schools are Malays.[40] Further, because Malay pupils profess Islamic, public schools focus on teaching Islamic education.

Third, Mohd Asri Zainal Abidin suggested that public schools be allowed to teach other religions in the afternoon session, where parents from different faiths can hire their own teachers. However, Muslim parents would not accept the suggestion out of the fear that their children could be influenced by the teaching of other faiths, even as parents from the other religions expressed a similar concern. Therefore, it is unlikely that this suggestion will be adopted, even though the president of the Malaysian Youth Council proposed that a special subject on different religions be introduced in schools and universities to allow students to learn about the various faiths of their peers in an attempt to promote unity and religious sensitivity among the different groups.[41]

Given the sensitive nature of religion, both Muslim and non-Muslim parents fear that public schools would turn into a place for the proselytization of religion. The Ministry of Education rejected the proposal to teach non-Islamic religions in public schools as politicians claimed that the proselytization of non-Islamic beliefs contradicted the Federal Constitution.[42]

Fourth, officials need to revise the curriculum to consider diversity through the study of comparative religion, civics and citizenship education, and multicultural education especially in the context of multicultural Malaysia. Making such a shift would hopefully create mutual respect, tolerance, and harmony. At the same time, co-curricular activities could be used to foster character building, leadership skills, responsibilities, and sensitivities to all citizens regardless of faith, culture, and/or race.

At present, feelings of mistrust, anger, tension, and misunderstanding that may eventually lead to racial conflict is a serious threat to the Malaysian community. In January 2020, a misunderstanding between Muslim and Hindu parents on the interpretation of a harvest festival threatened to destroy racial harmony.[43] The festival was a Tamil celebration for a harvest festival having nothing to do with religion. Prior to the incident, the Ministry of Education erred when its officials issued a letter to schools that described the Tamil harvest festival as a Hindu religious festival. The objective of the circular was to reduce Muslim parents' concerns over the participation of their children in the harvest celebration that took place in public schools.

The circular's content and advice to Muslim pupils followed the guidelines that were enacted by the Department for Islamic Development. Even so, the letter created an uproar among the Muslim-majority group. In fact, before this incident occurred but during the same month, officials at another public school were forced to remove some of the decorations that they had set up to celebrate the Chinese New Year.[44] In the latter case, the Ministry of Education had intervened with the statement that school officials could put up decorative items to celebrate the Chinese New Year because the decorative items did not represent any religion. The ministry's intervention succeeded in reducing tension between among parents, teachers, and pupils.

In December 2019, the Ministry of Education issued another administrative letter to encourage public schools to set up Islamic missionary clubs with the purpose of developing students' leadership qualities.[45] The ministry had directed all of the state education directors to collaborate with an Islamic foundation to establish the missionary clubs so that they could conduct Islamic evangelistic activities among public schools, teaching institutes, polytechnics, community colleges, and public universities. Although the ministry had planned to collaborate with the Islamic foundation to start this initiative, non-Muslim parents rejected this proposal because they perceived it as an attempt to promote the process of Islamization among educational institutions. Ministry officials denied this allegation claiming that the missionary clubs only involved Muslim pupils and that it did not infringe on the fundamental constitutional right to freedom of religion among non-Muslim pupils.[46]

Conclusion

Religion can be a highly emotive and divisive element in multiracial countries such that a limited understanding or in some circumstances ignorance about other religions can be risky. Such limited or nonexistent understandings can create misunderstandings that threaten national unity. On the other hand, there is greater tolerance and religious harmony if pupils from different faiths are able to learn about the faiths of their peers.

In Malaysian public schools, the teaching of religion concentrates on one religion, namely, Islam, making it a distinct feature in the nation's public school system. Private religious schools also place great emphasis on the teaching of Islam. During school hours, non-Muslim children study Moral Education while their Muslim classmates attend an Islamic education class. Thus, there are few opportunities for children to acquire better, more informed understandings of the religions of their peers.

Notes

1. www.agc.gov.my/agcportal/uploads/ files/Publications/FC/Federal%20 Consti%20(BI%20text).pdf.
2. www.agc.gov.my/agcportal/uploads/files/Publications/LOM/EN/Act%20 550.pdf.
3. Article 4, Federal Constitution.
4. Article 3(1), Federal Constitution.
5. Article 3(2), Federal Constitution.
6. Article 11, Federal Constitution.
7. Article 11(3), Federal Constitution.
8. Article 11(4), Federal Constitution.
9. Article 12, Federal Constitution.
10. Article 12(2), Federal Constitution.
11. Article 12, Federal Constitution.
12. Article 3, Federal Constitution.
13. Article 32, Federal Constitution.
14. Article 12(3), Federal Constitution.
15. Ibid.
16. www.agc.gov.my/agcportal/uploads/files/Publications/LOM/EN/Act%20 550.pdf, generally.
17. Section 8, Education Act 1996.
18. Section 9, Education Act 1996.
19. Section 18, Education Act 1996.
20. Section 18(2), Education Act 1996.
21. Section 18(3), Education Act 1996.
22. Section 50, Education Act 1996.
23. Section 34(1)(d), Education Act 1996.
24. Section 50(1), Education Act 1996.

25. Section 50(2), Education Act 1996.
26. Section 50(3), Education Act 1996.
27. Section 50(4), Education Act 1996.
28. Section 51, Education Act 1996.
29. Ibid.
30. Section 52, Education Act 1996.
31. Rosnani Hashim, *The Reformation of Muslim Education in Malaysia: Ensuring Relevance and Overcoming Challenges*. Retrieved April 25, 2020, from http://irep.iium.edu.my/35224/5/rh_imam_hatip_paper.pdf.
32. See *Meor Atiqulrahman bin Ishak and Ors v. Fatimah bte Sihi and Ors* (1994, 2005) 3 MLJ 61.
33. *Fatimah bte Sihi and Ors. v. Meor Atiqulrahman bin Ishak and Ors* (2005) 2 MLJ 25.
34. *Meor Atiqulrahman bin Ishak and Ors v. Fatimah bte Sihi and Ors.* (2006) 4 CLJ 1.
35. S. Khidhir, Malaysia's Religious Schools Under Fire, *The ASEAN Post*, September 6, 2019. Retrieved April 25, 2020, from https://theaseanpost.com/article/malaysias-religious-schools-under-fire.
36. Nur Hasliza Mohd Salleh, Heavy Hand of Religion Disrupting Studies at Government Schools, Say Helpless Parents, *Free Malaysia Today*, January 21, 2020. Retrieved April 28, 2020, from www.freemalaysiatoday.com/category/nation/2020/01/21/heavy-hand-of-religion-disrupting-studies-at-govt-schools-say-helpless-parents/.
37. Siti Kasim, What to Do with Religious Education, *The Star*, September 30, 2018. Retrieved April 25, 2020, from www.thestar.com.my/ opinion/columnists/siti-kasim-thots/2018/09/30/what-to-do-with-religious-education-the-right-place-for-theocratic-studies-is-not-in-public-schools/
38. Tajuddin Rasdi, A Radical Proposal on Religious Education, *Free Maylasia Today*, January 24, 2019. Retrieved April 24, 2020, from www.freemalaysiatoday.com/category/opinion/2019/01/24/a-radical-proposal-on-religious-education-and-why-we-should-say-yes/.
39. Ibid.
40. Malaysia Educational Statistics Quick Facts, *Educational Planning and Research Division* (Malaysia: Ministry of Education, 2018). Retrieved March 20, 2020, from www.moe.gov.my/en/muat-turun/laporan-dan-statistik/quick-facts-malaysia-education-statistics/563-quick-facts-2018-malaysia-educational-statistics/file.
41. Maszlee Rejects Having Schools Teach About Religions, Bernama, *The FMT News*, May 19, 2019. Retrieved April 25, 2020, from www.freemalaysiatoday.com/category/nation/2019/05/19/maszlee-rejects-having-schools-teach-about-religions/.
42. Rasdi, A Radical Proposal on Religious Education.
43. The New Straits Times, Uproar in Malaysia After Education Ministry Says Tamil Harvest Celebration Pongal Is a Religious Festival, *The New Straits Times*, January 15, 2020. Retrieved April 27, 2020, from www.straitstimes.com/asia/se-asia/uproar-in-malaysia-after-education-ministry-says-tamil-harvest-celebration-is-a-religious-festival.
44. Ibid.
45. Allowing Yadim to Preach in Schools Reflects Poor Use of Public Funds – Member of Parliament, *Borneo Post Online*, December 30, 2019. Retrieved March 28, 2020, from www.theborneopost.com/2019/12/30/allowing-yadim-to-preach-in-schools-reflects-poor-use-of-public-funds-mp/.

46. Education Ministry Denies 'Islamization', Says Missionary Club in Schools Only for Muslims, By Radzi Razak, December 24, 2019. Retrieved April 24, 2020, from www.malaymail.com/news/malaysia/2019/12/24/education-ministry-denies-islamisation-says-missionary-club-in-schools-only/1821992.

8 Perspectives on Law, Education, and the Place of Religion in Public Schools in Mauritius

Jeewan Ramlugun

Introduction

The Republic of Mauritius, a small island state in the Indian Ocean east of Madagascar off of the southeast coast of Africa, is governed within a framework of a vibrant multiparty parliamentary democracy. Mauritius gained its independence from Great Britain in 1968, at which time it adopted its Constitution as a free nation.[1] Mauritius is a multiethnic, multifaith, and multicultural society in which freedom of religious beliefs and practices are enshrined in its Constitution. In a small-scale society such as Mauritius, community cohesion and social stability are predicated on interreligious coexistence and mutual tolerance.

Mauritians historically are descendants of settlers, slaves, and indentured labourers originating from Europe, Africa, and Asia. These Mauritians brought with them their own distinctive traditions, heritages and faiths, worldviews, languages, and cultural mores and practices that have endured and contributed to a rich nationhood, altogether contributing to the island being considered an exemplary social mosaic.

"The 1968 constitution [implicitly] recognized four population categories: Hindus, Muslims, Sino-Mauritians, and the general population."[2] English is the official language in Mauritius, while French is the language of the mainstream media. In addition, Mauritian Indians generally speak Hindi and its dialect Bhojpuri alongside a minority of persons who speak Tamil or Telegu. The Hindu social stratification has survived in the form of the caste system, albeit on a less rigid basis, and is not occupation-based. The Muslim population, predominantly Sunnis who originated mainly from the Indian sub-continent, speak Hindi, Bhojpuri, Gujrati, Urdu, and Arabic. The early Chinese settlers were from the Canton region, speaking Cantonese, while the majority were of Mandarin origin from Hunan, adhering to Buddhism.

The general population in Mauritius comprises Franco-Mauritians and other settlers from Europe, as well as Creoles, mainly of black African origin most being adherents of the Roman Catholic faith.[3] As of July 1, 2020, the population of the Republic of Mauritius stood at approximately 1,266,000, corresponding to zero population growth[4] compared to a year earlier.[5] More specifically, in 2020 the population of Indo-Mauritians (meaning they are of Indian origin), by far the largest group, stood at 68%; Creoles (referring to those of African and Malagasy origin), 27%; Sino-Mauritians (those from China), 3%; and Franco-Mauritians (so called due to their French origins) 2%.[6]

In terms of its languages, Creole, a French derivative, is the lingua franca spoken by 86.5% of the population. There has been a growing call for making Creole a mainstream language in Mauritius, already introduced in parts of the media and in education, with increasing support for its use in the broadcasting of parliamentary debates. The other languages spoken in Mauritius are Bhojpuri, by 5.3% of the population, and French, by 4.1%. The remaining 4.1% include English, Mandarin, Cantonese, and various ethnic languages from India: Hindi, Telegu, Malayalam, Marathi, Urdu, and Tamil.[7]

Turning to religion, 48.5% of Mauritians are Hindu, 26.3% are Roman Catholic, 17.3% profess Islam, 6.4% follow other Christian faiths; and 3% are Buddhists or follow other religions. The other Christian faiths include adherents of Pentecostal Christianity, Seventh-Day Adventists, Anglicans, Presbyterians, the Church of Jesus Christ of Latter-day Saints (Mormons), Christian evangelicals, Jehovah's Witnesses, and the Assemblies of God. More than 95% of Muslims in Mauritius are Sunnis.[8]

Intra-ethnic languages and cultures in Mauritius, as in other nations, are identity defining, with overlapping intersections of inter-ethnic linguistic connectedness with the wider communities and other shared national consciousness signifiers. Some of the languages in Mauritius, particularly in the context of the island having been a former colony, carry status connotations. For instance, English signifies knowledge, whereas French signifies culture and Creole stands for egalitarianism.

Due to the multiplicity of religions, the government of Mauritius makes grant payments to religious groups according to the numbers of their followers. New religious groups with a minimum of seven members that are approved by the Registrar of Associations enjoy tax exemptions. The government grants religious missionaries residence permits for a maximum of three years. Interfaith dialogues and mutual intercommunity discourses are facilitated by the Council of Religions, which consists of 18 religious groups that participate jointly in religious festivals and rituals.[9]

As in the other chapters in this book, the remainder of this chapter examines the legal foundation for education and religion, the protection for freedom of religion or belief in education, judicial analysis of the freedom of religion in education, emerging issues, and a conclusion.

The Legal Foundation for Education and Religion

The Constitution

According to Chapter I, Section 2 of the Constitution of Mauritius: "This Constitution is the supreme law of Mauritius, and if any other law is inconsistent with this Constitution, that other law shall, to the extent of the inconsistency, be void."[10] As with other constitutional republics, the Constitution describes the other branches of the government, namely the Parliament or the National Assembly[11] and the Judicature or Court System.[12] The Constitution also sets forth the duties for officials such as the president and vice president of the republic.[13]

Parliament or National Assembly

Parliament is the supreme lawmaking institution in the Mauritian democracy, as long as its acts comport with the Constitution. In Mauritius, the parliament, or more properly, the National Assembly,

> comprises up to 70 members, 62 of whom are elected (60 from 20 three-member constituencies on the island of Mauritius plus two from the single constituency of Rodrigues). Up to eight additional seats are allocated to "best losers," to ensure representation of a variety of ethnic groups.[14]

In its *Role, Vision and Mission Statement,* the government explained that "The National Assembly together with the Presidency of the Republic is a parliamentary institution which plays a critical role in ensuring democracy."[15] In accordance with the Constitution of Mauritius, then, a separation of powers pertains between the legislature, the executive, and the judiciary.[16]

Judicial System

Not surprisingly in light of its history, the judicial system in Mauritius is based on the English common law and the French Napoleonic Code. The judicial system consists of the Supreme Court and the Subordinate Courts, namely the Intermediate Court, the District Courts, the Bail and Remand Court, and the Court of Rodrigues.[17]

The Supreme Court, comprising the Court of Civil Appeal and the Court of Criminal Appeal, has unlimited jurisdiction over any civil or criminal proceedings and the interpretation of the Constitution. The Intermediate and District Courts (Magistrate Courts) have jurisdiction over criminal and civil matters, while the Industrial Court handles employment matters.

The Legislative Process

Section 45(1) of the Constitution empowers the National Assembly in Mauritius to make laws subject to the Constitution.[18] 'As such, the judicial system may strike down or invalidate a law enacted by Parliament only if it infringes any of the provisions of the Constitution, including fundamental rights, or otherwise goes against any restriction or limitation the Constitution imposes.[19] Parliamentary lawmaking originates from bills debated in and passed by the National Assembly and assented to by the president of Mauritius.[20] If it is in accordance with the Constitution, the bill then becomes an act. "No law made by Parliament shall come into operation until it has been published in the Gazette, but Parliament may postpone the coming into operation of any such law and may make laws with retrospective effect."[21]

Office of the Attorney General

The Attorney General's Office interfaces with the legislature, the judiciary, and the executive. Officials in this office provide legal and legislative drafting services to the government while promoting the rule of law on behalf of both the state and the citizens.[22]

National Human Rights Commission

Within the National Human Rights Commission (NHRC), the Human Rights Division (HRD) is concerned with the protection of human rights as enshrined in Chapter II of the Constitution of Mauritius,[23] which is based mainly on the European Convention on Human Rights.[24] The NHRC operates on a human rights–based model of economic, social, and cultural development to enable citizens to enjoy a good quality of life based on human dignity and equality of treatment.

In terms of their relevance to education, the NHRC covers such rights in Chapter II of the Constitution as freedom of conscience; protection of freedom of expression; freedom to establish schools; and protection from discrimination in the public sector on the grounds of race, caste, place of origin, political opinions, colour, creed or sex. Officials of the HRD carry out investigations but have no power to resolve disputes; instead, its officers refer cases to the Supreme Court which takes the final decision.[25]

The Ministry of Education

The Ministry of Education oversees all aspects of education in Mauritius subject to the Education Act,[26] the primary law regulating elementary and secondary education in Mauritius. The goal of the ministry is to prepare the next generation of forward-looking and innovative leaders contributing to the transformation of the Republic of Mauritius into a high-ranking, prosperous nation while helping to create a cohesive, inclusive, and productive society through education and skills development for all.[27] The government guarantees free education to all by providing compulsory schooling until the age of 16.[28]

Protection for Freedom of Religion or Belief in Education

Mauritius is a democratic sovereign state within a multiethnic, multicultural, multilingual, and multireligious society. Not surprisingly, then, the fundamental rights to religion or belief, freedom of thought and expression, and the right not to hold a particular belief or religion, or to change belief or religion, are enshrined and safeguarded in the Constitution of Mauritius.[29]

Chapter II, Article 3 of the Constitution protects the fundamental rights and freedoms of the individual along with safeguarding the right to religious beliefs and practices. More specifically, Section 3.b protects "freedom of conscience, of expression, of assembly and association and freedom to establish schools." Chapter II, Article 11, which protects freedom of conscience, is essential in terms of protecting freedom of religion in education. To this end, Section 1 includes:

> freedom of thought and of religion, freedom to change his [*sic*] religion or belief and freedom, either alone or in community with others, and both in public and private, to manifest or propagate his [*sic*] religion or belief in worship, teaching, practice and observance.

In addition, Chapter II, Article 11 specifically addresses the status of freedom of opinion, thought, and conscience in Mauritius, elements that go to the heart of religion and education.

Section 2 of Article 11 adds that students, or, in the case of those who are minors:

> shall not be required to receive religious instruction or to take part in or attend any religious ceremony or observance if that instruction, ceremony or observance relates to a religion that he [*sic*] does not profess, and should be under no compulsion to receive religious instruction or to partake in any religious ceremony or observance relating to another religion.

Thus, without saying so directly, this provision protects students from being subjected to proselytizing in schools.

Chapter 11, Section 5(c) is of great importance to those who operate religious schools in Mauritius. Under this provision,

> [n]o religious community or denomination shall be prevented from making provision for the giving, by persons lawfully in Mauritius, of religious instruction to persons of that community or denomination in the course of any education provided by that community or denomination.

This provision ensures the rights of religious leaders to provide religious instruction in educational institutions.

Parties who claim that they were discriminated against on the basis of their religion can lodge complaints with the Equal Opportunities Commission, discussed above. The Commission can pursue remedies in court on behalf of aggrieved parties within the provisions of the Civil Judicial Procedures.[30] As a former British colony, beyond the Supreme Court, a party can seek further review at the level of the Privy Council of the United Kingdom.[31] Outside of the judicial system, the Ombudsman's Office is empowered to investigate the abuse of human rights complaints, including religion.[32]

Religion in the Schools

Private schools are commonplace in Mauritius. The prevalence of private schools came about because an ordinance of 1856 permitted the Government of Mauritius to support primary schools out of public funds, and further provision for primary schools, including non-Government primary schools. . . . [However], Roman Catholic authorities received no public subsidy for their secondary schools until 1947. The cost of running and administering the schools was met, and continued until 1977 to be met, very largely from fees paid by pupils attending the schools.[33]

Pursuant to the Education Act, "responsibility for controlling and directing the educational system of Mauritius was entrusted to a minister. Grants in aid to non-Government secondary schools were authorised. To qualify for a grant in aid such schools were required to be registered."[34] In addition, Article 14 of the Constitution guarantees the freedom of religious and other organizations to establish schools: "No religious denomination and no religious, social, ethnic or cultural association or group shall be prevented from establishing and maintaining schools at its own expense." Moreover, Chapter II, Article 14, Subsections 3–4 protect the parental freedom to send their child or children, which includes stepchildren or children who are adopted in a manner recognised by law, to non-state schools.

The Roman Catholic Education Authority (RCEA), which operates the largest system of religious schools in Mauritius through its diocesan office, has a network of 46 grant-aided primary schools, two Loreto privately paid junior primary schools, 17 grant-aided secondary schools, with one privately paid, and one technical school with substantive subsidies from the private sector.[35] As its core mission, the RCEA educates the head, the heart, and the soul. Officials in Catholic schools call their classes, catechisms or *cathéchèse*; for those students who are not of the Catholic faith, the schools offer Moral Values/Human Values classes. Since 2017, RCEA officials formalized the curriculum and created their own manuals of Religious Education and Intercultural Education integrating these subjects in the curriculum.[36]

At the primary level, there are religious instruction books for grades 1–3 and at the secondary level for grades 7 and 8. This instruction is compulsory for two periods per week. Students whose parents opt them out of religious instructions must attend intercultural education classes taught only in RCEA schools. Teachers of religious education participate in the in-service courses the Ministry of Education offers. Further, depending on the schools and on the regions, state primary and secondary schools access the services of religious education teachers from the Catholic diocese.[37]

Within the primary sector, the current zonal extent of religious instructions in Mauritius is as follows: zone 1, 53 out of 83 schools; zone 2, 51 out of 74 schools; zone 3, 32 out of 60 schools; and zone 4, 36 out of 41 schools.[38] The religious instruction timetable provides for three periods of 25 minutes in the primary sector, grades 2 to 6. Students whose parents choose not to have them take religious instruction are offered official reading time in class libraries and the sharing of storybooks. Religious study is not part of the secondary school curriculum in Mauritius, but Islamic studies and Hinduism are optional subjects at this level of education.[39]

Judicial Analysis of Freedom of Religion in Education

Generally

Unlike the United States, where litigation over religion and education is seemingly endless, Mauritius, like most other nations, has not experienced a large number of cases on this important topic. The human rights violations with reference to law, education, and religion that come to court in Mauritius do so by the nature of their evident departures from established statutes, constitutional stipulations, regulations, and covenants. While discriminatory practices involving matters of religion and faith in the human rights context can go undetected and unaccounted for, complaints that reach the court help to set the parameters of what is legally acceptable and normatively compliant with the Constitution and laws of Mauritius with regard to religious freedom in education as well as other spheres of life.

The relatively few cases involving religion and education in Mauritius, discussed below, focus on both the rights of employees and students. These cases are noteworthy because they confirm that the judicial system in Mauritius is available to safeguard religious freedom in education.

Litigation in Mauritius

Government Teachers' Union v. RCEA Authority[40]

The first of three cases involving the status and rights of teachers in Catholic schools arose when the Government Teachers' Union (GTU) sued the RCEA in a dispute where a school employee was subjected to disciplinary proceedings. The GTU argued that an RCEA official violated the Constitution on the ground that the employee was a public officer whose actions were subject to review by the Public Service Commission. In response, officials of the RCEA contended that the Public Service Commission had no jurisdiction over the appointment and disciplinary matters under the control of officials in the Catholic schools.

Ruling in favour of the RCEA, the Supreme Court of Mauritius was of the opinion that the employee worked in a Catholic school in a private rather than public capacity, and even though the school received governmental funds to help maintain its operations, this did not mean that its staff members were public officers. The Court thus entered a judgment in favour of the RCEA, rejecting the claim as being without merit.

Roman Catholic Diocese of Port St. Louis v. Minister of Education[41]

At issue in this case was whether the denominational schools run and administered by the RCEA, as recipients of government financial grants to help operate their schools, were free to hire staff members whose beliefs were sympathetic to and compatible with those of the Roman Catholic Church. The dispute arose when the GTU filed suit against the RCEA claiming that its employment practice violated the antidiscrimination provisions in Article II, Section 16, of the Constitution, which protect individuals from discrimination based on their creeds or religious beliefs and various other personal characteristics.

The RCEA maintained that despite the anti discriminatory language in the Constitution and regulations under the Education Act, its officials had latitude in the recruitment of its staff in order to preserve the specificity of its faith schools. To this end, officials of the RCEA pointed out that regardless of whether the grants they received are from public funds, in the past they enjoyed the freedom to ensure that the hiring and continued employment of all persons on their staff were subject to their acceptance of the Roman Catholic faith and its moral tenets in light of the specific religious character of the schools. At the same time, the RCEA denied that its officials ever discriminated in their recruitment of teachers on racial grounds. In its judgment, the Supreme Court agreed that because the RCEA was entitled to uphold its institutional specificity by hiring those who followed the teachings of the Roman Catholic Church, its officials had not engaged in discrimination.

Subramanien v. Government of Mauritius[42]

This case emerged as a challenge to a contractual agreement between the minister of education and Cardinal Margeot on behalf of the RCEA over the status and entitlements of teachers in state-aided primary schools. Under the terms of this agreement, the teachers who were employed in primary schools operated by the RCEA would be denied such benefits as transfers to and promotions within the state school system and in the public service. As a result of this agreement, teachers in the RCEA schools were unable to earn additional remunerations whereas these were available to other public employees.

The teachers filed suit, claiming that because they were public officers, they should have worked subject to the same rules, regulations, privileges, and rights as their peers in state schools. The teachers further claimed that under the disputed employment agreement, the RCEA deprived them not only of their constitutional right to acquired rights to property but also to the protection of the law. The Supreme Court of Mauritius dismissed the teachers' suit as lacking a legal foundation.

On further review, the Privy Council of Mauritius affirmed the dismissal in favour of the minister of education. The Law Lords agreed that the teachers did not meet the qualifications of a public officer as defined in various sections of the Constitution and statutes. The Law Lords added that because this case did not involve a constitutional issue, a constitutional remedy was unavailable to the teachers and that any relief they might have obtained would have to have been sought pursuant to contract or tort law.

Bishops of Roman Catholic Diocese of Port-Louis v. Tengur[43]

This case arose when a Hindu father filed suit alleging discrimination based on his concern that officials at a Roman Catholic secondary school or college, as they are called, would discriminate against his daughter, who was nearing the completion of her primary school education, when they reviewed her application for admission. The father challenged the practice of Catholic secondary school authorities that allocates 50% of their places in the first year of admission not only on the basis of geographical zonal criteria but also on the overriding principle of specificity, meaning that students must live in accordance with the Catholic creed. As a result of these criteria, the father claimed that his daughter, in competing for admission, was likely to be discriminated against vis-à-vis Catholic pupils who have an advantage over their non-Catholic peers.

In his complaint, the father went so far as to assure school officials that his daughter would be willing to participate in the religious activities that school officials conduct. School officials responded that they never practised any form of preferential treatment to pupils of Catholic faith in the allocation of the 50% of seats available in the secondary schools.

The Supreme Court of Mauritius entered a judgment in favour of the father. At the heart of its rationale, the Court was convinced that in light of the antidiscrimination provision in Article II, Section 16(3) of the Constitution that when students who are non-Catholic seek admission to the religious secondary schools, officials cannot treat them any differently from their peers who are Catholic. The Court explained that if officials had treated the Hindu student or other applicants differently due to their creeds or religious beliefs, their actions would have been discriminatory.

On further review before the Privy Council of Mauritius, the Lords of the Judicial Committee dismissed the appeal of officials of 12 secondary schools in Mauritius, which together have been called "the Catholic colleges."[44] After a detailed discussion of the history of and support for religious schools in Mauritius, the Law Lords rejected the appeal of the Catholic school officials as lacking merit.

Emerging Issues

The one overriding concern that has emerged in recent years in Mauritius is for the country to position itself as a locus for intercultural and interreligious dialogue.[45] To this end, officials at the University of Mauritius continue to offer a three-year part-time certificate course in peace and interfaith studies.[46] The program is designed to provide a basic understanding of the main underpinning concepts and challenges in regard to the promotion of national cohesion in pluralistic societies such as Mauritius by examining the place of faith communities in public life.[47] Supporters of such programs are hoping to propose a diploma-level course of study, with in-depth analyses of philosophy and aesthetics, aimed at teachers in primary and secondary schools. Such a program is conceived of as a means of providing teachers of religion and other beliefs the relevant deep subject knowledge, continually updated through continuous professional development.

At the same time, a second issue concerns the urgent need to review the way in which the subject of Religious Education is supported at various levels. Among the questions in need of consideration are whether the current statutory arrangements for the local determination of Religious Education curricula are effective, whether there is sufficient clarity about what constitutes learning in Religious Education and how the pupils' progress can be measured, and whether the provision for professional development in Religious Education is adequate.

The current practice of teaching Religious Education in state-funded schools in Mauritius in a way and in a mode truly representing both faith and nonfaith aspects remains a challenge. To this end, it is worth taking note of a ruling of the High Court in the UK in November 2015. In its order, the Court explained that Religious Education in state schools must be objective, critical, and pluralistic while their curricula and syllabi must include nonreligious worldviews such as humanism.[48]

It follows that the judgment from the UK leads to uncharted territories, such as when it comes to belief systems such as veganism, pacifism, secularism, atheism, non-theism, and others such as climate change. In addition, Catholic secondary schools in Mauritius, within their program of Education for Sustainability, the centrality of sustainability in environmental education, has been given much prominence in a class called Ecological Living in Action.[49] The leader of the Roman Catholic Church, Pope Francis, stressed a similar perspective during his visit to Mauritius in 2019.[50] In school settings, the teaching of religion, other eclectic beliefs, and values including distinct worldviews, in a scholarly rigorous way that enables critical inquiry, should all be integral to a well-rounded education for all students regardless of their level of schooling.

Were nonreligious belief systems, for example secularism, to become more widespread in Mauritius, school teaching programs would need to reflect and accommodate the attendant changing belief orientations over time. In this regard, it would help to undertake school surveys and research studies, with the endorsement of national educational ministries and authorities, on the extent of changing belief systems, so as to inform policy and strategy in respect of teaching of religion and other belief systems.

None of the preceding is meant to supplant existing beliefs and religious education curricula. Rather, these faiths and beliefs can, and should, be allowed to continue to retain, propagate, and perpetuate their distinctiveness. Yet, schools in these established faiths should become more inclusive in their teaching because inculcating a disciplined understanding of the multiplicity of belief systems, philosophical outlooks, and worldviews during students' formative years, and later in life, can only help to promote greater national cohesion grounded in a shared, overarching identity, aside from the separate religious and cultural affiliations. The effect of such an approach would be to render the social fabric in Mauritius less liable to fraying and splintering in the event of wider socioeconomic, political, or other extraneous adverse events or circumstances.

Conclusion

In dynamic and evolving societies such as Mauritius, the forces of change in their many facets can pose strains on traditions in the face of modernity or postmodernity. While Mauritius has a relatively recent history as a nation state, the various social groups that emanated from their ancestral origins brought along with them their respective time-honoured belief systems, worldviews, and ways of life. In their new, more geographically circumscribed setting, a harmonious confluence of diversities must work toward peaceful coexistence and social stability.

Religious freedom, the protection of liberty, and freedom of conscience, thoughts, and the right to hold other belief systems, within the protective ambit of human rights, have all served to maintain social cohesion in Mauritius as they have elsewhere. By way of its legislation and policy commitment, the government of Mauritius ensures equal representation of all communities in the civil service, including education, with no legal provision privileging one or another ethnic, racial, or religious group.

At the international and regional levels, Mauritius has not only acceded to the core human rights conventions such as the 1948 United Nations Declaration on Human Rights,[51] but it has also seen to it that those instruments, or at least the principles they represent, have to a large extent been incorporated into domestic law. Nevertheless, as is the case with any society, the Mauritian social fabric can be susceptible to fissiparous strains if mutual tolerance is compromised as, in isolated instances, its history bears testimony.

Instances of religious extremism culminating in violent action and the fomenting of communal tension have been isolated in Mauritius. Even so, they cannot be disregarded. The multiethnic social fabric of the island can be liable to serious fraying. Eternal vigilance needs to be in place, with religious and political leaders sparing no efforts to shore up mutual tolerance and peaceful coexistence. As such, guarding against complacency is critical, for despite great strides in the direction of intercommunal harmony, the tendency to exclusively or predominantly cooperate within distinct religious and ethnic boundaries, can militate against lasting wider national unity. Thus, as leaders and communities in Mauritius and elsewhere build cross-faith and cross-cultural bridges, they must avoid building walls at the same time, because religion can both unite and divide.

In a positive development, ecumenical and syncretistic movements are gaining ground in Mauritius, helping to foster even greater progress in this area while consolidating the collective conscience and the spirit of national solidarity. Importantly, schools and educational institutions, through their officials, generally play a pivotal part in instilling and promoting the values of tolerance and respect across cultures, religions, and other belief systems, within the overarching purview of an even-handed, impartial, enabling, and protective state.

The litmus test, as it were, is the effective extent to which the teaching of religions in schools can be both faith-affirming and faith-deepening while also being facilitative of critical reflection and of being open to, appreciative of, and respectful toward other faiths, beliefs, and/or world-views. It is only through an examination and evaluation of the religious and related teaching activities in schools over time that political, educational, and faith leaders can confirm whether the educational system in Mauritius is helping to achieve the wider societal goal of not only tolerance but also respect for the beliefs of others.

In order to ensure peaceful coexistence, leaders and adherents of different faiths and belief systems of all stripes and persuasions must ensure they are non-dominant and non-hegemonic, with the state playing a supportive yet impartial role. The precious mosaic of interreligious harmony in Mauritius, bar the exceptional intolerant strains, remains in a safe place and should be steadfastly preserved as a haven for religious freedom and other civic values and worldviews, in which schools can play a pivotal role as they teach about religion.

Notes

1. Constitution of Mauritius, as Amended. Retrieved from www.constituteproject.org/constitution/Mauritius2016.pdf?lang=en.
2. See Ethnicity, Religion, and Language, http://countrystudies.us/mauritius/10.htm. See also note 1.
3. See, e.g., www.gcatholic.org/diocese/country/Mu.htm.
4. Mauritius Inside Out, *The Population of Mauritius 2020 Estimated.* Retrieved from www.mauritiusinsideout.com/population-of-mauritius.html.
5. https://statsmauritius.govmu.org/Pages/Statistics/ESI/Population/Pop_Vital_Jan-Jun20.aspx.
6. Mauritius Inside Out, *The Population of Mauritius 2020 Estimated.*
7. Ibid.
8. Ibid.
9. See US Department of State, *Mauritius 2018 International Religious Freedom Report Executive Summary*, 1. Retrieved from www.state.gov/wp-content/uploads/2019/05/MAURITIUS-2018-INTERNATIONAL-RELIGIOUS-FREEDOM-REPORT.pdf See also www.dioceseportlouis.org/2013/06/07/father-goupille-although-on-some-issues-i-may-not-share-m-dultVhumuns-pinions-i-respect-him-as-a-mauritian-citizen-and-head-of-a-religious-federation/.
10. See note 1.
11. Ibid., Chapter V.
12. Ibid., Chapter VII.
13. Ibid., Chapter IV. See Chapter VI, The Executive, for descriptions of the roles of various ministries.
14. Commonwealth Governance, Constitution of Mauritius, www.commonwealthgovernance.org/countries/africa/mauritius/constitution/.
15. https://mauritiusassembly.govmu.org/SitePages/Index.aspx.

16. Mauritius Financial Network: Legal. Retrieved from www.mauritius-finance.com/en/legal ("In Mauritius, the Judiciary is vested with all the powers to administer justice. In line with the constitution which makes provision for an independent judiciary based on the concept of the separation of powers, Commonwealth Governance, The Judicial System."). See also www.commonwealthgovernance.org/countries/africa/mauritius/judicial-system/.
17. Commonwealth Governance, *The Judicial System*. Retrieved from www.commonwealthgovernance.org/countries/africa/mauritius/judicial-system/; see also the Supreme Court of Mauritius. Retrieved from https://supremecourt.govmu.org/SitePages/HomePage.aspx; https://supremecourt.govmu.org/Pages/Supreme-Court.aspx.
18. See note 1. See also https://mauritiusassembly.govmu.org/SitePages/Index.aspx.
19. Ibid.
20. Ibid., Article 46.
21. Ibid.
22. Ibid., Article 69; see also https://attorneygeneral.govmu.org/Pages/AboutUs/The%20Office/TheAttorneyGeneral.aspx.
23. National Human Rights Commissionhttps://nhrc.govmu.org/Pages/index.aspx; Mauritius: National Human Rights Commission. Retrieved from https://cfnhri.org/members/africa/mauritius/; National Human Rights Commission. Retrieved from https://informationmauritius.com/public-sector-guide/the-independent-bodies/the-national-human-rights-commission/.
24. www.echr.coe.int/Documents/Convention_ENG.pdf.
25. Mauritius, National Human Rights Commission; Human Rights Division.
26. The Role of the Ministry of Education is delineated in Part II of the Education Act. Retrieved from https://attorneygeneral.govmu.org/Documents/Laws%20of%20Mauritius/A-Z%20Acts/E/Education%20Act,%20No.%2039%20of%201957.pdf.
27. See generally https://govmu.org/EN/infoservices/education/Pages/default.aspx; Portal.mie.ac.mu/curriculum-development.
28. Republic of Mauritius, *Education and Training*. Retrieved from https://govmu.org/EN/infoservices/education/Pages/default.aspx.
29. See note 1.
30. http://eoc.govmu.org/English/Pages/default.aspx.
31. https://supremecourt.govmu.org/Pages/Judicial%20committee%20of%20the%20Privy%20Council.aspx.
32. www.locate-a-ombudsman.com/MauritiusOmbudsman.html.
33. https://mauritiusprivycouncilreports. blogspot.com/2004/02/bishops-of-roman-catholic-diocse-of.html, para. 6.
34. Ibid., para. 7.
35. Personal communication, on file with author and editor. Retrieved from www.dioceseportlouis.org/education/ecoles-primaires/; www.dioceseportlouis.org/education/colleges-secondaires/.
36. Ibid.
37. Ibid.
38. Ibid.
39. Ibid.
40. 1987 MR88.
41. 1991 MR 176.
42. https://mauritiusprivycouncilreports.blogspot.com/search?q=Roman+Catholic+Education+Authority+.

43. 2002 MR 116.
44. This judgment is available at appeal. Retrieved from https://mauritiusprivy councilreports. blogspot.com/2004/02/bishops-of-roman-catholic-diocse-of.html.
45. www.dioceseportlouis.org/2013/06/07/father-goupille-although-on-some-issues-i-may-not-share-m-dulthumuns-opinions-i-respect-him-as-a-mauritian-citizen-and-head-of-a-religious-federation/.
46. See https://uom.ac.mu/index.php/90-study-at-uom/398-full-list-of-under graduate-programmes-2019-2020.
47. Program details are available at https://uom.ac.mu/images/FILES/Programmes/FSSH/YR2019/Undergraduate/SH222A.pdf.
48. Judge Rules Government Broke the Law in Excluding Humanism From School Curriculum, November 25, 2015. Retrieved from https://humanism.org.uk/2015/11/25/judge-rules-government-broke-the-law-in-excluding-human ism-from-school-curriculum/.
49. Education for Sustainability. Retrieved June 17, 2014, from www.lemauricien.com/le-mauricien/education-sustainability-case-catholic-secondary-schools-mauritius-new-impetus-studies-appli/65129.
50. Pope Francis in Mauritius: Do Not Pit Economy Against Environment, Poor, *Catholic News Agency*, September 9, 2019. Retrieved from www.cathol icnewsagency.com/news/pope-francis-in-mauritius-do-not-pit-economy-against-environment-poor-43776; See also Pope Francis Teams Up with UN to Educate World on Sustainable Lifestyles, Gender Equality, Global Citizenship, December 28, 2020. Retrieved from www.lifesitenews.com/news/pope-francis-teams-up-with-un-to-educate-world-on-sustainable-lifestyles-gender-equality-global-citizenship.
51. www.un.org/en/universal-declaration-human-rights/index.html.

9 Separation of Church and State in Mexico Amid Debates Over Religion in the National Curriculum

Ricardo Lozano and Heriberto Lozano

Introduction

Education in Mexico, to the current day, continues to be affected by its unresolved past as well as enduring ethnic and class divisions present in the nation. This unresolved history of ethnic, cultural, and social divisions can trace its origins to the role the Catholic Church played during the colonial era. The first Spaniards arrived in Mexico in 1517, a year later reaching the gulf coast along what is now Veracruz. Hernán Cortez, who landed in 1519 with 11 ships and 550 men, succeeded in conquering the Aztecs within three years. Once Montezuma II was captured, Cortez named this land New Spain (Thomas, 2013).

Spain, like all other major colonial powers, provided education mainly for the ruling aristocracy. The Spanish intended to annihilate the traditional ways and culture of the Indigenous peoples of New Spain; however, numerous elements of these traditions and customs survived, thereby setting the stage for the birth of the new mestizo culture, which has elements from both civilizations but is characterized by its distinct individuality (MacLachlan, 2015). The unexpected emergence of this mestizo nation resulted in the internally conflicting culture and society characteristic of Mexico today.

In the Spanish colonies, including Mexico, education was provided solely by the Catholic Church. These institutions provided education in the classics for members of the upper class and clergy, whereas the peons and mestizos remained ignorant. The Mayans and Aztecs had their traditions trampled, for the most part, by the religious systems imposed by Catholic monks and priests (Sheridan, 1941).

Wary of the influence of the Crown and the Holy Roman Empire, the local Spanish attempted to establish their own plantation form of government in New Spain, one that exploited both the Indians and peasants (Spielvogel, 2007). The Roman Catholic Church and Spanish Crown, on the other hand, sought to establish a colonial system based on privilege formed and controlled through religious unification. The Catholic Church's intention was cultural genocide, often building their churches on sacred sites of the original inhabitants of the land (Tucker and Janick, 2018).

Missions and monasteries became the form of control over the local Indigenous population. Rural estates called *haciendas* surrounded these missions while monasteries functioned as self-sufficient centers of political and economic power. Within this system, members of the Franciscan order provided early education to natives and mestizo peasants consisting mainly of instruction in Catholicism (Turley, 2016). The Jesuits and Augustinians, on the other hand, provided the more classical education for Spanish immigrants and the *criollos*, that is, Mexican-born individuals of pure Spanish descent (Polzer, 1976).

Vasco de Quiroga, a liberal Catholic judge and bishop, is credited with starting the first school for the natives, the hospital-school of Santa Fe established on the outskirts of Mexico City in 1531 (Weaver, 2014). Viceroy Mendoza and Bishop Zumárraga established another school, the School of Santa Cruz de Tlatelolco, in 1536. With its focus on Latin, rhetoric, logic, philosophy, music, and native medicine, the school's student body comprised mainly the Spanish privileged class (Greenleaf, 2018). During the colonial times in Mexico, the small group of well-educated Indians was still held to an inferior status even by the illiterate Spaniards (Melvin, 2012).

In 1547, the Orphanage School of San Juan opened for the education of both Indian and mestizo youth. Further, in 1548, the Caridad School was established for orphaned mestizos. This was the beginning of a limited number of schools providing education for the female peasant youth (Catholic Encyclopedia, 1913). Nonetheless, few natives or mestizos benefited from these schools, as most learned the Spanish language and customs informally. Soon, this level of education and understanding of the Spanish language among the native and mixed-bloods frightened the Spanish with fears that continued formal education would lead to rebellion. Thenceforth, the education of the natives and mestizos was deemed undesirable by the colonial rulers (Marlow-Ferguson, 2002).

Alongside the education of the natives and mestizos being discussed by the Spanish rulers, the Royal and Pontifical University of Mexico opened in 1553, making it the first university in the North American part of the New World. Its main purpose was to educate the criollos for the Catholic clergy. During the colonial period, nearly 30,000 bachelor's degrees and more than 1,000 masters and doctorates were awarded, thus establishing New Spain's educated elite (Huck, 2017). In 1791, a second university was established in Mexico, in Guadalajara. Despite these advancements in education in the New World, by 1842 less than 1% of the Mexican population was educated and only about 33% of education was free (Manzanárez and French, 2004).

Under the haciendas system, major urban centers emerged, including Puebla, Guanajuato, Guadalajara, and Mexico City. Universities soon became established in these major urban trade centers. The Mexican-born criollos' resentment of Spanish influence germinated the seeds of revolution, resulting in the beginning of the war of independence in 1810. Mexico declared its independence from Spain in 1821, and in 1822 it proclaimed its own emperor, Agustín I. The empire was overthrown a year later when Mexico was declared a republic (Middleton, 2015).

Following wars with the north, first with Texas in 1836 and then with the United States between 1846 and 1848), a civil war (the War of Reform) between 1858 and 1861, and the attempt to establish a Mexican empire under Austrian Prince Maximilian, the liberals, under their Mexican leader Benito Juárez, brought about substantial reforms creating educational and economic opportunities for all, especially for the native and mestizo peasants (State University, 2020).

The birth of an independent republic guaranteed educational and social benefits for all. The Mexican government produced a Constitution in 1917 based on anticlericalism, land reform, nationalism, workers' rights, and secular education. The hemisphere's first university, the Royal and Pontifical University, then named the National Autonomous University of Mexico, was a multicampus facility throughout the country (Johnston, 1956). The new constitution provided greater powers to the federal government over education, including its structure and curricula. Religious (or parochial) schools were separated from public schools.

In 1921, the Secretariat of Public Education was created. At this time, a nationalistic theme was incorporated into all public schools in Mexico. This theme was a major feature of the revolution, one designed to obviate the foreign influence dictated by the Catholic schools (Priestley, 1920).

Marked changes occurred in Mexico following the revolution and World War I. These changes liberated the mestizos and Indians from their rural haciendas and pueblos, opening greater opportunities for their migration and integration into larger communities. Rural schools grew rapidly within these communities, thus providing greater educational opportunities for all Mexicans regardless of ethnicity or social class (State University, 2020).

Post–World War II industrialization saw two avenues of growth in Mexican education. One was in the direction of adequate training for the new industrial workers, and the other focused on higher education. A major project of the institutionalized revolution era (1946–1958) was the construction of the new University City built to house the National Autonomous University of Mexico (UNAM). Completed in 1952, the new campus of the UNAM sits on three square miles and was, at the time, one of the most modern group of structures in the world. As a result, a new intellectual movement emerged, moving toward objective scholarship and learning (Miller, 1989).

The educational efforts of the revolution of 1910 reduced illiteracy in Mexico from 77% in 1910 to less than 38% in 1960. Due to the rapidly growing Mexican population, this figure represented more than 13 million people (State University, 2020). In its attack on illiteracy, the Mexican government established a network of rural schools composed of prefabricated buildings. The government provided these buildings and the communities provided the land and labor, thereby increasing the cohesiveness of the local community and education, a process that continues to the present (State University, 2020). At this time, the Mexican government established the ongoing policy of a national, uniform curriculum. Compulsory textbooks provided in public schools, selected by the federal government, are free to all students.

Today, education in Mexico consists of three levels: primary, secondary, and higher education. Formal basic, compulsory education encompasses preschool, elementary, and secondary (K–12). Federal, state, and local schools provide 93% of basic education in the country, while private schools make up the remaining 7% (Monroy, 2020).

The Legal Foundation for Education and Religion

The Federal Government

Mexico is a federal republic formed by 31 states. Governmental powers are divided constitutionally between the executive, legislative, and judicial branches. The Constitution of 1917 guarantees personal freedoms and civil liberties while also establishing economic and political principles for the country.

The legislative branch is divided into an upper house (the Senate) and a lower house (the Chamber of Deputies). Senators serve six-year terms and deputies three-year terms; members of the legislature cannot be reelected for the immediately succeeding term. Three-fifths of the deputies are elected directly by popular vote, while the remainder are selected in proportion to the votes received by political parties in each of five large electoral regions. The president is popularly elected and limited to one six-year term, and is empowered to select a cabinet, attorney general, diplomats, high-ranking military officers, and Supreme Court justices who serve life terms.

Local Government

The Constitution delegates various powers to the 31 states. The state constitutions follow the model of the Federal Constitution in providing for three independent branches of government, executive, legislative, and judicial. Most states have a unicameral legislature called the Chamber of Deputies whose members serve three-year terms. Governors are popularly elected to six-year terms and may not be reelected. Because of Mexico's tradition of a highly centralized government, state and local budgets are largely dependent on federally allocated funds. Moreover, although such centralized control is no longer generally accepted, Mexico's main political parties still maintain locally dominant power bases in various states and cities.

At its most basic level, local government is administered by more than 2,000 units called *municipios* ("municipalities"), which may be entirely urban or consist of a town or central village and its surrounding communities. Members of *municipio* governments are typically elected for three-year terms.

Legal Foundations of Education in Mexico

Article 3 in Title I of Mexico's Constitution provides the framework for the configuration and philosophy of education in the country:

> All people have the right of education. The State – Federation, States, and Municipalities – will provide preschool, elementary, middle and high school education. Preschool, elementary and middle educations are considered as basic education; these and the high school education will be mandatory.
>
> Education provided by the State shall develop harmoniously all human abilities and will stimulate in pupils the love for the country, respect for human rights and the principles of international solidarity, independence and justice.

Article Three also establishes the duty of the states to ensure the quality of compulsory education:

> The State will guarantee the quality in mandatory education, in a way that educational materials and methods, school organization, educational infrastructure and the suitability of teachers and principals ensure the highest learning achievement of students.

Section I of Article Three of the Mexican Constitution establishes the separation of public education from any religious doctrine:

> According to the Article 24 regarding the freedom of religion, the education provided by the State shall be laical; therefore, state education shall be maintained entirely apart from any religious doctrine.

Section II of Article Three stresses the need for education to be science-based while also establishing education as the national guardian against ignorance, fanaticism, and prejudices:

> The guiding principles for state education shall be based on scientific progress and shall fight against ignorance and its effects, servitude, fanaticism and prejudices.
>
> Moreover, Section II of Article Three also establishes that education shall: Contribute to a better human coexistence, in order to strengthen the appreciation and respect for cultural diversity, human dignity, the integrity of the family, the convictions over society's general interest, the fraternity and equality of rights ideals, avoiding privileges based on race, religion, group, sex or individual.

Section III mandates the establishment of a national curriculum by the federal executive taking into consideration the views and opinions of the states as well as civil society, namely, parents and teachers:

I To fully comply with the provisions established in the second paragraph and under section II, the Federal Executive shall establish the syllabus for preschool, elementary and secondary education, as well as for teacher training colleges, to be applied throughout the country. To that end, the Federal Executive shall take into account the opinion of the States' and the Federal District's governments, as well as the opinions of civil society groups involved in education, teachers and parents, in accordance with the law.

Section VI addresses private versus public education: private persons may engage in education of all kinds and grades. However, as to elementary, secondary, and normal education, they must previously obtain, in every case, the express authorization of the state. This section further obligates all private educational institutions to conform to the provisions of Sections I and II and must be in harmony with official plans and programs:

VI Private entities may provide all kinds of education. In accordance with the law, the State shall have powers to grant and cancel official accreditation to studies done at private institutions. In the case of pre-school, elementary and secondary education, as well as teacher training college, private schools must:

a. Provide education in accordance with the same purposes and criteria established in paragraph second and section II, as well as to comply with the syllabus mentioned in section III; and

b. Obtain a previous and explicit authorization from the authorities, under the terms provided by the Law.

Article Three of the Constitution concludes, despite the national scope of its centralized education system, by establishing the authority and responsibility of the states and municipalities to establish appropriate funding and assurances of quality of education at the local level:

> The Congress of the Union, with a view to unifying and coordinating education throughout the Republic, shall issue the necessary laws for dividing the social function of education among the Federation, the States, and the Municipalities; for fixing the appropriate financial allocations for this public service; and for establishing the penalties applicable to officials who do not comply with or enforce the pertinent provisions.

According to the law in Mexico, children attend primary schools for six years before attending lower secondary schools. Students then have three options for their three years in upper secondary schools: they can receive a general certificate (*bachillerato general*), a certificate in technical studies (*bachillerato técnico*), or a certificate as a professional technician (*técnico profesional*; UNESCO TEVET Country Profile, Mexico, 2018, 5).

The Protection for Freedom of Religion or Belief in Education

As stated above, Mexico's public education operates under the principle of separation of church and state. Given this approach to public education in Mexico, this section addresses the government's position on freedom of religion. This principle attempts to establish the basis for the access to religious education in Mexico by means of private schools underwritten by religious associations.

Mexico's Constitution provides all persons with the right to exercise the religion of their choosing to or to not have a religion. This freedom includes the right to participate in ceremonics and acts of worship so long as they do not constitute offenses otherwise prohibited by law. Philosophical freedoms of conscience and religion have equal treatment by the state. Further, Congress may not dictate laws establishing or prohibiting any religion (Vargas, 1998).

According to the Mexican Law of Religious Associations and Public Worship, which applies to educational institutions, religious acts of collective worship should be conducted in places especially designated for these purposes. Individuals and/or groups wishing to conduct religious activities outside of places of worship must obtain permits to do so. In order to establish religious associations, each applicant must certify that the religious group observes, practices, propagates, or instructs on a body of religious beliefs; has conducted religious activities in the country for at least five years; has established permanent addresses in the country; and can prove that it has sufficient assets to achieve its purposes. Registered associations may freely organize their administrative structures and adopt rules concerning their governance and operations, including the training and selection of their clergy (Vargas, 1998; Goddard, 2012).

Religious associations may participate in public worship and conduct acts for the realization of their purpose lawfully and without profit. They may disseminate their doctrine in accordance with current regulations and participate in the creation and operation of private welfare, health, and educational institutions, provided these institutions are not for profit. In order to operate, religious groups are not required to register with the government. Registration is only required with the Directorate of Religious Associations (DGAR) to negotiate contracts, purchases, or rentals of land; to apply for official building permits; receive tax exemptions; or conduct religious meetings outside their places of worship.

Religious associations may not conduct political rallies of any kind. The federal government coordinates religious affairs through the Secretariat of the Interior (SEGOB). Within SEGOB, DGAR promotes religious tolerance, conducts conflict mediation, and investigates cases of religious intolerance. If a party presents an argument based on allegations of religious intolerance, DGAR may mediate a solution. If mediation fails, the parties may submit the issue to DGAR for binding arbitration or seek judicial redress. Each state in the country has offices with responsibility for religious affairs. The National Council to Prevent Discrimination (CONAPRED) is the federal agency responsible for ensuring nondiscrimination and equal opportunity. CONAPRED seeks to also prevent discrimination among religious groups.

The fact that the Constitution requires public education to be secular and independent of religious doctrine notwithstanding, religious groups may operate private schools, teach religion, and conduct religious ceremonies at their schools. Private schools affiliated with a particular religious group must be open to all students irrespective of their religious beliefs. Students in private schools are free not to participate in religious courses and activities if they are not associated with the school's religious group.

Despite the legal provision for the imparting of religious education through private schools endorsed by properly registered religious associations, a series of conflicts have arisen concerning the inclusion of topics deemed controversial in the national curriculum taught in schools throughout the country. These recent additions to the national curriculum have clashed with the views of conservative and religious groups. Among these additions to the national curriculum are the definition of what constitutes a family, the nonbinary definition of gender, and same-sex marriage. Private schools, as part of the national education system, must comply with the mandate to teach the national curriculum in its entirety, regardless of their affiliation with religious associations whose philosophies are in conflict with the teaching of these topics in their schools.

Judicial Analysis of the Freedom of Religion or Belief in Education

The DGAR works with state and local officials to mediate conflicts involving religious intolerance. While although the majority of these disputes occurred outside of context of public education, most of them concern entire families, thus affecting the freedom of school-aged children to attend schools and, therefore, to continue to exercise their constitutional right to education.

According to the US Department of State's International Religious Report (2018), between 2011 and 2018 CONAPRED reported 72 complaints of alleged acts of religious discrimination. Most of these cases involved individuals or groups from religious minorities – mostly entire families – who reported that members of the majority religious community in their vicinities deprived them of their access to basic services like water and electricity.

Municipal and state officials commonly mediate disputes between religious groups. However, some groups reported that officials rarely pursued legal punishments against offending religious leaders, preferring instead to reach informally mediated solutions. As reported in the Mexico profile published by Christian Solidarity Worldwide (CSW; 2018), informal mediated solutions regarding religious discrimination rarely led to changes in the status quo. Examples of these violations of religious freedom are as follows.

Protestants in the community of Cuamontax, in the State of Hidalgo, signed a conflict resolution agreement in mandating their participation in, and financial contribution to, Catholic festivals. The groups continue to report that there were insufficient resources devoted to federal and state agencies that work on religious freedom. Similarly, based on press reports, local authorities expelled an Indigenous family of ten from their village of Tajlovijho in the State of Chiapas after its members converted to evangelical Protestantism.

Representatives from federal, state, and municipal governments worked with members of an Indigenous community in Altamirano, also in the State of Chiapas, to resolve a conflict that began between community members and evangelical Protestant families who were expelled from the village for practicing a religion other than Catholicism. Under terms of a signed agreement, members of the displaced families returned but lived isolated from the main community.

CSW also included a follow-up reporting on a case that began in 2012 in the community of Yashtinin, San Cristobal de las Casas, Chiapas State. In 2012, village authorities detained 16 individuals and then expelled them from the community for converting from Catholicism to evangelical Protestantism. By 2015, 28 families had been forced to leave Yashtinin due to their religious beliefs. During the year, CSW representatives met with some of the displaced persons, learning that although authorities were notified of the situation and promised recourse, the individuals still were not allowed to return.

According to DGAR, Mexico's federal government continues to promote dialogue between religious actors with the stated goal of ensuring the exercise of religious freedom and resolving conflicts involving religious intolerance. In 2019, SEGOB launched the National Strategy for the Promotion of Respect and Tolerance of Religious Diversity. Government officials reported that the constitutionally mandated separation of church and state will not be impacted by this new strategy. The strategy is a combined effort by different elements of the government to work together and promote religious freedom. Actions included roundtables, workshops, and combined efforts to develop and implement trainings for state-level officials as well as courses for elementary school students with reference to religious freedom (SEGOB, 2019).

Also in 2019, the Commission for Human Rights in Mexico City (CDHCM) conducted the First Gathering for Cultural Diversity. Present at the event were representatives from CONAPRED, the federal Council to Prevent and Eliminate Discrimination in Mexico City, and the Secretariat of Public Education. During the event, the speakers acknowledged that religious minorities in the country faced prejudice at institutional levels. The participating institutions reiterated their commitment to eradicate discrimination and prejudices in the country. Religion was identified as one of the main causes of discrimination in Mexico, particularly in public settings and schools (CDHCM, 2019).

Emerging Issues

In matters or freedom of religion in schooling, the challenges faced by the Mexican public education system are complex. Despite the official separation of church and state in public education, conflicting understandings on ethics, morals, and values are constantly at odds, especially among groups promoting opposing ideas with regard to controversial issues such as same-sex marriage, gender identity, and abortion rights and their possible inclusion in the national curriculum.

The fact that the educational system in Mexico is centralized, making it uniform throughout the country, makes these debates even more heated. They are so heated because any change in curriculum, as minute as it might be, has an enormous potential to impact the collective understanding of right and wrong, truth, and the cultural identity of an entire generation of children in the country.

In addition to debates about the content of the national curriculum, a piece of legislation being currently debated concerns the rights of parents of children in public schools to decide whether their children can opt out of courses with contents contrary to their ethical, moral, or religious beliefs. The National Coalition of Parents (UNPF) and the National Front for the Family (FNF) have both vehemently opposed the inclusion of a gender ideology that, from their perspective, promotes the liberation of sexuality in minors without legal consequences for anyone. UNPF and FNF further expressed their unmistakable disapproval of these issues being presented in books and physical spaces funded by taxpayers (Siete24, 2020)

Another issue regarding religious education in Mexico concerns the somewhat recent and increasingly popular idea of homeschooling. Parents whose ideologies differ from those of the public education system, or who simply have confidence in their own abilities to provide their children with holistic educations with greater emphases on academics, athletics, the arts, or their religious values, have discarded Mexico's public and private educational systems by opting for the practice of educating their children at home.

Homeschooling is not closely monitored or regulated in Mexico, however. In fact, homeschooling is not mentioned in the General Law on Education or the recommendations for the validation of alternative models of basic education in the country. Both recognize that pursuant to Article 31 of the Constitution, homeschooling is not legal in Mexico. However, Article 26 of the Universal Declaration of Human Rights (UDHR; 1948) establishes that parents have priority when choosing the kind of education that shall be given to their children. Mexico, as a supporter of the UDHR (1948), tolerates the idea of parents educating their children at home.

In order to validate the homeschooling of their children with the Secretariat of Public Education, the body responsible for setting national curricular standards in all schools, public and nonpublic (Monroy and Trines, 2019), parents in Mexico have two distinct alternatives. Families can either take advantage of the different adult distance education programs offered by the Secretariat, have their children take their proficiency exams and validate their studies, or they can transfer credits from a foreign educational system that is accredited in a country where homeschooling is lawful (HSLDA, 2020).

Conclusion

The foundation on which Mexico was established as a nation was imprinted by the clashing of cultures, classes, and religions and was characterized by a sense of "them" and "us." Today, Mexico is not all that different. The ongoing struggle for identity permeates virtually all layers of Mexican society and culture. Education is the stage where these struggles materialize and are unmistakably clear.

Religion, in particular, is one of the bases on which Mexico's identity was founded. Some say that "to be a Mexican is to be a Catholic." Millions of non-Catholics in Mexico have lived under the shadow of the religion of the majority, the religion that provides the country with a sense of identity and unity. Religious minorities, which have been an integral part of Mexico's history, culture, and even its economy, have always had to adjust to the social norms established by the Catholic majority. Nevertheless, the separation of church and state established by the Mexican Constitution provides a more level field where all Mexicans can express their religions or nonreligious preferences freely.

The separation of church and state in Mexico, especially in the public education system, has allowed for a uniform structure, leaving all matters about religion to the individual outside of public school buildings. Mexico permits religious associations to be recognized, respected, and allowed to conduct acts of worship freely, as long as they do not interfere with the existing laws established in, and human rights protected by, its Constitution.

Private education is the provision by the Mexican legal system for religious associations to provide their adherents with access to education aligned with their values. This is, in theory, the solution to the problem of families providing their children with an education aligned with their religious views and values.

The challenge presents itself when Mexico's centralized educational system imposes a national curriculum to which all schools in the country must adhere. Religious schools have found ways around this issue by simply displaying the books provided by the Secretariat of Public Education on shelves where they are visible to everyone, authorities included, but using the curricula and materials of their preference, provided that they cover the basic academic requirements established by the national curriculum.

Families unable to afford the costs of private education have no other option but to send their children to public schools. The challenge faced by these families presents itself when the national curriculum includes viewpoints opposed to theirs. Some of these perspectives are signified by the inclusion of sex education (Chandra-Mouli et al., 2018; Huska, 2016), the idea of same-sex marriage, and the nonbinary understanding of gender in the national curriculum. Families, through the UNPF and the FNF, have challenged the authority of the public educational system to teach issues related to gender and sexuality to their children in public schools. The Secretariat of Public Education responded by stating that children should not be deprived of their right to a holistic approach to education, including sex education, through the public schools.

Parents unwilling or unable to send their children to private, religious schools have recently embarked on the quest for independent education through various homeschool models. These models allow parents to educate their children in manners in which their ethics, morals, and religious views are not compromised by the education their children receive.

The distinct public, private, and homeschool education systems present in Mexico today are a clear representation of the challenges faced by the nation regarding its cultural, social, economic, and religious identity. These challenges have been present from the moment the original inhabitants of the land faced the arrival of European conquistadores in the 1500s. Mexico's struggle to define its identity continues to this day. Education is clearly only one of the main stages where Mexico, as a nation, continues the struggle for the elusive idea of national identity and unity.

References

Catholic Encyclopedia. (1913). *An International Work of Reference on the Constitution, Doctrine, Discipline, and History of the Catholic Church.* New York: Encyclopedia Press.

Chandra-Mouli, V., L. Gómez Garbero, M. Plesons, I. Lang, and E. Corona Vargas. (2018). Evolution and Resistance to Sexuality Education in Mexico. *Global Health, Science and Practice,* 6(1), 137–149. Retrieved December 4, from www.ncbi.nlm.nih.gov/pmc/articles/PMC5878067/

Christian Solidarity Worldwide. (2018). *Mexico 2018 International Religious Freedom Report.* Retrieved July 6, 2020, from www.state.gov/wp-content/uploads/2019/05/MEXICO-2018-INTERNATIONAL-RELIGIOUS-FREEDOM-REPORT.pdf

Commission for Human Rights. (2019). *Instituciones Firman Compromiso a Favor de la Diversidad Cultural del País.* Retrieved June 17, 2020, from https://cdhcm.org.mx/2019/10/instituciones-firman-compromiso-a-favor-de-la-diversidad-cultural-del-pais/

Goddard, J. A. (2012). Meaning and Scope of the Restrictions Imposed by the Mexican Constitution on Ministers of Worship. *Brigham Young University Law Review,* 2, 705–728.

Greenleaf, R. E. (2018). *Zumarraga and the Mexican Inquisition, 1536–1543.* London: Papamoa Press.

HSLDA. (2020). *Legal Status and Resources on Homeschooling in Mexico.* Retrieved July 2, 2020, from https://hslda.org/post/mexico

Huck, J. D. (2017). *Modern Mexico.* Santa Barbara, CA: ABC-CLIO.

Huska, M. (2016). *Sex Education Battleground in Mexico.* Retrieved December 4, 2020, from https://notchesblog.com/2016/10/27/battleground-sex-education-a-struggle-for-moral-jurisdiction-in-mexico/

Johnston, M. C. (1956). *Education in Mexico.* Washington, DC: US Department of Health, Education, and Welfare, Office of Education.

MacLachlan, C. M. (2015). *Imperialism and the Origins of Mexican Culture.* Cambridge, MA: Harvard University Press.

Manzanárez, M. and L. French. (2004). *NAFTA & Neocolonialism: Comparative Criminal, Human & Social Justice.* Lanham, MD: University Press of America.

Marlow-Ferguson, R. (2002). *World Education Encyclopedia: A Survey of Educational Systems Worldwide.* Detroit, MI: Gale Group, Thomson Learning.

Melvin, K. (2012). *Building Colonial Cities of God: Mendicant Orders and Urban Culture in New Spain.* Redwood City, CA: Stanford University Press.

Middleton, J. (2015). *World Monarchies and Dynasties.* London: Taylor & Francis.

Miller, R. R. (1989). *Mexico: A History.* Norman: University of Oklahoma Press.

Monroy, C. (2020). *Education in Mexico.* Retrieved July 6, 2020, from https://wenr.wes.org/2019/05/education-in-mexico-2

Monroy, C. and S. Trines. (2019). *Education in Mexico.* Retrieved December 6, 2020, from https://wenr.wes.org/2019/05/education-in-mexico-2

Polzer, C. W. (1976). *Rules and Precepts of the Jesuit Missions of Northwestern New Spain.* Tucson, AZ: University of Arizona Press.

Priestley, H. I. (1920). *Modern Mexican History.* New York: Institute of International Education.

SEGOB. (2019). *Estrategia Nacional Para la Promoción del Respeto y la Tolerancia a la Diversidad Religiosa.* Retrieved, July 2, 2020, from www.gob.mx/segob/prensa/secretaria-de-gobernacion-presenta-estrategia-nacional-para-la-promocion-del-respeto-y-la-tolerancia-a-la-diversidad-religiosa-218341

Sheridan, John D. (1941). Education in the New Spain. *The Irish Monthly*, 69(811), 5–11. JSTOR. Retrieved June 3, 2020, from www.jstor.org/stable/20514825.

Siete24. (2020). *El gobierno debe educar sexualidad de niños, no los padres de familia: SEGOB.* Retrieved July, 4, 2020, from https://siete24.mx/vida-y-familia/el-gobierno-debe-educar-sexualidad-de-ninos-no-los-padres-de-familia-segob/

Spielvogel, J. (2007). *Western Civilization: A Brief History, Volume II: Since 1500.* Boston, MA: Cengage Learning.

State University. (2020). *Mexico, History and Background.* Retrieved July 4, 2020, from https://education.stateuniversity.com/pages/979/Mexico-HISTORY-BACKGROUND.html

Thomas, H. (2013). *Conquest: Cortes, Montezuma, and the Fall of Old Mexico.* New York: Simon & Schuster.

Tucker, A. O. and J. Janick. (2018). *Unraveling the Voynich Codex.* Cham, Switzerland: Springer International.

Turley, S. E. (2016). *Franciscan Spirituality and Mission in New Spain, 1524–1599: Conflict Beneath the Sycamore Tree (Luke 19:1–10).* London: Taylor & Francis.

UNESCO TEVET Country Profile, Mexico. (2018, November). Retrieved July 23, 2020, from https://unevoc.unesco.org/wtdb/worldtvetdatabase_mex_en.pdf

UN Universal Declaration on Human Rights. (1948). Retrieved July 2, 2020, from www.un.org/en/universal-declaration-human-rights/index.html

US Department of State. (2018). *Mexico 2018 International Religious Freedom Report.* Retrieved July 6, 2020, from www.state.gov/wp-content/uploads/2019/05/MEXICO-2018-INTERNATIONAL-RELIGIOUS-FREEDOM-REPORT.pdf

Vargas, J. A. (1998). Freedom or Religion and Public Worship in Mexico: A Legal Commentary on 1992 Federal Act on Religious Matters. *Brigham Young University Law Review*, 2, 420–481.

Weaver, J. (2014). *The Red Atlantic: American Indigenes and the Making of the Modern World, 1000–1927.* Chapel Hill, NC: University of North Carolina Press.

10 Law, Education, and the Place of Religion in Dutch Public Schools

Pieter W. Huisman and Stefan Philipsen

Introduction

Religion played an important role in the establishment of the Dutch system for primary and secondary education, which can be divided into two groups. First, there are private-denominational schools. Although these schools are not considered "public" under Dutch constitutional law, they are fully funded by the government as long as they comply with quality standards laid down by law. These schools not only make up the majority of the schools in the Netherlands, at over 60%,[1] but they almost always rely on a religious ethos as the foundation of their teachings. The intensity with which the ethos of schools plays a role in those teachings differs.

In practice, most private-denominational schools attach value to their religious ethos[2] even though it often does not play an explicit role in the daily teaching. In addition, there are some orthodox Christian, Jewish, and Islamic schools in which school communities unite around the religious ethos and in which the religious ethos colors every aspect of the schools' environments.

Private-denominational schools must offer the same national curriculum as public schools but can add religious teaching to the slate and have (to certain degree) more freedom in applying the standards of the national curriculum inside their classes. The quality criteria of the national educational inspectorate apply to all state-funded schools, regardless of whether they are public or religious. Private-denominational schools have, to a great extent, freedom to express their religious ethos in their teachings.

Second, there are public schools. These are truly public in the sense that they are maintained by the government and students have a right to access these schools. Contrary to private-denominational schools, public schools are not allowed to refuse students based on religious grounds. Article 23 of the Dutch Constitution[3] obliges the government to guarantee that public education is religiously neutral.[4] This chapter focuses mainly on these public schools. However, because the place of religion in public education and in the public schools can only be properly understood by contrasting it with private-denominational education, this chapter occasionally elaborates on the place of religion in private-denominational schools.

In recent decades, two contrasting developments have occurred with regard to the role of religion in society. These developments also affected the role religion plays in primary and secondary (public) education. First, due to migration and individualization, Dutch society has become many times more diverse with regard to religion. Yet, at the same time, Dutch society has become more secularized. In fact, studies show that over 50% of the Dutch population identify as having no religion.[5] Moreover, discussions about civics education have occurred in Dutch society for some time. The core of this discussion is formed by the idea that education should be more concerned with the transfer of values that are shared by all "Dutch" citizens. This discussion sometimes seems to be fueled by dissatisfaction with certain doctrines of religious minorities.

Against the preceding background, the next section of this chapter provides a general outline of the legal foundation for education and religion in public schools. The section focuses on the core legal provision, namely Article 23 of the Dutch Constitution. The chapter then expands on the way freedom of religion is protected in Dutch education law. The following section offers an outline of the most important case law on how freedom of religion is protected in Dutch education law. The chapter next provides a vista of emerging issues before concluding with a general observation.

The Legal Foundation for Education and Religion

The legal basis for the Dutch dual educational system, consisting of public and private-denominational schools, is rooted in Article 23 of the Constitution (hereinafter, Gw [abbr. for Dutch *Grondwet*]). The fourth section of this constitutional provision obliges officials in municipal governments to establish sufficient numbers of public schools. At the same time, the second section of Article 23 Gw grants all citizens who meet the quality requirements set by the government the right to establish schools and to teach in them according to their own understanding of "good education."

Article 23 Gw was born out of a long and heated political debate fueled by religious division. This debate is referred to as the "school struggle." The origin of this long-standing division in Dutch politics lay in the birth of the unified state of the Netherlands in 1795,[6] immediately after which the government took up the task of establishing a national system of education for the new country.

An important task of the new educational system in the unified state became the development of citizens through civics education. The notion of citizenship was thereby derived from the dominant Protestant religion and its morality. This led to a great deal of resistance from religious minorities, especially Catholics in the southern part of the country, who thought their religious freedom and natural right to educate their children was restricted. Further, Orthodox-Protestants in the north of the Netherlands also thought that their religious freedom was restricted; in their eyes, the religious views of the Protestant majority were too moderate, meaning that they wanted their own schools in which they could adhere to more dogmatic interpretations of the Bible.

For a century, the confessional parties, namely Orthodox-Protestants and Catholics, fought with the liberals over the role religion should play in education and to what extent government should facilitate religious education. The outcome was a "pacification," a national political agreement that created the dual education system in which religious minorities were granted the right to establish their own denominational schools, as stated above, fully funded by the government, and the municipal government would provide for religiously neutral public schools.

The dual educational system in the Netherlands aims to accommodate religious diversity. Religiously neutral public education provides a structure around which fully funded private-denominational schools can be established. Religious communities were thus given the freedom to design their own education as they see fit. From the end of the "battle for schools," they could allow their religious views to resonate in the teachings on their private-denominational schools. One of the arguments in favor of actively accommodating religious freedom was to try to ease religious tensions. It was a pragmatic solution designed to prevent greater conflict.

Insofar as the Constitution gave great freedom to private-denominational schools, the government was obliged to guarantee that public education respects every religious belief. Article 23, Section 3 Gw states that public schools should be neutral. However, the precise meaning of this requirement of neutrality, first incorporated in the Constitution in 1848, has been the subject of intense political debate during the "battle for schools." Soon after this requirement was incorporated in the Constitution, the question arose to what extent this requirement resulted in a positive obligation for the government to accommodate religious diversity actively, by for example establishing a public school for every religious minority.

With the recognition of the constitutional freedom of education and guaranteeing the right to full government funding of private-denominational schools, which was incorporated in Article 23, Section 5 Gw, it became clear that the requirement of neutrality should be interpreted primarily in a negative way. Put another way, it is an expression of the separation of church and state that makes clear that the government does not take sides in religious matters and cannot judge students or teachers based on their religion. Moreover, it means that admission to public schools must be without discrimination on the basis of religion or non-religious belief.

The constitutional guarantee of neutral public education as an expression of the separation of church and state is absolute. At the same time, the separation of church and state exists in many forms. The Dutch model of separation is much less strict than the church and state model adhered to by other countries such as the United States[7] or European countries such as France. In fact, the French system insists on a very strict separation between church and state while advocating for the absence of religion in public spaces.[8] The Dutch church and state model is much less strict and is often referred to as a model of "pluralistic cooperation."[9] This means that the government recognizes the value of religion for its citizens while its officials facilitate and support the possibility of persons expressing their existing religious diversity in public space. The full funding of private-denominational schools is an applied example of the expression of this church and state model.

The Dutch conception of the separation of church and state also influences the way in which public schools deal with religion. As mentioned earlier, this neutrality of public education, explained as the negative obligation to not select students and teachers on the basis of their religion, is absolute. However, this situation does not mean there is no place for religion in public schools. A typical example of this is that it is possible for students to receive religious or doctrinal education even in public schools.

Shortly after the dual educational system was established and before private-denominational schools were granted the right to full government funding in the Netherlands, some parents felt compelled to send their child to private-denomination schools even though public schools by then very often were of better quality. However, these parents considered a religious school education indispensable for their children. Because public schools were constitutionally obliged to be neutral, these parents had insufficient confidence that the religious education of their children would receive in the public schools, or worse, thought that neutral public education would ignore the religious educations of their young.

The Dutch legislature had recognized freedom of education. Even so, the legislature wanted as many children as possible to attend public schools. After all, those children would then remain directly within the sphere of influence of the government. For this reason, a pragmatic legal arrangement was proposed that would allow public schools to provide religious education during school hours. This religious or doctrinal education is funded by the national government.[10]

In order not to violate the constitutional requirement of neutrality, religious (doctrinal) education could be provided in public schools, but only to children of parents who so desired, for a limited number of hours, and the boards of these public schools could not formally organize or be responsible for the religious education of these children. School board officials had to outsource the teaching and planning of religious education to religious organizations such as churches, thereby treating the various denominations on an equal basis. More recently, this also includes nonreligious humanist education. The school boards did not appoint the teachers representing specific denominations. Further, these teachers cannot be members of regular staffs, and the school boards have no power to interfere with the religious doctrines these teachers teach. The only obligation for these school boards is that they must ensure that religious education is provided by teachers who meet the general competency requirements set by law, such as having didactical and pedagogical skills. This pragmatic scheme exists to this day.[11]

The idea of pluralistic corporation can also be recognized in the content of the curriculum of public schools. The constitutional requirement of neutrality of public education first requires passive neutrality.[12] Put another way, public schools must provide safe havens for all students and teachers of every religion. This means that the government must exercise restraint on subjects that directly or indirectly touch upon religion. After the Second World War, this fairly strict interpretation of the neutrality requirement gradually changed. Under the influence of a growing number of immigrants and an ever-increasing religious pluralism, the legislature realized that education cannot suffice without facilitating religious pluralism.

Two decades ago, the idea grew that educators in public education would actively have to teach children to deal with religious diversity while additionally instructing them on developing tools to live peacefully together in a pluriform society. The legislature therefore included this obligation in the educational legislation.[13] Public schools should not simply be "passively" neutral towards religion. Rather, educators in public schools must be actively pluralistic in the discovery of religions; this means to disperse knowledge about mainstream religions present in society. Per Article 23, Section 5 of the Dutch Constitution, this obligation also applies to private-denominational schools as a funding requirement.

The Protection for Freedom of Religion or Belief in Education

Freedom of religion in education is protected at different levels. First, the European Convention on Human Rights (hereinafter, ECHR)[14] should be mentioned. The ECHR is an international treaty and the most important human rights document on the European continent. The importance of the ECHR is underlined by the fact that an independent and specialized court oversees its application of the ECHR. Moreover, pursuant to Article 94 Gw, the ECHR has a direct effect in the Dutch legal order. Article 94 Gw declares that national law, including the Dutch Constitution, conflicting with treaties such as the ECHR, are considered void. The provisions of ECHR can, therefore, be characterized as the highest source of law in the constitutional hierarchy.

The right to education and the freedom of religion in education are mainly protected by Article 2 of the First Protocol to the ECHR (hereinafter, Protocol).[15] This article stipulates in the first sentence that everybody has the right to education. The second sentence adds that the state is obliged to respect the religious and philosophical freedom of parents. This means that states are obliged to ensure that the information transmitted in education that directly or indirectly touches on the religious or philosophical beliefs of parents and that the ECHR acknowledges is the whole curriculum is taught in an "objective, critical and pluralistic" way.[16]

The lower limit of this positive obligation is the negative duty of teachers not to indoctrinate students in education. More specifically, this means that if parts of the curriculum are not "objective, critical and pluralistic," parents have the right to have their children exempted from this part of a school's instructional program.[17] At the same time, the ECHR recognizes that the risk of indoctrination occurs in particular, but not exclusively, in religious education. The ECHR has repeatedly and explicitly ruled that member states must suppress any acts of proselytizing and must remain religiously neutral in that sense.[18]

Article 23 of the Dutch Constitution offers a second level of protection for the freedom of religion in education. As indicated above, Article 23, Section 3, Gw mandates that officials in public education shall pay due respect to each person's religion or belief.[19] Section 1 of Article 46, Section 1, of the Dutch Primary Education Act, clarifies and underlines this obligation by providing that "Public education contributes to the development of the pupils with attention for the religious, philosophical and social values which are present in the Dutch society and in recognition of the importance of the diversity of those values."[20] As such, public schools in the Netherlands are open to all children, and selection on the basis of their religion or belief is prohibited.

The requirement of Article 23, Section 3 of the Primary Education Act applies not only in selecting students and teachers but also in the way the curriculum is taught. Teachers in public schools cannot even try to proselytize students and must refrain from school prayer. As evidence of the importance of is the neutrality of Dutch public schools. Article 44, Section 2 of the Secondary Education Act affords the minister of education the power to suspend teachers who violate the principle of neutrality.

Besides the general requirement of neutrality, the legislation regarding primary and secondary education, which can be considered the third level of protection of religious freedom, contains no specific rules on the expression of religion through religious symbols. This includes religious clothing. Still, though, public school boards may formulate dress codes but must be aware that some clothing regulations may harm or disadvantage adherents of specific religions.

Dress codes resulting in the prohibition of, for example, headscarves and other clothing worn for religious reasons such as a turban, as is discussed later, or a *kirpan* (a religious dagger) may be at odds with the Equal Treatment Act,[21] because such a prohibition results in discrimination on the grounds of religion. This can also be true if the dress code does not aim directly at restricting religious clothing but only results in such a restriction in an indirect way, because the Equal Treatment Act prohibits both direct and indirect discrimination.

At this point, it is important to keep in mind that the Equal Treatment Act is an elaboration of Article 1 of the Dutch Constitution's provision specifying that all persons in the Netherlands should be treated equally in equal circumstances. Article 1 and the Equal Treatment Act prohibit distinctions due to religion, belief, political opinion, race, sex, or any other grounds. In addition, the Equal Treatment Act differentiates between direct discrimination related to distinctions directly based on one of the grounds of discrimination covered by the law.

The Equal Treatment Act also covers indirect discrimination that occurs when certain requirements, although neutral on their face, have a disparate impact on a group of people in relation to one of the prohibited bases for discrimination. The boards of public schools are never allowed to discriminate directly on the basis of religion. Direct discrimination is any act that restricts religious freedoms as its sole purpose. Indirect discrimination – acts indirectly disadvantaging freedom of religion – can be allowed as long as they are objectively justified.

A very specific and controversial part of the protection of freedom of religion on the third, or statutory, level is the protection offered by the Compulsory Education Act of 1969 (hereinafter, CEA).[22] The CEA obliges parents to enroll their children in schools and to make certain that they regularly attend their classes. However, the CEA does include an exception to this obligation for parents that have conscientious objections to the religious ethos of all of the schools within reasonable distances from their home; this exception includes religious objections against the nonreligious ethos of public schools.

Article 5, Clause b of the CEA offers objecting parents the possibility of opting out of their obligations under its provisions so they can engage in homeschooling their children. Even so, there is no formal obligation to homeschool children and the government does not oversee the manner in which parents educate their children once they have been granted exemptions. Even though possibilities to be exempted exist, the general idea behind the CEA is clear: in principle, every child should go to school. For this reason, courts have been very reluctant in granting exemption on the basis of conscience objections. This reluctance seems to have grown as the religious diversity in the Dutch society increases.

In order to apply for the exemption under Article 11a(1) of the CEA, parents must submit a letter to officials in the municipalities in which they reside before the first day of the month in which their children become eligible, specifically the age of six, for protection under the CEA. If parents do not comply with the requirements of the CEA, they can be criminally prosecuted.

In recent years, the Dutch Supreme Court, or *Hoge Raad*, the highest court in criminal cases, has followed a restrictive approach in the application of the exemption clause in the CEA. Parents can only be exempted if they have "serious objections" to sending their children to a school in the proximities of their homes and if these objections are founded in their religious or nonreligious beliefs. This means, for example, that parental objections to the pedagogical climates of schools cannot lead to exemptions from compulsory education. In addition, as illustrated in the next paragraph, the Supreme Courts scrutinize the claimed religious belief strictly.

At issue before the Supreme Court in 2020 was a parental claim alleging that the father followed a philosophy of life based on a "holistic point of view." The father characterized elements of his conviction as "open-mindedness with regard to the constantly new ways in which unity can manifest itself and accompany personal growth. Acceptance of any authority of religion, dogmatic or otherwise stands in the way of this, as is ideological neutrality."[23]

Rejecting the father's claim, the Supreme Court responded that not every subjective interpretation of personally held beliefs can count as a nonreligious belief protected by the exemption clause of the CEA or the freedom of religion.[24] According to the Court, objections should meet certain criteria; namely, that they are based on specific religious beliefs or philosophies, which means they attain a certain level of cogency, seriousness, cohesion, and importance. In addition, the court pointed out that serious objections remained relating to the ethos of a school in question. The Court thereby explained that an ethos is a fundamental orientation, derived from a specific religious belief or philosophy, that must be sufficiently concrete such that adequately serious objections are related to the education such a school can provide.

Rounding out its analysis, the Supreme Court was of the opinion that the objections the father put forward were insufficient to fall under the scope of the aforementioned criteria. In short, the court remarked that holism is too vague and subjective to be considered as a "specific" religion of philosophy and that his objections were not particularly concrete so as to entitle him to remove his daughter from the school.

The Supreme Court has also placed greater emphasis on the rights of the children in subsequent cases. The Court maintained that the right of parents in the religious upbringing of their children should be weighed against the rights of their children to attend school and interact with their peers.

In a case relating to the exemption under the CEA, the Court ruled that in the light of the freedom parents in the Netherlands have to choose one of the many private-denominational schools or establish a school themselves, where lessons are taught in a manner consistent with their religious or ideological views, and taking into account the freedom of parents to teach religion after school hours, a strict interpretation of the CEA that only allows exemptions for a very limited number of parents does not result in an infringement of the freedom of religion.[25]

Here it is also important to point to a limitation of religious freedom in schools that the Dutch legislature set on August 1, 2019, when it introduced a ban on clothing that conceals faces. Under this law, when dealing with public transport or government, health care, or educational buildings, individuals are no longer allowed to wear clothes, such as *burkas,* making their faces unidentifiable.[26] This partial ban on face coverings is intended to prevent them from being worn in places where it is necessary to recognize each other and see others' faces. More specifically, "face covering" refers to any item of clothing that prevents one's face from being identified including balaclavas, burkas, *niqab,* full-face motorcycle helmets, and masks. Often referred to as the burka or niqab ban, it is inapplicable to headscarves and/or hats.

The enactment of the partial ban on face covering was put in a new perspective when the Dutch government, in its fight against the coronavirus, obliged every citizen to wear masks in public indoor places.[27] This development makes it unlikely that the burka/niqab ban will be enforced in 2020 and 2021.

Judicial Analysis of the Freedom of Religion or Belief in Education

Most of the relevant cases on freedom of religion in public schools are not judicial in nature. Instead, they are decisions of the Netherlands Institute for Human Rights (NIHR),[28] the body charged with overseeing the compliance of schools with the Equal Treatment Act. Students, parents, and teachers can file complaints with the NIHR about actions and decisions of public school officials that might violate their rights under the Equal Treatment Act. Accordingly, this section discusses some of the most important decisions in this regard.

In a case before the NIHR, when two Islamic students in a public secondary school asked that they be allowed to use a classroom so they could pray during breaks, school board officials refused to grant this request. The students claimed that the deprivation of opportunities or space for prayer should be considered direct discrimination on the ground of religion. The students also argued that the neutral character of a public school did not offer a sufficient justification for this refusal to facilitate their religious freedom. Rejecting the claim, the NIHR reasoned that neither the text nor the parliamentary history of the Equal Treatment Act – or any other law for that matter – puts a positive obligation on the public school to provide rooms for prayer.[29] The NIHR added that because officials of the boards of public schools have the pedagogical and organizational freedom to operate the schools as they see fit, it is up to them whether to allow rooms to be set aside for prayer.

When it comes to rights of Muslims teachers in public schools to wear headscarves in classes, the NIHR decided that it is not, by definition, contrary to the ideologically neutral nature of public education as required by Article 23, Section 3 of the Dutch Constitution.[30] The NIHR acknowledged that it is true that the staff of public schools may be required to have an open attitude towards the different ideological and social values of their students and colleagues. Yet, the NIHR thought that even though Muslim teachers profess a particular religion, wearing a headscarf does not preclude them from being open-minded and able to teach in a manner consistent with the nature of schools as public educational institutions. Therefore, the NIHR concluded that preventing Muslim teachers from wearing headscarves in public schools constituted a prohibited form of direct discrimination.[31]

The situation is different, though, if teachers express their religious convictions actively and do not observe the restraint that the Constitution requires. For example, the NIHR upheld the dismissal of an activist Muslim intern who, contrary to the neutral character of public schools, did not leave enough room for students to form their own convictions on matters of faith. The NIHR accepted the school board's claim that because the behavior of the intern manifested an indirect form of discrimination, its action was objectively justified.[32]

To reiterate: the school boards of public schools have discretionary power to set specified rules for teachers, dealing, for instance, with the way they communicate with colleagues or should approach parents, even if this can be at odds with their religious convictions. One case dealt with a teacher who, since returning from a holiday in Morocco, refused on religious grounds to shake hands with her male colleagues. In this case, not only the NIHR but also the highest court for civil servants[33] was asked to determine where the fundamental right of the teacher ends and the autonomous authority of public school board officials begins.

Officials suspended and then fired the teacher because her conduct violated the school's codes of conduct. The NIHR observed that the dismissal involved indirect discrimination prohibited by the Equal Treatment Act because the teacher was willing to greet her male colleagues in a different way, such as by a friendly nod. The school board did not accept this judgment and persisted with suspending and dismissing the teacher. The question was whether the uniform greeting rule applicable at the school was compatible with the prohibition of discrimination and thereby requiring the balancing of interests. On the one hand, there is the neutrality of the school; on the other hand is the right of the teacher to have her religious freedom protected against unequal treatment.

The highest court for civil servants considered it important that

> the expression of faith for which protection is requested manifests itself in the open and affected others like pupils, parents and other third parties. The decision to not shake hands therefore directly affected the way in which the job was performed.[34]

In its order, the court emphasized the importance of the public school in preventing segregation and promoting a multicultural school community, finding that this outweighed the interest of the teacher. Although the obligation to shake hands was arguably a limitation of the teacher's freedom of religion, the court considered it appropriate and necessary.

In a more recent case, the Council of State, Administrative Jurisdiction Division, which has the highest authority in cases of admission or expulsion of students from public schools, was asked to resolve the refusal of public school officials for secondary education to allow a student to wear a *kirpan*, a religious dagger. The school board maintained that carrying weapons, or as stated in its code of conduct, "objects alike," was strictly prohibited. For religious reasons, the student, a member of the Sikh faith, contended that such a general prohibition of weapons would not apply to his mainly symbolic religious dagger. In addition, the student pointed out that the kirpan was smaller than a pen and hidden in a scabbard underneath his clothes. Even so, school board officials persisted in a zero-tolerance policy, suspending and later expelling the student.

In this case, the main issue was whether the board officials could ensure safety at school in accordance with their legal duty under Article 3b of the Secondary Education Act and whether this obligation could also result in a limitation of the student's religious rights. In its judgment, the Council of State weighed the individual right of the student to profess and promote a religion, in line with Article 9 ECHR and Article 6 Gw, against the general obligation of educational officials to ensure a safe school environment. The Council of State heavily relied on the jurisprudence of the ECHR, thereby assessing the measure on its legitimacy, necessity, and proportionality.

The Council of State made clear that the freedom of religion should be interpreted reasonably, meaning that the freedom to profess religion does not go so far as to allow religious actions to occur at any time and in any place one chooses. As such, the Council of State agreed that a total ban on weapons, including religious weapons, such as the kirpan, is allowed and outweighs the religious interests of the student.[35]

Considering the appropriate policy space of the school board, the Council interpreted the total ban as reasonable for considerations safety, effectiveness, and equal treatment between pupils.

Emerging Issues

As noted, private-denominational schools have the freedom to provide education grounded in their individual religious ethos. This freedom is part of an open and diverse society but also has limits set by governmental legislation and regulations. Recently, a debate emerged about a teaching method in Islamic primary schools regarding sexual diversity and interaction between boys and girls.

Encouraged by media coverage, the Inspectorate of Education was called on to investigate how educators in schools address topics in areas where their ethos may differ significantly from the prevailing views in society. To do this, approximately 80 schools – public and private but publicly funded, in primary and secondary education – were investigated.

The study revealed that in areas such as sexual diversity, the desired mode of interaction between boys and girls, and the respective roles of men and women, or the relationship between religious principles and prevailing views in society, schools take advantage of the freedom of education that they have at their disposal.[36] More specifically, the Inspectorate found that schools largely remain within the limits of the law. Inspectorate officials also learned that there was hardly any conflict with basic societal values in any of the schools they studied. The same was true for the instructional methods educators in the schools under investigation.

Although the Inspectorate's study demonstrated that freedom of education can exist, at the same time the government must be able to guarantee a minimum level of quality in all schools. This minimum level even touches on sensitive topics such as civics education. At the same time, the historical connection between religion and education is more and more considered as a troublesome by major parties in the Dutch Parliament. This also holds true for the church and state model of pluralistic corporation that has characterized Dutch public education for decades.

Residents in major Dutch cities more often call for a move towards a French model of strict separation of church and state. In this opinion, public schools should focus on what all Dutch have in common and teach the values we (should) share. Still, it must be remembered that public schools in such major Dutch cities as Amsterdam have a very mixed population in terms of different types of religions and racial and ethnic groups.

At this point, it is left to teachers to find a balance between the religious beliefs of students and the requirements of society. The confrontation between the views of pupils and the role of teachers to talk about sensitive subjects has led to a number of violent incidents,[37] following the killing of a French teacher over showing cartoons that had previously been published in the French magazine *Charlie Hebdo*.[38] These incidents will probably result in a call for a stronger focus on sensitive topics in private and public schools alike along with a greater emphasis on civics in education in all schools.

Conclusion

The Dutch educational system is arguably the most diverse educational system in the world. The Dutch system is based on the assumption that parents have the freedom to educate their children as they see fit. This holds in particular for parental choices with regard to the religious upbringing and education of their children. For this reason, the Constitution protects the freedom of education for private-denominational schools while also obliging the government to provide a system of public schools that accommodates religious pluralism in all kinds of ways.

At the same time, it must be acknowledged that the society in which the dual educational system was established is different from today's Dutch society. At that time, despite the religious diversity, society was still very homogeneous, as the various religions existing in 1848 differed slightly from each other and most citizens based their lives on very similar moral values. Such a situation is certainly not the case today. Instead of uniformity, today's society is characterized by a radical diversity in all areas of social life, in particular religion. Like many mature democracies, the Netherlands is learning how to respond to challenges engendered by immigration and how to cope with the political, social, and economic changes accompanying these shifts in society.

Ultimately, it will hold that the more diverse that society becomes, the more reason there is to counterbalance this diversity with a stronger focus on unity. Because education should at least partly serve that society, it will therefore always also have to guarantee a minimum basis of communality that every society requires. Diversity is very valuable but should not lead to the creation of *Paralellgesellschaften*, communities that neither interact with one another nor are able to understand each other.

In the near future, then, the pluralistic Dutch educational system will be dominated by the search for a balance between unity and diversity. Thus, officials in both public schools and private denominational schools each will have to take their part in finding this balance for the good of all of Dutch society.

Notes

1. Nigel Edwards, *Private Schools for Expats in the Netherlands, Wolters Kluwer Expat Briefing*, 2020. Retrieved from www.expatbriefing.com/country/netherlands/education/private-schools-for-expats-in-the-netherlands.html.
2. Onderwijsraad, *Meer ruimte voor nieuwe scholen* [Education Counsel, *More Space for New Schools*] (The Hague: Onderwijsraad, 2016).

3. The Constitution of the Kingdom of the Netherlands 2018 is available at www.government.nl/topics/constitution/documents/reports/2019/02/28/the-constitution-of-the-kingdom-of-the-netherlands. For an excellent commentary on the constitutional provision on education, see www.nederlandrechtsstaat.nl/grondwet/artikel.html?artikel=23##artikel23.
4. For additional background, see Freedom of Education, Government of the Netherland, n.d. Retrieved from www.government.nl/topics/freedom-of-education/public-authority-and-private-schools.
5. Ton Bernts and Jaontine Berghuis, *God in Nederland* [*God in the Netherlands*] (Utrecht: Ten Have, 2016); Hans Boutellier, *Het Seculiere Experiment* [*The Secular Experiment*] (the Hague: Boom Uitgevers, 2015).
6. For an detailed discussion and description of the Dutch political culture that resulted in this provision, see Arend Lijphart, *The Politics of Accommodation: Pluralism and Democracy in the Netherlands* (Berkeley: University of California Press, 1968).
7. See, e.g., the discussion in Chapter 18.
8. See extensively on this topic: Christopher Soper, Kevin den Dul and Stehpen Monsma, *The Challenge of Pluralism: Church and State in Six Democracies* (Lanham, MD: Rowman and Littlefield, 2017).
9. Ben Vermeulen, On Freedom, Equality and Citizenship, in Gaudreault Foblets and Dundes Renteln (eds.), *The Response of State Law to the Expression of Cultural Diversity* (Brussels: Peter Lang, 2010).
10. See Freedom of Education, Government of the Netherlands, n.d. Retrieved from www.government.nl/topics/freedom-of-education/public-authority-and-private-schools ("the state provides equal funding for both public-authority and private schools").
11. See Article 47 of the Secondary Education Act; available in Dutch. Retrieved from https://wetten.overheid.nl/BWBR0002399/2020-11-01. We point out that Section 2 of this Article still states: "The classrooms, heated and lit if necessary, are made available free of charge for training education." This provision stems from the time directly after it was made possible to receive religious education in public schools. At that time, school boards that were against religious education would turn off the heating in the winter as to prevent religious education to take place. Therefore, the law still explicitly states that the rooms in which religious education takes place should be heated.
12. Mentink and Vermeulen, Artikel 23 Grondwet [Article 23 Constitution], The Hague, 2011.
13. See Article 8 Primary Education Act. Retrieved from https://wetten.overheid.nl/BWBR0003420/2020-07-01.
14. The ECHR is available at www.echr.coe.int/Documents/Convention_ENG.pdf.
15. The First Protocol to the ECHR is available at www.coe.int/en/web/echr-toolkit/protocole-1.
16. ECtHR, December 7, 1976, nr. 5095;71, *Kjeldsen, Busk Madsen and Pedersen.*
17. ECtRM, June 29, 2007, nr. 15472;02, *Folgero et al. v. Norway.*
18. ECtHR, October 9, 2007, nr. 1448;01, *Hasan and Eylem Zengin.*
19. See also P.W.A. Huisman and A. de Wolff, The Place of Religion in Education in the Netherlands, in P. de Hert, J. de Groot and G. Lauwers (eds.), *Islam (Instruction) in State-Funded Schools* (Antwerp: European Association for Education Law and Policy, 2012), 179–194.
20. https://wetten.overheid.nl/BWBR0003420/2017-01-01#HoofdstukI (English translation).
21. https://mensenrechten.nl/sites/default/files/2013-05-08.Legislation%20Equal%20Treatment.pdf, Equal Treatment Legislation.
22. https://wetten.overheid.nl/BWBR0002628/2020-04-01.

23. Hoge Raad, June 30, 2020. Retrieved from http://deeplink.rechtspraak.nl/uitspraak?id=ECLI:NL:HR:2020:1157.
24. Ibid.
25. See Hoge Raad, September 15, 2015. Retrieved from http://deeplink.rechtspraak.nl/uitspraak?id=ECLI:NL:HR:2015:2577.
26. See Burqas Banned in Dutch Government Buildings – What Will It Mean in Practice? *Dutch News*, August 1, 2019. Retrieved from www.dutchnews.nl/news/2019/08/burqas-banned-in-dutch-government-buildings-what-will-it-mean-in-practice/. See also Netherlands: Burqa Ban Enters into Force, *Global Legal Monitor, US Library of Congress*, August 27, 2019. Retrieved from www.loc.gov/law/foreign-news/article/netherlands-burqa-ban-enters-into-force/.
27. Dutch Make Masks Mandatory as New Coronavirus Cases Taper, *Reuters*, December 1, 2019. Retrieved from www.reuters.com/article/health-coronavirus-netherlands-masks-idUSKBN28B4FO. See also Brin Andrews, Everything You Need to Know About the December 1 Mask Mandate, *Dutch Review*, November 24, 2010. Retrieved from https://dutchreview.com/news/coronavirus-news/everything-you-need-to-know-about-the-december-1-mask-mandate/.
28. The NIHR's Website. Retrieved from www.uu.nl/en/research/netherlands-institute-of-human-rights-sim.
29. NIHR Case 2000–51.
30. NIHR, December 22, 1999.
31. Prohibiting the wearing of headscarves in public schools does not result in a violation of the ECHR, February 14, 2001, nr. 42393/98 *Dahlab v. Switserland.* This is of course due to the fact that the ECHR must accommodate different models of state-church separation.
32. NIHR Case 2007–153.
33. Centrale Raad van Beroep, May 7, 2009, nr. LJN BI 2440.
34. Ibid.
35. Afdeling Bestuursrechtspraak Raad van State, June 12, 2019. Retrieved from http://deeplink.rechtspraak.nl/uitspraak?id=ECLI:NL:RVS:2019:1885, The Canadian Supreme Court in a similar case ruled otherwise; see *Multani v. Commission scolaire Marguerite-Bourgeoys* (2006) 1 S.C.R. 256, 2006 SCC 6.
36. Dutch Inspectorate, Themaonderzoek burgerschapsonderwijs en het omgaan met verschillen in morele opvattingen [Citizenship Education and Coping With Differences in Moral Standards], Utrecht, 2020.
37. Rotterdam Teacher in Hiding After Online Threats in Dispute Over 'Blasphemous' Cartoon, *DutchNews.Nl*, November 5, 2020. Retrieved from www.dutchnews.nl/news/2020/11/rotterdam-teacher-in-hiding-after-online-threats-in-dispute-over-blasphemous-cartoon/.
38. Tangi Salaün and Geert De Clercq, Teacher Knifed to Death in France After Showing Class Cartoons of Prophet Mohammad, *Reuters*, October 17, 2020. Retrieved from www.reuters.com/article/france-security-idUSKBN2712MP.

11 Challenging Voluntary Religious Instruction in New Zealand Schools

Keith Thompson

Introduction

The Secular Education Network in New Zealand (SEN) has made multiple complaints to the New Zealand Human Rights Commission,[1] alleging that the practice of allowing officials in state schools to close to allow religious instruction under the Education Act 1964 (NZ) (NZEA) leads to the bullying of students who are nonreligious. The SEN also asserted that the relevant provisions in that Act are inconsistent with the later provisions of the Bill of Rights Act 1990 (NZ) (NZBORA).

The New Zealand Ministry of Education's *Guidelines on Religious Instruction in State Primary and Intermediate Schools and Nga Kura* (hereinafter, *Guidelines*)[2] differentiate between religious instruction, religious observance, and religious education, and they also advise school boards that the religious instruction allowed under the NZEA is not inconsistent with the NZBORA. Indeed, the *Guidelines* go to some trouble to explain to school boards how they may design religious instruction programs that are consistent with both laws.

One of the SEN's witnesses in its 2017 Human Rights Review Tribunal case complained that his daughter was so bullied "after opting out of religious instruction class [at Red Beach School] that she ended up going to a different school."[3] That testimony contrasts with the author's own opt-out experience from Rosedale Intermediate School in Invercargill in 1968 at a time when there was a much higher level of religious observance in New Zealand. Yet, the SEN argument that allowing religious instruction in closed schools in the NZEA is inconsistent with the requirement that all teaching in state primary and intermediate schools have a "secular character"[4] also ignores considerable commentary suggesting that secular instruction is never neutral as SEN assumes.[5]

This chapter revisits the question of whether religious instruction in closed schools is inconsistent with the mandate that all state-sponsored primary and intermediate school education in New Zealand be secular in character, or whether it is otherwise time to change the law. Specifically, does freedom from religion, as opposed to freedom of religion, require that state schools in New Zealand never allow any religious manifestations at all, whether during or outside of school hours? This is not a chapter about private or integrated ethos schools in New Zealand. Rather, this chapter is only about the ongoing place of religion in state-sponsored primary and intermediate schools.

This chapter is divided into three parts. In the first part, I discuss the NZEA, my own experience in 1968 four years after the NZEA became the law, and the changes in the nature of religious observance in New Zealand in the meantime. In the second part, I discuss the Ministry of Education's current guidelines in the context of both the NZBORA and the relevant international human rights instruments. That discussion will also engage the SEN's argument that the NZEA is biased in favour of religion and will engage the contrary view that legislation that requires that education have a "secular character" is not neutral but rather biased in favour of either non-belief or atheistic belief.

In the third part, I suggest that even though the NZEA does not appear to have contemplated the arguments raised by the SEN and canvassed in the second part, it nonetheless strikes an enduring workable balance between religious belief and non-belief. That balance is well expressed in the *Guidelines* that the Ministry of Education issued in May 2019 after extended public consultation.

The chapter concludes by summarising the tolerance and accommodation that is required if human beings with different beliefs are to live together in peace. This vision of peace obliges us to find tolerant, respectful ways to live together in disagreement. The Ministry of Education has an obligation of continuous improvement, where the minority religious believers of the future are accommodated as well as their predecessors. This obligation requires the Ministry of Education to consider objections but resist ideas that would impose minority views on everyone in the alleged interests of laicist homogeneity. It is submitted that officials in the Ministry of Education have wisely resisted the SEN's demands for the removal of all religion from state schools, as their new May 2019 *Guidelines* enable the accommodation of diverse community interests. Significantly, these *Guidelines* also enable the preservation of New Zealand's 100+ year tradition of allowing religious instruction in state primary and intermediate schools.

Personal Reflections on the NZEA and Its Accommodation Regime

In *Worlds Colliding*, Rex Ahdar explained that New Zealand is a secular country. At the same time, he explained what that meant in New Zealand in 2001. In the words of reviewer Bill Atkin of Victoria University in Wellington:

> Ahdar argues that the place of Christianity has been receding in the West. In many countries, but not yet in Britain, there was an

> early de jure disestablishment or nonestablishment. The separation of church and state is a constitutional matter in the United States, but in New Zealand it is implicit and not complete. For example, Mr Speaker recites a Christian prayer each day in Parliament and Christmas, Good Friday, and Easter are public holidays. Recently, argues Ahdar, New Zealand has realised a cultural, de facto disestablishment. Whereas the moral authority of Christianity once flourished, it has now dissipated, with Christians in a minority situation.[6]

Though one might disagree with the view that the continuing existence of the Anglican state church in Britain means that there is no measure of disestablishment of Christianity in that country, that argument has no coordinates in New Zealand because there never was a state church requiring disestablishment to prove complete disestablishment. While there are questions whether anyone can exercise meaningful freedom of conscience and religion in a country where one religion is constitutionally established, this is not a question that has to be answered in this chapter insofar as the issue does not arise in New Zealand.[7]

Nor is the question Ahdar asks, after he defines the nature of religious establishment in New Zealand, directly relevant to the question this article has posed. How Christians should function in New Zealand society, where religion is de facto disestablished, is necessarily an individual question for each of those believers. Even so, I note that some of the SEN advocates who have engaged the New Zealand government on the future of the NZEA would appear to believe that all religious expression and perhaps all evidence of religious influence must be kept out of the public square if the secular purity of New Zealand's de facto secular state is to be preserved.

While I acknowledge and have elsewhere debated the Rawlsian view that comprehensive views must be kept out of the public square if we are to preserve and enhance the fragile consensus that sustains liberal democracy in the West,[8] I do not intend to engage in that debate here. Suffice to say that the Rawlsian vision is inconsistent with many of the premises of liberal democracy including the ideas of equality and freedom of speech.[9]

In this context, what do the SEN advocates mean when they say that allowing state school closure to enable religious education on the premises leads to the bullying of nonreligious students and that this practice is consistent with the NZBORA? The remedy the SEN advocates seek is the discontinuation of religious education on all state school premises, apparently because they believe this will prevent the bullying of nonreligious students and end inconsistency with the NZBORA. The implication of the first assertion is that there is a causal relationship between the conduct of religious education on state school premises and the bullying of non-religious students. And, despite the Ministry of Education's contrary position, the SEN's claim is that the practice is inconsistent with the NZBORA. I will examine those arguments separately in turn.

The first point that must be made about the alleged causal connection between state school closure to enable religious education and the bullying of nonreligious students is that the evidence presented was the anecdotal connection made by the parents of one child attending Red Beach primary school, just north of Auckland. No empirical evidence supporting that assertion was made. It thus presents as an assertion that the SEN advocates think speaks for itself. Absent contrary empirical evidence, anecdotal evidence in rebuttal seems appropriate.

The author was a New Zealand primary and intermediate school student in Dunedin and Invercargill when the NZEA was introduced in 1964. The new law that continued to allow school closure for religious education[10] was not compulsory, and the author's two primary schools[11] did not avail themselves of the opportunity to close to allow religious education. However, the author's intermediate school in Invercargill[12] did follow the "Nelson System," and the Reverend Blair Robertson from the Anglican Church was invited to provide religious education to the 41 students in his first form class during first period each Tuesday morning.

The author attended a minority Christian church during the 1960s, when mainstream Christian church attendance was greater that it is now. He attended the Reverend Robertson's first two classes and objected to the lessons being taught. With his parents' concurrence, he sought and obtained exemption from attending those classes for the next two years. He participated in all other class activities and made many friendships that have endured to the present day. In fact, in January 2017, close to the 49th anniversary of the establishment of that first form class, with others he organised a class of 1968 reunion with their 87-year-old teacher and contacted 36 of the 41 students, including 18 from as far away as Australia and the Republic of Ireland. At no time during that class was the author bullied on account of his withdrawal from religious education lessons or his minority religious belief, despite the fact that he was the only class member to seek and obtain an exemption from attendance.

Coincidentally, it also seems appropriate to observe that two of the author's grandchildren have attended Red Beach School north of Auckland and they have not reported bullying on account of their religious unorthodoxy either. These two anecdotal observations are consistent with New Zealand's operation of the Nelson System because it was first allowed in the Education Act of 1877.[13] Despite the SEN's revelation of some bullying at Red Beach School, it is noteworthy that there have not been many religious bullying stories from other New Zealand primary and intermediate schools during the intervening 120 years. This insight also suggests that it is not wise to generalise anecdotal experiences and it may not be constructive to seek empirical evidence that could prove or disprove a connection between religious education on school premises and bullying.

Now the legal point: is the Ministry of Education correct, contrary to the SEN's assertion, that religious education on school premises is not inconsistent with the NZBORA?

The Ministry of Education's Legal Obligation Under the *NZBORA*

As Ahdar reported in 2001, the NZEA 1964 simply "repeated the secular clause" that first appeared in the 1877 Education Act.[14] While the Nelson System, which allowed nondenominational biblical studies before the start of the school day, was not initiated until 1897, it was allowed under the 1877 Act because that Act provided that school buildings could be used for other purposes when they were not being used for public school purposes.[15] The NZBORA was passed and took effect in 1990. Not an entrenched Bill of Rights, NZBORA provides that it does not trump other inconsistent legislation. New Zealand courts are expressly denied the power to

> hold any provision of any [other] enactment to be impliedly repealed or revoked, or to be in any way invalid or ineffective . . . by reason only that the provision is inconsistent with this Bill of Rights.[16]

In deference to New Zealand's parliamentary sovereignty conventions, legislative inconsistency is to be dealt with by the attorney general. In fact, Section 7 requires the attorney general to bring the inconsistency of proposed legislation to the attention of the Parliament so that it can decide whether an amendment is required before new legislation is passed. While there is no reference to what happens in a case where inconsistency is discovered in existing legislation, such as that alleged by the SEN, the implication is that such matters are referred to the attorney general by the judges who discover the inconsistencies so that they can be dealt with by the Parliament in accordance with convention.[17]

There has been no attorney general referral to Parliament suggesting that the SEN's complaint against the Ministry of Education was correct in law, but for the sake of fulness, the NZBORA sections that the SEN may have had in mind are reviewed below to identify and discuss the SEN inconsistency argument. The NZBORA sections dealing with "Freedom of thought, conscience and religion" (s 13), "Freedom of expression" (s 14), "Manifestation of religion and belief" (s 15), "Freedom from discrimination" (s 19) and "Rights of minorities" (s 20) appear to be those the SEN advocates had in mind when they protested inconsistency.

But before I undertake a review, I note that the NZBORA anticipates inconsistency in theory or practice. Therefore it provides both that the rights and freedoms recognised under the NZBORA "may be subject to reasonable limits prescribed by law" (s 5) and that other legislation be interpreted in a manner "consistent with the rights and freedoms contained in this Bill of Rights" if such interpretation is possible (s 6).

The freedom of thought, conscience, and religion recognised in s 13 is not defined. While the definition of each of these ideas is notoriously difficult, it is widely accepted that the protection of this freedom includes protection of the freedom of those who do not believe in the precepts of an organised religion and of those who affirm that there is no God, or other transcendent principle with canons of conduct attaching or not.[18]

Is the Ministry of Education's established practice of allowing religious education in state schools when those schools are not being used for other purposes (in accordance with s 78 of the NZEA) inconsistent with any interpretation of this freedom? Although Henry VIII found a way to get inside the mind of Thomas More by requiring him to swear the 1534 Oath of Supremacy recognising Henry as head of the church in England, it is not suggested that any provision of the NZEA or any practice of the New Zealand Ministry of Education requires anyone to do anything in breach of their conscience.

At its highest, the SEN bullying assertion holds that other students at Red Beach School chose to harass the child of a SEN protester on grounds of nonreligious belief and that the Ministry of Education's practice contributed to that harassment. To the writer's knowledge, it has not been suggested that Red Beach School or the Ministry of Education condones bullying on any grounds whatever, and certainly not if that harassment was somehow premised on the basis of thought, belief, or religion.

While it took Henry VIII some time to find a way to detect Thomas More's thoughts, it is less difficult to detect speech and manifestations of religion and belief under ss 14 and 15 of the NZBORA. By their nature, they can be detected by others using their five physical senses. Is there anything that the Ministry of Education does or has authorised under the NZEA, the Nelson System, or otherwise, that prevents nonreligious believers from manifesting their nonbelief as anticipated by the United Nations (UN) Human Rights Committee's broad ecumenical definition of freedom of thought, conscience, or religion or the lack of it? The answer is no. Even though the SEN advocates may not agree with the Ministry of Education policy that continues to allow religious education on state school premises when school is not in session, that practice does not interfere with nonreligious practice or belief.

The freedom from discrimination that is protected under s 19 of the NZBORA is the discrimination set out in s 21 of the Human Rights Act 1993 (NZ). They are – subject to identified exceptions – discrimination in employment, the provision of goods and services, the provision of land, housing, accommodation, access to educational institutions on grounds of sex, marital status, religious belief, ethical belief, colour, race, national or ethnic origin, disability, age, political opinion, employment status, family status, or sexual orientation.

The SEN does not appear to have suggested that the Ministry of Education has discriminated against those for whom it advocates on any of these grounds. It is possible that if the SEN wished to provide out-of-school hours classes for students who wanted to learn about a nonreligious life, following the ministry's guidelines, individual school boards might have made school premises available. Perhaps discrimination and NZBORA issues would arise if such premises were not made available despite significant community interest, but no such allegation was made. The only complaint was that in providing this facility to students who wanted to learn about religion or whose parents wanted them to so learn, the Ministry of Education was breaching the NZBORA.

With respect, after considering the legislation listed above, it is easy to agree with the ministry's assessment that religious instruction when a school is closed under s 78 of the NZEA does not offend the NZBORA. While the ministry has not explained its decision, the SEN appears to have been asking the ministry to close down a practice that has recognised this manifestation of religious freedom for more than 100 years. In that context, the SEN's request presents as an ironic example of intolerance of religious belief and manifestation because the SEN's claim was that the ministry was aiding and abetting intolerance on grounds of conscience and belief. Because the SEN's claim could only be satisfied if the ministry shut down this expression of other people's religious freedom, it presents as an effort to deny the religious freedom guaranteed in the NZBORA.

To restate the issue in another way, insofar as everyone, including a nonreligious believer, has a conscience and belief system to protect, absolute freedom of thought, conscience, and religion is impossible. This is because the absolute protection of one individual's thought, conscience, and religion would require human rights enforcement authorities to shut down the manifestation of religious belief of every other person with whom the first person disagreed. This insight explains why the NZBORA includes a limitation before it sets out any of the freedoms it was established to protect. The limitation provides that "the rights and freedoms in [the *NZBORA* are] subject to such reasonable limits prescribed by law as can reasonably be justified in a free and democratic society" (s 4). The limitation in the NZBORA is intended to prevent the use of the idea of freedom of thought, conscience, and religion being used to shut down the freedom of thought, conscience, and religion.

Human rights are an interdependent compound. Because we can never completely avoid interacting with other people in human society, practical human rights observance requires give and take, tolerance, and hopefully even respect. While it is regrettable that any public school student in New Zealand would be the subject of bullying and there are rules in every public school to prevent it, rules to prevent the perceived indirect causes of that bullying will never be practical. The need to protect freedom of thought, conscience, and religion under UN instruments and the NZBORA and Human Rights Act 1993 (NZ), require that we can only pass laws proscribing offensive behaviour. The attorney general is required to advise Parliament that the passage of any future law intruding into freedom of thought, conscience, and religion would breach the NZBORA rule that new law should not be "inconsistent with any of the rights and freedoms contained in" (s 7) the NZBORA.

The New Zealand Ministry of Education's *Guidelines*[19] were published in May 2019 following a public consultation process that ended on December 7, 2018. The *Guidelines* explain how primary and intermediate school boards can implement religious instruction programmes in their schools without breaching the NZBORA and the Human Rights Act 1993 (NZ). The *Guidelines* go to some lengths to spell out in plain English what respect for the rights and freedoms of others under the NZBORA and the Human Rights Act 1993 (NZ) mean in practice. For example, they provide:

> If a board chooses to close their school to allow religious instruction to take place, they must also comply with New Zealand's human rights laws. What this means in practice is that religious instruction must be done in a way that does not discriminate against anyone on the basis of their religious or non-religious beliefs.
>
> The guidelines provide practical advice for boards on how to enable the closure of schools for the allowance of religious instruction programmes, while doing so in a way that keeps the rights of diverse students, and their families and whānau, at the centre of their decision making to reduce the possibility of discrimination.[20]

The *Guidelines* clearly differentiate between "religious instruction" and "religious education." Religious instruction is nonneutral, endorses specific faiths, and is not a part of the Ministry of Education's curriculum. Religious education is the neutral examination of information about religion and related cultural practices, which form a valid part of the ministry's social science curriculum.[21]

The *Guidelines* make careful recommendations intended to ensure that religious instruction teachers cannot be mistaken for members of the relevant school's permanent secular staff.[22] And, it is clear that school boards are not obliged to offer religious instruction and should conduct transparent public consultation to measure interest before they make any decision to do so.[23] The *Guidelines* are also clear that religious instruction can only occur at times when the school is closed in accordance with s 78 of the *NZEA* continuing the rule that was set in s 84 of the Education Act 1877 (NZ).

An Assessment of the *NZEA's* Success in Accommodating Freedom of Thought, Conscience, and Religion

It will already be obvious that the author is a fan of what the New Zealand government did in 1877 and 1964 when it passed those Education Acts, as well as what the Ministry of Education did in 2018–2019 when it conducted a public consultation and set *Guidelines* for the future of religious instruction in state primary and intermediate schools. But in this section, I want to put those achievements in a larger context so that the wisdom involved can be better appreciated.

In 1964, when the New Zealand government chose to retain the Nelson System allowing religious instruction in state primary and intermediate schools, the UN was still wrestling with how to turn the Universal Declaration of Human Rights 1948 into a binding treaty or convention. Although there was optimism that a treaty would follow quickly after Eleanor Roosevelt succeeded in having the Declaration approved by the UN without a dissenting vote in the wake of WWII, the optimism faded. Eventually, the would-be treaty was divided in two, as the International Covenant on Civil and Political Rights and the International Covenant on Cultural Economic and Social Rights were approved in 1966, two years after the New Zealand government had approved continuation of its 1877 law initiative.

The prescience of those 1877 legislators should not surprise us. These were legislators in the same country that led the world in extending suffrage to women.[24] They were clearly thinkers. Despite English apron strings, they were able to cut their own cloth. They did not copy England and establish a state church. As Ahdar explained, New Zealand did not just happen upon its religious disestablishment model. In the 19th century, New Zealand actively sought out a way to accommodate the diverse religious beliefs of its inhabitants so they could live together in peace when they disagreed.[25] That search and efforts to find a respectful solution can be seen in Captain Hobson's response to Bishop Pompallier's Catholic "What about us?" question at Waitangi in February 1840.[26] It can be seen in what Ahdar has identified as two active decisions to maintain disestablishment in 1840, beginning with the Treaty of Waitangi, and in 1877 with the Education Act 1877 (NZ).[27] And it has endured despite the decline of active Christian church attendance since the second half of the 20th century.

Australia has made some similar decisions. In their constitutional conventions during the 1890s, the Australian framers chose to acknowledge God in the Preamble to their Constitution[28] but provided that there could be no establishment of a state church.[29] Yet, despite the SEN-like atheist litigation in 1981, the Australian High Court found that the Commonwealth government was not in breach of constitutional prohibitions when it funded Australia's extensive network of independent religious schools, even though that was anathema in the United States.[30]

The respectful accommodation of religious difference has always seemed to come more easily in New Zealand, however. The NZBORA was passed without significant dissent in 1990, and there was no opposition from the mainstream churches. That easy passage to the statutory protection of religious liberty stands in stark contrast to the efforts to pass the Religious Discrimination Bill 2020 (Cth). Although Tasmanian Attorney General Andrew Inglis Clark recommended a complete Bill of Rights in Australia at federation in 1901, his co-framers were concerned that would dilute the White Australia Policy.

American-style prohibitions on establishment and Commonwealth law that would prohibit the free exercise of religion were passed to make certain Patrick Glynn's recognition of Almighty God in the Preamble did not lead to establishment. Even so, the High Court has always interpreted these "protections" narrowly so that by themselves, they have not protected conscientious objection to compulsory military training[31] or the Cabinet's decision to wind up the Jehovah's Witness Church in South Australia because it preached pacifism during WWII.[32] In that same spirit, the Whitlam/Murphy attempt to establish human rights protections under the International Convention on Civil and Political Rights (ICCPR), including religious freedom in the 1970s stalled, the Howard government ignored the Human Rights and Equal Opportunity's Commission recommendation for a Religious Freedom Act in 1998. Further, the Rudd government rejected the Brennan Commission's 2010 recommendation that Australia pass a UK/NZ style Bill of Rights Act was rejected because it would "hand power to 'unelected' judges and override parliamentary sovereignty."[33]

While other commentators argued that mainstream Christian religious opposition was a large factor in the Rudd government's rejection of the 2010 Brennan recommendation, unsuccessful collective religious opposition to the same-sex marriage plebiscite in 2017 may be the final key to the passage of comprehensive religious discrimination legislation in Australia. For finally, religious Australia seems to have accepted that religious freedom legislation might prevent the erosion of freedom of religious expression and practice. Note however, that as of this writing, the Religious Discrimination Bill 2020 (Cth) has not been finalised as legislation. The official reason that the two public consultations have stalled is the advent of the COVID-19 pandemic. But the passage of this Religious Discrimination legislation was a Morrison government election promise and the 2022 election deadline is coming up fast.

New Zealand never experienced any of those religious freedom birthing pains. Even though the Nelson System did not take advantage of the closed school provision in the 1877 version of the Education Act until 20 years after it was passed, the New Zealand legislature still understood respectful religious freedom well enough to draft enabling provisions to work as soon as the appropriate operating system was conceived. What is even more remarkable is that the 1877 wording did not require amendment when the 1964 version of the Education Act was passed, and as the 2019 *Guidelines* attest, it is a respectful religious freedom solution that still works in the 21st century. This is no small accomplishment.

Conclusion

While the idea of religious freedom is simply expressed in a number of international human rights instruments, it is not an easy concept to put into practice. In a modern pluralistic society, it is not easy to please everyone all the time. The New Zealand Ministry of Education has not been able to satisfy the SEN. Those advocates wanted the ministry to terminate religious instruction in schools that has been occurring since 1897.

Using anecdotal evidence, the SEN claimed that the practice was contributing to the bullying of nonreligious students. Yet, the discontinuation of this almost traditional practice in New Zealand would have cancelled a practice approved by many parents who allowed their children to receive instruction in schools that they wanted. The ministry thus faced a dilemma. If it acceded to the SEN's demands, it would have cut off a historical practice approved by law and which was apparently tolerated by many in society. If the ministry allowed religious instruction to continue in schools in accordance with current law, they would have offended the SEN and its supporters. The dilemma was complicated by the SEN's argument that allowing religious instruction in schools was inconsistent with NZBORA and the Human Rights Act 1993 (NZ).

It is submitted that the ministry followed a wise course. Although it did not disclose the advice steps it took, it appears that the ministry obtained advice to determine whether the SEN's assessment of the legal status of religious instruction in New Zealand's primary and intermediate schools was correct. Having determined that the practice did not breach the NZBORA, the ministry released a discussion paper to determine both the popularity of the religious instruction programme and how it should be adjusted in light of changes in social mores. The submissions received obviously did not mandate abolition of the programme but did suggest the advisability of the *Guidelines* for school boards that may have lacked understanding of the relevant law, how to manage community interest, and the best ways to engage with their communities if they chose to retain or implement religious instruction practices in accord with the NZEA.

This course enabled respectful dialogue in New Zealand society to continue. It shows that religious freedom does not need to be privatised and it does not need to be a zero-sum game. School boards are best qualified to recognise what their school communities want. They are not obliged to implement religious instruction programmes, nor must they capitulate to minority groups who would like to see all religious expression removed from the public square. The Ministry of Education's management of challenges to the Nelson System presents as a template for allowing diverse community groups to participate in public school communities further afield. The ministry's solution also suggests that religious belief is an aspect of New Zealand's community diversity that can be accommodated with sufficient effort.

Notes

1. For example, see Dubby Henry, *Secular Education Network Challenging Bible in Schools Through Human Rights Tribunal*, May 2, 2017. Retrieved from www.nzherald.co.nz/nz/news/article.cfm?c_id=1&objectid=11848793.
2. Ministry of Education, *Guidelines on Religious Instruction in State Primary and Secondary Schools and Nga Kura*, May 2019. Retrieved from www.education.govt.nz/our-work/consultations/recent-consultations/consultation-on-draft-guidelines-on-religious-instruction-in-state-primary-and-intermediate-schools-me-nga-kura/ ("*Guidelines*"). These guidelines were issued following a consultation which closed on December 7, 2018. For details of the consultation draft guidelines, see Ministry of Education, *Draft Guidelines on Religious Instruction in State Primary and Intermediate School*. Retrieved from www.education.govt.nz/assets/Documents/Consultations/Draft-Religious-Instruction-Guidelines-for-consultation.pdf.
3. Henry, *Secular Education Network Challenging Bible in Schools Through Human Rights Tribunal*.
4. Ibid.
5. For example, in his 2017 Acton Lecture for the Centre for Independent Studies, Iain Benson observed that the political state can never be neutral: "[T]he state may operate impartially but that is not the same as 'neutrally.' Laws and policies, or the refusal to adopt laws and policies are necessarily moral decisions of some sort or another and so the idea of 'neutrality' while comforting to the morally phobic is an illusion" (Civic Virtues and the Politics of "Full Drift Ahead," *The Centre for Independent Studies*, May 4, 2017, Sydney, Australia. Retrieved from www.cis.org.au/app/uploads/2017/06/op155.pdf. Benson has elsewhere observed that "all persons are believers and all have faith. The question is not whether they are believers but, rather, what they believe in." He then warned that when "[c]ontemporary atheists" assert that they have no beliefs, that assertion is normally a prelude to the further assertion that "their kinds of beliefs . . . should have public recognition" and be the default neutral belief system (The Confusions of "Secularism" and "Secular," in *International Center for Law and Religion Studies* (Provo, Utah, n.d.). Retrieved from www.iclrs.org/content/blurb/files/Benson,%20Canada.pdf).
6. Bill Atkin, *Book Review of Worlds Colliding, Conservative Christians and the Law* (Aldershot: Ashgate Dartmouth, 2001) in *Journal of Church and State*, 45(1) (Winter 2003), 172–173, 172. Ahdar in fact suggests that there were two early de facto Christian disestablishments in New Zealand, the first occurring when the Treaty of Waitangi was signed on February 6, 1840, including confirmation (at the instance of Catholic Bishop Pompallier) that Maori of all religions "would have the protection of the British Government" (ibid., 9), and the second from 1897 when state schools became allowed to provide "religious . . . teaching on a limited basis. . . [by the] 1877 Education Act" (ibid., 13).

7. Note that Cole Durham and Brett Scharffs explore this question in great detail in *Law and Religion, National, International and Comparative Perspectives*, 2nd ed. They conclude that religious establishment by itself does not dilute free exercise of conscience and religion. Other factors, including the degree of cooperation between church and state, have a much greater impact on practical freedom of conscience and religion. Indeed, it is arguable that despite Anglican establishment in Britain, British citizens enjoy more religious freedom than US citizens despite the constitutional prohibition on establishment in that country.
8. Anthony K. Thompson, Should "Public Reason" Developed Under US Establishment Clause Jurisprudence Apply to Australia? *UNDALR*, 17 (2015), Article 6, 107–134. Retrieved from http://researchonline.nd.edu.au/undalr/vol17/iss1/6/.
9. Ibid., 121–125, where I note such criticisms of Rawls' idea of public reason by Jeremy Waldon, John Finnis, and Steven Smith.
10. Ahdar in note 6, 13. The practice of closing schools to allow for limited religious education had been going on for nearly 100 years by the time the 1964 version of the Education Act was passed and was known as the Nelson System.
11. Mornington Primary School in Dunedin and Invercargill North Primary School.
12. Rosedale Intermediate School.
13. Rex Ahdar in note 6, 13, reports that the practice of closing states schools to allow limited mostly Protestant education, "was the brainchild of a Nelson clergyman, the Rev JH McKenzie and commenced in 1897."
14. Ibid.
15. Ibid., citing s 84(3) of the Education Act 1877 (NZ).
16. NZBORA, s 4.
17. The UK Human Rights Act 1998, which followed the New Zealand template in depriving the judiciary of the right to overrule inconsistent legislation and deferring to parliamentary sovereignty conventions, goes further than the New Zealand template, and in s 4 it directs judges who discover inconsistency in existing legislation while adjudicating other matters to refer them to the Parliament for review. Grant Huscroft has noted that the New Zealand Court of Appeal announced in *Moonen v. Film and Literature Board of Review*, 2 (2000) NZLR 9, 17, that it does have "the power, and on occasions the duty" to issue declarations of incompatibility (Grant Huscroft and Paul Rishworth (eds.), Rights, Bills of Rights, and the Role of Courts and Legislatures, in *Litigating Rights, Perspectives from Domestic and International Law* (Oxford: Hart Publishing, 2002), 13). When Elin Weston wrote about the effectiveness of the UK *Human Rights Act 1998* in 2015, she reported that there had been 29 declarations of incompatibility since the Act took effect in October 2000. But she was not particularly complimentary about Parliament's ongoing willingness to avoid legislation that breaches human rights norms, since these "issues are frequently matters of great political controversy, and almost always involve political decisions" (The Human Rights Act 1988 and the Effectiveness of Parliamentary Scrutiny, *King's Law Journal*, 26(2) (2015), 262, 281, 283–284).
18. In paragraph 2 of General Comment 22, the United Nations Human Rights Committee has stated Article 10 protects theistic, nontheistic, and atheistic beliefs as well as the right not to profess and religion or belief. The terms "belief" and "religion" are to be broadly construed. Article 18 is not limited in its application to traditional religions or to religions and beliefs with

institutional characteristics or practices analogous to those of traditional religions. The Committee therefore view with concern any tendency to discriminate against any religion or belief for any reason, including the fact that they are newly established or represent religious minorities that may be the subject of hostility on the part of a predominant religious community (Forty-Eighth Session, 1993. Retrieved from www.equalrightstrust.org/ertdocumentbank/general%20comment%2022.pdf).

19. Ministry of Education, *Draft Guidelines.*
20. Ibid., 3. See also the "Summary," 5.
21. Ibid., 3–4.
22. Ibid., 10–11.
23. Ibid., 5–9.
24. New Zealand Women and the Vote, *Ministry for Culture and Heritage,* December 20, 2018. Retrieved from https://nzhistory.govt.nz/politics/womens-suffrage.
25. Ahdar in note 6, 9–18.
26. Ibid., 9.
27. Ibid., 9–18.
28. *Convention Debates,* February 7, 1898, 655–657, February 8, 1898, 658–663 and then again on March 2, 1898, 1732–1779 and on March 17, 1898, 2474. See Parliamentary Library, *Australasian Federation Conference: Third Session: Debates,* Parliament of Australia, 1898. Retrieved from http://parlinfo.aph.gov.au/parlInfo/search/display/display.w3p;adv=yes;db=CONSTITUTION;id=constitution%2Fconventions%2F1898-1103;orderBy=customrank;page=0;query=australasian%20federation%20conference;rec=8;resCount=Default.
29. On April 6, 1897, 1,201 electors from Victoria, South Australia, Tasmania, and New South Wales prayed "that neither the Federal Government nor any State Parliament sh[ould] make any law respecting religion or prohibiting the free exercise thereof." On April 7, 1897, 1,663 electors from Victoria, South Australia, and New South Wales delivered a very similar petition. On April 12, 1897, 2,606 residents of New South Wales, Victoria, South Australia, and Tasmania prayed similarly. And finally on April 20, 1897, 2,337 persons from New South Wales, Victoria, South Australia, and Tasmania prayed that "no state in the Commonwealth should be allowed to make any law respecting religion or prohibiting the free exercise thereof." See Parliamentary Library, *Australasian Federation Conference: First Session: Debates,* Parliament of Australia, 1897. Retrieved from http://parlinfo.aph.gov.au/parlInfo/search/display/display.w3p;adv=yes;orderBy=customrank;page=0;query=exercise%20religion%20Dataset%3Aconventions;rec=12;resCount=Default. The matter was settled by the introduction of American "free exercise of religion" language into the federal Constitution, but after debate, the prohibition only applied to the federal government (*Convention Debates,* February 7, 1898, 655–657, February 8, 1898, 658–663 and then again on March 2, 1898, 1732–1779, and on March 17, 1898, 2474. See Parliamentary Library, *Australasian Federation Conference: Third Session: Debates,* Parliament of Australia, 1898. Retrieved from http://parlinfo.aph.gov.au/parlInfo/search/display/display.w3p;adv=yes;db=CONSTITUTION;id=constitution%2Fconventions%2F1898-1103;orderBy=customrank;page=0;query=australasian%20federation%20conference;rec=8;resCount=Default.
30. *Attorney General* (*Vic*); *Ex rel Black v. Commonwealth* (*DOGS Case*) (1981) 146 CLR 559.
31. *Krygger v. Williams* (1912) 15 CLR 366.

32. *Adelaide Company of Jehovah's Witnesses Inc v. Commonwealth* (*Jehovah's Witnesses Case*) (1943) 67 CLR 116.
33. Mike Head, The Rudd Government Rejects Human Rights Charter, *Treaty Republic*, May 24, 2010. Retrieved from https://treatyrepublic.net/content/rudd-government-rejects-human-rights-charter.

12 A Legal Framework for Teaching Religion and Ethics in the Polish Education System

Marta Ponikowska-Stejskal and Boguslaw Przywora

Introduction

Religion and the Catholic Church played a significant role in the process of Poland's regaining its independence in 1989. In addition, the "reintroduction of religious education to public schools was one of the socially significant components of the democratization process of Polish law on religion initiated in 1989."[1] In light of these two important realities, over the years the issue of religious freedom in the public education system has attracted the attention from both academia and public policy analysts. Accordingly, this chapter examines Polish education and constitutional statutory law. The chapter also reviews case law from the Polish Constitutional Court and other courts on religion in the public school system. Moreover, the chapter discusses in more detail issues related to religion and ethics classes, personal development education programs, and religious freedom of teachers in Polish public schools.

By providing relevant quotations and analysis, this chapter reviews Polish education and constitutional statutory law as well as the most important case law from the Polish Supreme Court and Constitutional Court on religion and ethics in the state school system. The quotes presented here are designed to serve as a basic introduction to the Polish legal context for international readers.

The Legal Foundation for Education and Religion

The legal foundation for education and religion in Poland belongs mainly to constitutional and administrative law. Officials in state schools in Poland are obliged to organize religion classes on request of those who are interested in authorized institutions, namely, churches or religious organizations. The development and approval of religion coursebooks and curricula are at the competence of the respective churches or religious organizations registered in Poland that do not fall under the supervision of the Ministry of Education. The ministry is only informed about curricula and coursebooks; it cannot influence their content. Religion classes can be supervised by the officials of the churches or religious organizations, or the ministerial authorities responsible for pedagogical supervision of state schools.[2]

Under the current regulations in Poland, school authorities can organize two hours of religion classes per week.[3] The first factor in this process is that teachers of religion, regardless of whether they are lay or religious, who hold these positions, must follow the Teachers Charter, the law regulating the rights and obligations of teachers in Poland. Additional provisions governing employment of religion teachers are included in the bilateral agreements between Poland and each church or religious community operating in the nation.

The second factor influencing the organization of religion classes in state schools in Poland is the number of students in one class who are willing to participate in these courses. More specifically, if a class of at least seven students cannot be formed, then school officials shall organize joint religion classes for more than one class[4] because pupils attending state schools in Poland have the freedom to decide whether to continue to attend religion classes. It is important to note that having the opportunity to make such a decision depends on the ages of students. The Ordinance of the Minister of National Education on the Conditions and Methods of Organizing Religious Education in Public Schools and Kindergartens[5] regulates the manner in which religion and ethics classes are organized. This is discussed further below.[6]

Article 70 of the Constitution of the Republic of Poland, April 2, 1997,[7] guarantees the right to education for everyone ("education in the state schools shall be free of charge"), the parental right to choose school for their children, and the right of citizens and institutions to establish schools, higher, and further education institutions. The specific manner of fulfilling all the educational rights and obligations identified in Article 70 is provided in the education law and statutes.[8]

Article 53 of the Constitution of the Republic of Poland guarantees freedom of conscience and religion for everyone including "freedom to profess or to accept a religion by personal choice as well as to manifest such religion, either individually or collectively, publicly or privately, by worshipping, praying, participating in ceremonies, performing of rites or teaching; as well as freedom of 'possession of sanctuaries and other places of worship for the satisfaction of the needs of believers as well as the right of individuals, wherever they may be, to benefit from religious services.' " In addition, Article 53 addresses parental rights to ensure the moral and religious upbringing of their children in accordance with their convictions. Plus, it guarantees the rights of churches or legally recognized religious organizations to teach religion at schools without infringement of the freedom of religion and conscience. This Article further guarantees that no one shall be compelled to participate in religious practices or disclose religious convictions or belief.[9]

Article 25 of the Republic of Poland provides that relations between the state and churches should be governed by principles of cooperation and respect for autonomy of the churches. Under this Article, all churches and religious organizations have equal rights. The State shall ensure freedom of expression in the public life and stay impartial in matters related to religion and personal convictions. Article 25 reveals the way in which the relations between the State and churches or religious organizations shall be determined.[10] This constitutional guarantee with regard to the functioning of churches and religious associations includes the obligation to create institutional and procedural frameworks for the realization of the rights of these entities on equal bases. This includes a framework for the teaching of religion and the realization of religious freedom on individual bases.

Following the Constitution, two most important laws in Poland of education are the School Education Act of September 7, 1991, and its amendments,[11] and the Law on School Education, December 14, 2016.[12] The preamble to the Law on School Education, December 14, 2016, provides that "[t]eaching and upbringing – respecting the Christian system of values – accepts universal ethics as its fundaments."[13]

The qualifications of religious teachers are determined mainly by two acts. The first act is the Agreement Between the Polish Ecumenical Council and the Minister of National Education of April 3, 2019, on the professional qualifications required for religious teachers from churches associated with the Polish Ecumenical Council.[14] The second act, the Regulation of the Minister of National Education of April 14, 1992 (Regulation of April 14, 1992), on the conditions and method of organizing religious education in public schools, is the most important act when it comes to detailed rules on how religion classes in public schools are supposed to operate.[15]

The organization of religion classes in kindergartens, primary schools, and secondary schools is described in § 1.1 of the Regulation of April 14, 1992:

> In public kindergartens and kindergarten wards in public primary schools, hereinafter referred to as "kindergartens," religion teaching is organized at the request of parents. Religion and ethics classes are organized in public primary and secondary schools, hereinafter referred to as "schools";
>
> 1) in primary schools – at the request of parents;
> 2) in secondary schools – at the request of either parents or students themselves; after reaching the age of majority, students decide to receive religious instruction and ethics.[16]

The curriculum for religion classes must be reviewed by officials of the Ministry of Education in line with § 4 of the Regulation of April 14, 1992:

> Teaching religion takes place on the basis of programs approved by the competent authorities of the Catholic Church, the Polish Autocephalous Orthodox Church and the superior authorities of other churches or religious associations and presented to the Minister of National Education for information. The same principles apply to religion textbooks.[17]

The Regulation of the Minister of National Education of April 14, 1992, also sets the rules on the qualifications of religion teachers. According to § 6 of the Regulation of April 14, 1992, these standards are determined and set by the appropriate authorities of the Catholic Church, the Polish Autocephalous Orthodox Church, and the superior authorities of other churches or religious associations in consultation with the minister of national education. According to § 7.3 of Regulation of April 14, 1992:

> A religion teacher may run socio-religious and ecumenical organizations on the school grounds, pursuant to the principles set out in art. 56 of the Act on the Education System. He is not entitled to any additional remuneration for running the organization.[18]

Pursuant to § 9.1 of the Regulation of April 14, 1992, grades students receive for their religion or ethics classes are to displayed on their school certificates:

> The grade for religion or ethics is placed on the school certificate immediately after the grade for exercising. In order to eliminate possible manifestations of intolerance, do not include data that would indicate which classes of religion (or ethics) the student attended. 2. Grade for religion (ethics) has no effect on promoting the student to the next class. 3. The grade for religion (ethics) is issued according to the grade scale adopted in the given class.[19]

Section 11 of the Regulation of April 14, 1992, further established rules for the supervision of religion classes. According to this Regulation, supervision visits during religion lessons are allowed for the inspectors appointed by diocesan bishops of the Catholic Church, competent authorities of the Polish Autocephalous Orthodox Church, and officials of other churches and religious organizations authorized to visit religion lessons. Section 11 provides that supervision over the teaching methodology and compliance with the programs for religion and ethics is conducted by the heads of schools and pedagogical supervision employees;

the details of these provisions are set out in separate regulations.[20] The Regulation of April 14, 1992, further established the legal basis for the presence of the cross in school premises:

> A cross can be placed in the school rooms. At school, you can also say a prayer before and after class. Praying at school should be an expression of the students' common aspirations and tact and tenderness on the part of teachers and educators.[21]

On one final matter, § 10 of the Regulation of April 14, 1992, sets the conditions and method of organizing religious education in public schools:

> Students attending religious education have the right to be exempt from school in order to attend three-day Lenten retreats, if the retreat is the practice of a given church or other religious association. During the retreat, the school is not exempt from carrying out educational function.[22]

Article 19.2.10 of the Law on Guaranteeing Freedom of Conscience and Belief adds further clarification in stating that "[a]n fulfilling their religious functions, churches and other religious associations may in particular teach religion."[23] Moreover, under Article 20.3 of this law, "[t]eaching religion to public school pupils and kindergarten pupils public may also take place in schools and kindergartens."[24]

Touching on the issue of organizing religious education, The Law on Guaranteeing Freedom of Conscience and Belief stresses three major points. The first item is the equality of all churches and religious organizations officially functioning in Poland. The law makes it clear that school officials have the right to offer religious education classes "in accordance with the decision of parents or legal guardians."[25] Second, the law specifies in Article 19.2.12 that all churches and religious organizations in Poland have the right to operate schools): "[i]n fulfilling their religious functions, churches and other religious associations may in particular undertake educational and teaching activities."[26] Third, the law ensures that private, tuition-based Catholic and other faith-based schools can function as nonpublic schools. Such nonpublic schools "are supervised by the State with regard to the quality of activities and their compliance with national legislation, though supervision is more extensive in the case of public schools than non-public schools."[27]

Given the fact that Catholic religion has predominant status, it is important to mention the Concordat between Poland and the Holy See of 1993 that was ratified in 1998 as an important source of the law on education and religion. The Concordat recognizes parental rights with regard to the religious education of their children, obliging the State to guarantee that teaching of religion can be arranged in preschools as well as public elementary and secondary schools. At the same time, the Concordat establishes the principle that the Catholic religion curriculum and textbooks shall be determined by ecclesiastical authorities who inform the appropriate state officials of their choices.

The Concordat between Poland and the Holy See additionally requires teachers of religion to hold a so-called *missio canonica,* a type of authorization issued by diocesan bishops. Holding a *missio canonica* equals the right to teach religion such that its loss leads to withdrawal of the right to work in Catholic schools. Under the terms of the Concordat, detailed provisions about the training and preparation of religion teachers shall be agreed on between the competent state authorities and the Bishop's Conference of Poland. Religion teachers must then observe Church laws and regulations with regard to religious instruction and related matters. In line with the Concordat's provisions, the Catholic Church enjoys the liberty to organize catechesis for adults under the ministry for the academic community.[28]

Concomitantly, Polish law respects the international law binding it in the field of religion and education, particularly Article 9 of the European Convention on Human Rights (ECHR) and Article 2 of its Protocol No 1,[29] and Article 18 of the International Convention on Civil and Political Rights (ICCPR).[30]

According to Article 9 of the ECHR:

> Everyone has the right to freedom of thought, conscience and religion which includes freedom to change religion or belief and freedom to manifest his religion or belief, in worship, teaching, practice and observance, either alone or in community with others and in public or private. Limitations of the above freedoms can be only applied in case it is necessary to protect public safety, order, health or morals or for the protection of the rights and freedoms of others.[31]

Article 2 of the Protocol No. 1 to the ECHR declares:

> No person shall be denied the right to education. In the exercise of any functions which it assumes in relation to education and teaching, the state shall respect the rights of parents to ensure such education and teaching in conformity with their own religious and philosophical convictions.[32]

Pursuant to Article 18 of the ICCPR:

> Everyone shall have the right to freedom of thought, conscience and religion, which include freedom to have or to adopt a religion or belief of his choice, and freedom, either individually or in

community with others and in public or private, to manifesthis religion or belief in worship, observance, practice and teaching.[33]

The ICCPR specifies that no one shall be subject to coercion which would impair freedom to have or to adopt the religions or beliefs of their choices. Similar to Article 9 of the ECHR, these freedoms can be subject of limitations necessary to protect public safety, order, health and morals or fights and freedoms of others. The ICCPR obliges state parties to have respect for the liberty of parents and legal guardians to ensure the religious education of their children according to their own convictions.

The Protection for Freedom of Religion or Belief in Education

The Polish Constitution guarantees the right of parents to ensure their children a moral and religious upbringing and teaching in accordance with their convictions, while taking into account the freedom of conscience and belief of their children. As stated in Article 48.1 of the Constitution:

> Parents shall have the right to rear their children in accordance with their own convictions. Such upbringing shall respect the degree of maturity of the child as well as his freedom of conscience and belief and also his convictions.[34]

In addition, pursuant to Article 53.3 of the Constitution:[35]

> [p]arents shall have the right to ensure their children a moral and religious upbringing and teaching in accordance with their convictions. Parental rights are limited by the child's right to have own religious convictions and beliefs, as well as child's age.[36]

In its judgment U 10/07 of December 2, 2009, the Polish Constitutional Court explained:

> The Constitutional Court is aware of the fact that in specific cases, given the dominant position of the Roman Catholic faith in the religious make-up of Polish society, the choice of an additional subject (religion or ethics) by parents or pupils may not be entirely free, but may be taken under pressure from "local" public opinion. The free choice of the additional subject depends to a large extent on the respect for the principles of pluralism and tolerance for different convictions and beliefs in local communities. In specific cases in which external pressure – impinging on the free choice – was

exerted it would have been the result of a low level of democratic culture. This important issue, while it is noted by the Constitutional Court, lies outside its jurisdiction.[37]

Judicial Analysis of the Freedom of Religion or Belief in Education

In order to understand the legal issues associated with the teaching of religion in public schools in Poland in the context of the implementation of guarantees concerning the protection of religious freedom and the principles related to the separation of the state from religious associations, it is important to review relevant judicial judgments. In particular, the standard developed on the basis of constitutional provisions and international agreements by the Constitutional Tribunal is significant. This current standard is consistent with the provisions of the 1997 Constitution of the Republic of Poland.

The first of these judgments is the decision of the Constitutional Tribunal of January 30, 1991 (K. 11 /90), on the return of religious instruction to schools.[38] The Tribunal reviewed the Instruction of the Minister of National Education of both August 3, 1990, on the return of religious instruction to schools during the 1990/91 academic year and August 24, 1990, about the return of religious instruction to school in the 1990/91 school year. In its analysis, the Tribunal established principles of cooperation with Churches and Religious Associations outside the Roman Catholic Church that are not inconsistent with Article 2 of the Act of July 15, 1961, on the Development of the Educational System.[39]

In its rationale, the Tribunal interpreted the Instruction of the Minister of National Education dated August 3, 1990, as consistent with Articles 18(3) and 19(1) of the Act of May 17, 1989, on the Relation of the State to the Catholic Church in the Republic of Poland.[40] The Tribunal added that both Instructions are consistent with Articles 1, 3 and 67 Paragraph 2 and Article 82 Paragraph 2 of the Constitution of the Republic of Poland, as well as with Article 2 Point 4 of the Act of May 17, 1989, on Guarantees of Freedom of Conscience and Religion.[41]

The Tribunal decided that point 4 of the Instruction of the Minister of National Education of August 3, 1990, and point 7 of the Instruction of August 24, 1990, were not inconsistent with Article 9(1) and (2) and Article 23(1)(4) of the Act of January 23, 1982, adding that the Teachers' Charter[42] is consistent with Articles 1 and 3 of the Constitution. The Tribunal emphasised that Minister's Instructions do not violate Articles 2(4) and (5) of the Act on Guarantees of Freedom of Conscience and Religion in connection with Article 67(2) and Article 82(1) of the Constitution. Rather, the Tribunal was convinced that the Instructions fulfilled the content of these legal norms by creating organizational conditions for all stakeholders to voice their opinions on the opportunities for religious instruction created by the law. The Tribunal emphasized that such opportunities derive from inherent, inalienable human rights and freedoms, points well established in international law.

In the Tribunal's view, the alleged violation of Article 9(1) and (2) of the Teachers' Charter Act with respect to qualification requirements for teachers of religion was unfounded. During the proceedings, the Minister of National Education explained that the qualifications of religion teachers are adequate because the requirements about the content of teaching are an internal matter of churches. Accordingly, the Minister maintained that decisions about catechists and their qualifications belong to Church authorities.

The Tribunal noted that the challenged provisions did not violate the principles of separation of Church and State, secularism and State neutrality, or the related notion of non-subsidizing of churches. It observed that the Minister of National Education's Instructions do not violate these principles because they only define the conditions for making premises available in schools. The Tribunal next rejected the argument that the return of voluntary religious instruction to schools consists in its integration into curricula, then indicating that remunerating religion teachers cannot be equated with subsidising churches or other religious associations.

It is also worth acknowledging the decision of the Constitutional Tribunal of April 20, 1993 (ref. U 12/92), on the guarantee of freedom of conscience and religion on the conditions and manner of organizing religious instruction in public schools. This case delineated the approach to religious instruction while establishing standards.[43] The Tribunal reasoned that the procedure for issuing the Regulation of the Minister of National Education of April 14, 1992, on the conditions and manner of organising religious instruction in public schools was consistent with the objective set by the legislator and did not violate Article 12(2) of the Education System Act of September 7, 1991.

In this order the Tribunal rejected the allegation that Church officials violated Article 10, paragraph 2, of the Act on Guarantees of Freedom of Conscience and Religion which stipulates that churches and other religious associations should not be subsidised by the State or its organisational units, as unfounded. The Tribunal added that paying salaries to religion teachers cannot be equated with subsidising churches or other religious associations. Concomitantly, the Tribunal rejected the argument that the regulation of the Minister of National Education privileged one religion in Poland. Instead, the Tribunal believed that the Act creates equal conditions for all, including non-believers who would not want to attend religion classes because it introduced ethics courses that can be attended by believers who opt out of or choose to go to religion classes.

The judgment of the Constitutional Tribunal of May 5, 1998 (ref. K 35/97), in which it stated that Article 6, point 3, Article 7, point 4,

Article 8, point 2, Article 9, point 2, Article 10, point 2, Article 11, Article 12, point 2 and Article 13, point 2 of the Act of June 26, 1997, amending the Act on Guarantees of Freedom of Conscience and Religion and amending other laws, are consistent with Article 25, paragraph 1 and Article 32, paragraph 1 of the Constitution, is noteworthy. The Tribunal asserted that the regulation met the need to ensure religious education by smaller churches and religious associations because it grants them the right to include the grade for religion in the school certificates issued by public schools, if religion is taught therein in agreement with officials in the schools the pupils attend. The court further remarked that the requirement of organizing religion classes in catechism for at least three students was not excessive especially if they lack students in one grade or school.

Finally, the Tribunal wrote "This understanding of the principle of equal rights of churches and religious associations further supports the position that the mere deletion from the Acts on the relationship between the State and individual churches and religious associations of provisions concerning the inclusion in certificates of public schools of marks from religion conducted in catechism classes does not violate the principle of equal rights of churches expressed in Article 25 of the Constitution, nor the principle of equal treatment of citizens formulated in Article 32 of the Constitution."[44]

The Polish administrative and civil courts have also analyzed freedom of religion and belief in education. In the judgment of the Supreme Administrative Court of March 27, 2019, signature I OSK 1959/18,[45] it stressed that there is no relation between the number of students attending religion classes and the amount of teaching hours of religion:

> The period of teaching religion lessons may be reduced only with the consent of the diocesan bishop of the Catholic Church or the superior authorities of other churches and other religious associations. A smaller number of people in the group may not affect the number of hours of teaching religion in kindergartens and schools.

The organization of religion classes was subject of the Judgment of Voivodship Administrative Court in Gliwice of February 6, 2019.[46] The court reviewed provisions of the Regulation of April 14, 1992, expressing the opinion that

> the kindergarten and school are obliged to organize religion lessons for a group of not less than seven students within a class or group of pupils of the kindergarten, which means that the rule is to organize religion lessons within the class or kindergarten class, and the only circumstance allowing for exempt from this rule is the number of students or pupils in a given class less than seven people. As it stems

> from the second sentence of § 2 para. 1 of the regulation (Regulation of the Minister of National Education of April 14, 1992 on the conditions and method of organizing religious education in public schools), when in one class or kindergarten group there is less than 7 students willing to attend religion classes, then religion lessons are organized in an inter-class or inter-class group.[47]

In addition, the Court clarified the way of in which the number of hours in religion classes are calculated. The Court wrote:

> Pursuant to § 8 Sec. 1 of the Regulation of the Minister of National Education of April 14, 1992 on the conditions and method of organizing religious education in public schools, teaching of religion in public schools of all types generally takes place in the amount of two lessons per week. Thus, in the case of 10 groups, organized on the basis of the education of children in individual classes, middle school, high school, it is 20 hours a week, not 8 hours a week, calculated for each educational stage.

A recent case on religion and education highlights the tensions between faith-based and atheist points of views in the Polish society. Oftentimes, the courts deal with cases of citizens or institutions seeking to undermine the position of religious education in the Polish education system by excluding religious elements in the schools. The judgment of the Court of Appeal of Gdansk City of November 26, 2014[48] highlighted that:

> Although the state school is a non-denominational school, and therefore, it is not allowed to introduce religious elements into its functioning, example of such an activity is the blessing of the school flag, there is no legal provision forbidding such activity, nor can it be derived from the neutrality of the education system. Despite the existence of the aforementioned principle of neutrality of the state schools, one can find in its functioning religious elements such as religion teaching at school, or the presence of crosses symbolizing the Catholic religion in classrooms in many schools.[49]

In examining the conflicts between believers and atheists, research reveals that, on the one hand, the legal solutions do tend to improve such situations.[50] On the other hand, legislation fails to protect the rights of various religious and social groups sufficiently. Neither does case law safeguard the access rights to teaching about the worldview assumptions of believers by including instruction about their perspectives in school lessons for children. Research also shows that whole persons who are members of the Roman Catholic Church have privileged positions with regard to some of these issues; they acquired this status due to cultural practices and pragmatic considerations rather than legal judgments and/or regulations.

Emerging Issues

The Office of the Polish Ombudsman[51] assessed the current state of play in the field of religious education in the public schools. Based on the findings about the situation in the public schools, the Ombudsperson pointed to activities taking place in the Polish schools evidencing discrimination in the legal relationship between religion and education.[52]

The first of two emerging issues, according to one of the Polish legal opinion-making centers, is that "[r]ecently, more and more parents (especially in large cities) decide not to send children to classes in religion or ethics."[53] In the last five years, for example, perhaps the most discussed issue related to education and religion focused on the concerns of parents about religion classes, the displays or exposition of religious symbols in classrooms, and Christmas nativity plays in the public school. It remains to be seen how this situation plays itself out in coming years.

The current state of play in the field of religious education in the public schools was assessed by the Office of the Polish Ombudsman. According to findings of the report of the Ombudsman, officials in 70.4% of schools of the schools surveyed automatically sent students to Roman Catholic religion lessons. If students or their parents did not wish them to anticipate in these lessons, only 41.4% reported this orally while only 29% did so in writing. Moreover, "[a]lmost half of the school principals (42%) stated that the[y did] not inform students and their parents about their right to choose minority religion lessons."[54]

Based on these data on the situation in public schools with regard to minority religions, the Office of the Ombudsman uncovered evidence of discrimination in the field of religion and education in a variety of forms.

Among the key findings of the Ombudsman were the lack of effective actions by school officials or governing bodies to include minority religion lessons in the schools, the failure to enter grade forms of the religion of religious minorities on their school certificates, not remunerating teachers of religion who provided instruction on the minority denominations, and a general reluctance in dealing with concerns relating to the organization of minority religion lessons.[55] In particular, it must be stressed that the availability of religious minority and ethics classes within the educational system has improved significantly in recent years. However, the recommendations of the Polish Ombudsman remain valid, primarily concerning further improvement of organizational solutions and school practice such as the wider availability of ethics lessons in schools.[56]

A related issue that emerged was the right of teachers of religion to become classroom teachers. In 2018 the Ministry of National Education presented a draft of a regulation that foresaw the introduction of the possibility of entrusting the duties of regular classroom teachers to the specialized teachers of religion.

The introduction of the proposed change in the Regulation of April 14, 1992, caused officials of the Helsinki Foundation of Human Rights (HFHR) to express doubts about the compatibility of such a practice with the Constitution of Poland and the secular nature of its public educational system. More specifically, a report by the HFHR feared that such a change violated provisions in the Polish Constitution relating to freedom of conscience and religion in Article 53, the right of parents to raise their children in accordance with their own beliefs in Article 48, and the principle of ideological state impartiality in Article 25. The HFHR also voiced concerns that the possible change may lead to unequal treatment of students in elementary school students in violations of Articles 70(1) and 32 of the Polish Constitution.[57] Consequently, the minister of national education withdrew the draft from further consideration at that time.

In 2020 and 2021, it is worth keeping in mind that significant impediments or restrictions have emerged with regard to the delivery of religious or ethics classes due to COVID-19 restrictions.[58] In the majority of instances, these classes are delivered through distance learning.[59]

Conclusion

"In contrast to many European countries. Poland is seen as exceptionally religious. This is confirmed by various studies showing a high level of religious beliefs and religious practices."[60] At the same time, the secularization of the European society coupled with the development of international policy and norms that are often against freedom of religion and belief of Christians can be observed. Given the above, a new scope of legal analysis has been developed that maintains that some norms of international law and policy are not in line with the religious freedom guaranteed in the Polish legal system.

Themes that scholars analyzing Polish law on both education and religion raise currently focus around three themes: the form of withdrawal from religious classes, marks for religion classes on the public school certificates of students, and the number of pupils necessary for school officials to organize religion classes. Our analysis of the legal foundation for education and religion in Poland demonstrates that the national educational system guarantees freedom of both of these rights while not infringing on human rights. The difficulty in understanding the argument between academicians alleging breaches of human rights and those defending the status quo lies in a different understanding of definitions, such as the scope of the curriculum and whether it should contain materials about reproductive health.

Despite the fact that the legal basis for religious freedom in educational premises is clearly regulated in both Polish education law and case law,[61] some parents who do not belong to the Catholic Church – traditionally the denomination of the majority of society – make claims against the presence of the religion in the school life. Observing development of the case law, there appears to be a growing need for reconciliation between believers and nonbelievers whose children attend public schools. Put another way, the "laws in the books" that lay down very solid guarantees for freedom of religion and belief in the Polish public schools are not always equal to the "law in practice."

Religious practices in Poland do not arise due to misconduct by school directors or the lack of the rule of law in the field of religious education. Rather, it occurs because Polish society is traditionally and overwhelmingly Catholic. This fact does bring and will continue to result in many more administrative or civil law cases with regard to parents or their children who claim that they are subjected to discrimination because they are not Catholics or Christians.

In light of such potential conflict, one academician suggested that "[p]erhaps more emphasis should be placed on the subject of ethics, introducing the science of religion, which seems to be a golden mean or the best solution in the current crisis of values, so as not to discourage young people from benefiting from the possibility to study religion."[62] Thus, legal scholars can play an important role in analyzing and promoting "the third way," one of reconciliation, to help parents and students who are of non-Christian denominations feel more safeguarded by the law[63] so they do not adopt confrontational approaches towards teachers and school directors in Poland's public schools.

Notes

1. P. Stanisz, *Religion and Law in Poland* (Kluwer Law International, 2017), 171; P. Goliszek, *Religious education in Polish public preschools and schools,* "Teka Komisji Prawniczej PAN Oddział w Lublinie," Volume XIII (2020) no. 2, 180–181, Retrieved from tkp.edu.pl/wp-content/uploads/2020/12/Goliszek_sklad.pdf, 06.05.2021; see also P. Sobczyk, *Shaping the legal position of religion as a subject in public education],* [in:] Religion and ethics in public education, J. Krukowski, P. Sobczyk, M. Poniatowski (eds.) (2014); also: D. Szczepaniak: Freedom of conscience and religion and religious education in the light of the case law of the European Court of Human Rights, Retrieved from HYPERLINK"http://www.repozytorium.uni.wroc.%20pl/Content/%2078949/05.%20Damian_Szczepaniak.pdf" www.repozytorium.uni.wroc. pl/Content/ 78949/05. Damian_Szczepaniak.pdf, 63–64.
2. Section 11 of the Ordinance of the Minister of National Education on the Conditions and Methods of Organizing Religious Education in Public Schools and Kindergartens, April 14, 1992 (with later amendments), Journal of Laws 1998, no. 117, item 759 and no. 162, item 1126.

3. Ibid., item 759, para. 8.
4. Ibid., item 759, second sentence of § 2 para. 1.
5. Ibid., no. 117, item 759 and no. 162, item 1126.
6. See Regulation of April 14, 1992, and accompanying text.
7. Polish Constitution, April 2, 1997, Journal of Laws 1997, no. 78, item 483.
8. See B. Banaszak, Commentary on Art. 70, in B. Banaszak (ed.), *The Constitution of the Republic of Poland Commentary* (2012); see L. Garlicki, M. Derlatka, Commentary on Art 70, in M. Zubik (ed.), *The Constitution of the Republic of Poland Commentary, Vol II* (2016); see M. Florczak, Commentary on Art 70, in P. Tuleja, *The Constitution of the Republic of Poland Commentary* (2019); see The Case Law of the Constitutional Court: The Judgment of the Constitutional Court of 5.06.2014 r., K 35/11, OTK-A 2014, no. 6, item 61; The Judgment of the Constitutional Court of 22.06.2015 r., SK 29/13, OTK-A 2015, no. 6, item 83.
9. See P. Sarnecki, Commentary on Art 53, in L. Garlicki and M. Zubik (eds.), *The Constitution of the Republic of Poland Commentary, Vol II* (2016); Commentary on Art 53, in P. Tuleja, *The Constitution of the Republic of Poland Commentary* (2019); A. Syryt, *Standards of Religious Freedom in the Jurisprudence of the Polish Constitutional Tribunal*, in P. Szymaniec (ed.), *Dimensions of Religious Freedom in Contemporary Europe*, 222–236 (2017); see The Case Law of the Constitutional Court: The Judgment of the Constitutional Court of 7.10.2015 r., K 12/14, OTK-A 2015, no. 9, item 143; The Judgment of the Constitutional Court of 10.12.2014 r., K 52/13, OTK-A 2014, no. 11, item 118.
10. See B. Przywora, The State Impartiality in Religious and Ideological Matters in the Light of the Provisions of the Constitution of the Republic of Poland and the Jurisprudence of the Constitutional Tribunal, Scientific Journal of the Management Faculty of GWSH 2013, no. 1, item 31–37; see W. Brzozowski, *Worldview Impartiality of Public Authorities in the Constitution of the Republic of Poland* (2011); see P. Tuleja, Commentary on Art 25, in P. Tuleja, *The Constitution of the Republic of Poland. Commentary* (2019); See the Constitutional Court case: The judgment of the Constitutional Court of 14.12.2009 r., K 55/07, OTK-A 2009, no 11, item. 167; The judgment of the Constitutional Court of 2.12.2009 r., U 10/07, OTK-A 2009, no 11, item. 163.
11. School Education Act of September 7, 1991 with amendments.
12. Law on School Education of December 14, 2016, with amendments.
13. Ibid.
14. Agreement Between the Polish Ecumenical Council and the Minister of National Education of April 3, 2019, on the Professional Qualifications Required of Religious Teachers From Churches Associated in the Polish Ecumenical Council, Journal of Laws of 2019, item 9.
15. Regulation of April 14, 1992, Journal of Laws 1998, no. 117, item 759 (with further amendments).
16. Ibid.
17. Ibid.
18. Ibid.
19. Ibid.
20. Ibid.
21. Ibid.
22. Ibid.
23. Journal of Laws, 1989, no. 25, item 155.
24. Ibid.
25. K. Zielińska and M. Zwierżdżyński, Religious Education in Poland, in Derek Davis i Elena Miroshnikova (eds.), *The Routledge International Handbook of Religious Education* (London: Routledge, 2013), 264–271.

26. EACEA, *Organisation of Private Education in Poland.* Retrieved from https://eacea.ec.europa.eu/national-policies/eurydice/content/organisation-private-education-56_en.
27. Ibid.
28. Concordat between the Holy See and the Republic of Poland Signed July 28, 1993 [Ratified February 23, 1998], Dz.U. z 1998 r., no. 51, item 318; see also A. Abramowicz, Right to Religious Instruction in Public Schools and Kindergartens and the Principle of Equal Rights for Religious Associations, Studies in Religious Law, 236–237; see also J. Krukowski, *Polish Concordat: The Meaning and Implementation* (1999).
29. www.echr.coe.int/Documents/Convention_ENG.pdf.
30. www.ohchr.org/EN/ProfessionalInterest/Pages/CCPR.aspx.
31. www.echr.coe.int/Documents/Convention_ENG.pdf (dostęp: 4.05.2021 r.); see M. A. Nowicki, Commentary on Art 9, in *Komentarz do Konwencji o ochronie praw człowieka i podstawowych wolności [in:] Wokół Konwencji Europejskiej. Komentarz do Europejskiej Konwencji Praw Człowieka, wyd. VII,* Warszawa 2017; see also ECHR's *Buscarin and others v. San Marino of 18.02.1999,* The Grand Chamber, § 34; see also *Case Sodan v. Turkey of 02.062016,* Section II, No. 18650/05, § 38; *Case Jakóbski v. Poland of 7.12.2010,* Section IV, No. 18429/06, § 44.
32. www.echr.coe.int/Documents/Convention_ENG.pdf (dostęp: 4.05.2021 r.)
33. www.ohchr.org/EN/ProfessionalInterest/Pages/CCPR.aspx (dostęp: 4.05.2021 r.); see W. Sobczak, Commentary on Art 18, in R. Wieruszewski (ed.), *International Covenant on Civil (Personal) and Political Rights Commentary* (2012).
34. Article 48.1 of the Polish Constitution, April 2, 1997, Journal of Laws 1997, no. 78, item 483.
35. Ibid.
36. Regulation of April 14, 1992 and accompanying text.
37. The judgment of the Constitutional Court of December 2, 2009 (case no. U 10/07).
38. OTK ZU 1991, poz. 2.
39. Dz. U. Nr 32, poz. 160 ze zm.
40. Dz. U. Nr 29, poz. 154 ze zm.
41. Dz. U. Nr 29, poz. 155 ze zm.
42. Dz. U. Nr 3, poz. 19 ze zm.
43. OTK ZU 1993, poz. 9.
44. The judgment of the Constitutional Tribunal of 5 May 1998 (ref. K 35/97) OTK ZU 3/1998, item 32.
45. The judgment of the Supreme Administrative Court of March 27, 2019, signature I OSK 1959/18.
46. Judgment of Voivodship Administrative Court in Gliwice of February 6, 2019, signature IV SA/Gl 685/17.
47. Ibid.
48. Judgment of the Court of Appeal of Gdansk City of November 26, 2014, signature V ACa 729/14.
49. Ibid.
50. See Ombudsman's Office, Accessibility of Minority Religion Lessons and Ethics Lessons Within the School Education System, Analysis and Recommendations, *The Principle of Equal Treatment: Law and Practice,* 17 (2015), 49.
51. Ibid., 49.
52. Ibid.
53. Ordo Iuris, *Ignoring Religion Lessons to the Detriment of Students,* March 4, 2020, from https://ordoiuris.pl/edukacja/ignorowanie-lekcji-religii-ze-szkoda-dla-uczniow-analiza-ordo-iuris.

54. Ombudsman Office, Accessibility of Minority Religion Lessons and Ethics Lessons Within the School Education System, Analysis and Recommendations, *The Principle of Equal Treatment: Law and Practice*, 17 (2015), 49.
55. See ibid., 49.
56. See Ombudsman Office, Accessibility of Minority Religion Lessons and Ethics Lessons Within the School Education System, Analysis and Recommendations, *The Principle of Equal Treatment: Law and Practice*, 17 (2015), 51. Retrieved from www.rpo.gov.pl/sites/default/files/BIULETYN_RZECZNIKA_PRAW_OBYWATELSKICH_2015_nr_6.pdf.
57. Helsinki Foundation of Human Rights, *Religion Teachers as Class Tutors*. Retrieved from www.hfhr.pl/katecheci-jako-wychowawcy-klas/.
58. See Ombudsman Office, *Information on the Activities of the Ombudsman in 2020 and on the State of Play of Human and Civil Freedoms and Rights*, 1 (2021), 183–184. Retrieved from www.rpo.gov.pl/sites/default/files/Informacja_RPO_za_2020.pdf, 4.05.2021r.
59. See M. Moulin-Stozek, Polish Education Law: Evaluation of Its Response to COVID-19, in C. Russo (ed.), *Yearbook of Education Law*, 303–310ā (Cleveland, Ohio: Education Law Association, 2020); M. Plebańska, A. Szyller, and M. Sieńczewska, 2020, June, Report – Remote Education in the Times of Covid-19. Summary of the Results of the Survey of the Faculty of Pedagogy, University of Warsaw, Warsaw, pp. 13–14. Retrieved from files.librus.pl/articles/00pic/20/07/09/librus/a_nauczanie_zdalne_oczami_nauczycieli_i_uczniow_RAPORT.pdf.
60. K. Zielińska, et al., Sacred or Profane? Human Rights in Religious Education in Poland, in: Anders Sjöborg and Hans-Georg Ziebertz (eds.), *Religion, Education and Human Rights Theoretical and Empirical Perspectives* (2017), 14. Retrieved from ndl.ethernet.edu.et/bitstream/123456789/3140/1/44.pdf.
61. M. Stożek and M. Ponikowska, Governance, Constitutional Rights and Emerging Issues in Polish Education Law, in C. Russo (ed.), *Handbook of Comparative Education Law* (2018).
62. M. Judycka, *Dylematy religijne w polskiej szkole, Z problemów bezpieczeństwa: Prawa człowieka*, Redakcja naukowa: Tadeusz Jasudowicz, Janusz Gierszewski, Przemysław Zientkowski (2012), 15.
63. See B. Przywora, *Normative Model of Unpaid Pre-Litigation Legal Aid in Poland* (2019), 414–421.

13 Law, Education, and Religion in South African Public Schools

Marius H. Smit

Introduction

The accommodation of religion in public schools is an ongoing and contentious issue in most pluralistic societies.[1] Although religion has lost much of its impact on social life in many Western countries, freedom of religion and respect for religious diversity is still a moral tenor of society. Many sceptics equate religion with superstition or blind faith and unreasonable beliefs,[2] while anti-theists assert that all religions are harmful and should not be taught to children.[3]

Critics of religion opposed to the teaching of or practice of religion in schools contend that science is the only way to know things, all religions are man-made, religion is unscientific, and that religions cause wars and lead to violence in society and harm social relationships between people.[4] Ironically, research by atheists who oppose Christianity shows that Christian faith counters superstitious thinking such as belief in astrology, magic, fate or "luck."[5] It should always be borne in mind that most religions are merely superficially similar but that all religions differ fundamentally on core beliefs, practices, and doctrines.[6]

Perhaps Christian apologists have most cogently countered arguments by critics of religion by demonstrating that Christianity is based on reasonable faith, that is rational proof, factual evidence, and personal experience;[7] science was born of Christianity;[8] and that the Bible and the Judeo Christian worldview coherently accord with science and are confirmed by science.[9] Many of the arguments of anti-theists are philosophically illogical, fallacious, and/or habitually rely on straw-man caricatures and ignorance of theology.[10] Lennox explains that "secular scientists" have a specious grasp of the supernatural and of "God"[11] and a reductionist understanding of science and reality.[12] Phillips and Axelrod determined that only 0.3% of all wars in human history were caused by religious conflict,[13] and many renowned scientists affirm that science and religion are not incompatible but are in fact in partnership.[14]

In view of the fact that 62% of the world's population, or approximately 4.4 billion people, regard themselves as religious,[15] it is clear that religion plays a major role in the lives of many people. In *Christian Education South Africa v. Minister of Education*, Constitutional Justice Sachs eloquently elaborated on the importance of freedom of religion, conscience, belief, and opinion in schools as follows:

> Religion regulates human behaviour and sets the moral rules for what is acceptable for society. Religion concerns the believers' capacity to determine concepts of self-worth, views of society and the world. It determines their work ethic and sense of responsibility, and founds the distinction between right and wrong. In general, schools with an ethos of religious freedom tend to develop a culture of tolerance and respect, experience increased levels of kindness, support and participation and gain a framework for individual growth and social stability.[16]

South Africa is a multireligious society where the majority, or 79.8% of people, self-identify as Christian and approximately 15% of the population have no religion. Islam is the religion of 1.5% of South Africans, Hinduism 1.2%, African traditional belief 0.3%, Judaism 0.2%, and other beliefs 0.6%.[17] For most religious people, including schoolchildren, religion is not just a mere question of belief or doctrine. Rather, religion is a part of a way of life, how they understand and experience reality and, in many cases, the essence of human dignity, life, and existence.

Many liberal Western democracies nonetheless struggle with the idea of accommodating religious diversity in their public educational systems in a manner that is fair, equitable, and equal to the satisfaction of parents and students, on the one hand, and the state and other role players, on the other.[18] Ultimately, it boils down to the challenge of allowing religious diversity in a manner that respects the plurality of heterogeneous communities. In view hereof, this chapter aims to discuss the legal principles underpinning religion education and the Co-operative Model of accommodating religious observances in public schools in the multireligious context of South Africa.

The Legal Foundation for Education and Religion

In terms of Section 15(2) of the Constitution of South Africa, everyone has the right to freedom of religion, belief, conscience, thought, and opinion. Religious observances may be conducted at state and state-aided institutions such as public schools, colleges, and universities in South Africa, in terms of Section 15(2).[19] This section places three conditional requirements on the manner in which religious observances may be conducted at state or state-aided institutions, namely that:

1. Those observances follow rules made by the appropriate public authorities.
2. They are conducted on an equitable basis.
3. Attendance at them is free and voluntary.

Section 7 of the South African Schools Act[20] specifically provides that religious observances may be conducted at public schools, as it echoes the conditions of the Constitution, by requiring that religious observances (1) should follow rules made by the school governing body; (2) are conducted on an equitable basis; and (3) attendance at them is free and voluntary.

The Co-operative Model of Accommodating Religion in Public Schools

In terms of the "Co-operative Model," the state does not establish or favour a particular religion. Rather, the state co-operates with religious communities by permitting religious observances at state and state-aided institutions, subject to specified constitutional provisos.[21] In order for the Co-operative Model to function optimally, a measure of tolerance and resilience among diverse religious and nonreligious communities and individuals is required.

Most public schools in South Africa have an ethos that is religious in orientation and thus they allow for religious observances to be contacted on fair and equitable bases. A core aspect of the Co-operative Model is that attendance at and participation in religious observances at public schools must be free and voluntary. The requirement of "free and voluntary" goes hand in hand with the prohibition of indoctrination or coercive inculcation of a specific worldview or religious doctrine.

Legislation and guidelines by the provincial and national departments of education in South Africa contain provisions that prohibit the indoctrination of students while promoting critical thinking and freedom of expression.[22] Indoctrination is the antithesis of academic freedom. Indoctrination is defined by the *Oxford Dictionary*[23] as compulsory or forceful, closed, not open and transparent, and fake communication of a doctrine or dogma in a manner that does not allow for alternative views and critical thinking. Indoctrination is a process of teaching a person or group to accept a set of beliefs uncritically.

In order to avoid indoctrination and proselytization, the National Policy on Religion and Education makes the following distinctions:[24]

- Religious training (or religious instruction) – Instruction in a particular religion or worldview with the view to establish belief, to convert, or proselytise a person to a particular religion or to strengthen that belief by way of upbringing.
- Religion education – A school subject that is part of a curriculum or course to study different religions, their holy or sacred texts, special days, beliefs and rituals.
- Religious observances – The practice of customs, rites, and traditions of religious characters manifesting belief that are in accordance with it, such as prayer, reading of sacred texts, meditation and reflection

on sacred texts, praise and worship, witnessing, fasting, and other dietary observances, dress, observance of days of the calendar year that are of special significance, gathering of adherents and religious rituals.
- Religious orientation – The ethos, life- and worldview, directional choice, and/or foundation of beliefs. Ethos is the characteristic belief system and spirit of a person, community, culture, or era as manifested in its attitudes and aspirations; the prevailing character of an institution.

Based on these distinctions it follows that religious instruction or religious training, evangelizing or proselytizing by educators or other school personnel is not allowed in public school classrooms because the students are captive audiences and attendance is neither free nor voluntary. Religious instruction or religious training is the responsibility of parents and their religious community; for example, as members and leaders of churches, mosques, temples, and/or synagogues).

The Format and Content of Religion Education in the Curriculum

Religion education does not promote a single religion. Instead, religion education pursues a balanced approach to teaching and learning about religion in order to increase understanding, create capacity for empathy, and eventually develop powers of critical reflection on problems of moral concern.[25] All public schools in South Africa include education about the constitutional right to religious freedom and respect for the rights of others as well as tolerance for cultural and religious diversity as part of the Life Skills (namely the Foundation Phase and Grades R to 3)[26] and Life Orientation (covering Intermediate, Senior, and FET Phases, Grades 4 to 12) subjects.

The subjects of Life Skills and Life Orientation address skills, knowledge, and values for the personal, social, intellectual, emotional, and physical growth of learners. Depending on the learning phases, age groups, and grades of learners, the Curriculum Assessment Policy Statements (CAPS) prescribe subtopics addressing themes such as religions of the world, worldviews, and moral choices under main topics such as "Development of the self in society," "Health, social and environmental responsibility," and "Constitutional rights and responsibilities."[27] Because it is inappropriate for public schools to provide confessional or sectarian forms of religious instruction or to proselytize learners,[28] to date no case in South Africa has been litigated to determine whether parents may decide on behalf of their children to opt out of Life Orientation classes in public schools.

The Rights of Parents and Legal Guardians to Determine the Religious Upbringing of a Child

In terms of the South African common law, parental authority to decide on the nature and content of the education and religious instruction that their minor children should receive arises *ex lege* by virtue of parentage of children born to or adopted by the parent(s).[29] Parents are the primary educators of children and have the parental power and legal duty to care for, maintain, support, raise, and educate their children.[30] It follows, therefore, that parents should have the first right to determine what type of upbringing, language, religion, culture, and education would be best for their child or children. It is an established legal principle that the custodial parent can decide in which religion to raise the child(ren), irrespective of the other parent's religion or wishes.[31]

South Africa has ratified international treaties circumscribing the rights and duties of parents, including the International Covenant on Civil and Political Rights (ICCPR), the Convention against Discrimination in Education, the United Nations Convention on the Rights of the Child (CRC), and the African Charter on Human and People's Rights.[32] Section 39(1)(b) of the South African Constitution states that international law must be considered when interpreting its Bill of Rights. All these treaties identify the family as the fundamental group unit of society and must be recognized and preserved by the state.[33] The state, in turn, has the duty to respect parental autonomy to determine the language, culture, education, and religion of the family, unless the best interests of children are affected due to abuse, neglect, and/or exploitation.[34] The child is the bearer of all fundamental rights, not autonomously, but as directed and led by their parents according to their ages, level of maturity, and evolving capacities.[35]

Parental powers are limited by lawful and judicially sanctioned state actions, the best interests of the child, the maturing child's relative capacity, and the child's interests in life, survival, and development.[36] However, the rights of parents or children are not absolute in terms of South African law: the High Court of South Africa is the upper guardian of all children. As such, the High Court has inherent jurisdiction to decide on all matters concerning children.[37]

Public Funding of Schools – No Strict Separation Between "Church" and "State"

The South African state has a constitutional obligation to provide basic education to all and must fund public schools from public revenue on an equitable basis in order to ensure the proper exercise of the rights of learners to education and to redress past inequalities in educational provision.[38] Public schools are funded by the state from national taxation according to a quintile system based on the socioeconomic contexts of the school community in which the school is situated.

Under the amended Norms and Standards for School Funding, schools are ranked and categorized from quintiles 1 to 5, where 1 is the poorest and 5 the wealthiest; more funds are allocated to the poorest schools and the poorest provinces. Quintiles 1 to 3 are so-called no-fee schools that may not charge any school fees. Quintile 4 and 5 schools are, in essence, semi-independent or self-governing public schools that may charge additional school fees.[39] In terms of Section 48 of the Schools Act, the minister of education may subsidise independent schools. The provincial departments of education are legally entitled to and do subsidise faith-based independent schools from time to time.

The Protection for Freedom of Religion or Belief in Education

South Africa has a long history of religious observance in public schools in all sectors of its population. During the constitutional negotiations in the early 1990s, the parties were acutely aware of the strict separation between the secular state and religion that in the United States had developed into an intolerance of anything religious in the public realm. As a result, the drafters of the South African Constitution steered the constitutional ship on a religious course diametrically opposed to that of the United States. South Africa follows the co-operative approach, which avoids strict separatism between church and state while allowing religious observances at state institutions insofar as they comply with the South African Constitution, the South African Schools Act, and relevant provincial legislation.

However, in order for the Co-operative Model to function optimally, a measure of tolerance and resilience is required among diverse religious and nonreligious communities and anti-theistic individuals. In the matter of *Wittmann v. Deutscher Schulverein, Pretoria and others*,[40] Van Dijkhorst J explained that

> the concept 'religion' when used in section 1 of the [Interim] Constitution is not neutral. It is loaded with subjectivity. It is a particular system of faith and worship. It is the human recognition of superhuman controlling power and especially of a personal God or gods entitled to obedience and worship (The Concise Oxford Dictionary). It cannot include the concepts of atheism or agnosticism, which are the very antithesis of religion. The atheist and agnostic is afforded his protection under the freedom of thought, belief and opinion part of this section. There is conceptually no room for him

under the freedom of religion part. Freedom of religion does not mean freedom from religion.

Judicial Analysis of the Freedom of Religion or Belief in Education

South African jurisprudence has noteworthy court decisions on matters such as religious activities in public schools, limitation or containment of unlawful religious practices, and tolerance and accommodation of non-harmful religious customs and traditions in public schools.

Legality of Religious Observances and Religious Activities at Public Schools – The Randhart Case

The right to conduct religious observances such as public prayer, reading from holy scriptures, singing hymns, and giving sermons in public schools in South Africa remained uncontested for approximately two decades after the promulgation of the Schools Act. However, this right came to the fore when, in 2017, the controversial and much anticipated case of *Organisasie vir Godsdienste Onderrig en Demokrasie* [ORED; Organisation for Religions Education and Democracy] *v. Randhart Primary School and others* about religion and worldviews at public schools, was heard in the Johannesburg High Court. ORED (or "the Applicant") applied for six declaratory orders and 71 interdicts against public schools inter alia to prohibit the following religious activities:

- Commencing school during assemblies with Bible reading and prayer.
- Any references to God – more specifically, the Christian God – in the school song or anthem.
- Referring to Christian values in the school's code of conduct.
- Teaching the biblical version of creation according to Genesis or creation science at public schools.
- Attending of Christian School Association activities during break time.
- Distributing Bibles by the Gideons organisation at schools.
- Singing religious songs or hymns.
- Evangelizing students at schools or during class or school time.
- Formulating a school's mission within a Christian framework.
- Distributing Christian literature.
- Making a room available at the school for prayer.
- Allowing Christian activities and clubs at schools.
- Advertising a public school as a "school based on Christianity."
- Displaying slogans and references to God on school insignia.

The case received widespread media attention as many religious communities from various religions united their efforts to launch a public awareness campaigns in favour of religion at schools. The respondent schools, the national minister of education, and amici curiae (i.e. "friends of the court," which included Christian denominations, the Jewish Council, Islamic Organisation, FEDSAS, and Afriforum) contested the application.

ORED argued that all religion and religious activities were in contravention of the Constitution and wanted them banned from public schools. However, the Applicant could not substantiate all its averments with convincing evidence and proof of unfair or unconstitutional conduct by Randhart ("the Respondents"). The court commented on the absence of sufficient proof and the exaggeration of many claims by the Applicant.

On the other hand, the Respondents and amici provided copious volumes of affidavits and proof that, by and large, public schools across the country have managed to comply with the constitutional and legislative requirements of equitable and fair accommodating of students from diverse religious and cultural backgrounds. This evidence showed that students, parents, and the Christian, Muslim, Hindu and Jewish faith-based communities were able and willing to tolerate and accommodate diverse religious expression and observances. The Respondents contended that the school governing bodies and local school communities were ultimately in the best position to arrange and manage the fair accommodation and toleration of religious diversity.

Van der Linde J, on behalf of the full bench court, refused to grant a single interdict, which is somewhat revealing. Even so, the court granted two declaratory orders. First, the court held that it offends Section 7 of the Schools Act for public school officials to promote that their schools adheres only to one or predominantly one religion to the exclusion of others. Second, the court declared it unlawful for officials in public schools to signify that they promote the interest of only one religion in favour of others. In other words, the court held that *in casu* all of the listed religious observances and practices at the public schools were lawful and constitutional, but that public school authorities may not brand or market their schools as exclusively "Christian schools," for instance, or that their schools predominantly adhere to single religion.

The judgment in *Randhart* is a victory for allowing religious observances in public schools as well as a recognition of religious diversity in South Africa. Far from removing religion from schools, the judgment directs public schools to create proper policies providing space for students from various religious traditions to observe and express their religious beliefs. This is in keeping with the constitutional right to freedom of religion rather than freedom from religion.

In its reasoning, the court in *Randhart* specifically held that South Africa is not a secular state and, accordingly, that the education system is not secular. The court ruled that ORED had followed the incorrect legal procedure by failing to cite all interested parties as respondents and by neglecting to utilize or exhaust the internal provincial dispute resolution mechanisms in terms of provincial legislation and regulations. The court dealt with the core issues of fairness to religious observances in schools and whether public school authorities may hold their school out as having particular religious ethos by invoking the legal principle of subsidiarity, as discussed in the next section.

The Principle of Subsidiarity and Implications for Schools

In *ORED v. Randhart Primary School and others,* the court held that an applicant that contends that religious conduct at a public school is unconstitutional must either found its case on a contravention of an applicable rule of the school governing body or, if it avers that the conduct is unconstitutional despite being consonant with the school governing body rules, it must contest the relevant rules as being unlawful or unconstitutional. In other words, the correct procedure would be either to contest the legality of the religious conduct at issue or the school governing body rules or policies at the local level of each particular public school. This means that public school internal dispute mechanisms as well as provincial dispute mechanisms should be exhausted before the courts may be approached.

Carpenter[41] explains that the legal principle of subsidiarity means that the power of decision-making and conduct originally rests with the lower echelons or local entities and this authority is delegated "upwards" at the discretion of the latter, not at the discretion of the central authority. The essence of subsidiarity is the recognition that specified responsibilities and powers do not belong to the centre but to the lowest hierarchical level. Carpenter explains that the principle of subsidiarity, which applies in South Africa, simply means that it is wrong for the central functionaries to usurp the autonomy of local functionaries or for parties to litigate national and general legislation before specific legislation and community policies were first contested. In this regard the higher echelons and central powers play a "subsidiary" role, hence the term "subsidiarity," insofar as they provide support and, possibly, take over the functions of the lower functionary if the latter is unable to perform them adequately.

Unlawful Acts in the Name of Religion May Be Prohibited

At times, the exercise of religious practices by parents and educators acting in loco parentis, or in the place of the parent, may be unlawful or unconstitutional. For instance, in the matter of *Christian Education*

South Africa v. Minister of Education, the Constitutional Court held that prohibition of corporal punishment at schools in terms of Section 10 of the Schools Act is constitutionally valid.[42] The Court decided that the limitation of the freedom of religion of parents to require corporal punishment for their children in terms of the proportionality test of Section 36 of the Constitution was justified and reasonable, as the physical safety and security rights of learners outweighed the religious beliefs about corporal punishment. This case thus affirms that under specific circumstances religious beliefs that may result in unlawful acts, such as violent jihadi extremism or Rastafarian use of marijuana, can be limited or prohibited in accordance with the Constitution.

Religion, Cultural Practices, Freedom of Expression, and School Rules

The purposeful constitutional measure to allow for religious observances at public schools and the tolerance of religious diversity has, on occasion, conflicted with school rules. In *MEC for Education, Kwa-Zulu-Natal v. Pillay*, the Constitutional Court upheld the right to freedom of expression of a student at Durban Girls High School to wear a golden nose stud to school, in keeping with her South Indian family traditions and culture.[43]

Religious and cultural freedom of expression by learners in schools should be accommodated as long as it does not result in the substantive disruption of school discipline or unlawfully harm the reputation of a person. The Court in *MEC for Education, Kwa-Zulu-Natal v. Pillay* instructed the school governing body to revisit its school code of conduct and school uniform policy by providing for an exemption mechanism to allow for cultural dress or religious practices if the circumstances do so merit. In so ordering, the Court demonstrated that a satisfactory balance between the law and free exercise of religion could thus be achieved.

Emerging Issues

Since 1994 South Africa has experienced fundamental transformation that involved deep-rooted and radical changes to societal mores and the views of many. The liberal Western ideas undergirding individualism, secularism, and radical progressivism have also taken root in South African society and its political establishment. As a result, the National Department of Basic Education has implemented some controversial policies such as the recent compulsory Comprehensive Sexuality Education in the Life Orientation subject, with lesson books for learners that include illustrations of naked boy and girl bodies (Grades 4–6, ages 9–11); decisions about sex (Grade 7, age 12 years); illustrations of safe sex, contraceptive methods (Grade 8, age 13 years); and male and female genitals (Grade 10, age 16 years).[44] The high unwanted pregnancy and birth rates among adolescents, high incidence of sexual violence, and HIV infections among teenagers are the reasons for this policy.[45]

Many conservative, religious parents and educators object to the age inappropriateness of some of the content as well as the objectionable underlying values that inadvertently arouse curiosity, experimentation, and even encourage promiscuity, attitudes that accept the inevitability of early sexual activity of learners as a given while ignoring or underemphasizing traditional religious values of abstention and sex in marriage only. Freedom of Religion South Africa (FORSA) has garnered support and mobilized concerned parents who are lobbying for the right to have their children opt out of these lessons about sex. This is an emerging issue that will probably result in litigation or protest action.

Another example of contentious curriculum content is the compulsory teaching of the neo-Darwinian theory of evolution in the life science subject; approximately 30% of the content of the life sciences or biology subject in the Grade 12 curriculum is evolution theory.[46] The a priori assumptions or worldview on which the evolution theory is based is natural materialism.[47] The two main worldviews in modern science, namely natural materialism and theistic creationism,[48] are discordant and lead to incompatible scientific interpretations of the same phenomena or data, especially in the fields of biology or life sciences and geosciences. Many life science teachers hold religious objections, making them apathetic or sceptical of neo-Darwinian evolution.[49] Deckard, DeWitt, and Patana demonstrate that freedom of religion, thought and conscience, and academic freedom of students are inhibited by secular indoctrination in the classroom.[50]

An array of scholars and scientists contend that the evolution theory is in a crisis[51] and that multiple scientific proofs refute the evolution theory. First, the primary axiom of neo-Darwinian theory is that evolution is the result of random natural selection and mutation. However, according to Sandford, these basic mechanisms of evolution do not give rise to new genetic material, because natural selection reduces, removes, and eliminates genetic information[52] and mutation damages or destroys, harms, impairs, and/or reduces pre-existing genetic information.[53] Even beneficial mutation, gene duplication, and polyploidy are not viable mechanisms for evolution as these methods still require the presence of pre-existing genetic information.[54] In other words, evolution theory is fatally flawed as it does not explain where the initial genetic information came from or how the first single-celled organism acquired complex genetic information. Thus, neither natural selection nor mutation is a viable mechanism for evolution to occur.

Second, the impossibility, based on mathematical probability calculations and information science, that undirected "evolution" of the even the simplest single-celled organism such as *Mycoplasma genitalia* could ever occur by random unguided natural processes.[55] Third, the repeated discovery of soft tissue such as red blood cells, DNA, and protein in "fossilised" dinosaur bones contradicts the assertion that dinosaurs became extinct 65 million years ago.[56] Fourth, the irreducible complexity of every organic cell and many other features of living organisms point to the inevitable, namely intelligent design.[57] Fifth, there is a complete absence of gradualism and the "instantaneous" appearance of new kinds of animals and plants throughout the fossil record.[58] Finally, there is the absence of any visible or testable empirical evidence that shows one kind of organism evolving into another kind of organism.[59]

One-sided dogmatic teaching of evolution theory that excludes religious perspectives can result in indoctrination if the content of lessons and teaching methods do not allow for alternative views and critical thinking by students.

Conclusion

ORED v. Randhart Primary School and others affirms that the Co-operative Model of allowing religious observances in public schools in South Africa is workable. However, school governing bodies must develop policies and may not brand themselves as exclusively or predominantly for one religion. In accordance with the principle of subsidiarity, school governing bodies must determine appropriate school rules to allow for a reasonable, fair, and equitable accommodations of religious and worldview diversity among learners.

The issue of secularisation of the curriculum, the extent to which conflicting worldviews or contentious lessons content are tolerated and accommodated in public schools and in classrooms remains a burning issue, insofar as conflicting interests, values, worldviews, and religious or cultural traditions are certainties in pluralist societies and liberal democracies. Thus, controversial ideas in schools and classrooms should be tolerated and even nurtured to the extent that any negative academic or legal consequences are minimal or negligible. However, unconscionable ideas or harmful teaching should be contested if the resultant harm surpasses acceptable thresholds. Part of the right of learners to religious freedom is to opt out of lessons about controversial topics. Instead of indoctrinating learners with compulsory learning of one-sided dogma, they should be taught to think critically about the controversy by studying the evidence of contested scientific theories.

Notes

1. Marius H. Smit, Religion in South African Public Schools – The Case of *ORED v. Randhart Primary School*, *The Indian Journal of Labour Economics*, 49 (2019).
2. Jerry A. Coyne, *Faith vs Fact: Why Science and Religion Are Incompatible* (New York: Viking, 2015), vii, 43; Robert L. Park, *Superstition: Belief in the Age of*

Science (Princeton: Princeton University Press, 2008); W. Sumner Davis, *Just Smoke and Mirrors – Religion, Fear and Superstition in our Modern World* (Bloomington: iUniverse, 2003); Michael Shermer, *Why People Believe Weird Things: Pseudoscience, Superstition, and Other Confusions of Our Time* (London: Palgrave Macmillan, 2002).

3. Daniel C. Dennett, *Breaking the Spell: Religion as Natural Phenomenon* (2007); Richard Dawkins, *The God Delusion* (2006); Sam Harris, *End of Faith* (2004).
4. Christopher Hitchens *God Is Not Great* (2011); Richard Dawkins, well-known atheist and a caustic opponent of Christ-ianity, described students in Christian schools as "taught superstitions drawn from ancient scriptures." The Root of All Evil? Episode 2: The Virus of Faith, *channel4.com/culture*, 2006.
5. W. S. Bainbridge and R. Clark, Superstitions: Old and New, *The Skeptical Inquirer*, 4(4) (1980), 18–31. This research by atheists showed that conservative Christians, who are the most likely to reject Darwinism, were the most likely to reject "occult and pseudo-scientific notions." Conversely, surveys showed that regions poor in Darwin-rejecting churches had the most cults, occult activity, and superstition.
6. Irving Hexham, *Understanding World Religions: An Interdisciplinary Approach* (2011).
7. William Lane Craig, *Reasonable Faith: Christian Truth and Apologetics* (2006).
8. Stacy Trasancos, *Science Was Born of Christianity* (2014).
9. Kurt P. Wise, *Faith, Form and Time: What the Bible Teaches and Science Confirms About Creation and the Age of the Universe* (2002).
10. Jason Lisle, *Discerning Truth: Exposing Errors in Evolutionary Arguments* (2010).
11. Peter S. Williams, *A Sceptic's Guide to Atheism: God Is Not Dead* (2013); Ravi Zacharias, *The Real Face of Atheism* (2004).
12. John C. Lennox, *Gunning for God – Why the New Atheists Are Missing the Target* (2011); John C. Lennox, *God's Undertaker – Has Science Buried God?* (2009).
13. Charles Phillips and Allan Axelrod, *Encyclopedia of Wars Vol. I–III* (2005).
14. Philip Clayton, *Religion and Science: The Basics* (2012); Stephen Jay Gould, *Rock of Ages: Science and Religion in the Fullness of Life* (2011); Henry F. Schaefer, *Science and Christianity: Conflict of Coherence?* (2004).
15. WIN Gallup Global Index of Religiosity and Atheism, 2017. Retrieved from www.http://gallup-international.bg/en/Publications/2017/373-Religion-prevails-in-the-world.
16. *Christian Education South Africa v. Minister of Education* (2000) JOL 7320 (CC) (Sachs J) para. 36.
17. Statistics South Africa, Statistical Household Survey, 31, 2015.
18. Charles Glenn, Historical Background in Conflicts Over Religion in Public Schools, in: J. L. M. Lopez-Munitz, J. De Groof and G. Lauwers (eds.), *Religious Education in Public Schools: Study of Comparative Law – Yearbook of the European Association for Education Law and Policy*, vi (2019), 302.
19. Act 104 of 1996.
20. Act 84 of 1996.
21. Department of Basic Education, *National Policy on Religion and Education Policy*, para. 3–4, 2003.
22. For example: s 10 of the North-West Schools Education Act; s 9 of the Northern Cape School Education Act; s 4(1)(m) of Limpopo Province School Education Act; s 5(1)(a), (d) of the Gauteng Education Policy Act.
23. Oxford Dictionary. Retrieved from www.https://en.oxforddictionaries.com/.
24. Department of Basic Education, *National Policy on Religion and Education Policy*, para. 15.

25. Ibid., para. 23–26.
26. Department of Basic Education, *National Curriculum Statement* (2011), 1–3.
27. Department of Basic Education, *Curriculum and Assessment Policy Statements: Grades R-3, Grades 4–6, Grades 7–9, Grades 10–12* (2011).
28. Department of Basic Education, *National Policy on Religion and Education Policy*, para. 21.
29. E. Spiro, *Law of Parent and Child* (1985), 4th ed., 76.
30. Ibid., 88.
31. P. J. Visser and J. M. Potgieter, *Introduction to Family Law* (1996), 206.
32 Marius H. Smit, School Choice and School Funding Reform in South Africa, *Journal for Contemporary Roman-Dutch Law*, 83(2) (2020), 362.
33. A. Moyo, *Balancing Child Participation Rights, Parental Responsibility and State Intervention in Medical and Reproductive Decision-Making Under South African Law* (PhD thesis, UCT, 2014), 1 (hereinafter, Moyo PhD thesis).
34. Ibid., 136–148.
35. Ibid., 148.
36. Ibid.
37. *Terblanche v. Terblanche* 1992 (1) SA 501 (W).
38. *Governing Body of the Juma Musjid Primary School v. Essay* NO 2011 (8) BCLR 761 (CC); SA Schools Act, s. 34 (1996).
39. Smit, School Choice and School Funding Reform in South Africa, 372–373.
40. *Wittmann v. Deutscher Schulverein, Pretoria* 1998 (4) SA 423 (T), 446, par G-H.
41. Gretchen Carpenter, *Cooperative Government, Devolution of Powers and Subsidiarity: The South African Perspective*, Seminar Report on Subnational Constitutional Governance (1999), 43–54.
42. *Christian Education South Africa, Christian Education South Africa v. Minister of Education*, para. 75–83.
43. *MEC for Education, Kwazulu-Natal v. Pillay* 2008 (1) SA 474 (CC) (Langa CJ).
44. Department of Basic Education, *Scripted Lesson Plans for Comprehensive Sexuality Education* (2019). Retrieved from www.gov.za.dbe.
45. Department of Basic Education, *Basic Education Department Releases Scripted Lesson Plans to the Public to Allay Fears Regarding Comprehensive Sexuality Education* (2019). Retrieved from www.gov.za.dbe.
46. F. Clitheroe, N. Singleton, E. Dempster and S. Marsden, *Focus CAPS Life Sciences Grade 12 Learner's Book* (2018).
47. Natural materialism is the worldview premised on the assumption that there is no metaphysical realm and that the physical realm of nature and matter is all that exists. Natural phenomena may, according to the natural materialist worldview, only be scientifically explained and researched with reference to present-day natural processes and therefore, any possible reference to metaphysical or "religious" explanations such as specific revelation, general revelation, miracles, and divine creation are excluded per definition.
48. Theism (theistic creationism) is the worldview that is premised on the assumption that the metaphysical or spiritual realm exists together with the natural realm as part of reality and everyday actuality. In terms of the theistic worldview the meta-physical or spiritual realm is part and parcel of science, nature and the cosmos and thus forms part of legitimate scientific enquiry.
49. A. Chinsamy and E. Plaganyi, Accepting Evolution. *International Journal of Organic Evolution*, 62(1) (2008).
50. S. W. Deckard, D. DeWitt and J. Patana, The Role of Educational Factors on College Students' Creation Worldview, *Creation Ex Nihilo Technical Journal*, 17(71–73) (2003).

51. Michael Denton, *Evolution: Still a Theory in Crisis* (2016); S. Mazur, *The Altenberg 16: An Expose of the Evolution Industry* (2010).
52. John Sandford, *Genetic Entropy and the Mystery of the Genome* (2008), 123.
53. Ibid., 15–33.
54. Robert Carter, Can Mutations Create New Information? *Journal of Creation*, 25(2) (2011), 92–98.
55. John Glass, Nacyra Assad-Garcia, Nina Alperovich, Shibu Yooseph and Matthew Lewis, Essential Genes of a Minimal Bacterium, *Proceedings of the National Academy of Sciences* 103(2) (2006), 425–430. https://doi.org/10.1073/pnas.0510013103.
56. Mary H. Schweizer, J. L. Wittmeyer and J. R. Horner, Soft Tissue and Cellular Preservation in Vertebrate Skeletal Elements from the Cretaceous to Present, *Proceedings of the Royal Society B: Biological Sciences*, 274 (January 22, 1667, 2007), 183–197.
57. Michael Behe, *Darwin's Black Box* (1996); Steven Meyer, *Darwin's Doubt – the Explosive Origin of Animal Life and the Case for Intelligent Design* (2013).
58. Stephen Gould and John Eldredge, *Natural History* (1977), 22–30.
59. William Moyers, 2004, Richard Dawkins was asked by Bill Moyers during an interview whether evolution has been observed. Dawkins answered: "Evolution has been observed. It's just that it hasn't been observed while it's happening." Retrieved from www.pbs.org/moyers/journal/archives/dawkins_now_flash.html.

14 Law, Education, and the Place of Religion in Spanish Public Schools

Javier García Oliva and Helen Hall

Introduction

The treatment of religion in Spanish schools is a perennial source of controversy, both socially and politically.[1] Religion is a topic of conversation best avoided in gatherings of friends or extended family because it is a subject bound to provoke strong and clashing sentiments. This is undeniably one facet of the deeply rooted divisions and alliances between left and right in the Spanish nation and the traditionally strong association between the Catholic Church and the right as well as anticlericalism and the left.[2]

Of course, such broad generalizations were always a gross oversimplification of reality, and even in the 20th century assumptions tended to break down at a grassroots or individual level. Further, it is undeniably the case that old categories are increasingly crumbling, as Spanish society evolves as a complex and pluralistic context, set within a culturally dynamic Europe and a global marketplace of ideas.

Keeping the preceding important considerations in mind, it is still unquestionable that the left/right division in relation to religion and politics in Spain was never merely a myth or stereotype, nor is it by any means dead. Moreover, even if ailing, the monster is more than capable of revival, with new movements emerging at both ends of the political spectrum.[3] This background is important because it explains the ebb and flow of legislative policy on religion in schools, which we shall see in the succeeding section, as legal arrangements were scrapped and recast every time that the political tide turned.

Given that this pattern is ongoing with the current regime of Pedro Sánchez, acknowledging it remains a pragmatic necessity when addressing the bigger picture in Spain.[4] It also renders addressing the overarching constitutional provisions relevant to both ideological freedom and education, which set out the rules governing this seemingly eternal game of political football, and also the boundaries of the pitch within which play must take place.

It should also be remembered that the state level is not the only one at which political and administrative decisions may be made in Spain, and that the strategies adopted by regional authorities – in particular "autonomous communities," the category of substate entity enjoying the greatest degree of self-determination – may have a significant impact on the implementation of nationally applicable provisions and the overall educational experience of students.[5] Consequently, while for the purposes of this chapter the aim is to give an overview of the Spanish picture, it is critical to appreciate that there is huge diversity at the grassroots level.

The Legal Foundation for Education and Religion[6]

In common with other Western European paradigms, the Spanish model evolved over time from a position in which the education of children was a matter exclusively for parents to arrange however they saw fit, in accordance with their economic resources and family inclinations, to one in which the state acknowledged a duty to ensure that all children received a minimum level of education during their formative years. In order to achieve this system, public authorities were required to guarantee that there was adequate provision in terms of the number of educational institutions and also to take responsibility for standardizing the quality of provision, at least to some degree. As such, the state's assumption of responsibility was a secularizing agenda, which deliberately stepped away from reliance on religious organizations, or in other words, religiously neutral education must be made available to all and financed by the public purse.

As discussed further below, though, the Spanish constitutional paradigm has long recognized the right to "freedom of teaching/instruction," envisaging this as being vested both in individual citizens and social groups that enjoy the freedom to set up educational institutions. Consequently, private faith schools are necessarily accepted as part and parcel of the education law landscape, given that their establishment is a fundamental right. For this reason, commentators such as del Valle have described the clash between religious and secular teaching on the ground as a tension between state and confessional schooling.[7]

As might be anticipated, the right to education in Spain is deemed an individual right that guarantees every young person a place in a state educational institution. The provision of this service and its constitutional status have been judicially recognized,[8] and are unambiguously set out in the text of Article 27.5 of the Constitution. Such a right is universal and is not dependent on citizenship or other legal status. The *Ley Orgánica 4/2000, sobre derechos y libertades de los extranjeros en España* was modified, in compliance with the decision 236/2007 of November 7, of the Constitutional Court,[9] to recognize the right of all minors to enjoy equal benefits in respect of both compulsory and post-compulsory levels of teaching. Still, this right must not be delivered in a way which would render its uptake an affront to other guaranteed freedoms, meaning that the treatment of religion in the public arena must be sensitive to the ideological perspective of individual students and their families.

The upshot of the above considerations, at least for the purposes of this chapter, is that young people must be in receipt of full-time education to a minimum standard and the default option for provision of this will be state-funded educational institutions. Moreover, confessional schools are permitted as a matter of constitutional guarantee and, crucially, the Spanish Constitution acknowledges the right of parents to elect for their children the religious and moral education that is in accordance with their own convictions.[10]

So, how does this acknowledged claim to state-funded education and teaching of religious and moral values in accordance with parental conviction play out in terms of the current statutory framework? The various rights that are recognized by Article 27 of the Spanish Constitution have been both implemented and fleshed out by various *Leyes Orgánicas*,[11] which have passed through the state legislature as the wheel of political fortune has turned. The earliest significant step in this long path was the now repealed *Ley Orgánica 5/1980, 19th July, del Estatuto de los Centros Docentes* (LOECE).

The Spanish Constitutional Court was called on to consider the LOECE while it was in force, in 5/1981, February 13. This ruling confirmed that it was not unconstitutional for a private educational institution to adopt a particular religious ethos. In addition, the judgment clarified to a certain extent the balance of power between communities concerned with providing education in accordance with a designated faith tradition and the scope for them to intervene in the administration of institutions funded by public authorities.

The next major enactment was the *Ley Orgánica 8/1985, 3 July, reguladora del Derecho a la Educación* (LODE). In common with its predecessor, this law met with opposition from some quarters and faced a challenge. The Constitutional Court examined the new framework in its decision 77/1985, June 27, particularly in relation to the possibility of establishing a system of financial agreements with private educational institutions. Subsequently, the *Ley Orgánica 1/1990, 3 October, de Ordenación General del Sistema Educativo* (LOGSE) was approved. Both this law and the LODE were partially repealed and modified by the *Ley Orgánica 2/2001, 23 December, de Calidad de la Educación* (LOCE), which was in turn repealed by the *Ley Orgánica 2/2006, 3 May, de Educación* (LOE).

Going the way of seemingly all Spanish enactments on education and religion, the *LOE* regime was subjected to major reworking by the *Ley Orgánica 8/2013, 9 December, de Mejora de la Calidad Educativa* (LOMCE), and then further tweaked in 2015. It would not help this discussion to relate the minutiae of this dance between right and left and the intricacy of every step. The chapter shall shortly examine the stage that Spain has currently reached, bearing in mind of course that the dancers remain in motion. However, what is worth noting is that there have been recurring themes in the back and forth, and these remain life issues: the content of compulsory teaching for all students, the shape of subjects in which pupils may opt in or out, and the role of religious communities in relation to educational provision.

All of the various categories of state and nonpublic schools, such as international, vocational, and online schools), are potentially battlegrounds in which these issues may be fought out legally. As noted above, the freedom to establish teaching centres is recognized by Article 27.6 of the Constitution and vests in both natural and juridical persons. The LOE distinguishes, in its Article 108, three different types of educational institutions: state centres, which must by definition be controlled by public administrations; private schools, which may belong to either a natural or juridical person; and publicly subsidized private schools.

Fully private and publicly subsidized private schools are entitled to establish their own religious ethos, as is recognised in Article 115 of the LOE. Clarifying its decision of 5/1981 in relation to the terms "ethos" and "own character," the Constitutional Court has declared that the two labels are synonymous. Less helpfully, though, the Court did not offer much commentary or insight in respect of what these two interchangeable terms actually mean. In other words, $X = Y$, but the value of both X and Y remains a subject for debate. The judges contented themselves with observing that "ethos" amounts to an expression of the ideological character of a school, which encompasses both pedagogical and educational aspects of the particular institution.

It is clear at least that the designation of an ethos enables parents to choose schools in harmony with their personal convictions, thereby promoting their constitutional rights in this regard. It also allows officials in the schools, as institutions, to make certain specifications for staff members, limiting their freedom as instructors and employees in ways that might otherwise be legally problematic.

The Protection for Freedom of Religion or Belief in Education

The present Constitution of 1978 was a key part of Spain's transition from a dictatorship to a free and democratic state.[12] Consequently, it cannot be overemphasized that the text enshrined in this document and the wider project of transition were part of a collective endeavour embraced and enabled by representatives across the political spectrum. We are bound to recognize tussles between left and right over the interpretation of the Constitution. Yet, this should not be misconstrued as a suggestion that any element within mainstream Spanish politics is seeking to reject its most basic tenets of modern society. Article 1 sets out equality, liberty, and political pluralism as fundamental values of the juridical system, rights that have not been contested in any of the legal or political battles that have been fought since the 1980s.

Spain's contemporary constitutional settlement, consequently, recognizes fundamental freedoms within its own framework.[13] It also obliges state actors to respect the international human rights instruments that Spain has ratified. For present purposes, Articles 8, the Right to Private and Family Life; Article 9, the Right to Freedom of Religion and Belief; and Article 2 of Protocol 1, the Right to Education of the European Convention on Human Rights (ECHR) are of particular relevance. The text of Article 2, Protocol 1 provides that:

> No person shall be denied the right to education. In the exercise of any functions which it assumes in relation to education and to teaching, the State shall respect the right of parents to ensure such education and teaching in conformity with their own religious and philosophical convictions.

As the case law of the Strasbourg Court makes clear, though, this right is clearly subject to reasonable limitations, and the state enjoys a wide margin of appreciation.[14] The thrust of this right is to ensure that children and young people are not subjected to indoctrination in the course of public education; still, this does not mean that parents are entitled to demand à la carte provision in every respect to suit their personal worldview. Rather, public education is a collective project, such that a degree of give and take related to both available resources and societal values is acknowledged as appropriate by international law.

The United Nations Declaration on the Rights of the Child is also important in this arena, in particular Article 28, on the Right to Education, and Article 14, on the Right to Freedom of Conscience. The latter is especially significant because Article 9 of the ECHR makes no provision for the inchoate capacity of younger students, whereas Article 14 UNCRC explicitly provides:

> State Parties shall respect the rights and duties of parents, and where applicable, legal guardians, to provide direction to the child, in the exercise of his or her right in a manner consistent with the evolving capacity of the child.[15]

Although giving parents a "piggyback" right is not entirely unproblematic in terms of declaring the freedoms and dignity of minors as individuals, it is a pragmatic acknowledgment of the reality in practical terms where younger students are concerned. This provision is also very much in line with the Spanish model, which as shall be seen, places considerable emphasis on the ideological freedoms of parents to direct their children's spiritual and ethical formation, even when they are in receipt of publicly funded education.

It is fair to observe that at a constitutional level, Spain, in general terms, marches in step with international law where schooling is concerned. It is important to bear in mind that as Valero Estarellas asserts, it was never the intention of either the contracting states, or the Strasbourg Court, to interpret Article 9 in a way that would impose uniformity in the context of education and state neutrality;[16] instead, there are several acceptable models that allow breathing space for cultural and political differences between states. Bearing this in mind, Spain can be said to fit within the designated parameters and to be broadly aligned with the aims of the transnational norms.

As this chapter has shown, within the catalogue of fundamental rights contemplated by Chapter II of the Spanish Constitution, those concerning education are included in Article 27. As discussed above, this proclaims not only the right to education itself but also the freedom of instruction, which facilitates the pursuit of pluralism within this field. The same article explicitly sets out the right of parents to choose religious and moral education for their children in compliance with their own convictions.[17] This is logical, given that as Celador Angón argues, in the broader context of Article 9 of the ECHR, freedom of religion and conscience is of limited value if it does not encompass the right to transmit ideas, beliefs, and opinions.[18] While the education of children is only one facet of such transmission, it is a highly significant one.

The lack of explicit mention of the rights vested in the students in this provision is regrettable from a human rights perspective, although the wording of Article 14 of the UNCRC renders it more readily defensible than it might otherwise have been. Nevertheless, where older students are concerned, there are potential issues should a clash arise between the perspectives of pupil and family, in light of the Article 9 of the ECHR and Article 14 of the UNCRC rights, which the young person enjoys. If young people are able to make independent choices, riding roughshod over their expressed wishes to decline or to participate in religious instruction is not compatible with the liberty and dignity of the individuals concerned.

Setting aside these questions of the rights of children versus parental rights, one can observe that this facet of Article 27 serves as constitutional justification for the incorporation of religious teaching in state institutions.[19] As long as the instruction is not enforced on families who wish to refuse it, the offering of such provision can be construed as fulfilling, rather than infringing, a freedom based on constitutional and international law. Of course, permissibility and desirability are separate questions and the mere fact that a political choice may be open within an overarching framework does not signify that it should be adopted as optimal in policy terms.

In addition to the text of Article 27, it is key to bear in mind the express right to religious and ideological freedom recognized by Article 16 of the Spanish Constitution, which effectively functions as the domestic equivalent of Article 9 of the ECHR. This encompasses both individual and communal liberty to manifest religious and ideological beliefs. It may be limited, but no further than is necessary for the protection of public order. As Mantecón observes, it is recognized that the right to religious freedom is not, and should not be, conceived of in absolute terms, but at the same time it should not be lightly set aside.[20]

The content of Article 16 was built on by the *Ley Orgánica 7/1980* of July 5, on Religious Freedom. Article 2 of the *Ley Orgánica* recognizes the right to receive and deliver religious teaching orally, in writing, or through any other medium. It reiterates the right to choose for oneself and for minor children (*no emancipados*) religious education and instruction that is in accordance with personal beliefs and values. This provision encompasses both school and nonschool settings, thereby effectively safeguarding the rights of parents to send their children to a Hebrew school or madrassa outside of school hours.

Intimately related to this is the right of religious denominations to disseminate their own tenets, a right that is also expressly embraced. It is stated that in order to properly and effectively facilitate enjoyment of these rights, public authorities must adopt the measures necessary to enable religious education within state educational institutions.[21] This is distinct from the right vested in religious denominations, as well as all other juridical persons, to fund their own teaching institutions, provided these operate in conformity with constitutional principles. This caveat is important because the constitutional values and human rights safeguards mean that faith groups by no means enjoy carte blanche, even within the private sector.

Nevertheless, one could not deny that the balance of competing interests and duties is particularly delicate in the state arena. As this chapter demonstrates, according to the principle of pluralism as understood in the Spanish model, any indoctrination on the part of the state is prohibited. Consequently, although required to provide religious education, the state may only deliver teaching that is essentially critical, objective, and pluralistic in nature. Further, in compliance with the principle of religious neutrality,[22] no denomination may be accorded any official status.

Without a doubt, the historical model of Catholic confessionalism in Spain has been left behind in this regard and a more separatist approach has been adopted.[23] Yet, as commentators like Diez argue, this does not mean that all vestiges of the legacy of institutional Catholicism have been completely erased in sociological terms.[24] Nevertheless, as a matter of juridical intent, such a system prohibits any confusion or intermingling of religious and state functions. The requirement of neutrality demands that the state abstain from any approach to religious education that might be construed as supporting a particular faith as normative or operating in a way that excludes other perspectives. Needless to say, this is easier to state in the abstract than to make manifest in practice. The difficulties of implementing concrete policies are explored in the next section as we move to consider judicial treatment of these questions.

Judicial Analysis and Administrative Treatment of the Freedom of Religion or Belief in Education

Religious Education

As this chapter shows, the Constitution does not simply protect the exercise of religious freedom in schools but also enables minors to receive religious education in the state educational sector.[25] One avenue through which this has been actively pursued lies in the agreements signed by the state and various religious bodies.

As far as the Catholic Church is concerned, the Agreement on Teaching and Cultural Affairs with the Holy See (1979) provides in its Article II that every educational stage from primary to secondary (excluding university and other tertiary institutions) include the teaching of Catholic religion offered on comparable terms to those in place for other fundamental subjects.[26] However, importantly, it was also agreed that such teaching would not be compulsory. As Ferreiro demonstrates, all sides of the debate recognize that religious education as it is currently conceived in Spain is not simply an academic subject such as chemistry or history, but it has a dimension of passing on the tenets of a faith.[27] Therefore, as one might expect from the previous discussion, families have a right to opt in to Catholic religious education but are not obliged to accept it.

Nevertheless, it must be stressed that other groups that have signed agreements with the state – so far encompassing Jewish, Muslim and Protestant religious bodies – are not in a completely parallel position.[28] This is a practical attestation of the special cultural position of the Roman Catholic Church and the functional cooperationism of the Spanish Constitution. Where each of the minority faith agreements is concerned, Article 10 guarantees, again from primary to secondary stages, the right in both state and publicly funded private schools to receive religious education in respect of the faith in question, but only insofar as the exercise of this right does not contravene the ethos of the educational institution the student attends.[29]

The LOE includes the study of religion within the block of required subjects for primary education while recognising social and civic values as an optional subject (Art. 18). The LOE follows the same pattern for secondary education but substitutes ethical values for social and civic values as the optional subject in Article 24. Religion is also offered within the baccalaureate equivalent qualification at the end of secondary education, highlighting the intellectual and academic importance of it as a discipline.

Dress and Symbols

Because there is no legal prohibition on the wearing of religious symbols in schools, controversies akin to those in other jurisdictions of head covering and jewellery have not arisen to the same degree in Spain as in France, Belgium, and other jurisdictions. The majority of conflicts have taken place at the administrative level. However, for instance, the courts were required to make such a determination in 2012, rendered by the *Juzgado de lo Contencioso-Administrativo de Madrid.*[30] This ruling concerned an appeal by the parents of a Muslim student against the decision of the educational authorities of the Region of Madrid. The dispute arose when the student transferred from one school to another, because officials in her original school did not allow her to wear the type of Islamic covering that she wished to adopt.

The regional Court of Madrid found, basing its reasoning on judgments of the Court of Strasbourg, that the prohibition of the veil in this instance did not amount to a breach of the girl's religious freedom. The court concluded that on the facts it came within the requirements established by the ECHR, finding that the policy school authorities adopted was necessary in order to protect fundamental rights of others as well as the public order. The public order considerations the court addressed were identified with the non-confessional nature of the state as acknowledged by Article 16.3 of the Constitution. This decision has been widely criticized by commentators such as Cañamares, particularly in light of the absence of concrete evidence about the need to protect third parties.[31] Cañamares contended that it was not clear whose interests were being put in jeopardy by the student's being permitted to adopt religious dress.

One factor which exacerbated the lack of clarity was the terminology that the court used, as the word "veil" conveys limited information about the nature of the garment in question. How restrictive the desired religious dress was for movement and how much loose-flowing material it involved may have been relevant factors in terms of health and safety or concerns of the kind raised in the UK *Begum* case, where Muslim members of a school community were resistant to reforming the uniform policy to allow more conservative clothing, as they were concerned about peer pressure to comply.[32]

It seems highly unlikely that school authorities would resist any form of head covering and, for instance, it would seem manifestly cruel and unreasonable to deny a child who had lost her or his hair due to illness the opportunity to wear a hat or scarf if this made the student feel more comfortable. Therefore, if some forms of head covering were potentially acceptable, what was the problem with the one being put forward in this instance? Had the court provided more precise detail, it would have been helpful in determining what was really happening and ultimately the persuasiveness of the reasons given for upholding the decision in this particular case.

Of course, it should be remembered that in addition to the potential for cases to turn on their facts, and the particular circumstances of a given student or school, the Spanish system does not operate on the basis of precedent. Thus, it ought not to be assumed that another tribunal faced with a pupil wishing to wear religious dress and facing a school-based prohibition would lead to a similar conclusion.

Dietary Requirements

With regard to dietary requirements in the Agreement with the Islamic Commission of Spain, its Article 14 declares that "the food . . . of Muslim pupils in state and publicly-funded private schools, who request it, will try to be adapted to the Islamic religious precepts, as well as fasting dietary requirements." As has been seen, this accommodation is a duty imposed on the relevant public authorities unless it causes harm or undue pressure on the provision of service of a school community as a whole.

It might have been expected that a similar requirement would have been in place in respect of the agreement with the Jewish community, but this was not the case. It is also worth observing that once again, pupils seeking to assert their rights in front of the courts have not fared well from reported cases. For example, a decision of the Superior Court of Justice of Madrid of June 16, 2015, rejected a Muslim student's complaint about the lack of provision for his dietary needs by a school canteen.[33] The court declared that insofar as this food service was voluntary, the student was free to look for another school that was more responsive to his specific requests.

The outcome of this decision does seem to be an unfortunate one. The reluctance of a court to impose undue burdens on the provision of voluntary services is understandable given the risk of such benefits simply being withdrawn to the detriment of the entire community, with the possibility for creating social tension in the process. At the same time, though, the state-level agreement is of very little value to families if school authorities can too easily slough off the duties that it apparently imposes. Because the experience of sharing food and social interaction over meals with fellow students is critical for building up community ties, facilitating this where possible is highly positive for social cohesion.

Moreover, the greater the level of understanding and flexibility on both sides, the greater the possibility of coming to a mutually satisfactory conclusion. For example, if school authorities faced budgetary or ethical obstacles to providing halal meat, they could perhaps ensure that there was always a vegetarian option available in the canteen, because this would be religiously acceptable to the majority of Muslims. There is also the reality that many Spanish school canteen meals, such as egg and chips, are actually meat-free by accident, if not design, but this requires a certain degree of knowledge and willingness to seek a solution.

It is perhaps also worth noting that reported case law does not amount to sociological research, because this is not its function. Although the cases appear unpromising in terms of religious freedom when it comes to meeting dietary or dress requirements, the dearth of litigation might actually reveal that, generally speaking, Spanish school authorities are willing to find solutions on the ground. One cannot positively assert that this is the situation, and of course, it is possible that the reported cases are simply the tip of a grubby iceberg, and that many more students feel that their religious freedoms have been infringed within the educational system but lack the financial resources, or perhaps even the emotional energy, to go as far as issuing proceedings. In reality, more academic work needs to be done in this area, ideally of an interdisciplinary nature, in order to better understand the sociological context within which the current Spanish provisions are operating.

Religious Instruction

With regard to religious instruction, teaching in relation to the Catholic faith is universally available, but optional, rendering litigation about its provision is relatively unlikely. In contrast, the availability of religious education in one of the minority faiths is contingent on resources and compatibility with the ethos of the institution, so it is a more likely source of conflict in relation to delivery. Again, imposition is not an issue, given that it is provided in response to a request.

It should be noted that aligning religious education with students' own spiritual backgrounds available in state schools is not per se necessary to comply with either the requirements of Spanish Constitutional Law or the international law obligations that the state has undertaken to respect. In fact, the lack of specific provision for those whose faith is not covered by an accord with the state demonstrates this to be the prevailing interpretation within the Spanish paradigm. Given the immense religious diversity found in the 21st century, it would be unrealistic to guarantee tailored religious education to any faith tradition that a parent might nominate. Nevertheless, having entered into specific agreements, the Spanish state has generated a legitimate expectation that these will be respected, and appropriate religious instruction should be offered unless there are strong reasons rendering this impractical.

As this chapter has demonstrated in the Spanish context, issues around access to education and faith go far beyond religious instruction. There are also questions around the school environment and how welcoming it may be for pupils from distinctive religious or ideological backgrounds. Matters such as the ability to join peers in dining rooms for meals or the willingness to accommodate religious dress may affect the accessibility of some schools to some pupils. Addressing this on the ground is complicated because pragmatic decisions do have to be made when financial resources need to be expended or where competing interests are at stake. Nevertheless, the flexibility accorded to school authorities to manage practical and logistical challenges involved in delivering their statutory obligations should be not be a cloak to cover capricious uses of discretion or unnecessary restrictions on religious freedom.

Emerging Issues

Undeniably, the largest emerging issue on the horizon in the Spanish paradigm concerning religion and education relates to the current reforms of Prime Minister Pedro Sánchez. From the beginning of his administration, he openly promoted a secularizing agenda, setting the tone by eschewing all Christian symbols from the ceremonial oaths and assumption of office. For current purposes, the most significant proposal is that of removing religious education from the curriculum, a move that would, it goes without saying, drive a coach and horses through a large section of the foregoing discussion.[34]

As suggested above, such a step would also be in keeping with the swinging pendulum of policies between left and right in Spain. While the Sánchez administration would be no more culpable than any of its predecessors, it is regrettable that both ends of the political spectrum are more anxious to push their own agendas in this sphere rather than to try to create a reasonable, middle-ground solution that might endure beyond the political shelf life of its implementing regime, while assisting young people to understand their own ideological or spiritual heritages, that of their country, and that of their neighbours.

In late November 2020, the so-called Ley Celaá (taking its name from the government minister of education) narrowly made it through a very divided Parliament, by a majority of just 29 votes, achieving a place in the statute book.[35] However, the future of the this legislation remains in doubt because it is facing challenges in the Spanish Constitutional Court by the rightwing Partido Popular and its allies.[36] If the law survives in its current form, it will:

1. Make education in civic and ethical values compulsory in primary and secondary schools. This course will focus especially on promoting knowledge of, and respect for human and childhood rights, and in particular the principle of equality between men and women.
2. Remove the obligation to take an alternative course to Religion if students do not opt for it, and discount the grade attained for Religion in calculating a grade average and determining access to university courses.[37]

In addition to the current legal action, it is already apparent that there will be ongoing challenges and wrangling in relation to the details and implementation of the statute along with attacks on its compatibility with constitutional and international law. Students opting for religion will be materially disadvantaged because in secondary education it will not boost their marks. Consequently, time devoted to the study of religion will not pay the dividends of other subjects. Spending time studying religion will now effectively be optional, given that no alternative class need be taken instead, and it will not be advantageous in terms of marks attained. The change will also have a disproportionate effect on students who are already disadvantaged academically such as, for example, due to their additional learning needs or the challenges of studying in their second or third languages. Thus, young people already stretched in tackling subjects needed for grades are less likely to regard extra commitments as justifiable because these will drain their time but not enhance their final marks.

Further, the content of the new civic and ethical values course is likely to be seen as controversial by some socially and religious conservative groups. Those whose beliefs conflict with gender equality, for instance, might even go so far as to argue that it is a form of state indoctrination, given that they have no possibility of opting out and are effectively being presented with an ideology that young people are being encouraged to accept. This is not to suggest that such claims would be justified or successful, but due to the level of dissatisfaction that the policies will generate in some quarters, the idea of them escaping challenge by litigants seems somewhat fanciful.

Conclusion

At the constitutional level, the position of Spanish law is settled and well understood in the sense that there is overwhelming support for human rights and religious liberty for both parents and pupils. Nonetheless, drilling down beneath this, the picture is much more complicated. The teaching of religion in schools has been bouncing backwards and forwards like a ping-pong ball from the early days of democracy onwards and shows no signs of settling down. This is regrettable from the perspective of both students and the wider society.

It would be difficult for any educationalist to assert that this kind of polemical bun-fight is a conducive environment in which to develop a curriculum that will be academically rewarding. Neither is it likely to equip future citizens to engage in a nuanced way with a world of diverse perspectives, an open and plural society, or the rich cultural heritage that is the patrimony of all Spaniards.

At the same time, for as long as the treatment of religious instruction remains such a deeply divisive issue and a talisman for both left and right, it is very difficult for Spanish society as a whole to engage in a balanced debate around the treatment of faith and conscience in schools more broadly. While religion is a rallying battle cry for substantial sections of the political landscape, any measured or reasonable discussion about policy is going to be hard to come by. This is extremely unhelpful for citizens with tangible problems and concerns, whether these relate to diet, dress, or other matters.

Going forward, the medium- and long-term aspiration for the Spanish legal framework must be to find an escape from the Groundhog Day scenario of each incoming regime marking its territory and tearing down the flags of its predecessor. A structure that is broadly acceptable to both left and right needs to be found. The conflicts of the 20th century in this regard need to be allowed to recede into history so that the challenges of a vibrant, open country in the 21st century can be adequately addressed.

Notes

1. J. García Oliva and F. Cranmer, Education and Religious Symbols in the United Kingdom, Italy and Spain: Uniformity or Subsidiarity? *European Public Law*, 19(3) (2013), 555.
2. S. Payne, *Spain's First Democracy: The Second Republic 1931–1936* (Madison: University of Wisconsin, 1993), 81–124.
3. Un informe de la Iglesia culpa a Podemos de "empeorar" el anticlericalismo en España, *El Diario*, November 16, 2016. Retrieved July 20, 2020, from www.eldiario.es/sociedad/libertad-religiosa-denuncia-anticlericalismo-espana_1_3739211.htm; Spanish Elections: How Far Right Vox Party Found Its Footing, *BBC News*, Novermber 11, 2019. Retrieved from July 20, 2020, from www.bbc.co.uk/news/world-europe-46422036.
4. J. Luxmore, Spanish Church Seeks Accord with the Socialists, *The Tablet*, July 1, 2020. Retrieved from www.thetablet.co.uk/news/13097/spanish-church-seeks-accord-with-socialists.
5. Spanish Constitution, Arts. 137 and 143.

6. For a general overview of this topic, see S. Cañamares and J. García Oliva, Spain, in C. J. Russo (ed.), *Handbook of Comparative Education Law* (New York: Rowman & Littlefield, 2018), vol. III, 117–1404.
7. J. M. González del Valle, *Derecho Eclesiástico Español* (Madrid: Civitas, 2005), 317–318.
8. July 10, 86/1985, *Fundamento jurídico tercero.*
9. Ibid.
10. Article 27 of the Spanish Constitution reads as follows:

    1. Todos tienen el derecho a la educación. Se reconoce la libertad de enseñanza.
    2. La educación tendrá por objeto el pleno desarrollo de la personalidad humana en el respeto a los principios democráticos de convivencia y a los derechos y libertades fundamentales.
    3. Los poderes públicos garantizan el derecho que asiste a los padres para que sus hijos reciban la formación religiosa y moral que esté de acuerdo con sus propias convicciones.
    4. La enseñanza básica es obligatoria y gratuita.
    5. Los poderes públicos garantizan el derecho de todos a la educación, mediante una programación general de la enseñanza, con participación efectiva de todos los sectores afectados y la creación de centros docentes.
    6. Se reconoce a las personas físicas y jurídicas la libertad de creación de centros docentes, dentro del respeto a los principios constitucionales.
    7. Los profesores, los padres y, en su caso, los alumnos intervendrán en el control y gestión de todos los centros sostenidos por la Administración con fondos públicos, en los términos que la ley establezca.
    8. Los poderes públicos inspeccionarán y homologarán el sistema educativo para garantizar el cumplimiento de las leyes.
    9. Los poderes públicos ayudarán a los centros docentes que reúnan los requisitos que la ley establezca.
    10. Se reconoce la autonomía de las Universidades, en los términos que la ley establezca.

11. The *leyes orgánicas* own a hierarchically superior position to ordinary laws and regulate, as stated by Article 81 of the Constitution, the development of fundamental rights and public freedoms, amongst other subjects.
12. A detailed explanation of the political and religious background of Spain can be found on J. Martínez-Torrón, *Religion and Law in Spain: International Encyclopaedia of Laws: Religion* (Alphen on the Rhine: Wolters Kluwer, 2013), 17–33.
13. Article 10.1 of the Spanish Constitution declares that "1. The dignity of the person, the inviolable rights which are inherent to the person, the free development of the personality, the respect for the law and the rights of others are the foundation of the political order and social peace."
14. See, for example, *Campbell v. Cousins v. UK.* App. No. 7511/76, 7743/76, 4 Eur. H.R. Rep. 293 (1982); *The Belgian Linguistic Case Application, no. 1474/62; 1677/62; 1691/62; 1769/63* (1994).
15. UNCRC Article 14 (2).
16. M. J. Valero Estarellas, Autonomía de las Confesiones Religiosas, Neutralidad del Estado y Prohibición de Arbitraridad, en la Reciente Jurisprudencia del Tribunal Europeo de Derechos Humanos, in: *Libertad Religiosa, y Neutralidad del Estado y Educaación: Una Perspectiva Europea y Latinoamericana* (Aranzadi: Pamplona, 2019), 55–78, 77.
17. Spanish Constitution Article 27(3).

18. O Celador Angón, *Libertad de Conciencia y Europa: Un estudio sobre las tradiciones constitucionales comunesy el Convenio Europeo de Derechos Humanos* (Madrid: Fernando de los Rios, 2011), 87–88.
19. In this sense, see M. Rodríguez Blanco, Manifestaciones del derecho fundamental de libertad religiosa, in: *La libertad religiosa en España: XXV años de vigencia de la Ley Orgánica 7/1980, de 5 de julio. Comentarios a su articulado* (Granada: Comares, 2006), 74–78.
20. J. Mantecón, *El derecho fundamental de libertad religiosa: Textas, comentarios y bilografía* (Pamplona: Eurosa, 1996), 93.
21. This chapter uses the term "state" rather than "public" in order to refer to schools owned by public authorities. The term "public" is confusing in the United Kingdom, where it is used for private educational establishments, and we wanted to avoid any confusion. Further, it should be borne in mind that education is a devolved matter in Spain, and therefore "state" as an adjective has been used to refer to both the "state" and the regional authorities.
22. Spanish Constitution Article 16(3).
23. Although, considered holistically, the Spanish Constitution is now undoubtedly a hybrid, cooperationist paradigm, and by no means one of thoroughgoing separatism. Article 16(3) states: "There shall be no State religion. The public authorities shall take the religious beliefs of Spanish society into account and shall consequently maintain appropriate cooperation with the Catholic Church and the other confessions."
24. G. Diez, La Educación Religiosa en España: ¿Contribución al diálogo intercultural o factor de conflicto entre religiones? *Estudios sobre las Culturas Contemporáneas,* 14(28) (2008) 11, 18.
25. González del Valle, *Derecho Eclesiástico español,* 331.
26. Agreement Between Spanish State and Holy See of 3 January 1979 Concerning Education and Cultural Affairs (ratified 4 December 1979; B.O.E. no. 300, 15 December 1979).
27. J. Ferreiro, *Profesores de Religión de le enseñaza publica y Constitución Española* (Barcelona: Atelier, 2004), 74.
28. These agreements were approved by an ordinary law in the Spanish Parliament, so that the Law 24/1992, November 10, approves the Agreement Between the State and the Federation of Evangelical Entities of Spain (FEREDE); the Law 25/1992 approves the Agreement with the Federation of Jewish Communities; and the Law 26/1992 approves the Agreement with the Islamic Commission of Spain.
29. M. Moreno Antón, *La enseñanza religiosa no católica en la escuela pública, La enseñanza de la religión en la escuela pública: Actas del VI Simposio Internacional de Derecho Concordatario* (Granada: Comares, 2013), 329–374.
30. 35/2012, January 25.
31. S. Cañamares, La inclusión de los otros: la simbología religiosa en el espacio público, in *La inclusión de los otros: símbolos y espacios de la multiculturalidad* (Granada: Comares, 2012), 99–120; M. Alenda, *El símbolo religioso en el Estado laico español* (Valencia: Tirant, 2016); J. Martínez-Torrón, La cuestión del velo islámico en la jurisprudencia de Estrasburgo, *Derecho y Religión* (2009), 87–109.
32. *Begum v. Denbigh High School* UKHL 15, 1 AC 100.
33. *Tribunal Superior de Justicia, Sala de lo Contencioso,* N°. de Resolución: 388/2015.
34. Socialist Pedro Sanchez Becomes First Spanish Prime Minister to Be Sworn in Without a Bible, *The Telegraph,* June 2, 2018. Retrieved August 6, 2020, from

www.telegraph.co.uk/news/2018/06/02/socialist-pedro-sanchez-sworn-new-spanish-pm/.

35. BOE Ley Organica 3/2020.
36. El PP recurre ante el Tribunal Constitucional la "ley Celaá", *El Pais,* March 29, 2021. Retrieved May 7 2021, from https://elpais.com/sociedad/2021-03-29/el-pp-recurre-ante-el-tribunal-constitucional-la-ley-celaa.html.
37. ¿Qué propone la "ley Celaá" de educación? *El Confidencial,* June 17, 2020. Retrieved August 6, 2020, from www.elconfidencial.com/alma-corazon-vida/educacion/2020-06-17/educacion-ley-celaa-propuestas_2642755/.

15 Sweden Exemplifies How Religion Is Taught in a Secular State

David Ryffé

Introduction

In early March 2020, a hate campaign was launched against a municipal school in Tierp, north of Stockholm, Sweden.[1] The cause of the campaign was a lesson about Islam where young children had the task of writing a text about Islam from a fictional perspective in the form of "confessing" themselves to that religion. An excerpt from a notebook circulated in alternative media that said, among other things, "I belong to Islam" and "I pray in the mosque," even though the child was not Muslim. This was perceived by some as so provocative that the school was reported to the police as proselytizing, even though this was used as a pedagogical tool regarding the teaching of all of the major religions in the world.[2]

Earlier, in the year 2019, various private schools with religious orientations received extensive criticism from the Swedish school inspectorate, in some cases due to extensive lack of objectivity in regard to religion. One of those schools even lost its permission to engage in teaching.[3] Because private schools in Sweden are financed by public funds and must follow the same regulations as public schools, this raises many questions about the clash between freedom of religion and the right to education as well as about how religion is, and should be, taught.

Over the past decade or so, the educational landscape in Sweden with regard of religion has changed, not least due to extensive immigration. At the same time, officials have discovered that a few schools, both private and public, have become dominated by different Christian communities. The domination by these Christian communities has led to an extensive impact on the content of what is being taught overall in those schools, not the least of which in terms of teaching about religion and related subjects are, for instance, sports and sex education.[4]

Even though the focal point of this chapter is on how religion is taught and to what extent religion may be manifested in publicly funded schools in Sweden, there is no clear divide between breaches with the curriculum regarding religion as a school subject and the religious expressions in schools with more confessional approaches. Therefore, these issues should be seen as two different aspects of how religion is actually taught. However, in mainstream schools, the teaching about religion is not seen as a problem itself, even though various academicians have pointed out that religion in Swedish schools is taught in a far too descriptive way and that the instruction about religion should rather be about cultural aspects of religion.

What is to be taught regarding the school subject of religion is described in the curriculum,[5] which in Sweden has the legal status of an ordinance and is therefore subordinate to the Education Act.[6] The curriculum also includes general values for all of education as well as some aspects to be considered about how different subjects are taught.

Education is, by default, a complex endeavor, and even more so when it comes to balancing religion and science in a so-called secular state. The overall aim of education in Sweden, as described both in the Education Act and in the associated curriculum, is that students should study on a scientific basis, to reflect, and to be critical.[7] The selection of subjects and their core content has been determined by the state, based on what could be called a "political belief system," about what knowledge serves the best interests of the state. This belief system, which is sometimes incorrectly described as objective, often ends up in conflict with different religious belief systems.

Even if Sweden is often described as a "secular state," one could argue that it depends on how religion is defined. In *The Godless People: The Post-Christian Swedes and Religion* (2015), the Swedish professor David Thurfjell argues that the idea of Sweden as a secular country, apart from religion, is a chimera.[8] Instead, he argues, religious beliefs have transformed from that of the church to that of the individual. From a legal standpoint, this reflects on how freedom of religion is to be understood in a Swedish context.

The Swedes still believe both in a traditional sense and in a more undefined spiritual way, and one should note that almost 6 million people, out of a population of about 10 million, are members of the Church of Sweden.[9] Still, the idea of Sweden as a secular country has played a crucial role in how the legal framework about education has taken shape. Also, the idea of the secular state is in many ways at the root of the many controversies that arise when it comes to religion, education, and how religion is taught in publicly funded schools.

Because education and religion are both seen as core social values worth defending in a modern democracy, the legal framework protecting these fundamental rights sometimes has to deal with "opposing" rights regarding values in conflict with each other. The remainder of this chapter, then, examines the interplay between religion and education in Swedish schools.

The Legal Foundation for Education and Religion

The Swedish educational system has been torn between secular and religious values ever since the end of World War II. The same goes for a majority of the developed parts of the world, even though Sweden might have taken state secularism further than most other countries.

When the United Nations (UN) adopted the Universal Declaration of Human Rights in 1948, Article 26, the right to education,[10] was one of the most difficult issues on which world leaders had to agree.[11] Would the right, in practice, accrue to the state, which could design education according to the needs of the labor market, or would the right accrue to parents and guardians, who could thereby choose educations for their children in accordance with their beliefs? That the right to education should accrue to the child itself was hardly even a thought until the UN Convention on the Rights of the Child was adopted in 1990.[12]

If possible, matters of religion and education proved even more difficult to unite in a pan-European context, meaning the European Convention on Human Rights (ECHR),[13] which did not include the right to education at all in its first implementation. The ECHR is considered domestic law since Sweden joined the European Union in 1995. The right to education was added on to the ECHR in an Additional Protocol two years later, such that individuals' freedom of religion came to trump the state's interest in defining the content of education.[14] This led to Sweden invoking a dispensation to the provision on the right to education when it was finally adopted.[15] According to the dispensation, it would generally not be possible for parents and guardians to renounce specified teachings for religious reasons.

The ECHR has a special legal status in Sweden, as it stands above all domestic law but the Constitution. However, because Sweden has had the dispensation mentioned above, the relationship between freedom of religion and the right to education is still a contentious subject where, to this day, there is no legal clarity.

Freedom of religion in the Swedish context is defined in the Constitution as a negative right, to the extent that the state must not restrict individuals' right to practice their religions.[16] For those parts of religious activity or religious life also relating to freedom of speech and/or freedom of assembly, restrictions can be made by law provided they meet the requirement of "satisfying purposes acceptable in a democratic society."[17] Both freedom of religion and freedom of speech are defined in relation to the state, meaning that the public must not intervene against individuals. At the same time, the Constitution states that those who act as a public officials must observe objectivity and impartiality in their positions as representatives of the state, which limits the ability of the officials, including teachers, to express religious conviction within the framework of their service.[18]

It follows from the Education Act[19] that any Swedish public school must be nondenominational and that private schools financed by public funds must not provide confessional education.[20] The distinction between these different forms of schooling is that teaching and education have different legal meanings. Teaching is the part of the education covered by the curriculum and is usually conducted under the guidance of one or more teachers. On the other hand, education is a broader concept encompassing all elements of students' school days. The latter means that education can be considered to include breaks, dining situations, and voluntary activities in connection with school activities.

For public schools, which are normally operated by municipalities, it is therefore only the curriculum that defines the actual content of religious education. The curriculum is usually selected by various authorities on authorization by law, such that even if it is a formality, the government has the final say on what is taught. The contents of the curriculum are developed by the National Agency for Education, which is also a major policymaker. Because the Agency is bound by the demands relating to objectivity and impartiality, religious issues have very little place in policymaking.

In private schools, teaching about religion, as to content and scope, is similarly bound by their curricula, but there is also room for both religious deepening, prayer, and other activities in close connection to the actual teaching. In practice, this can be expressed as prayer before or after lessons, in-depth study of religious texts after school, or celebrations of various holidays with religious affiliations. At the same time, as there is some room for confessional content in the activities conducted in connection with schools, a "negative freedom of religion" follows to the extent that no one can be forced to participate in such activities even though, in reality, there may be a feeling or sense of social compulsion to participate. The negative aspect of freedom of religion also prohibits all forms of proselytizing.

Because elementary schooling is compulsory for all Swedish children, there is no way to opt out of teaching about religion that is in line with the curriculum, which sets high demands on teachers not to conduct teaching in a way that can be perceived as preaching or as missionary work for one or the other belief. The requirement of objectivity is supplemented by a fairly comprehensive regulation about discrimination, which should be understood to the extent that it is not just discrimination from an activity. Discrimination can thus be understood both directly and indirectly that, in practice, means that students must not be disadvantaged by norms that are objectively regarded as neutral, but which, in practice, work disadvantageously for specific individuals or groups with, for instance, sharing the same religious affiliation.[21]

A practical and legal problem linked to the controversies between the right to education, religious affiliation, and the teaching about religion, in a broader sense, is how the teaching is organized. Because the teaching itself must not include confessional elements, boys and girls cannot be separated on religious grounds and there may be no coercion regarding how to dress or behave beyond what is required by general rules or standards. Nor may the content of the education deviate from the curriculum or the scope of other subjects in parts that can be perceived as conflicting in relation to particular religious points of view. Typical problems that have led to critiques from the authorities are that officials in some schools with "religious profiles" avoid relating objectively and scientifically to, for example, sex education, life knowledge, and, to a certain extent, social sciences regarding the relationship between secular and divine laws.

The curriculum itself, as to the subject of religion, dictates which areas of religion and religious life and philosophy must be dealt with in classes.[22] Interestingly, in the Swedish context, despite a secular basic notion, there is a clear overweight in Christian doctrine. Also, the subject of religion as a whole relates very descriptively to the various world religions to an extent that might be provoking to those who acknowledge specific religions: the Jewish counterpart to a church is a synagogue, Muslims are expected to make a pilgrimage to Mecca, and the Christian symbol is a cross. How a religion can be defined, how it can be understood in a broader cultural context, what unites different religions, and where the dividing lines go are addressed in very modest terms in the curriculum, which has been criticized in a number of academic works.[23]

The Protection for Freedom of Religion or Belief in Education

As mentioned in the introduction, the issue of religious education in schools encompasses opposing freedoms and rights. Freedom of religion must be understood partly as it is expressed in the Swedish Constitution and partly as explained in the ECHR because these are two separate sources of law, albeit with somewhat different meanings, that still bind the actors in the school system.

The constitutional freedom of religion is guaranteed in the second chapter of the Instrument of Government, the main act of the Constitution, which states that everyone "has the freedom to practice his religion alone or together with others."[24] This right is usually interpreted very narrowly and means almost a right to believe what one wants in situations where the surroundings are not affected; in addition, it is a right not to be discriminated against or persecuted because of one's beliefs. Freedom of religion is thus a kind of protection against discrimination as a result of one's religious beliefs. The freedom, or the "right," includes both a negative aspect, which means that the public cannot discriminate against individuals, and a positive aspect, which means that the state must ensure that no one is exposed to discrimination or harassment by other individuals as a result of their religions.

While other rights deriving from the Constitution may be restricted by regular law, if there is a legitimate interest that can be considered acceptable in a democratic society, freedom of religion is absolute and therefore cannot be restricted.[25] In practice, though, multiple rights interact when one actually chooses to practice a religion in the form of rites, gatherings, sermons, or the like. In such cases, it is the question of conduct that must be assessed according to freedom of expression, freedom of assembly, and freedom of association.[26] These are also constitutionally protected but can be restricted by legislation. For example, religious attire and religious symbols are protected under the freedom of speech, and religious gatherings are protected by freedom of assembly. The protection of the individual is therefore weaker when it comes to religious expression in a public context than when the religion is practiced privately, which is in line with the general Swedish view of religion as an individual concern.

The ECHR can be understood as an addition to the constitutional rules and provides in Article 9 that

> Everyone has the right to freedom of thought, conscience and religion; this right includes freedom to change his religion or belief and freedom, either alone or in community with others and in public or private, to manifest his religion or belief, in worship, teaching, practice and observance.[27]

Each state that has signed the ECHR has a margin of appreciation, meaning that the rules must be interpreted in the light of the social and cultural context of the Contracting State. Insofar as the Swedish Constitution stipulates that no domestic law may conflict with the Convention, laws governing schools must be interpreted in the light of the ECHR and its more dynamic rules regarding, among other topics, religion.[28] Yet, the second paragraph of Article 9 indicates that states have the authority to restrict freedom of religion if the constraints officials impose follow from domestic law and can be seen as necessary in a democratic society in the interests of public safety; for the protection of public order, health, or morals; and/or for the protection of the rights and freedoms of others.

An illustrative example of how these two parallel rights, arising from two different sources of law, are applied alongside the issue of education, which nevertheless shows the weight of religious freedom, is a ruling by the Supreme Court in the case of Pastor Green.[29] The pastor gave a sermon to his congregation, which was broadcasted on the radio and reproduced verbatim in a local newspaper, in which he consistently condemned homosexuals. According to Pastor Green's presumption, homosexuals could not be seen as Christians and that they should be punished. Pastor Green was indicted for incitement against a group of people, a criminal provision that constitutes a statutory exception to, among other things, freedom of expression.

When Pastor Green's case reached the Supreme Court, it found that he could very well be liable on account of the exception in the freedom of expression in the form of the criminal provision. The Court added that in the event of the judgment was appealed to the European Court on Human Rights, it was likely on the basis of Article 9 of the ECHR that Sweden would have been found to have violated the Convention. Pastor Green was therefore acquitted on the basis of the meaning of the rights as they are to be understood according to ECHR. Therefore, the freedom of religion could be understood as a stronger freedom, or right, in the ECHR than in the Swedish Constitution.

In an educational context, though, the outcome would most likely have been different. The Swedish dispensation with respect to the right to education that follows from the ECHR's first Additional Protocol, Article 2, states that Sweden does not accept such a right that takes into account the parents' or custodians' beliefs. Therefore, only with the freedom of religion as expressed in the Swedish Constitution can the beliefs of parents or custodians be taken into account. As mentioned above, this should be understood as the students having the right to belong to whatever religion they wish, but this does not mean a right to "practice" religion within the framework of the teaching.

From teachers' perspective, the same regulation as in the previous paragraph means that, within the framework of both teaching and education, teachers must not express their own religious beliefs in a way that can serve as missionary work because religious freedom should also be understood as freedom from religion. This is especially important when it comes to situations where one party, namely the adult teacher, is an authority and the student is in a subordinate position.

The curriculum not only governs the substantive content of what is to be taught but also discusses how the teaching should take place. Objectivity is a key point for the students' entire education, which also follows from the Education Act because it severely limits the ability of teachers to angle instruction in accordance with their own religious views.

The parents' ability to choose education for their children that is consistent with their own religious beliefs depends on the "free choice of schools" that makes it possible to select independent schools with religious orientations.[30] Although parents or guardians may choose such education for their children, there are strict requirements on the voluntary nature of individual students to participate in the religiously embedded activities that surround the teaching, such that it is not possible to force the children to participate if they do not want to do so. The aspect of freedom of religion, which also implies a freedom from religion, thus belongs to the students and not their parents or guardians. Therefore, because teaching elements must not deviate from the curriculum even in such independent schools, students who have achieved certain levels of maturity and insight are free to choose not to follow their parents' beliefs and so receive more secular education, even in independent schools with religious orientations.

In summary, religious freedom is rather weak in an educational context, both for teachers and for students, because there is no room for religious elements in the teaching itself. The teaching of religion should follow the elements of the curriculum and therefore include all world religions on more or less equal terms with some kind of benefit to Christianity because it played a crucial role in the development of Swedish society and Swedish culture. Regarding one's own religious identity, there is no possibility of banning religious attire or religious symbols such as the cross, the veils, or the kippah insofar as these are attributes covered by freedom of expression in combination with freedom of religion, which thereby strengthens the image of the Swedish view on religion as something highly individual rather than cultural.

The right to education derives from the Swedish Constitution, the Education Act, and the first Additional Protocol to the ECHR. Yet, nowhere in these legal documents are any qualitative or quantitative measures presented. The upshot is that it is not clear what the right actually means. Out of other provisions of the Constitution, regarding requirements for objectivity and based on the rules about equality in the Education Act,[31] as well as that the ECHR should be interpreted with a margin of appreciation, it is a reasonable interpretation that the right to education should be understood, among other things, as a right to an objective education free from religious elements but with the possibility of a religious imprint on a school as a whole.

Judicial Analysis of the Freedom of Religion or Belief in Education

A wide range of controversies have touched on religion and education in recent years, but since the opportunities to sue schools or their representatives are limited in terms of educational activities, only a few of those controversies have reached the Swedish courts. An infringement of the ECHR shall primarily be tried by domestic courts and may be brought before the European Court of Human Rights only if all domestic remedies are exhausted.[32]

In the Swedish legal system, the guiding state bodies, especially the National Agency for Education, play decisive roles in shaping policies where the legislation is not clear. One such example is that graduations have traditionally been allowed to take place in churches and that a specific Christian hymn is sung. The National Agency stated that such a way of celebrating graduation may continue if it is the school staff, and not a priest, who leads the ceremony; it added that the Christian hymn has become a cultural element rather than a religious one, even though this has been criticized by families with other religious beliefs and by atheists.[33]

Another form of legal guidance comes from decisions of the supervisory authority, the Swedish School Inspectorate, which sometimes includes sanctions and whose decisions cannot be appealed.[34] In a case from 2019, the School Inspectorate made a directed supervision of a school in Jukkasjärvi, a sparsely populated municipality in northern Sweden, where a religious group called *laestadians* had come to exert a great influence over the school's teaching. During the inspection it became clear that various compulsory elements about sex education, dancing, drama, and music were not practiced in accordance with the curriculum; further, the school, consistent with the laestadians' own beliefs, did not convey the values of all people equally and, for instance, did not teach knowledge and understanding of those with different sexual orientations.[35]

The School Inspectorate directed school authorities, on the threat of administrative fines, to rectify the deficiencies because the religious interpretation of the content of the education that led to the current situation was not in keeping with either the curriculum or the law. At the follow-up, the supervisory authority concluded that the municipality had taken its responsibility and had changed the teaching back to the way it was before the religious group had "intervened."

What is particularly interesting about the case is that it concerns a public school in a small town where a religious group, with no formal connections to the school, exerted a great influence through indirect threats of social isolation if the teachers did not adapt teaching based on the group's own values rather than those conveyed through the curriculum. Even so, the School Inspectorate held the municipality to account because its officials were responsible for the teaching.

Another case, which has been a "serial" in the Swedish administrative courts for many years, concerned an Orthodox Jewish family's eventual right to homeschool their children in accordance with their religious beliefs.[36] From the family's point of view, the basic question was both how religion was taught and how it was taken into account with regard to the teaching of all other school subjects. However, the judicial system instead considered other aspects of the curriculum because there is little room, from a legal point of view, to consider precisely the question of how religion is taught, especially in cases where religion can be considered to encompass all aspects of life.

The parents had moved to Sweden in 1991 and started a private school six years later, primarily for their own children. The school was closed down in 2007 when the number of students was considered too low and because the parents had been homeschooling their own children with help from a Jewish online school. This setup was approved by the municipality until the new Education Act came into force in 2011, at which time the rules about homeschooling changed. An important factor behind the parental appeal of the decision of municipal officials not to allow homeschooling any longer was that the children, by their peculiarities, could not be safe in ordinary school environments. Further, the parents complained that the actions of municipal officials violated Article 9 of the ECHR.

The Administrative Court rejected the parental appeal, but the Court of Appeal granted them the right to homeschool their children with reference to the Education Act, which states that the teaching can be given in a different way if there are very special reasons to do so.[37] The court thereby considered the parents' religious peculiarities as constituting such special reasons even though the preliminary work to the provision – which is of great legal significance in the Swedish legal system – states that a school should be comprehensive, factual, and thereby designed for all students to participate, regardless of which religious or philosophical views they and their parents or guardians accept.[38]

Municipal authorities appealed the judgment to the highest administrative court, where the case was set for trial in 2013. Although the education the children were receiving was considered a satisfactory alternative to ordinary school, the court pointed out the importance of their receiving social training in a social context. The issue of "social training" has been tried in court in previous cases and includes, in addition to meeting with other children from other backgrounds, the importance of a critical perspectives on different school subjects, such as the meaning and relevance of religion.[39] Against this background, the Court did not consider that there were such exceptional reasons as to override that need and that homeschooling should not be allowed.

The case later began anew when the family continued to educate their children via homeschooling despite the previous decisions and court rulings.[40] In April 2014, municipal officials charged the family with threats of administrative fines to ensure that they fulfilled their duties at two designated municipal schools. When the family, on the same grounds as stated in the previous process, did not comply with the request, the municipal officials applied for the court to sentence the penalty. The district court, in December 2017, decided to impose a penalty on each parent of SEK 301,500 (approximately USD 30,000) for not complying with the school duty by ensuring the rights of their children to be educated.[41] The family appealed against the judgment, but their application was rejected in June 2018.[42]

The case shows that the right to education, free from religious connotations, trumps the freedom of religion when it comes to the setup of education. Also, the possibilities for homeschooling do not include religious placements, thereby demonstrating that it is not possible for parents to opt their children out of "secular schools" even if they are deeply religious.

Emerging Issues

The legal questions about the place of religion in Swedish compulsory education continue to grow as Swedish society itself is increasingly polarized. On the one hand, the increasing number of immigrants – and second-generation immigrants – with more vivid faiths than the average Swede, are asking for an increase in private schools with religious curricula for their children. On the other hand, advocates for a growing nationalism have started to apply a stricter view on secular and objective education as a "tool" for assimilation.

One such example of the latter is that two municipalities have initiated local policies that prohibit the use of a veil or headscarf, which in reality is targeting young Muslim women even though that is not mentioned in the decision.[43] Such policies are in direct violation of various laws and the municipalities have no mandate to issue such binding policies. Yet, municipal officials have still put the question up for a vote in the town council, where a majority voted for such a prohibition. For the street-level educational bureaucrats such as teachers and principals, that is a big problem because they find themselves in positions to either go against their employer, the municipality, that made the decision based on a democratic, local vote, or to possibly be charged with violating national laws and international conventions. This could be seen as a fragmentation of the legal landscape where the same rules do not apply all over the country, which, if it spreads to other areas of the law, may result in even bigger problems for the legal system and the Swedish people.

Another growing problem on the matter of religion is the number of requests for exemptions from participation in specific activities called for in the curriculum, such as dancing, singing, and swimming, due to religious reasons. The Education Act addresses the possibility that parents and students may obtain exemptions, but it is unclear about the extent to which religious beliefs can qualify as special as called for in the law. Even more troubling is that it is principals who make such decisions themselves. In private schools with religious profiles, it would be more likely that principals grant such exemptions if they are in line with the religious believes that the school stands for and there is hardly any supervision on these matters. Also, in public schools there have been cases where principals do not want to get in conflict with religious minority groups and have therefore granted exemptions, even though they do not believe in such segregating measures, because they are in direct violation of the curriculum.[44]

Besides these two issues regarding religion and education, the National Agency for Education is investigating whether the subject of religion should remain in the curriculum in its current form or if there should be a reduction.[45] A growing number people believe that Sweden, like France, should completely remove religion as a school subject and more clearly distance itself from all religious expressions in the school environment – including religious items of dress worn by students that are currently protected by the Constitution.

Conclusion

Sweden is an odd bird in terms of the state's relation to religion, at least compared to other northern European countries. With a development where religion has largely come to be regarded as "individual" rather than social, while education is seen as a key task for the state, religious freedom has a relatively weak position in relation to compulsory schooling and the right to education on a scientific basis.

Religious freedom means, in reality, that an individual cannot be prevented from acquiring a certain belief and exercising it privately. Conversely, religious practice in public contexts is subject to specified restrictions, not least in schools. Although Sweden's educational system, through the publicly funded private schools, enables education in accordance with specific beliefs, the teaching is strictly limited to the content of the curricula. At the same time, both religious attributes and religious customs must be strongly linked to the choices of individual students or children rather than those of their parents or guardians. In public schools, there is no opportunity whatsoever for religious imprinting of either teaching or education at large.

Religious education in Sweden can be seen partly as directly linked to the teaching of religion and partly from a religious perspective to consider all school subjects through the scope of religious belief. Although the latter is a natural part of both education and teaching for sections of society that have chosen to live more active religious lives, their opportunities are limited by the requirement of objectivity and impartiality in the Constitution that is reflected in both it, the Education Act, and the curricula.

A seemingly increasing polarization between secular and religious forces in Sweden has raised the issue of religious expression and religious teaching wherein incompatible values have come into conflict with each other. The public leaves little or no room for religious "character" of the teaching which, in turn, has resulted in a variety of legal conflicts. Secular and the divine law are in some respects incompatible, and in a pronounced secular state the secular law always takes precedence. For religious parents or guardians and their children, though, the relationship between the worldly and the divine can be the opposite, where the divine is given precedence, which implies a somewhat "silent revolt" against the current system.

In a legal system such as Sweden, where the courts generally play a minor role in education-related issues, even when linked to religious matters, the various state authorities play a central role. Because these authorities, like the representatives of the schools, are bound by the requirements of objectivity and impartiality and have directives to strive for all schools to comply with the requirements of science, the curriculum trumps religious freedom as understood in a broader perspective. However, through the supervision of school activities, it is noted that the conditions in practice do not always correspond to these ambitions. Although there are direct prohibitions and associated sanctions, there are attempts to proselytize on the part of teachers, as well as religious considerations in teaching, both in terms of content and the form of teaching. The law, therefore, is not fully capable of keeping religious elements out of schools in Sweden.

Cases

Gothenburg Court of Appeal, 207–18
Gothenburg Court of Appeal, 208–18
Supreme Administrative Court, HFD 2013 ref 49
Supreme Administrative Court, RÅ 1990 ref. 60
Supreme Administrative Court, RÅ 1990 ref. 111
Supreme Court, NJA 2005 p. 805

Notes

1. Arbetarbladet, Tierps skola anklagas för att försöka omvända barn till islam – här är föräldrarnas fina gest efter hatdrevet mot lärarna, *Arbetarbladet*, March 5, 2020.
2. See, for instance, Tierps kommun reagerar på uppgifter om muslimsk konvertering – hotar att polisanmäla kritiker, *Samhällsnytt*, March 5, 2020.
3. The School Inspectorate's decision SI-2019:3330.
4. Hällebergs school in Ljungskile, Jukkasjärvi school in Jukkasjärvi, and Labora School in Långaryd.
5. Ordinance (SKOLFS, 2010, 37) about the curriculum for primary school, preschool class and leisure home (2011), revised 2018 ("The Curriculum").
6. Instrument of Government (1974, 152), Ch. 8, sec. 1.
7. The Education Act (2010, 800), Ch. 1, sec. 5 and The Curriculum, p. 7.
8. David Thurfjell, Det gudlösa folket – De postkristna svenskarna och religionen, *Norstedts*, 2015, 60–62.
9. Medlemsutveckling 2018–2019, per församling, kommun och län samt riket, p. 35.
10. www.un.org/en/universal-declaration-human-rights/index.html.
11. Klas Roth, Artikel 26: ett principiellt yttrande om utbildning, In: Thomas Englund (ed.), *Utbildning som medborgerlig rättighet: Föräldrarätt eller barns rätt eller?* (Daidalos, 2011), 17–32. Retrieved from oru.diva-portal.org/smash/get/diva2:382356/FULLTEXT03.pdf
12. www.unicef.org/child-rights-convention/convention-text-childrens-version.

13. www.echr.coe.int/Documents/Convention_ENG.pdf.
14. Ninni Wahlström, Internationella konventioner och debatten om friskolor i Sverige, in Thomas Englund (ed.), *Utbildning som medborgerlig rättighet: Föräldrarätt eller barns rätt eller?* (Daidalos, 2011), 87–128. Retrieved from oru.diva-portal.org/smash/get/diva2:382356/FULLTEXT03.pdf.
15. Prop. 1953:32 on the Ratification of the Additional Protocol to the Council of Europe Convention on the Protection of Human Rights and Fundamental Freedoms, p. 11.
16. Instrument of Government (1974, 152), Ch. 2, sec. 1 and 20–25.
17. Ibid., sec. 21.
18. Ibid., Ch. 1, sec. 9.
19. Education Act (2010, 800).
20. Education Act (2010, 800), Ch. 1, sec. 6–7.
21. Labour Court, Judgment nr 51/18 and The Discrimination Act (2008, 567), Ch. 1, sec. 4, 6 and The Education Act (2010, 800), Ch. 6, sec. 2.
22. This is further described in the syllabus or curriculum about religion in various parts of this chapter.
23. Edgar Almén, Presentation and Problem Inventory: Religious Education in Sweden, in Edgar Almén and Hans Christian Øster (eds.), *Religious Education in Great Britain, Sweden and Russia* (Linköping: University Electronic Press, 2000), 89.
24. Instrument of Government (1974, 152), Ch. 2, Sec. 1.
25. Ibid., in relation to Ch. 2, sec. 20–21.
26. Ibid., Ch. 2, sec. 1.
27. www.echr.coe.int/Documents/Convention_ENG.pdf.
28. Instrument of Government, Ch. 2, sec. 19.
29. Supreme Court, NJA, 2005, 805, pp. 14–15.
30. The Education Act (2010, 800), Ch. 10, sec. 30, 35.
31. Ibid., Ch. 1, sec. 9.
32. European Convention on Human Rights, Article 35.
33. The National Agency for Education, *Skol- och förskoleverksamhet i kyrkan eller annan religiös lokal, juridisk vägledning*, 2012, 5. Retrieved from https://www.riksdagen.se/sv/dokument-lagar/dokument/kommittedirektiv/konfessionella-inslag-i-skolvasendet_H6B115.
34. The Education Act 2010, Ch. 28, sec. 18.
35. The School Inspectorate's decision, 430–2018:11604.
36. Supreme Administrative Court, HFD 2013 ref 49.
37. The Education Act 2010, Ch. 24, sec. 23.
38. Prop. 2009/10:165. The new Education Act – for knowledge, freedom of choice and security, pp. 523–524, 885.
39. Supreme Administrative Court, RÅ 1990 ref. 111 and RÅ 1990 ref. 60.
40. Gothenburg Court of Appeal, cases no. 207–18, 208–218.
41. Ibid., 10.
42. Ibid., 1.
43. See decisions by the municipalities in Staffanstorp and Skurup.
44. SOU 2019:64 *Nya regler för skolor med konfessionell inriktning*, 126–127.
45. The National Agency for Education, Dnr 2019:173, 2019:770.

16 Religious Education in Taiwan's Public Schools

Chih-Hung Chou

Introduction

Taiwan is a free, pluralistic society in which people practice different religious beliefs and belong to many religious organizations that are active in society. Because the Constitution and government of Taiwan guarantee religious freedom, all faiths are free to spread and develop. On the basis of the freedom of religion guaranteed by the Constitution,[1] no state religion has been established, and all religions in Taiwan are equally protected and directly guaranteed.

During the late 19th century, Christian missionaries introduced the earliest Western-style education in Taiwan by opening schools based on their own religious purposes. Consequently, Taiwan's first private schools, including Oxford College in 1882, Tamsui Girls School in 1884, and Chang Jung Senior High School in Tainan in 1885,[2] were operated by missionaries and staff from Christian denominations to provide religious education for students. In the early days of Japanese rule, religious education in church schools was still respected and remained available until the end of World War II.

In the years since 1945, Taiwan's original Japanese-era educational system was replaced by the education system of the Republic of China. This transplanted educational system from China had been influenced since the 1920s by the Movement for the Repossession of the Power to Education, that is the Non-Christian Movement and/or the Anti-Christian Movement. The tradition against religious education was thus formed. Religious education based on faith-based teachings was prohibited not only in public schools but also in private schools. Even schools run by religious groups were required to provide secular instruction while having to avoid espousing religious beliefs or making courses on religion, such as those on religious teachings, mandatory for all of their students. As a result, religious education was not only unavailable in public schools at all levels in Taiwan, but it was also restricted even in private schools that the various religious groups had established.

The situation with regard to religious education in Taiwan has changed since the beginning of the 21st century because the restrictions that had been placed on religious education in private schools have been relaxed. Still, religious education in public schools is subject to strict limits.

In light of the guarantee of freedom of religion, including freedom of religious education, in the 1947 Constitution of the Republic, this chapter examines the status of the latter in Taiwan. More specifically, the chapter examines whether officials in public schools are free to implement religious education and, if so, what kind of programs they can permit. As such, the remainder of this chapter focuses on the relationship between and among the Constitution, various statutes, and religious education in Taiwan's public schools.

The Constitution of Taiwan and Religious Education

Article 13 of the Constitution of the Republic of China, promulgated in 1947, guarantees that "[t]he people shall have freedom of religious belief" in accordance with the J. Y. Interpretation No. 573.[3] Article 13 thus refers to the freedom people have to believe, or not to believe, in any religion of their choice as well as the freedom to participate, or not participate, in any religious activities. Further, it means that the state shall neither encourage nor forbid any specific religion, just as it may not grant favorable or unfavorable treatment to any people who profess specific religious beliefs. The scope of this protection extends to the freedom of inner belief, freedom of religious activity, and freedom of religious association.[4]

The constitutional guarantee of the people's freedom of religious belief in Article 13 of the Constitution is designed to preserve self-development and self-realization of the human spirit of the people as well as making social and cultural diversity a tangible reality. Therefore, as noted above, the government of the Republic of China and its officials shall abide by the principles of neutrality and tolerance neither by encouraging or forbidding any specific religion nor affording favorable or unfavorable treatment to any people having specific beliefs.

At the same time, Article 7 of the Constitution guarantees that "[a]ll citizens of the Republic of China, irrespective of sex, religion, race, class, or party affiliation, shall be equal under the law." Therefore, if the state, though various enactments and/or actions of officials, forbids a specific religion or treats it and its followers unfavorably, such actions would run counter to the principles of religious neutrality and religious equality.

It is important to note that while the Constitution does not mention freedom of religious education, general constitutional doctrine ensures the guarantee of freedom of religious belief as including multiple rights. Most notably, these guarantees protect freedom of religious belief, covering both belief and nonbelief in religion. Moreover, this covers the freedom not to express an attitude as to which one's religious beliefs, or lack thereof, are based, the freedom to propagate one's own religion, and, importantly for this chapter, freedom of religious education. This last item includes the freedoms to implement religious education and to receive, or refrain from participating in, religious education. Finally, this Article introduces the principle of separation of church and state that is prominent in and the guarantee of freedom of religious conduct.[5]

As reflected in Figure 16.1, the so-called religious education implies both a broad and a narrow meaning.[6] Broadly distinguished, religious education includes religious knowledge education or academic research, religious sentiment education, and sectarian education. Religious education in a broad sense includes religious sentiment education and sectarian education carried out by specific religious sects for the transmission of their particular teachings.

In the narrow sense, religious education includes the teachings of a specific religion or sect for the study of that religion and providing instruction designed to prepare priests or religious personnel of particular religions. Here it is important to acknowledge that religious sentiment education and sectarian education belong to, or are covered by, the notion of religious teaching whereas religious knowledge education or academic research comes under the heading of teaching about religion.[7]

Another important point emerges with regard to the state in Article 7 of the Constitution, according to which "All citizens of the Republic of China, irrespective of sex, religion, race, class, or party affiliation, shall be equal before the law." Clearly, then, religion must be treated equally under the law. Therefore, the state, through its laws and officials, must do two important things. First, the state must adopt the principle

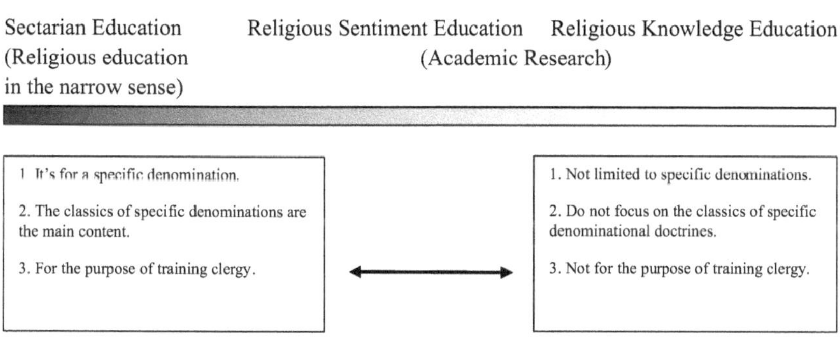

Figure 16.1 The Types of Religious Education

Source: Chou, Chih-Hung, Religious Education in the Stage of Higher Education, in *Academic Freedom and the Legal System of Higher Education* (Taipei: Higher Education Publishing Company, 2002), pp. 315–316.

of separation of church and state, maintaining a distance from religion as well as not supporting or opposing particular religions. Second, the state must adopt the position of religious neutrality toward all religions by demonstrating an attitude of tolerance with regard to the religious beliefs of the people such that governmental, including school, officials cannot arbitrarily interfere with their activities unless there is a legal basis present and legitimate reasons for doing so.

Under these provisions, the state must maintain religious neutrality in the establishment of public schools, meaning those supported by the public service budget, based on the principles of separation of church and state as well as equal treatment of religion. Because all nationals of Taiwan, irrespective of their religious beliefs, have the right to attend public schools based on their abilities, these students are likely to hold to different religious beliefs. As with the government, because they are ultimately state officials, administrators and other staff members in public schools must act based on the constitutional principles of religious neutrality and religious equality. Additionally, religious education, which embrace the teachings of the content of particular religions, cannot be offered in public schools unless educators act in accordance with the outline of the National Basic Education Curriculum of the state for 12 years. Under this curriculum, addressing education on religion and the education of understanding religion is assumed to be teaching about religion.

The Educational Fundamental Act in Taiwan and Religious Education

Since the Movement for the Repossession of the Power to Education in the 1920s, the educational system in the Republic of China has adopted a restrictive attitude towards religious education.[8] To this end, the Beijing government set out "the rule of accreditation for Foreigners donation schools"[9] in 1925. This law stipulated both that school officials may not have the goal of disseminating religion (Art. 5) and religious subjects may not be included in compulsory subjects (Art. 6).

Clause 8 of the Private Schools Ordinance of 1933[10] states that

> Private schools are not allowed to take religious subjects as compulsory subjects and to do religious propaganda in their classrooms. In schools established by religious groups, students may not be forced or persuaded to attend if there is a religious ceremony. Religious ceremonies are not allowed in primary schools and their equivalents.

Following revisions, the text changed but the basic content is not much different.

When the Private Schools Act was enacted in 1974, its Article 8 stipulated that "private schools are not allowed to take religious subjects as compulsory subjects. Students may not be forced to participate in religious ceremonies in schools established by religious groups."[11] When it was amended in 1984, Article 8 of the Private Schools Act (1984) read, "Private universities or colleges, with the approval of the Ministry of Education, may establish religious colleges or institutions. Private schools may not compel students to participate in any religious ceremony."[12] In practice, though, in line with Article 2 of the Rules of the Private Schools Act,

> religious colleges or departments established under Article 8, paragraph 1, of this Act shall be for the purpose of religious academic research and shall not be aimed at the educational purpose of a particular religion or the training of clergy of a particular religion.[13]

As such, restrictions remain on religious education in private schools.

Along the same line, Article 6 of the Educational Fundamental Act, enacted in 1999, mandates that "Education shall be based on the principle of impartiality."[14] The Act continues:

> Schools may not engage in promotional or other activities for any specific political group. Neither the competent education administrative authority nor any school may force school administrative personnel, teachers, or students to participate in any political group or political activity.[15]

However, this provision is considered to be in violation of the freedom of religion guaranteed by the Covenant on Civil and Political Rights because it limits individual religious rights.[16]

Pursuant to another law, the Private Schools Act, Section 9, which was separately amended in 2004 declares:

> A private university or religious legal person who, in order to train clergy and religious personnel and grant religious degrees, shall apply to the Ministry of Education in accordance with the relevant regulations and, upon approval, establish a religious college.

Moreover, officials in private schools may not compel students to participate in any religious ceremony (para. 2).[17]

Article 7 of the Private Schools Act, amended in 2008, stipulates that officials in "Private schools may not compel students to attend any religious ceremony or to take religious courses." Article 8 maintains that officials of a "school or religious legal person may apply to the Ministry of Education for permission to establish religious colleges in order to train clergy and religious personnel and to grant a religious degree."[18] Consequently, when religious colleges were allowed to open, they had the opportunity to allow for religious education and granting degrees for the study of religion.

Thus, the Educational Fundamental Act Article 6 was amended in 2013 to read:

> (1) Education shall be based on the principle of impartiality.
> (2) Schools may not engage in promotional or other activities for any specific political group. Neither the competent education administrative authority nor any school may force school administrative personnel, teachers, or students to participate in any political group or political activity.
> (3) Public schools may not engage in promotional or other activities for any specific religion or belief. Neither the competent education administrative authority nor any public school may force school administrative personnel, teachers, or students to participate in any religious activity.
> (4) Private schools may organize specific religious activities aligned with the purpose for which the school was established or with the specific nature of the school; they shall respect the wishes of school administrative personnel, teachers and students to participate in such activities, and may not treat any person in a discriminatory way because they do not participate. However, religious colleges shall be governed by the Private School Law.[19]

From the time of this law's enactment, officials in private schools other than the religious colleges may permit specified religious activities consistent with the purposes of their institutions or the nature of running their schools. At the same time, though, these officials must respect the will of administrative personnel, teachers, and students to participate and shall not treat any of them in a discriminatory manner if they choose not to participate because adopting such an approach safeguards the freedom of religion of administrators, teachers, and students. However, religious neutrality should remain in public schools such that school employees may not distribute propaganda, proselytize, or engage in activities for specific religious beliefs. As a corollary, under the provisions of this act, school administrators, teachers, and/or students must not be compelled to participate in any religious activity. This, of course, also includes the inability to carry out religious education or religious teaching.

Public Schools and Religious Education

Public schools are not permitted to allow their employees to distribute propaganda, proselytize, or engage in activities designed to carry out religious education for specific religious beliefs in accordance with the Educational Fundamental Act.[20] Still, public schools inevitably have religious content in accordance with the provisions of the Outline of the 12-year National Basic Education Curriculum.[21] As a part of social life and beliefs related to the development and self-realization of individual personalities, religion classes must provide relevant content in education to meet the needs of students. Therefore, the religious education implemented in public schools should mainly be teaching about religion and the education of understanding religion rather than the practice of religion; this approach is called teaching about religion.

Religious Education in the Formal Curriculum of General Public Schools

In accordance with the Outline of the 12-year National Basic Education Curriculum,[22] in the field of social learning, teachers must emphasize that students "understand and respect the uniqueness and subjectivity of the historical development of different cultures, religions, ethnic groups, races and genders."[23] Regarding the life education in the field of comprehensive activities, it is important that students can master philosophy, life and death issues, and the basic meaning of religion as well as its relationship to life. Teaching students in this manner should help them to establish their ultimate beliefs in life as they learn about the views of religious or ethnic beliefs with regard to suffering and death as well as the perspectives of different disciplines or religions on personality integration and spiritual cultivation. In so doing, the 12-year National Basic Education Curriculum should provide guidance on the content of religion in education.

Religious Activities in the Informal Curriculum of General Public Schools

As noted, religious classes or religious teachings are not allowed in public schools. Even so, religious groups often seek to promote religious beliefs or teachings through various activities in public schools.[24] These activities usually occur outside of the official curriculum of public schools, such as during morning time before class, after-school activities or after-school care time, and are provided by volunteers who are not school employees. At present, the cooperation between officials in religious groups and in public schools is aimed at assisting in character education, moral education, life education, and gender equality education.

Controversial activities have, for example, been promoted in public schools by the Buddhist Compassion Relief Tzu Chi Foundation in its teaching of "Jing Si aphorisms." There are also local chiefs who use public schools to conduct Buddhist examinations.[25]

In another incident, in October of 2019, some worried parents and representatives of the political parties conducted a joint press conference, "Classroom or Church?" questioning the Rainbow Moms, a group that purportedly helped out in primary and secondary schools during morning time. The concerns arose because the Rainbow Moms are a part of a strong religious group, the Rainbow Family Life Education Association, which claimed that their entry into the schools was a kind of "life education" and that there was no religious stance on campus activities. However, this content of the "life education" the Rainbow Moms provided was reflected in religious songs such as "There's no Santa Claus, only my Lord Jesus."[26]

In response to the activities of the Rainbow Moms, Taiwan's Ministry of Education repeatedly stated that Article 6 of the Educational Fundamental Act is clear that "public schools may not engage in propaganda or activities for a particular religion or belief. The competent educational administration and public schools shall not compel school administrators, teachers and students to participate in any religious activity."[27]

Public Schools Commissioned by Religious-Related Groups

Another recent challenge has emerged with regard to religious education in public schools. This incident occurred when local government officials, responding to the provisions of the Act Governing the Commissioning of the Operation of Public Schools at Senior High School Level or Below to the Private Sector for Experimental Education[28] entrusted the operations of public schools to private individuals and groups. Because these commissioned private groups include various religious organizations, it seems likely that officials in the entrusted public schools may inevitably develop religious curricular content or educational objectives.

The first of two questions that arose with regard to these commissioned schools addressed whether there is a risk that local governments and public schools will violate Article 6 of the Educational Fundamental Act in permitting such arrangements. The second concerns whether private trustees of such public schools can be restricted from being religious groups and whether they should be committed to the avoidance of distributing propaganda, engaging in proselytization, or conducting activities associated with particular religions.

Content and Limitation of Religious Education in Public Schools

Public schools subject to the principle of separation of church and state and the requirements of religious neutrality are not allowed to offer religious teachings of specific religions. However, educators in public schools are not completely prohibited from teaching about religion mainly because they should think about the need to implement religious education from the perspective of students' right to education. Educators should also allow some education about religion because they need to consider the need to do so from the perspective of the rights of students to be educated.

Based on the needs of individual personality development and self-realization in students, the choice of places as well as the methods and patterns of education should be an extension or continuation of the right to education. To this end, the choice of religious education should belong to the exercise of the right to education and be guaranteed by the Constitution. Of course, the opportunity to take advantage of religious education is exercised by the parents or local guardians of students in light of the best interests of their children. Needless to say, the state should respect the choice of parents or their legal representatives.[29]

Another rationale supporting the inclusion of some teaching about religion in public schools is that in a multicultural society, it should be a subject of great significance not only to the "religious self-realization" of religious believers. At the same time, such classes should be useful to those students who have no religious beliefs or different religious beliefs. Instruction on this subject matter should be provided through the implementation of religious knowledge education for the different faiths students and their families practice with the intent of generating understanding and tolerance – a main goal of modern education.

It is important to recall that education is intended to promote mutual understanding, respect, and care for all people as well as different religious beliefs and religious groups. Appropriate religious knowledge and education in students is thus necessary to achieve this goal. Therefore, acting in a manner consistent with the law, educators in public and private schools should develop curricula that takes the ages, maturity levels, and judgments of their students into account. With this information, educational officials should add appropriate content in their religious education curricula that comply with the principle of separation of church and state. Moreover, educators should respect the freedom of religion of students not to be coerced by acting in a manner similar to the German *Prinzip der Freiwilligkeit* (voluntary principle), thereby respecting the wishes, or personal choices, of students and their parents.

In order to maintain religious neutrality in public schools, administrators and teachers are obliged to avoid or limit the ability of religious and related groups or individuals to use volunteer and noncurricular time to engage in propaganda or proselytizing type activities in order to promulgate the teachings or values of their particular religions. Otherwise, if educators in public schools fail to maintain neutrality, they risk the possibility of violating the principle of equality in Article 7 of the Constitution, Article 13 of the principle of freedom of religious belief, and the principle of religious neutrality under Article 6 of the Educational Fundamental Act.

An Emerging Issue: Religious Groups Interfere With the Educational Content of Public and Private School Curricula

Attempts by religious groups to influence the content of school curricula continue. For example, in the consolidated petitions of Huei-Tai-12674 filed by Chia-Wei Chi and Huei-Tai-12771 filed by the Taipei city government regarding the constitutionality of same-sex marriage, the Constitutional Court announced J.Y. Interpretation No. 748 on May 24, 2017. The heart of the ruling of the Court is as follows:

> the provisions of Chapter II on Marriage of Part IV on Family of the Civil Code do not allow two persons of the same sex to create a permanent union of intimate and exclusive nature for the purpose of living a common life. The said provisions, to the extent of such failure, are in violation of the Constitution's guarantees of both the people's freedom of marriage under Article 22 and the people's right to equality under Article 7. The authorities concerned shall amend or enact the laws as appropriate in accordance with the ruling of this Interpretation within two years from the date of announcement of this Interpretation. It is within the discretion of the authorities concerned to determine the formality for achieving the equal protection of the freedom of marriage. If the authorities concerned fail to amend or enact the laws as appropriate within the said two years, two persons of the same sex who intend to create the said permanent union shall be allowed to have their marriage registration effectuated at the authorities in charge of household registration, by submitting a written document signed by two or more witnesses in accordance with the said Marriage Chapter.[30]

This decision made Taiwan the first country in Asia to legalize same-sex marriage. However, because religious groups raised objections to same-sex marriage, a referendum was put before the voters as "Case 11 of the National Referendum: Do you agree that the Ministry of Education and schools should not implement education about LGBTQ as stipulated in the Enforcement Rules for the Gender Equity Education Act[31] at primary and secondary levels?" The referendum, which proposed to ban education about the rights and status of those in the LGBTQ community in gender equity education in public and private schools, was approved with 67% of the votes.[32] Thus, this referendum was an example of religious groups' interference in educational content not only in public schools but also in private educational institutions.

As a result of the referendum, religious groups also objected to content about same-sex marriages in school curricula. Therefore, because the referendum was legally binding on the Ministry of Education, it amended the provisions of the Enforcement Rules for the Gender Equity Education Act[33] and deleted the terms relating to education about persons in the LGBTQ community. Even so, in schools, it is up to the teachers whether the content of gender equality education actually includes education about LGBTQ.[34]

Conclusion

Taiwan guarantees freedom of religious belief and the rights of students to education in compliance with the constitutional principle of separation of church and state in addition to the principle of religious neutrality and tolerance. Officials in Taiwan's public schools can permit teaching about religion in the implementation of religious education, however, offering knowledge of religion in curricula and fostering tolerance among students to respect different religions. Consequently, officials in public schools cannot permit the distribution of propaganda or proselytizing activities by or on behalf of particular religions. Further, students cannot be forced to accept particular religious beliefs or participate in religious ceremonies, teachings, or activities based on specific religions if they do not wish to do so.

At the same time, educators in private schools may, in accordance with their religions, distribute propaganda and/or engage in proselytizing activities of their faiths, practice religious teachings, and even establish religious colleges to train clerics and other key personnel. This distinction is permissible because public and private schools have different legal guarantees and restrictions available to them with regard to the implementation of religious education – another concrete manifestation of the state's neutral and tolerant attitude towards religion.

To sum up, the relationship between religion and education in Taiwan remains complex. All religious groups wish to spread their doctrines through education because they have been able to offer some degree of religious education through the establishment of private schools. Public schools that are, on the other hand, required to adhere to religious neutrality cannot avoid constantly being tested by religious groups and the influences they exercise in Taiwan. Therefore, in the future, Taiwan will likely continue to face many disputes and challenges relating to religious education in public schools.

Notes

1. The Constitution of Taiwan. Retrieved from https://law.moj.gov.tw/Eng/LawClass/LawAll.aspx?PCode=A0000001. For a more annotated version, see Retrieved from www.constituteproject.org/constitution/Taiwan_2005.pdf?lang=en.

2. See Chih-Hung Chou, *Research on the Freedom of Private Education and the Legal System of Private Schools* (Taipei: Xuelin Cultural Business Co., Ltd., November 2005), 77.
3. https://cons.judicial.gov.tw/jcc/en-us/jep03/show?expno=573.
4. See J. Y. Interpretation No. 490. Retrieved from https://cons.judicial.gov.tw/jcc/en-us/jep03/show?expno=490.
5. Ji-dong Lin, *Interpretation of the Constitution of the Republic of China, Article-by-Article* (Taipei: San-min Book Co., 1982), Vol. I, revised in the first edition, 194–196.
6. According to the analysis of Japanese scholars, the content of religious education usually must touch on three parts, namely: religious knowledge education, religious sentiment education and sectarian education, or, to divide religious education into a broader range of religious education, including the abovementioned three, and specific sectarian education, narrower religious education. See Hiroshi Satoshi, The Idea of Religious Education, compiled by the Japanese Religious Society, *The Theory and Practice of Religious Education* (Tokyo: Suzuki Press, 1985), 12–36.
7. See Chih-Hung Chou, Religious Education in the Stage of Higher Education, in: *Academic Freedom and the Legal System of Higher Education* (Taipei: Higher Education Publishing Company, 2002), 315–316.
8. Chou, *Research on the Freedom of Private Education and the Legal System of Private Schools*, 65–66.
9. Ibid.
10. There is no official English version, which in Chinese is「私立學校，不得以宗教科目為必修科，及在課內做宗教宣傳。宗教團體設立之學校內如有宗教儀式，不得強迫或勸誘學生參加；在小學及其同等學校並不得舉行宗教儀式。」The Ministry of Education ed., *Education Acts and Rules* (Taipei: Zheng-zhong Book Company, 1953), 31.
11. There is no official English version, which in Chinese is「私立學校不得以宗教科目為必修科目。宗教團體設立之學校內如有宗教儀式，不得強迫學生參加。」the Act in Chinese. Retrieved from https://lis.ly.gov.tw/lglawc/lawsingle?0063474D9C7F000000000000000000A00000000200FFFFFD00^01721063110500^00068001001
12. Ibid.
13. As amended in 2011, the Act. Retrieved from https://law.moj.gov.tw/ENG/LawClass/LawAll.aspx?pcode=H0020045.
14. Ibid.
15. Ibid.
16. www.ohchr.org/EN/ProfessionalInterest/Pages/CCPR.aspx.
17. https://law.moj.gov.tw/ENG/LawClass/LawAll.aspx?pcode=H0020001. The Private Schools Act Enforcement Rules. Retrieved from https://law.moj.gov.tw/ENG/LawClass/LawAll.aspx?pcode=H0020002.
18. There is no official English version which in Chinese is 第七條：「私立學校不得強制學生參加任何宗教儀式或修習宗教課程。但宗教研修學院不在此限。」第八條第一項：「學校法人為培養神職人員及宗教人才，並授予宗教學位，得向教育部申請許可設立宗教研修學院；其他經宗教主管機關許可設立之法人，亦同。」. Article 7 of the Private Schools Act, amended in 2014, stipulates that "The private schools shall not force students to participate in any religious rituals or take any religious courses. However, religious schools are not bound by this article." Retrieved from https://law.moj.gov.tw/ENG/LawClass/LawAll.aspx?pcode=H0020001.
19. https://law.moj.gov.tw/ENG/LawClass/LawAll.aspx?pcode=H0020045.
20. Ibid.

21. Curriculum Guidelines of 12-Year Basic Education, Ministry of Education, November 2014. Retrieved from http://english-taiwan.com/uploads/9/3/1/6/93160956/2019_curriculum_guideines_-_core_competencies.pdf. For a commentary on this curriculum, see Hao Chen and Hsin-Hsien Fan, *Education in Taiwan: The Vision and Goals of the 12-Year Curriculum* (The Brookings Institute, November 11, 2014). Retreived from www.brookings.edu/opinions/education-in-taiwan-the-vision-and-goals-of-the-12-year-curriculum/. For a commentary on this curriculum.
22. Ibid.
23. Ibid.
24. Min-feng Chen, *When the Holy Good of Religion Reaches the Campus, Why Should Education Be Passed?* September 19, 2016. Retrieved from https://opinion.udn.com/opinion/story/8806/1970114.
25. Journalist Wen-an Su, Shan-shan Wu reported from Taipei, 1995–06–18, *Christian Tribune*, "Recently, 800,000 primary and secondary school students in the country participated in the 'Fo Guang Shan World Buddhist Examination,' due to the high visibility and mobilization of the organizers, some schools semi-forced students to participate, causing parents' protests." Source: *Christian Tribune*. Retrieved from www.ct.org.tw/1141008#ixzz6PardbgBl.
26. Spy Mom, *No Problem Without Mission? The Doubts Behind the Rainbow Mom's 'Religious Propaganda' Entering Campus*, December 12, 2019. Retrieved from www.thenewslens.com/article/126849; Public News Network, *Parents Accuse Rainbow Love Association to Go to School to Promote Religion*, October 29, 2019. Retrieved from https://news.pts.org.tw/article/452336.
27. https://law.moj.gov.tw/ENG/LawClass/LawAll.aspx?pcode=H0020045.
28. This act is retrieved from https://law.moj.gov.tw/ENG/LawClass/LawAll.aspx?pcode=H0070062.
29. Universal Declaration of Human Rights Article, 26, "3. Parents Have a Prior Right to Choose the Kind of Education That Shall Be Given to Their Children." Retrieved from www.un.org/en/universal-declaration-human-rights/index.html. See also the International Covenant on Economic, Social and Cultural Rights, Article 13, "3. The States Parties to the Present Covenant undertake to have respect for the liberty of parents and, when applicable, legal guardians to choose for their children schools, other than those established by the public authorities, which conform to such minimum educational standards as may be laid down or approved by the State and to ensure the religious and moral education of their children in conformity with their own convictions." Retrieved from www.ohchr.org/EN/ProfessionalInterest/Pages/CCPR.aspx.
30. The opinion is retrieved from https://cons.judicial.gov.tw/jcc/en-us/jep03/show?expno=748.
31. The act is retrieved from https://law.moj.gov.tw/ENG/LawClass/LawAll.aspx?pcode=H0080067.
32. For coverage in English, see Michael K. Lavers, Taiwan Voters Reject Same-Sex Marriage in Referendum, *The Washington Blade*, November 28, 2018. Retrieved from www.washingtonblade.com/2018/11/24/taiwan-voters-reject-same-sex-marriage-in-referendum/. For a story in Chinese, see retrieved from https://web.cec.gov.tw/referendum/cms/p_result/29618.
33. The Enforcement Rules for the Gender Equity Education Act (2012). Retrieved from https://law.moj.gov.tw/ENG/LawClass/LawAll.aspx?pcode=H0080068. Article 13 of the Enforcement Rules declares that the curriculum related to gender equity education referred to the second paragraph

of Article 17 of the Act shall cover courses on affective education, sex education, and education about LGBTQ to enhance students' gender equity consciousness.

34. Article 13 of the Enforcement Rules for the Gender Equity Education Act (2019): The curriculum related to gender equity education referred to the second paragraph of Article 17 of the Act shall cover courses on affective education, sex education, different gender, gender characteristics, gender temperaments, gender identity, and sexual orientation, and prevention and handling of sexual assault, sexual harassment, and sexual bullying on campus to enhance students' gender equity consciousness.

17 The Legal Basis of Religious Education in Turkey

Bilgen Kiral and Erkan Kiral

Introduction

People have some basic rights and freedoms that are inherent, meaning they cannot be delegated, cannot be given up, and cannot be replaced because they are essential to being human. One of the most important developments in the field of human rights flows from the promulgation of United Nations (UN) Universal Declaration of Human Rights (UDHR) in 1948. With this Declaration, the status of individual and group human rights gained importance as a cross-border, international issue mandating that national governments and leaders respect the rights of their citizens. Moreover, the subsequent widespread acceptance of such other international instruments as the European Convention on Human Rights (ECHR) and the European Union Charter of Fundamental Rights (EUCFR) led pioneering efforts in attempts to secure human rights for all.

During the 21st century, among the most important human rights are those to live freely, to education, to freedom of religion, and to thought and expression, as well as the right to establish associations. These rights are important because they can help to guarantee the fulfillment of individuals' spiritual needs. Yet, many wars and conflicts have been fought and violence continues to erupt over the lack of protections for such fundamental human rights as those to education and freedom of religion, the latter two being the subject of this chapter and book.

Aware of their importance, this chapter examines the rights to education and freedom of religion in Turkish schools. Following this introduction, the chapter highlights major international documents to which Turkey is a signatory nation. The chapter then examines the legal basis of religious education in primary, which includes what are traditionally called middle schools in other countries, and high schools in Turkey as well as *imam-hatip* schools in the national education system before briefly exploring an emerging issue. The chapter ends with a brief conclusion.

International Foundations of Religious Education

It is important to review some of the most important international documents to understand how they helped to provide the legal basis of religious education in Turkey. The underlying rights to freedom of religion and conscience began to find a place in international texts in the middle of the 20th century.

The UN Charter (1945), the UDHR (1948), the ECHR (1950), the United Nations Convention on the Rights of the Child (UNCRC, 1989), and the Declaration on the Elimination of All Forms of Intolerance and of Discrimination Based on Religion or Belief (1981) are the most well-known international instruments signed by Turkey's leaders and approved by their counterparts in many countries. Moreover, Turkey has adhered to these international documents in establishing its national legal texts. As such, the remainder of this section briefly reviews key elements of these documents as they relate to freedom of religion and conscience.

United Nations Charter

The Charter, also known as the UN Treaty, was signed on June 26, 1945, by the leaders of 51 countries, including Turkey; it entered into force on October 24, 1945. The first article of the Charter establishes its intent "to achieve international cooperation in solving international problems of an economic, social, cultural, or humanitarian character, and in promoting and encouraging respect for human rights and fundamental freedoms for all without distinction as to race, sex, language, or religion." As can be understood from this article, one of the aims of the UN Charter is to ensure that everyone benefits from human rights and fundamental freedoms without any discrimination based on religion.

Universal Declaration of Human Rights

Article 2 of the UDHR, which was accepted as one of 30 articles in the session of the UN General Assembly in Paris on December 10, 1948, prohibits all discrimination on various grounds, including religion. Freedom of religion and conscience are covered under a separate heading in Article 18; pursuant to this article, individuals have the right to change their religions or faiths while everyone can teach and practice their faiths and explain them to others. In short, Article 18 guarantees that individuals have the right to live their religious faiths as they wish.

The UDHR contains explanatory statements on how religious teaching should be conducted. To this end, the second paragraph of Article 26 stipulates that teaching should encourage understanding and tolerance among all nations as well as their constituent racial, ethnic, and religious groups; paragraph 3 adds that parents have the right to determine the type of education their children will receive. The UDHR also identifies important rights for religious education in the context of freedom of religion and conscience. In particular, Article 18 protects areas of freedom including teaching, while Article 26, paragraph 3 affords parents the right to educate their children according to their religious beliefs.

European Convention on Human Rights

The leaders of the nation members of the Council of Europe signed the ECHR in Rome on November 4, 1950; it entered into force in 1953. Turkey ratified the Convention on March 10, 1954, but only conditionally because its leadership had reservations that it might violate the provisions of the law of Tevhîd-i Tedrîsât, or the Law on the Unification of its Educational System.

At the same time, though, Turkey recognized the rights of its citizens as individuals to petition to the European Court of Human Rights on January 28, 1987, accepting its compulsory jurisdiction on January 28, 1990 (Turan, 2012). Article 9 of the ECHR addresses freedom of religion and conscience. Article 9, paragraph 1, for example, acknowledges that

> [e]veryone has the right to freedom of thought, conscience and religion; this right includes freedom to change his religion or belief and freedom, either alone or in community with others and in public or private, to manifest his religion or belief, in worship, teaching, practice and observance.

Paragraph 2 then maintains that the

> [f]reedom to manifest one's religion or beliefs shall be subject only to such limitations as are prescribed by law and are necessary in a democratic society in the interests of public safety, for the protection of public order, health or morals, or for the protection of the rights and freedoms of others.

Declaration on the Elimination of All Forms of Intolerance and of Discrimination Based on Religion or Belief

The UN adopted this declaration in the General Assembly in resolution 36/55 of November 25, 1981. One of the most important articles of this declaration in the context of freedom of religion and belief is Article 5, which includes the rights of children. Paragraph 1 of Article 5 specifies that parents have the right to raise their children according to their religions or beliefs as well as to teach them the faith and the moral system in which they believe their young children should be raised. Beyond this,

Paragraph 2 dictates that children shall not be compelled to receive education contrary to their religious or philosophical beliefs and impliedly those of their parents.

Article 6 addresses freedom of thought and conscience. In so doing, this declaration is a clear expansion of other international documents on human rights and fundamental freedoms. From the point of view of religious education, this document clearly emphasizes a variety of freedoms from the establishment of religious institutions to the education of children in accordance with the religions or beliefs of their parents.

United Nations Convention on the Rights of the Child

The UN General Assembly unanimously approved the UNCRC on November 20, 1989; it entered into force on September 2, 1990. The UNCRC includes provisions relating to the civil, political, social, cultural, and human rights of children. Although the rights of children have been set out in various international documents, this convention is very important because it is the first legally binding independent document on its signatories in the history of law focusing exclusively on the rights of children.

Article 14 of the UNCRC directly addresses the rights of children to belief as follows:

1. States parties respect the right of the child to freedom of thought, conscience, and religion.
2. States parties respect the rights and duties of the parents and, when applicable, legal guardians, to provide direction to the child in the exercise of his or her right in a manner consistent with the evolving capacities of the child.
3. Freedom to manifest one's religion or beliefs may be subject only to such limitations as are prescribed by law and are necessary to protect public safety, order, health or morals, or the fundamental rights and freedoms of others.

When an overall assessment of the international dimension of freedom of religion and conscience is made, it can clearly be seen that all of the international documents that are in force in Turkey emphasize the rights of children to religious freedom either directly or indirectly. As to religious education, other international documents, especially Article 2 of the Additional Protocol No. 1 of the ECHR, afford individuals the right to religious education; it also protects those who do not have any religious beliefs and/or do not wish to receive religious education and training. In addition, parents have the right to request that state officials provide religious education and training for their children.

National Foundations of Religious Education

This section reviews the most important legal documents in Turkey addressing religious education for children: the Constitution of 1924, 1961, and 1982; the 1924 Law on Unity of Education (the Law of Tevhîd-i Tedrîsât); and the 1973 Basic Law of National Education. All of these instruments emerged after Turkey was proclaimed a Republic in 1923.

The Constitution of 1924

This was the first constitution adopted by the Grand National Assembly of Turkey after the establishment of the state of the Republic of Turkey; it was adopted on April 20, 1924. This Constitution, Chapter 5, Article 70, addresses freedom of religion and conscience: "As rights and freedoms, the privilege of people, conscience, thinking, speech, publication, travel, contract, work, possession, use of property and rights, assembly, establish association and partnership, are among the natural rights of Turks." Article 75 declares that "no one can be condemned for his philosophical belief, religion and sect. All kinds of religious ceremonies are free, not to be found in contradiction with security and decency ceremonies and laws." According to Article 80, "All kinds of education are free under the supervision and control of the government and within the framework of the law."

To reiterate, Article 70 guarantees freedom of religion and conscience while Article 75 safeguards freedom of religion, conscience, and worship along with making it clear that there are registration requirements or restrictions on religious education. Article 80 declares that all kinds of education, including religious education, must be provided under state supervision. In terms of religious education, these articles were among the most important legal sources until the 1961 Constitution was adopted even though it did not contain a special section; religious education was covered by the Law of Tevhid-i Tedrisat number 430, on March 3, 1924.

The Law of Tevhid-i Tedrisat, or the Unification of the Educational System

The Turkish Grand National Assembly adopted this law on March 3, 1924 after the nation was proclaimed a republic. The Tevhid-i Tedrisat law is one of the reform statutes protected under Article 174 of the 1982 Constitution, with the expression "it cannot be understood and interpreted as being against the Constitution." The relevant articles of the law of Tevhid-i Tedrisat constituting the source of important changes in state education in the Republic of Turkey are highlighted as:

> Article 1. All science and education institutions in Turkey are affiliated to the Ministry of National Education.
> Article 2. All madrasahs and schools managed by the Ser'iye and Efkaf Vekaleti, the Ministry of Religious Affairs and Pious Foundations, or private foundations affiliated with the Ministry of National Education.
> Article 3. In the budget of the Ministry of Religious Affairs and Pious Foundations, the savings belonging to schools and madrasahs will be transferred to the budget of the Ministry of National Education.
> Article 4. The Ministry of National Education will open a Faculty of Theology at the university to train high religious professionals; it will also open separate schools for religious services such as imamate and oratorics.
> Article 5. As of the date of the publication of this law, military secondary schools and high schools affiliated to the National Defense and orphanages which are linked to the Ministry of Health were affiliated to the Ministry of National Education with their budgets and training staff. The links of the education groups in these secondary and high schools was arranged by alternating between the ministries to which they belong to while the teachers who were affiliated with the army will continue in this relationship.

The importance of the Tevhid-i Tedrisat law is that educational institutions that provided education under the foundation of the Ottoman Empire were affiliated with Ministry of National Education. In this way, educational institutions became more institutionally democratic. Based on Article 4 of this law, a faculty of theology in Darulfunun and 29 imam-hatip (religious) schools, were established to train imam orators, preachers, and clergymen in 1924. These two educational institutions were later closed later due to lack of students. In terms of religious education, this law sought to address religious education in general schooling by integrating the two (Turan, 2012).

The Constitution of 1961

This Constitution, which came into effect after the military coup in 1960 and entered into force with Law 334 on July 9, 1961, has many articles regulating education. Paragraph two of Article 10 granted the state the duty to fulfill the conditions necessary for the development of the material and spiritual existence of its people. Paragraph one of Article 14 stated that everyone has the right to life, to develop their material and spiritual existence, and to freedom of person. Importantly, Article 50 guarantees state-provided education.

Article 19, which is very important in terms of the regulation of freedom of religion and conscience, reads:

> 1. Everyone has the freedom of conscience, religious belief, and opinion.
> 2. Worship, religious rites, and ceremonies, which are not contrary to public order or general morality or laws issued for these purposes, are free.
> 3. No one can be forced to worship, to participate in religious rites and ceremonies, and to explain his religious beliefs and convictions; cannot be condemned for his religious beliefs and convictions.
> 4. Religious education and learning depends only on the will of the individuals and on the wishes of the legal representatives of minors.
> 5. No one shall exploit or abuse religion or religious feelings or things religion held sacred by religion in any manner whatsoever, for the purpose of personal or political interest or influence, or for even partially basing the fundamental, social, economic, political, and legal order of the State on religious tenets.

These provisions apply to real and legal persons who fall outside of this prohibition or incite others in this way.

The 1961 Constitution was important because it advanced beyond the 1924 Constitution as the first to guarantee religious education and teaching in its Article 19, Section 4. Under this provision, religion courses taught in schools became elective, subject to the permission of students and/or their parents or guardians as their legal representatives. At the same time, this paragraph placed a restriction on officials in the educational system by making religious educational optional.

The Constitution of 1982

This Constitution came into force with Law 2709, dated November 7, 1982. This Constitution guarantees freedom of religion and conscience while including religion classes among compulsory courses in primary and secondary schools. The freedom of religion and conscience, in Article 24 of the 1982 Constitution, is as follows:

> 1. Everyone has the freedom of conscience, religious belief and opinion.
> 2. Acts of worship, religious rites and ceremonies can be conducted freely, as long as they do not violate the provisions of Article 14.

3. No one can be forced to worship, to participate in religious rites and ceremonies, to reveal their religious beliefs and convictions; cannot be condemned and blamed for their religious beliefs and convictions.
4. Religious and moral education and training must be carried out under the supervision and control of the state. Religious culture and moral education are among the compulsory courses taught in primary and secondary education institutions. Other religious education and training depends only on the individual's wishes and on the request of the legal representative of the minors.
5. No one shall exploit or abuse religion or religious feelings or things religious held sacred by religion in any manner whatsoever for the purpose of personal or political interest or influence or for even partially basing the fundamental, social, economic, political, and legal order of the State on religious tenets.

As can be seen, this section protects both the freedoms of religion and conscience while permitting religious education and teaching. In so doing, this provision acknowledges that religious education was to be taught in the Religious Culture and Moral Knowledge courses among the compulsory courses in primary and secondary schools (Aydın, 2007). These courses, which were taught as "Religious Knowledge and Moral" between 1976 and 1982, were merged under the name "Religious Culture and Moral Knowledge" once the 1982 Constitution came into force (Turan, 2012).

Basic Law on National Education

This law came into effect after the adoption of the 1982 Constitution. The Basic Law on National Education 1739 was adopted on June 14, 1973, and was amended by Law 2842 on June 16, 1983. As a result of the amendment, Article 12 titled "Secularism" was modified to read: "Secularism is essential in Turkish national education. Religious culture and moral education are among the compulsory courses taught in primary schools and high school and equivalent schools." A change in 1990 introduced some exceptions to the requirement relating to religious instruction (Kaymakcan, 2006). These modifications afforded those belonging to non-Islamic religions the right to refuse to attend these classes if they wished. However, neither the law nor the Ministry of National Education identified a compulsory class or a moral course for those who were exempt from this requirement.

The Basic Law of National Education is the legal basis for imam-hatip high schools discussed earlier, which include religious education.

Pursuant to Article 32, the Ministry of National Education opened these educational institutions in the secondary education system in order to implement preparatory programs both to train students to perform religious services such as imamate, orator, and teaching the Qur'an course as well as to prepare pupils to enter universities. This article led to accepting the Religious Culture and Moral Knowledge course as being among compulsory classes in primary and high schools.

At the same time, this article changed the name of imam-hatip schools to imam-hatip high school, while imam-hatip school programs were rearranged to fit into those of high schools. Thus, the graduates of imam-hatip high school gained the right to enter some of the universities and all colleges affiliated with the Ministry of National Education.

Summary of Turkish Law and International Documents on Religious Educations

As a result of this analysis of national and international documents in the context of religious education, the following conclusions can be drawn:

1. Parents have the right to determine the religious educations of their children.
2. Parents have the right to live out their religious beliefs and teach their children as they see fit.
3. Religious education is compulsory in Turkish schools. Even so, parents have the right to ask school officials to exempt their children from the Religious Culture and Moral Knowledge courses so that they can take courses in accordance with their own faiths.
4. Individuals do not have the right to judge others in society due to their religious beliefs.
5. The state will prevent all kinds of discrimination in society while providing freedom of religion and conscience.
6. Parents who wish to have their children educated in religious schools can send them schools providing religious education.
7. It is the responsibility of the state to provide religious education in order to prevent misinterpretations of others' beliefs, different perspectives, and religious divisions.
8. It is the responsibility of parents and the state to respect the religious days of others and to teach their children to do the same.

As discussed above, the Turkish legal system protects freedom of religion and conscience in line with both the relevant internationally accepted documents and its own national laws. Indeed, these texts reflect the continuation of efforts in Turkish law to safeguard religious freedom in education by complying with the internationally accepted and signed instruments and by having the state and appropriate officials adopt specific measures to protect the interests of all.

Religious Education in Turkey

Religious education was provided in mosques, madrasahs, *tekke*, *enderun*, and *sıbyan* schools during the establishment and rising periods of the Ottoman Empire before the emergence of the Republic. Along with the westernization that occurred in Turkey after the Tanzimat – a period of reform during the Ottoman Empire starting in the middle of the 19th century – education was offered in schools under various names such as madrasahs, *rustiye* or middle school, *idadî* or high school, and *sultanis*, which were middle plus high schools. Sultanis were Western-style schools during the periods of stagnation and decline. Accordingly, religious education was offered in different forms before the Republic, sometimes under the supervision of the state and other times under the direction of different institutions and individuals.

With the adoption of the law of Tevhid-i Tedrisat in 1924 shortly after the proclamation of the Republic, all schools were placed under one roof, so to speak, while religious education was completely transferred to the Ministry of National Education. In accordance with Article 4 of the law of Tevhid-i Tedrisat, imam-hatip high schools and a theological faculty opened in Istanbul in order to meet the religious needs of society. However, these schools were closed shortly thereafter due to reasons such as the lack of students (Buyrukcu, 2007).

In general, religion classes were taught two hours a week as “Quran and Religion Lessons” in primary schools in 1924; in 1926, this instruction was reduced to one hour per week starting from grade 3. In 1929, students in grades 4 and 5 of elementary schools along with grades 1 and 2 of middle schools, and grades 1 and 2 of teacher schools received one hour per week of instruction. These religion lessons were completely abolished in city elementary and middle schools in 1931–32 and in village primary schools in 1938 (Yilmaz, 2003).

The revival of formal religious education in Turkey began in 1948 with the development of elective religious courses in primary schools. This revival increased with the opening of imam-hatip courses in the same year and a theological faculty in Ankara in 1949. Since 1950, the movement to teach religious courses in schools developed gradually in such a way that it was divided into two as religious and moral courses.

Since the academic year of 1974–1975, a course on morals became compulsory in grades 4 and 5 of elementary schools; grades 1, 2, and 3 in middle schools; and grades 1 and 2 of high schools. Even so, religion courses were offered as optional. As stated in Article 24 of the 1982 Constitution, which was adopted after the military coup of September 12,

1980, religion classes were among the compulsory courses taught in primary and high schools (Yilmaz, 2003). Today, the Religious Culture and Moral Knowledge course is compulsory in public primary and general high schools from grades 4 to 12 for two hours per week (Head Council of Education and Morality, 2020).

Because Turkey's religious education policies are an important and sensitive issue, its leaders have made various arrangements over time. For instance, the Religious Culture and Moral Knowledge lesson curriculum was rearranged with the renewal of its educational programs in 2018. In determining the content of the Religious Culture and Moral Knowledge course, educational leaders and policymakers adopted an approach that can be described as non-sectarian, meaning that it not based on any particular sectarian perspective, does not involve sectarian discussions, and is designed to lead to an understanding of religion (Ministry of National Education, 2018). The framework for this focuses on the root values of Islam based on basic sources of knowledge of this religion. The goals of these lessons are to provide students with sound knowledge of religion and morality, develop their basic skills, and thereby contribute to the realization of the general goals of national education.

The 29 imam-hatip schools that opened in 1924 grew to 34. Yet, these schools were closed systematically two to three months after they opened due to lack of students. By the end of the 1925–1926 academic year, all of these schools other than those located in Istanbul and Kutahya had closed. The imam-hatip schools in Istanbul and Kutahya closed in 1930 (Ocal, 2008).

New imam-hatip schools opened for in seven provinces on October 17, 1951 based on Article 4 of the Unification of Education Law. In the following years, the number of these schools increased. In 1973, after the enactment of the Basic Law of National Education, which changed the names of these schools to "imam-hatip high schools" whose graduates had the right of entry to universities, the number of schools grew into the hundreds and the number of students reached hundreds of thousands. Eventually, the Turkish Grand National Assembly passed a law known to the public as the "8-year uninterrupted compulsory education law" on August 16, 1997. Once this law was published and put into effect in the Official Gazette as Law 4306, the middle school parts of imam-hatip high schools were closed (Law on Amendment to Primary Education and Education Law and Some Laws, 1997).

The Primary Education and Education Law and the Law Amending Some Laws introduced a 4 + 4 + 4 system in education in 2012, allowing for the reopening of the middle schools within the imam-hatip high schools. Based on the available data, there were 1,624 imam-hatip high schools in Turkey educating 605,869 students, of whom 266,692 were boys and 339,177 girls, and employing 46,812 teachers. There were 3,394 imam-hatip middle schools educating 358,859 boys and 402,926 girls, for a total of 761,785 pupils being instructed by 43,112 teachers (2018–2019 Ministry of National Education Formal Education Statistics). As can be seen, the Republic of Turkey provides a wide range of opportunities from primary to high school to meet the religious education requirements of its students and their parents.

An Emerging Issue

Religious education in the Republic of Turkey is offered under the supervision and control of the state. The reason why the state took control over religious education is to prevent improper practices, interpretations, and distortions of different faiths. As discussed above, compulsory religious education applies to all students in primary and high schools studying in Turkey.

If a family's religion is not Islam, then parents can request to have their children exempted from compulsory religious education. Students who are exempted from the Religious Culture and Moral Knowledge course typically work on assignments of their own choices under the supervision of a teacher. In a matter likely to cause controversy, this law is inapplicable to parents who belong to different sects such as Shiism, hold to mystical beliefs such as Alevism, or are atheists. Because the exception applies only to families of different religions, it remains to be seen how this plays out. Of course, if parents are denied opportunities to exempt their children from this course, then they have the option of seeking judicial remedies so that their children can be excused from these classes (Efe, 2016). Discussions about this issue have been ongoing (Dogan, 2017).

Conclusion

Regardless of where they live, the expectations of society and especially of parents for their children are increasing day by day. At the same time, as in all areas of education and as reflected in this volume, discussions on the nature of religious education manifest themselves differently in just about all countries. In general, the discussions on the scope of religious education in Turkey can be summarized as follows.

The primary institutions providing religious education in the Turkish National Education system are imam-hatip schools that were created to train imams to teach such classes and offer religious services (Aslamaci, 2013). In addition to training imams, these schools prepare students for higher education (Aslamaci, 2017). Consequently, some of the students in the imam-hatip schools who were expected to prepare to become imams did not enroll in the theology faculty but instead chose to pursue other studies in the university system. Not surprisingly, this situation has led to discussions about the function of imam-hatip schools.

As noted, religious education in Turkey is provided under state supervision and control in all primary and high school students in order to ensure that students are not taught improper practices, interpretations, and distortions of various faiths. However, as discussed above, controversy is likely to arise over which parents can have their children excused from these classes.

In light of national and international documents on the rights to education and freedom of religion, it is clear that all nations and their officials have the duty to not only avoid interfering with the beliefs of individuals but also to take steps to ensure that all persons enjoy freedom of belief. In light of the international consensus as well as national law to ensure this right, the government in Turkey has taken the necessary measures to establish an atmosphere of mutual respect in society while promoting freedom of religion and conscience, especially in the education of its students.

References

Aslamaci, I. (2013). Evaluation of Religious Culture and Ethics Knowledge Courses in Terms of Pluralism. *Hikmet Yurdu Journal, 6*(12), 267–282.

Aslamaci, I. (2017). The Problems with the Quality of the Religious Education Offered at the Imam-Hatip Schools: A Qualitative Research Based on the Opinions of the School Administrators. *Turkish Studies, 12*(10), 49–80.

Aydin, M. Z. (2007). Discussions of Religion Classes at School (History of Religion Courses in Turkey, Theoretical Structure, with Some Country Comparison). *C. U. Theology Faculty Journal, XI*(2), 7–51.

Buyrukcu, R. (2007). *Professional Religious Education in Turkey with Institutional Change and Development Dimensions.* Isparta: Faculty Pub.

Charter of the United Nations and Statute of the International Court of Justice, San Francisco. (1945). Retrieved November 15, 2019, from www.treaties.un.org/doc/Publication/CTC/uncharter.pdf

Constitution of 1924. Law Number: 491. (1924, April 20). Retrieved January 25, 2020,from www.anayasa.gov.tr/tr/mevzuat/onceki-anayasalar/1924-anayasasi/

Constitution of 1961. Law Number: 334. (July 9, 1961). Retrieved December 11, 2019, from www.anayasa.gen.tr/1961ay.htm

Constitution of 1982. Law Number: 2709. (1982, October 18). Retrieved November 11, 2019, from www.mevzuat.gov.tr/MevzuatMetin/1.5.2709.pdf

Convention for the Protection of Human Rights and Fundamental Freedoms. (1950). Retrieved December 12, 2019, from www.rm.coe.int/1680063765

Convention on the Rights of the Child. (1989). Retrieved November 17, 2019, from www.ohchr.org/en/professionalinterest/pages/crc.aspx

Declaration on the Elimination of All Forms of Intolerance and of Discrimination Based on Religion or Belief. (1981). Retrieved November 10, 2019, from www.ohchr.org/EN/ProfessionalInterest/Pages/ReligionOrBelief.aspx

Dogan, P. U. (2017). A Qualitative Study on the Characteristics of a Non-Confessional Program Design. *Kirikkale Journal of Islamic Sciences Faculty, 2*(3), 127–154.

Efe, H. (2016). The Last Words of EHRC to Turkish Government: "Recognize the Alevis Officially." *Alevisim and Bektashism Research Journal, 14*, 81–99.

Ilkogretim ve Egitim Kanunu ile Bazı Kanunlarda Degisiklik Yapilmasına Dair Kanun [The Primary Education and Education Law and the Law Amending Some Laws]. (1997). Law Number and Date: 4306, 16.08.1997. Retrieved December 2, 2019, from https://www.mevzuat.gov.tr/MevzuatMetin/1.5.4306.pdf

Ilkogretim ve Egitim Kanunu ile Bazı Kanunlarda Degisiklik Yapılmasına Dair Kanun [The Primary Education and Education Law and the Law Amending Some Laws]. (2012). Law Number: 6287. (2012, March 30). Retrieved December 5, 2019, from www.resmigazete.gov.tr/eskiler/2012.04.20120411-8.htm

Kaymakcan, R. (2006). Thoughts on Religious Education Policies in Turkey. *EKEV Academy Journal, 10*(27), 21–35.

Milli Egitim Temel Kanunu. Law Number and Date: 1739 and 14.6.1973. (1973). Retrieved January 12, 2020, from www.mevzuat.gov.tr/MevzuatMetin/1.5.1739.pdf

Ministry of National Education. (2018). *Curriculum of Religious Culture and Moral Education*. Ankara: MEB Pub.

Ministry of National Education Formal Education Statistics. (2019). Retrieved January 10, 2020, from www.sgb.meb.gov.tr/www/icerik_goruntule.php?KNO=361

Ocal, M. (2008). History of Religious Education Literature in Turkey. *Turkey Research Literature Journal*, 6(12), 399–430.

Talim ve Terbiye Kurulu Baskanligi [Head Council of Education and Morality]. (2020). Retrieved January 15, 2020, from www.ttkb.meb.gov.tr/www/haftalik-ders-cizelgeleri/kategori/7

Tevhid-i Tedrisat Kanunu [Tevhid-i Tedrisat Law]. Law Number and Date: 430/3.3.1340. (1924). Retrieved January 9, 2020, from www.mevzuat.gov.tr/MevzuatMetin/1.3.430.pdf

Turan, I. (2012). Legal Basis of Religious Education in Turkey in Terms of National and International Law. *Ondokuz Mayıs University Review of the Faculty of Divinity*, 32, 77–109.

Universal Declaration of Human Rights. (1948). Retrieved January 5, 2020, from www.un.org/en/universal-declaration-human-rights/

Yilmaz, H. (2003). *Religious Education and Social Peace*. Istanbul: Insan Pub.

18 Legal Issues Surrounding the Teaching of Religion in Public Schools in the United States

Charles J. Russo

Introduction

According to the opening 16 words of the First Amendment to the United States Constitution, enacted in 1791 as part of the Bill of Rights, "Congress shall make no law respecting an establishment of religion, or prohibiting the free exercise thereof."[1] Yet, as reflected by the vast amount of litigation over the First Amendment Religion Clauses, there is little agreement over the meaning of what are known as the Establishment and Free Exercise Clauses, particularly over the role, if any, of religion in public education.

Disputes over the First Amendment Religion Clauses are so common that hardly a year goes by without the Justices reviewing a case on the relationship between the Religion Clauses and education. At the same time, the Justices refuse to review many cases involving religion with implications for public schools. This much is clear, though: the Court has made it clear that while educators in public, or state-funded, schools can teach about religion, they may not teach religion, making them walk a fine line.

Addressing this fine line, in *Abington v. Schempp* and *Murray v. Curlett* (*Abington*),[2] a case about prayer and Bible reading in public schools discussed in greater detail below,[3] the Supreme Court pointed out in dicta[4] that

> it might well be said that one's education is not complete without a study of comparative religion or the history of religion and its relationship to the advancement of civilization. It certainly may be said that the Bible is worthy of study for its literary and historic qualities. Nothing we have said here indicates that such study of the Bible or of religion, when presented objectively as part of a secular program of education, may not be effected consistently with the First Amendment.[5]

In his concurrence in *Abington*, Justice Brennan observed that

> [t]he holding of the Court today plainly does not foreclose teaching about the Holy Scriptures or about the differences between religious

> sects in classes in literature or history. Indeed, whether or not the Bible is involved, it would be impossible to teach meaningfully many subjects in the social sciences or the humanities without some mention of religion."[6]

Courts continue to reach mixed results over the appropriate place of teaching about religion and other subjects in public school curricula because they have failed to develop a workable measure balancing the impermissible practice of the teaching of religion and the constitutionally acceptable approach of teaching about religion as an academic subject.

Against the background outlined in the preceding paragraph, then, the remainder of this chapter is divided into four substantive sections and a conclusion. The second section examines the legal foundation of education in the United States, focusing on Supreme Court cases because it is often the final arbiter of what is constitutionally permissible with regard to religious activities in public schools. This chapter combines its third and fourth sections because it is virtually impossible to distinguish the way in which the American legal system safeguards the right to religious freedom in education and the multitude of cases setting the boundaries on the status of religion in public schools. The chapter then examines emerging issues surrounding the teaching of religion in public schools before rounding out with a brief conclusion.

The Legal Foundation for Education and Religion

As noted, the US Constitution is the law of the land. As the primary source of law, the Constitution provides the framework within which the entire American legal system operates. Consequently, all actions of federal, state, and local governments such as public school boards, including state constitutions, statutes, and regulations as well as directives from federal agencies (commonly referred to as ministries in the other nations represented in this book), school policies and curricula, plus common law judgments, must ultimately comply with the Constitution as interpreted by the Supreme Court. As a democratic republic with a bifurcated system of federal and state of governments, while state and local agencies have some ability to offer guidelines, again, they are ultimately subordinate to judgments of the Supreme Court.

As a common law (or judge-made law) jurisdiction, jurists in the United States must "interpret the law,"[7] examining issues that may have been overlooked in the legislative or regulatory process or that may not have been anticipated when statutes were enacted. Common law involves the concept of precedent, the idea that a majority ruling of the highest court in a given jurisdiction is binding on lower courts within its purview. Thus, a ruling of the Supreme Court is binding throughout the United

States, while decisions of state supreme courts are binding only in their given jurisdictions.

The importance of the US Constitution notwithstanding, it is silent with regard to education. Moreover, pursuant to the Tenth Amendment, "[t]he powers not delegated to the United States by the Constitution, nor prohibited by it to the States, are reserved to the States respectively, or to the people," thereby making education primarily a concern of individual states. Later, in its only case on school finance, *San Antonio Independent School District v. Rodriguez*,[8] the Court emphasized that "[e]ducation, of course, is not among the rights afforded explicit protection under our Federal Constitution. Nor do we find any basis for saying it is implicitly so protected."[9] On matters related solely to state law such as curricula, funding, and a myriad of other topics, state law is supreme.

Because matters involving constitutional rights, such as whether religion can be taught in public schools, along with state and local regulations addressing this and related questions, the federal courts have primary responsibility for resolving such disputes. While state courts can hear First Amendment disputes on matters involving religion, they cannot limit or restrict rights conferred by the Constitution or judgments of the Supreme Court.

Jurisprudence related to the First Amendment Religion Clauses has created a great deal of confusion over the appropriate standard of reviewing the actions of officials in public schools. As such, it is necessary to engage in a quick review of the various tests it created. The Justices initially enunciated the two-part purpose and effect test in *School District of Abington Township v. Schempp* and *Murray v. Curlett* (*Abington*),[10] wherein they invalided prayer and Bible reading in public schools. The Justices later expanded the two-part test in *Abington* in *Lemon v. Kurtzman* (*Lemon*),[11] thereby creating the seemingly ubiquitous tripartite Establishment Clause test.

Lemon, from Pennsylvania, and its companion case, *Earley v. De Censo*, set in Rhode Island, dealt with the boundaries of governmental aid to supplementing the salaries of teachers in religiously affiliated nonpublic schools. In its analysis, the Court created a new test by adding a third element, excessive entanglement, from *Walz v. Tax Commission of New York City*,[12] wherein it had upheld New York State's practice of providing state property tax exemptions for church property used in worship services.

Under the *Lemon* test, governmental action must "[f]irst have a secular legislative purpose; second, its principal or primary effect must be one that neither advances nor inhibits religion; finally, the statute must not foster 'an excessive government entanglement with religion.' "[13] The Court's failure to offer a clear rationale why *Lemon* – a test whose first two parts came from cases on prayer and Bible reading while the third originated in a disagreement over state tax exemptions for churches – should have become such a widespread measure for cases ranging from the limits of state aid to faith-based schools as well as a wide array of disputes involving religious activities such as teaching about the Bible and prayer.

What become known as the *Lemon* test has long been the Supreme Court's primary standard when resolving cases involving the relationship between the government qua public schools and both state aid – a voluminous topic well beyond the scope of this chapter and book – to faith-based institutions and questions involving religious practices in public schools. However, the viability of the *Lemon* test may be in question in light of the Court's recent judgment in *Espinoza v. Montana Department of Taxation* (*Espinoza*)[14] because the Justices avoided this tripartite test in its rationale.[15] In *Espinoza*, the Court ruled that state officials could not deny generally available benefits, in this case tuition tax credits, to faith-based institutions and people of faith in state-funded programs, essentially treating them as second-class citizens solely because they are religious.[16]

Particularly in cases involving religious activities such as prayer, the Supreme Court has occasionally relied on two other tests. In *Lynch v. Donnelly*,[17] albeit in a nonschool case about the inclusion of a nativity scene in a Christmas display on public property in Rhode Island, Justice O'Connor's plurality opinion (one in which a clear majority of a court did not join) created the endorsement test over the status of religious activity in public settings. Under this measure, courts invalidate governmental actions that appear to endorse a particular faith by allowing such practices as public religious displays in schools.

In addition, the Supreme Court occasionally relied on *Lee v. Weisman*,[18] in which it ignored *Lemon* but made two points in striking down school-sponsored graduation prayer. First, the Court invalidated prayer because the state, through a public school principal in Rhode Island, not only selected the rabbi to pray but also gave him guidelines to offer nondenominational benediction and valedictory remarks. Second, the Justices feared that the prayers were psychologically coercive to the graduating students and others because, as captive audience, they may have been forced against their wills to be part of a ceremony from which they were not genuinely free to be excused.[19]

Against this background, the next section of the chapter provides a brief review of the judicial developments leading to a discussion of key litigation on issues associated with teaching about religion in public schools.

Protection for Freedom of Religion or Belief in Education

At this point, it is important to address two preliminary matters. First, because public schools in the United States cannot include teaching about religion in their curricula, unlike in many of the other national policies analyzed in this book, the question of whether parents can opt their children out of religious instruction is a moot point in the United States. As noted and discussed below, the Supreme Court had reasoned that while educators in public school cannot teach religion, as a subject involving faith and acceptance by believers, it they can engage in the academic study of religion in subjects such as history and literature.

The second important preliminary matter is that it must be kept in mind that the First Amendment explicitly prohibits only Congress from making laws establishing religion. As such, in 1940, the Supreme Court applied the First Amendment to the states through the Fourteenth Amendment in *Cantwell v. Connecticut* (*Cantwell*).[20] Although not involving education, *Cantwell* is noteworthy because in invalidating the convictions of Jehovah's Witnesses for violating a statute against the solicitation of funds for religious, charitable, or philanthropic purposes without prior approval of public officials, it marked the first time the Court extended the First Amendment to the states by incorporating it into the Fourteenth Amendment. Following *Cantwell*, individuals have the same rights against their state and local governments as they do when they sue the federal government over their First Amendment right to freedom of religion.

In 1947, the Supreme Court resolved its first case directly involving the First Amendment and education, in *Everson v. Board of Education* (*Everson*).[21] In *Everson*, the Court upheld constitutionality of a law from New Jersey that permitted local boards to make rules and contracts to transport children to and from their faith-based schools on the basis that it did not violate the Establishment Clause.

Following *Everson*, the Supreme Court has reviewed more cases on the First Amendment Religion Clauses than any other subject involving education, with, as acknowledged, rarely a year passing without the Justices hearing such a dispute. Moreover, while the litigation involving the First Amendment tends to be classified as being primarily based on the Establishment or Free Exercise Clauses, the cases often overlap because no clear line separates the two.

An important point to keep in mind when reviewing Supreme Court cases on religion is the ongoing split in terms of whether jurists are separationists or accommodationists.[22] Separationists, or liberals, support the Jeffersonian metaphor calling for erecting a "wall of separation" between church and state[23] – language not appearing in the Constitution. This is the perspective most often associated with the Supreme Court since Justice Black's opinion introduced it in *Everson*, particularly on religious activities in public schools, some of which involve the subject of this book, legal issues over teaching religion in these schools. The Court seems to have moved away from this perspective on matters of aid, a topic beyond the scope of this volume.[24]

On the other hand, accommodationists, often called originalists, textualists, or conservatives,[25] largely reject the notion of a "wall of separation" between Church and State, preferring what may be better described as a chain-link fence separating the government and religious activities. Accommodationists generally maintain that the government can permit aid to meet the needs of children who attend faith-based, or nonpublic, schools under the Child Benefit Test. The Child Benefit Test – again, a topic beyond the scope of this chapter – is a legal construct standing for the proposition that state aid such as for transportation and textbooks is acceptable because it primarily assists students rather than their faith-based schools. Moreover, accommodationists do not oppose all interactions between the government and religious schools insofar as they are more favorably disposed to the possibility of prayer at a public school graduation and religious activities in public schools.[26]

The accommodationist end of the Supreme Court bench, which now apparently represents the majority, has ruled that states cannot deny generally available benefits to faith-based schools or believers simply because of their religious natures.[27] Still, unlike nations such as Australia, the Netherlands, and South Africa that allow direct financial aid to fund the operations of faith-based schools, even the accommodationists have disfavored states from granting direct monetary assistance to religious institutions. As such, the remainder of the chapter focuses on issues about the teaching of religion exclusively in public schools, meaning those supported entirely by state monies.

Judicial Analysis of the Freedom of Religion or Belief in Education

In light of the wide array of cases involving issues associated with teaching about religion in public schools in the United States, this section highlights litigation under headings identifying the nature of the disputes.

Using Public School Facilities for Teaching Religion Classes

A year after *Everson*[28] upheld the constitutionality of aid under the Child Benefit test it created in its First Amendment jurisprudence, the Supreme Court addressed whether public school officials could allow faith leaders to teach classes about the religious tenets of their faiths in their buildings. In the program at issue in *People of State of Illinois ex rel. McCollum v. Board of Education of School District No. 71, Champaign County* (*McCollum*),[29] a school board in Illinois allowed a Jewish rabbi, Catholic priests, and Protestant teachers to provide religious instruction to children whose parents agreed to have them take part in the program. Under the program, all students were released from their classes with their religion instructors notifying their regular teachers if they were absent. Students who did not attend religious instruction went to other classrooms to engage in secular studies.

In an opinion written by Justice Black – the member of the Court who had introduced the "wall of separation metaphor" a year earlier in *Everson* – the *McCollum* Court ruled in favor of the mother who challenged the program. Reversing an earlier decision to the contrary, the Justices invalidated the program for two reasons. First, the Court was of the opinion that allowing the classes to be taught violated the First Amendment because it allowed religious leaders to use tax-supported public school facilities to be used to disseminate their faith-based doctrines. Second, the Justices determined that by allowing the program to operate, public school officials afforded religious groups invaluable, impermissible aid, essentially assisting them by making students available pursuant to Illinois' compulsory education laws.

Release Time

Supreme Court Case

In 1952, in *Zorach v. Clauson* (*Zorach*),[30] the Supreme Court upheld the constitutionality of a statute from New York permitting the practice known as "release time," whereby officials dismissed students from their public schools so they could attend religious classes elsewhere, usually in faith-based schools. The Court affirmed that officials were free to accommodate the religious wishes of parents by releasing their children at their request, allowing the practice to continue because public schools were not used for religious instruction. In its analysis, the Court compared the practice of "release time to allowing acceptable excuses for students who were absent for religious reasons."[31]

Lower Court Cases

The Second Circuit subsequently upheld the denial of the claim of a mother in New York who objected to release time involving the local public school her children attended, even though they did not take part in the program.[32] The court affirmed that the program passed Establishment Clause scrutiny because it did not use public funds or offer on-site religious instruction in public schools, participation was purely voluntary, and educators did not coerce or pressure students to take part in the classes.

On a different issue involving release time, the Fourth Circuit upheld the rejection of a challenge to such a time program in South Carolina that allowed students to receive academic credit for taking part in the religion classes.[33] Relying on both *Zorach* and *Lemon*, the court upheld the program as constitutional because it did not evidence an impermissible religious motive, its principal effect did not advance religion, and it did not result in excessive entanglement insofar as students could earn academic credit regardless of their religion, faith, or denomination.[34]

The Use of Sacred Texts in Teaching About Religion in Public Schools

Considering the central place the Bible occupied in the lives of the earliest Christian colonists in what became the United States, it is a bit surprising that the first case involving the discontinuation of reading in schools did not take place until well into the 19th century. At that time, the Supreme Court of Ohio invalidated an ordinance that directed a board to have school days start with readings from the King James Bible because the judiciary should not have entered into matters of educational governance and that the Bible was not part of common law in the United States.[35]

Modern Supreme Court Jurisprudence

The status of the Bible was at issue in the companion cases of *School District of Abington Township v. Schempp* and *Murray v. Curlett*,[36] suits originating in Pennsylvania and Maryland, respectively. At issue in *Abington*, the lead case, was whether starting the day in public schools with a reading of ten verses from the King James Bible and the recitation of the Our Father or Lord's Prayer as part of the opening of a school day violated the Establishment Clause. Parents and their children objected to both practices because the doctrines expressed in these activities were contrary to their own religious faiths.

The Supreme Court invalidated both practices under the Establishment Clause as applied to the states via the Fourteenth Amendment. The Justices were of the view that by allowing reading from and relying on the Bible and allowing prayer, school officials violated the principle of governmental neutrality pursuant to which neither states nor arms thereof such as school boards, can aid any or all religions and all have the right to make personal religious choices free from state compulsion. In its judgment, the court relied on the two-part test, discussed earlier: "[t]he test may be stated as follows: what are the purpose and the primary effect of the enactment? . . . [T]o withstand the strictures of the Establishment Clause there must be a secular legislative purpose and a primary effect that neither advances nor inhibits religion."[37]

Lower Courts on Bibles in Public Schools

After an initial flurry of cases on Bible study in public school curricula, litigation of this issue has slowed down. The courts largely invalidated plans to offer classes about the Bible because they were skeptical that the courses could pass the *Lemon*, endorsement, and/or psychological coercion tests.

The then Fifth Circuit,[38] in a case from Alabama, held that a school board could not offer a Bible as literature class because its primary effect was to advance religion in violation of the Establishment Clause.[39] Similarly, a federal trial court in Tennessee prevented one school board from offering Bible study classes in elementary schools because their natures, intents, and purposes were not primarily history, literature, or otherwise secular insofar as they were of a religious nature that tended to advance Christianity.[40] Conversely, the court allowed a second board to offer such a class because it had guidelines in place ensuring that it did not violate the Establishment Clause. Further, a federal trial court in Mississippi prevented a board from offering Bible study classes because they violated the Establishment Clause under the *Lemon*, endorsement, and coercion tests.[41]

A case with a twist from Florida addressed a challenge to a two-semester course on the Bible as history and literature class. A federal trial court allowed a board to permit the proposed class on the Old Testament because it offered a secular purpose for doing so. Yet, the court enjoined the board from permitting the New Testament course to continue because in light of the inclusion of references to the resurrection of Jesus in classes, the court found it difficult to conceive how the account of the resurrection or of miracles could be taught as secular history.[42]

On an issue relating to logistics of Bible study in public schools, the Eighth Circuit upheld an earlier order invalidating a program in Arkansas, in which students left their regular classes to attend Bible study courses taught by volunteers who were neither acting on behalf of any church nor school employees, because it had the principal effect of advancing Christianity.[43] In a like case, the Sixth Circuit affirmed that a program a board in Tennessee sponsored that allowed students from a local Christian college to teach weekly Bible classes for children in grades K–5 violated the Establishment Clause because it failed all three parts of the *Lemon* test.

Use of Sacred Texts in Teaching About Other Faiths

Islam

In a case from California, the Ninth Circuit affirmed the dismissal of a challenge to the use of curricular materials in a unit of a social studies class because it covered Islam. Among other activities, the students were required to memorize verses from the Qur'an and recite the Five Pillars of Faith.[44] The court concluded that insofar as the activities "were not. . . 'overt religious exercises' that raise[d] Establishment Clause concerns,"[45] the case was without merit.

More recently, the Fourth Circuit addressed whether assignments about Islam violated the Establishment Clause among other charges. The disputed material was part of a world history unit designed to introduce students to the religion, politics, and culture of Muslims. When a student in Maryland, on the advice of her father, refused to participate in a fill-in-the-blank assignment because she had to write "There is no God but Allah and Muhammed is the messenger of Allah,"[46] one of the Five Pillars of Islam, they unsuccessfully challenged the project. The court affirmed that the fill-in-the-blank assignment regarding Islam had a secular purpose, its primary effect was not to endorse any religious belief, and it did not result in excessive entanglement with religion.[47]

Hinduism

An advocacy group representing parents of Hindu children sued the California state board of education and department of education alleging discrimination in the history–social science standards and framework for sixth and seventh grades, in violation of various rights including the Establishment and Free Exercise Clauses. Affirming a grant of summary judgment in favor of the state, the Ninth Circuit held that the discussion of Hinduism did not violate the parents' rights absent allegations that the materials penalized, interfered with, or otherwise burdened their rights to the free exercise of religion. The court also agreed that materials did not implicitly endorse Judaism, Christianity, or Islam, nor did they disparage Hinduism in violation of the Establishment Clause, because they acknowledged divine origins of Hinduism. The court also rejected the challenge to the description of the caste system as a religious belief, singling out Hindus for negative treatment because the framework dictated that "[t]eachers should make clear to students that [caste] was a social and cultural structure as well as a religious belief."[48]

Origins of Humankind

Starting with the so-called Scopes Monkey Trial, including two Supreme Court cases, conflicts continue over the origins of humankind between those whose religious beliefs compel them to accept the Genesis account of creation as written and those who subscribe to Darwin's theory of evolution. In *Scopes v. State*,[49] the Supreme Court of Tennessee overturned a teacher's conviction for violating a state law prohibiting the delivery of instruction about evolution because it contradicted a literal acceptance of the creation account in Genesis. In the underlying dispute, the court invalidated the fine imposed on the teacher but left the statute in place.

Epperson v. Arkansas, the first of two Supreme Court cases, involved a high school teacher in the state's challenge to a 1928 state law making it "unlawful for a teacher in any state-supported school or university 'to teach the theory or doctrine that mankind ascended or descended from a lower order of animals,' or 'to adopt or use in any such institution a textbook that teaches' this theory."[50] Teachers who violated the statute could be dismissed. The Court invalidated the law because it failed *Abington*'s purpose and effect test insofar as it placed primacy on the Genesis account of creation in its attempt to forbid teaching of Darwin's theory of evolution.

In a second case from Arkansas calling for balanced treatment in instruction on the biblical account of creation should evolution be included in curricula, a federal trial court in Arkansas invalidated such a statute.[51] The court reasoned that the because the law's goal was to introduce the biblical version of creation into public school curriculum, its purpose was to advance religion, while its reliance on Genesis meant that it had the primary effect of advancing a particular religious belief, namely Christianity, and the ongoing involvement of state officials in the matter created excessive and prohibited entanglement with religion.

Edwards v. Aguillard,[52] the second Supreme Court case, involved a challenge to Louisiana's Balanced Treatment for Creation-Science and Evolution-Science in Public School Instruction Act. The act prohibited the teaching of "evolution-science" in public elementary and secondary schools unless accompanied by instruction on "creation-science." The Court invalidated the act both because it lacked an identified secular purpose and its primary purpose was to advance a particular religious belief, thereby impermissibly endorsing religion.

At issue in a second case from Louisiana was a school board's having adopted a resolution disclaiming the endorsement of evolution after it failed to introduce "creation-science" into its curriculum as a legitimate scientific alternative.[53] The Fifth Circuit affirmed that insofar as the primary effect of the disclaimer was to protect and maintain a particular religious viewpoint, namely Christianity, it violated both the second prong of *Lemon* and the endorsement test.[54]

In Pennsylvania, a federal trial court invalidated a school board policy that would have required students to hear a statement mentioning intelligent design as a newer religious alternative to Darwin's theory of evolution. As in the previous case, the court held that the policy violated both the endorsement and the effects, or second, prong of *Lemon*.[55]

Not surprisingly, state courts have been unsympathetic to claims of teachers who refused to teach about evolution. For example, the Supreme Court of South Dakota affirmed the nonrenewal of a biology teacher's contract because he devoted too much time to creationism or religion in his class but failed to cover basic principles in accordance with the board's policies and guidelines that had been explained to him.[56] Later, an appellate court in Minnesota upheld the reassignment of a biology teacher to a different class because he refused to provide instruction about evolution.[57]

Emerging Issues

Religious objections to teaching some aspects of human sexuality and related topics are often hot-button issues in public schools. Consequently, litigation in this regard has arisen over programming about AIDS and sex education as well as family lifestyles. In a related emerging issue, it remains to be seen whether controversy will arise should the proposed federal Equality Act become law.

In a case from Connecticut, the Second Circuit affirmed that school officials did not violate the Free Exercise Clause when they rejected a father's request to excuse his son from a mandatory health education course that included lessons on family life and development as well as AIDS, assigning the student a failing grade for refusing to do.[58] The court agreed that the father's objection was without merit because officials acted on the rational basis of promoting the health and welfare of children in providing such instruction.

Another representative case arose in Kentucky, where a student and his parents failed in their claim over the denial of their request that he be excused from a significant portion of diversity training, much of which was devoted to issues of sexual orientation and gender harassment, because he believed homosexuality to be sinful. The Sixth Circuit affirmed that the student's subjective belief that he would have been disciplined for violating his school's policy against making stigmatizing or insulting comments about the sexual orientation of peers was neither supported by the concrete acts of officials nor did it constitute "injury-in-fact" allowing his claim that educators violated his right to the free exercise of religion to proceed.[59]

On another matter, the First Circuit affirmed a grant of summary judgment in favor of a school official in Massachusetts in a case that addressed material about same-sex marriage in an elementary school curriculum. The court agreed that school officials did not significantly limit either their rights of parents or their children to the free exercise of religion when teachers used books portraying diverse families, including those in which both parents were of the same gender. The court pointed out that students were neither required to read the books nor did they endorse same-sex marriage "or even address these topics explicitly, but merely describe[d] how other children might come from families that look different from one's own."[60]

The previous cases involved subjects addressing sexuality education broadly and related matters for which there is a broad consensus combined with the undisputed public health need to include these topics in school curricula. An emerging issue that may be contentious as this book heads to press concerns the proposed federal Equality Act, which is designed to ban "discrimination based on sex, sexual orientation, and gender identity in a wide variety of areas including public accommodations and facilities [and] education."[61]

The House of Representatives approved the bill by a vote of 224–206, along party lines, on February 25, 2021,[62] but it is uncertain whether it will pass in the Senate.[63] Provisions in the Act that are likely to lead to controversy in school settings include granting access to "a shared facility, including a restroom, a locker room, and a dressing room, that is in accordance with the individual's gender identity."[64] If it becomes law, the Act would also present challenges to religious freedom[65] because under its terms, "[t]he Religious Freedom Restoration Act of 1993 (42 U.S.C. 2000bb *et seq.*) shall not provide a claim concerning, or a defense to a claim under, a covered title, or provide a basis for challenging the application or enforcement of a covered title."[66]

In addition to President Biden's having made it clear that "he wants the act to become law within 100 days,"[67] a goal he failed to reach, he issued an executive order mandating that "[a]ll persons should receive equal treatment under the law, no matter their gender identity or sexual orientation."[68] This means that athletes who are transgender now have the opportunity to compete in the sports genders with which they identify. As might be expected, such changes are likely to be controversial in schools. Moreover, if these and related practices are adopted in schools, while also making their way into curricula, it remains to see what challenges the executive order and the Equality Act, if it is enacted, are likely to face from parents and advocacy groups based on their long-held, sincere religious beliefs and other grounds.

Conclusion

When addressing legal issues surrounding how religion is taught in American public schools as well as the other nations covered in this volume, the maxim of Heraclitus, "that you cannot step into the same river twice"[69] readily comes to mind. In other words, in the litigious common law jurisdiction known as the United States, as new topics and issues emerge, they are almost certain to lead to litigation. Moreover, new cases may well overturn established precedents both because of factual differences in the disputes but also because newer rulings are likely resolved by different groups of jurists whose understandings of and attitudes toward the law differ from those of their predecessors.

At this point, one can only imagine what issues will emerge in coming decades. Still, this much is certain: new disputes will arise whatever modifications occur with regard to teaching about religion in public schools in the United States that will contribute to the seemingly endless supply of litigation on this crucial topic.

Notes

1. U.S. Const., amend. I.
2. 374 U.S. 203 (1963).
3. See notes 35–37 and accompanying text.
4. Dicta are nonbinding statements courts make in their rationales that are not part of their holding but which may be accorded some weight in terms of what their judgments mean.
5. *Abington*, 374 U.S. at 225.
6. *Id.* at 300 (J. Brennan, concurring).
7. For an article on the judicial process, see Charles J. Russo, Judges as Umpires or Rule Makers? The Role of the Judiciary in Educational Decision Making in the United States, *Education Law Journal*, 10(1) (2009), 33–47.
8. 411 U.S. 16 (1973).
9. *Id.* at 35.
10. 374 U.S. 203, 222 (1963). The Court noted that "[t]he test may be stated as follows: what are the purpose and the primary effect of the [legislative] enactment? . . . [T]o withstand the strictures of the Establishment Clause there must be a secular legislative purpose and a primary effect that neither advances nor inhibits religion." *Id.*
11. 403 U.S. 602 (1971).
12. 397 U.S. 664 (1970).
13. *Id.* at 612–613. As to entanglement, particularly with governmental assistance, the Court added three factors to take into consideration: "we must examine the character and purposes of the institutions that are benefitted, the nature of the aid that the State provides, and the resulting relationship between the government and religious authority." *Id.* at 615.
14. 140 S. Ct. 2246 (2020).
15. *Id.* at 2265, where Justice Thomas referred to *Lemon* as "this Court's infamous test."
16. For another recent case reaching a like outcome, see *Trinity Lutheran Church of Columbia v. Comer*, 137 S. Ct. 2012 (2017).
17. 465 U.S. 668, 687 (1984).
18. 505 U.S. 577 (1992).
19. *See also Santa Fe Independent School District v. Doe*, 530 U.S. 290 (2000) (invalidating prayer prior to the start of high school football games but completely ignoring *Lee* and its psychological coercion test).
20. 310 U.S. 296 (1940).
21. 330 U.S. 1 (1947), *reh'g denied*, 330 U.S. 855 (1947).
22. *See* Jim Dey, Durbin to Supreme Court on Gun-Rights Case: Back Off or Else, *The News-Gazette* (Champaign-Urbana, IL), August 20, 2019, 2019 WLNR 25388738 (identifying "the [C]ourt's five conservative justices [as] John Roberts, Samuel Alito, Neil Gorsuch, Brett Kavanaugh and Clarence Thomas. . . [and its] four liberals – Stephen Breyer, Sonia Sotomayor, Elena Kagan and Ruth Bader Ginsburg."). *See also* Steve Mazie, Barrett Moves Court to Right, *The Times-Tribune* (Scranton, PA), November 30, 2020, 2020 WLNR 34120333 (reporting that "with the death of Justice Ruth Bader Ginsburg in September and Barrett's ascension to the bench the tide has turned. . . [as] the court's staunchest conservatives have a five-vote majority.").
23. Thomas Jefferson's letter of January 1, 1802, to Nehemiah Dodge, Ephraim Robbins, and Stephen S. Nelson, A Committee of the Danbury Baptist Association. 16 Writings of Thomas Jefferson 281 (Andrew Adgate Lipscomb & Albert Ellery Bergh, eds. 1903) popularized the metaphor of the "wall of separation." Jefferson wrote: "Believing with you that religion is a matter

which lies solely between man and his God. . . . I contemplate with sovereign reverence that act of the whole American people which declared that their legislature should 'make no law respecting an establishment of religion, or prohibiting the free exercise thereof,' thus building a wall of separation between church and state."

24. *See, e.g.*, notes 15 and 16 accompanying text.
25. Carrie Severino, Perspective: Trumpism's Next Act, *The Gazette* (Colorado Springs, CO), November 15, 2020, 2020 WLNR 32590051 (writing that "all three of President Trump's appointments to the Supreme Court [Gorsuch, Kavanaugh, and Barrett] are unabashed originalists and textualists. The president's paramount judicial legacy is a court that finally has a majority of originalists, a goal that was a long time coming.").
26. *See, e.g.*, note 18. In a scathing dissent, the late Justice Scalia wrote: "The Court's argument that state officials have 'coerced' students to take part in the invocation and benediction at graduation ceremonies is, not to put too fine a point on it, incoherent."). *Lee* 505 U.S. at 636.
27. Notes 14–16 and accompanying text.
28. Note 21 and accompanying text.
29. 333 U.S. 203 (1948).
30. 343 U.S. 306 (1952).
31. New York City's public schools continue to permit release time. See *Regulation of the Chancellor, A-630, Religious Accommodation of Students.* Retrieved from www.schools.nyc.gov/docs/default-source/default-document-library/a-630-english.
32. *Pierce ex rel. Pierce v. Sullivan W. Cent. Sch. Dist.*, 379 F.3d 56 (2d Cir. 2004). For like outcomes, see *Smith v. Smith,* 523 F.2d 121 (4th Cir. 1975), *cert. denied,* 423 U.S. 1073 (1976) and *Lanner v. Wimmer,* 662 F.2d 1349 (10th Cir. 1981).
33. *Moss v. Spartanburg Cnty. Sch. Dist. No. 7,* 683 F.3d 599 (4th Cir. 2012), *cert. denied,* 568 U.S. 1011 (2012).
34. Ohio (Ohio Rev. Code Ann. § 3313.6022 (West 2014)) and Tennessee (Tenn. Code. Ann. § 49–2–130 (West 2015)) subsequently enacted laws permitting students to earn academic credit for the religious classes they take during release time.
35. Apparently the earliest recorded case on the Bible in public schools was *Board of Educ. of Cincinnati v. Minor,* 23 Ohio St. 211 (1872) (upholding a board's vote to discontinue Bible reading in public schools). *But see Wilkerson v. City of Rome,* 110 S.E. 895 (Ga. 1922) (refusing to invalidate an ordinance calling for a board to have school days start with readings from the King James Version of the Bible).
36. Note 2.
37. *Minor,* 23 Ohio St. at 222.
38. When the Fifth Circuit Court of Appeals Reorganization Act of 1980, §§ 9, 9(2), 28 U.S.C.A. § 41, became law, Alabama moved from the Fifth to the Eleventh Circuit.
39. *Hall v. Board of Sch. Comm'rs of Conecuh Cnty.*, 656 F.2d 999 (5th Cir. 1981).
40. *Wiley v. Franklin,* 497 F. Supp. 390 (E.D. Tenn. 1980)
41. *Herdahl v. Pontotoc Cnty. Sch. Dist.*, 933 F. Supp. 582 (N.D. Miss. 1996).
42. *Gibson v. Lee Cnty. Sch. Bd.*, 1 F. Supp. 2d 1426 (M.D. Fla. 1998). Kentucky has since enacted a statute empowering boards to offer an elective course in social studies about the "Hebrew scriptures" and/or the New Testament. Ky. Rev. Stat. § 156.162 (West 2017).
43. 725 F. Supp. 1503 (W.D. Ark. 1989), *aff'd,* 923 F.2d 857 (8th Cir. 1990), *cert. denied,* 499 U.S. 922 (1991).

44. *Eklund v. Byron Union Sch. Dist.*, 2006 WL 1519184 (Appellate Petition, Motion and Filing) (U.S. 2006). *Petition for a Writ of Certiorari* (No. 05–1539) at 3–13.
45. *Eklund v. Byron Union Sch. Dist.*, 154 Fed. App'x 648 (9th Cir. 2005), *cert. denied*, 549 U.S. 942 (2006) (internal citations omitted), *quoting Brown v. Woodland Joint Unified Sch. Dist.*, 27 F.3d 1373, 1382 (9th Cir. 1994) (affirming that a program which asked children to discuss witches or create poetic chants and pretend they were witches or sorcerers did not require them to practice the "religion" of witchcraft in violation of the Establishment Clause or California Constitution).
46. *Wood v. Arnold*, 915 F.3d 308, 312 (4th Cir. 2019), *cert. denied*, 140 S. Ct. 399 (2019).
47. *See also Doe v. Cape Henlopen Sch. Dist.*, 759 F. Supp. 2d 522 (D. Del. 2011) (allowing the claim of a Muslim mother to proceed where issues of fact remained over whether a fourth-grade teacher's use of Christmas readings class violated her daughter's rights under the state constitution's preference clause, essentially the equivalent of the federal Free Exercise Clause).
48. *California Parents for Equalization of Educ. Materials v. Torlakson*, 973 F.3d 1010 (9th Cir 2020.
49. 289 S.W. 363 (Tenn. 1927).
50. 393 U.S. 97, 98–99 (1968).
51. *McLean v. Arkansas Bd. of Educ.*, 529 F. Supp. 1255 (E.D. Ark. 1982).
52. 482 U.S. 578 (1987).
53. *Freiler v. Tangipahoa Parish Bd. of Educ.*, 185 F.3d 337 (5th Cir. 1999), *reh'g en banc denied*, 201 F.3d 602 (5th Cir. 2000), *cert. denied*, 530 U.S. 1251 (2000).
54. *See also Selman v. Cobb Cnty. Sch. Dist.*, 449 F.3d 1320 (11th Cir. 2006) (vacating and remanding in favor of a school board in Georgia for additional evidentiary inquiries and new fact-finding after it ordered educational officials to place stickers on biology textbooks describing evolution as a theory).
55. *Kitzmiller v. Dover Area Sch. Dist.*, 400 F. Supp. 2d 707 (M.D. Pa. 2005). *See also COPE v. Kansas State Bd. of Educ.*, 821 F.3d 1215 (10th Cir. 2016), *cert. denied*, 137 S. Ct. 475 (2016) (affirming the denial of a claim that Kansas' new science standards sought to establish a nonreligious worldview because the advocacy group purportedly promoting the religious rights of parents and students lacked standing).
56. *Dale v. Board of Educ., Lemmon Indep. Sch. Dist. 52–2*, 316 N.W.2d 108 (S.D. 1982).
57. *LaVake v. Independent Sch. Dist. No. 656*, 625 N.M.2d 502 (Minn. Ct. App. 2001), *review denied* (2002), *cert denied*, 534 U.S. 1081 (2002).
58. *Leebaert v. Harrington*, 332 F.3d 134 (2d Cir. 2003).
59. *Morrison v. Board of Educ. of Boyd Cnty.*, 521 F.3d 602 (6th Cir. 2008), *cert. denied*, 555 U.S. 1171 (2009).
60. *Parker v. Hurley*, 514 F.3d 87, 106 (1st Cir. 2008), *cert. denied*, 555 U.S. 815 (2008).
61. Summary: H.R.5–117th Congress (2020–2021). Retrieved from https://www.congress.gov/bill/117th-congress/house-bill/5/text.
62. *Ibid.*
63. Nicholas Wu, *Equality Act with LGBTQ Protections Passes House, Faces Uncertain Future in Senate, USA Today*, February 25, 2021. Retrieved from https://www.usatoday.com/story/news/politics/2021/02/25/equality-act-lgbtq-protections-passes-house-heads-senate/6816645002/.
64. H.R. 5 Equity Act Sec. 1101(b)(2).
65. For a commentary on point, see Jim Denison, Equality Act: Why It's a Perilous Threat to Religious Freedom, *Christian Post*, January 28, 2021. Retrieved

from https://www.christianpost.com/voices/equality-act-why-its-a-perilous-threat-to-religious-freedom.html.

66. H.R.5, Equality Act, 117th Congress (2021–2022), Sec. 1107, Claims. Retrieved from https://www.congress.gov/bill/117th-congress/house-bill/5/text.
67. David Crary and Elana Schor, Biden Promises LGBTQ Protections, Arkansas Democrat Gazette (Little Rock), November 29, 2020, 2020 WLNR 34152710.
68. Joseph R. Biden, *Executive Order on Preventing and Combating Discrimination on the Basis of Gender Identity or Sexual Orientation*, January 20, 2021. Retrieved from www.whitehouse.gov/briefing-room/presidential-actions/2021/01/20/executive-order-preventing-and-combating-discrimination-on-basis-of-gender-identity-or-sexual-orientation/. See also Ebony Bowden, Biden Sparks TERF [Trans-Exclusionary Radical Feminist] War with Gender Discrimination Order, *New York Post*, January 21, 2021. Retrieved from https://nypost.com/2021/01/21/joe-biden-sparks-terf-war-with-gender-discrimination-order/; Samantha Schmidt, Emily Wax-Thibodeaux and Moriah Balingit, Biden Calls for LGBTQ Protections in Day-One Executive Order, Angering Conservatives, *Washington Post*, January 21, 2021, 2021 WLNR 2062633.
69. Plato, *Cratylus* (C.D.C. Reeve, trans.) (Indianapolis: Hackett, 1998), 33.

19 Summary and Recommendations for the Teaching of Religion in Public Schools

Charles J. Russo

Introduction

As reflected in the opening paragraphs of this volume, and throughout the chapters, religion continues to play a vital role in societies throughout the world. Aware of the importance that religion occupies in so many cultures, national governments, either explicitly by incorporating them into their own domestic laws, or implicitly in line with internationally agreed to instruments, have enacted legal protections via constitutions, statutes, regulations, and litigation; in addition, national and local educational agencies have implemented their own regulatory safeguards. As to case law, not surprisingly, the United States, a highly litigious society, has had more case law examining controversies associated with teaching about religion in public schools than all of the other nations combined. All of these legal documents offer degrees of protection for both dominant, or majority, and minority religions when addressing instructional or curricular issues in elementary and secondary public or state-funded schools.

In reviewing that status of legal issues associated with teaching about religion in public schools in the nations discussed in this volume, the remainder of this chapter is divided into two substantive parts. The first part briefly summarizes the relationship between and among education, law, and religion in the nations covered. Because some of the many issues that have been litigated in the United States and/or other nations have not necessarily resulted in case law elsewhere, this chapter does not review every controversy from each of the nations studied in this volume. In addition, because topics, whether current or emerging, such as the qualifications and status of individuals who may be eligible to teach religion in state-funded public schools in Brazil, Hungary, Italy, and Poland, traditionally Roman Catholic nations, or the rights of parents to opt their children out of what may be mandatory religious education in public schools in other nations, are not much of an issue, if at all, in most of the countries studied in this book, they are not discussed in detail here or later in this brief chapter.

The second part of this chapter offers recommendations on how to enhance legal protection for freedom of education in religion. The chapter rounds out with a brief conclusion.

Summary

Initial Considerations

As noted, all of the nations covered in this book protect freedom of education and religion under domestic law, often in some conjunction with international instruments. These nations safeguard educational and religious freedom in varying degrees, thereby allowing a range of instruction about religious issues in public schools. Accordingly, this part of the chapter presents a brief overview of the scope or protection provided for freedom of religion in education.

All of the nations reviewed in this volume are signatories to an array of international documents. Even so, these legal and educational systems place varying degrees of reliance on these instruments domestically. For example, England incorporated the European Convention on Human Rights (ECHR) through its Human Rights Act 1998 into its domestic schema of education laws. In this way, there is a degree of constitutional protection for religious rights in England because primary and secondary legislation in the UK must be interpreted in compliance with the rights identified in the ECHR, with the High Court or above empowered to issue a declaration of incompatibility otherwise. Italy, Spain, Sweden, and Turkey, too, place great weight on the ECHR. In addition, Italy and Turkey have complied with judgments of the European Court of Human Rights in matters dealing with religious freedom.

Against this background, all of the legal systems in the countries discussed in this volume ensure a measure of religious freedom in their national constitutions and/or by incorporation of international instruments and, as in the case of Canada, explicitly within a constitutionally embedded Charter of Rights. Concomitantly, neither Australia nor England has written bills of rights despite the fact that religious schools are numerous and widespread in both nations.

Australia lacks comprehensive, national protection of fundamental rights and freedoms, but safeguards are present in its Constitution, albeit by limiting federal power to make laws establishing a state church or prohibiting the free exercise of religion. Moreover, it is important to keep in mind that while the provision on religious freedom in its Constitution is reminiscent of its counterpart and model, the First Amendment to the US Constitution, Australian courts have interpreted its language restrictively. The upshot is that in Australia, there is a gap in the protection of fundamental rights and freedoms generally and religious freedom specifically.

When viewed on a spectrum, the national systems discussed in this book can be classified into one of three different groupings according to the receptiveness to teaching about religion in public schools. At the one end, the United States maintains the most stringent form of a wall of separation between religion and education in state-funded public schools, with the courts placing tight restrictions on what may be taught. Canada is not far behind its neighbor to its south insofar as the close historical relationship between institutionalized Judeo-Christianity and public education has all but vanished. Still, notable exceptions remain, as exemplified by the presence of publicly funded Roman Catholic denominational schools in multiple provinces.

In addition, Australia maintains an uneasy balance of separation between religion and state education. The relationship between religion and public education remains in Brazil and Italy but is not as strong as it has been in the past. In Brazil, the change is due to the secularity of the state and the growth in the freedom of religion. Similarly, in Italy, some of this change is due to the impact of immigration and what can be described as a growing secularization that is impacting European society as a whole. New Zealand law requires all teaching in state primary and intermediate schools to have a secular character but does allow teaching about religion. In like manner, Spain has abandoned its historical model of Catholic confessionalism in public schools and has adopted a more cooperationist approach. Mexico continues to maintain its clear separation between religion and education in its public schools. Taiwan also adopts a model of separation of church and state but allows objective teaching about different religions.

In the middle grouping, Mauritius, is perhaps the most religion-friendly of the three countries in this category. Together with the Netherlands and Sweden, these three nations have religiously diversified populations, with the latter two being impacted by growing immigrant populations. The educational systems in these three nations permit a greater degree of optional teaching about religion in public schools than nations in the first grouping.

The third group of nations is more favorably disposed toward teaching about religion in public schools, even if the content of classes is sectarian or confessional in nature. Not surprisingly, in light of the resurgence in religious freedom broadly in post-communist Hungary and Poland, they fit in this classification because religion occupies an important role in schooling for many. In addition, South Africa is more religion-friendly than most nations in this volume, permitting teaching about religion in public school curricula.

A bit further on the spectrum, Malaysia and Turkey have adopted the most religion-friendly governmental perspective, mandating instruction about the dominant faith, Islam, in public schools. In fact, Malaysia has different categories of public schools and religious schools that are established by governmental agencies that focus on teaching of the Islamic faith. Students who are not Muslim must attend compulsory moral studies classes.

Teaching About Religion Classes in Public School Classes

Insofar as the content of curricula has a great deal to say about the role (or lack thereof) that religion occupies in schools, the wider marketplace of ideas, and societies, it should not be surprising that some nations afford religious education greater freedom in public education than others. Government schools in Australia allow for a range of activities that may touch on religion, including teaching of religious education classes and religious seminars to support for religious student clubs. Given Brazil's confessional character, there is neither a common national basis for the subject of religion nor curricular components defined nor training courses for teaching religious education. Still, Brazil does permit optional religious education as a specific topic in elementary education, but the need remains to establish parameters on how religious-confessional material can be defined and how minority religions such as those of Afro-Brazilians can be protected.

Canada permits education about religion that does not indoctrinate students in particular faiths. This approach is important because it is designed to help students navigate in a culturally and religiously diverse modern world fraught with misunderstanding, tension, and conflict about matters of faith. A key feature of the system in England is the ensured place of religion within the academic life of schools. Religious education is a compulsory element of the basic curriculum in all maintained schools in England, while there is a statutory requirement obligating students to take part in a daily act of collective worship. While there is freedom of choice concerning participation in such religious elements of school life, it is significant that it is exercisable through opting out or withdrawal rather than opting into such parts of school life.

Hungary's 2012 Constitution has stabilized schools, now permitting teaching about religion in public education but making this course of study optional. Italy is starting to enact legislation providing for optional religious education for different denominations in an experimental way, especially in the realm of orthodox minorities. This approach mainly follows the pedagogical models already in use and inspired by Italy's Catholic experience. While Malaysian law expressly prohibits the teaching of other religions to students who profess the Islamic faith, requiring its instruction in public schools, it mandates classes on Moral Education for those who are not Muslims.

Mauritius, which allows teaching about religion in public primary and secondary schools, is a well-functioning pluralistic, multiparty, democratic secular state. Consequently, freedoms of thought, conscience, expression, belief, and religion in education are enshrined in law and are constitutionally protected. Mexico continues to maintain its clear, constitutionally mandated separation between church and state in public schools. Nonetheless, officially recognized religious institutions can legally provide religious education in Mexico through the private schools they sponsor. The law in the Netherlands allows neutral, non-biased teaching about religion in public schools as educators seek to design programming that is responsive to, and mindful of, the growing religious pluralism in their public schools.

In New Zealand, guidelines from its Ministry of Education differentiate between religious instruction, religious observances, and religious education in state primary and intermediate schools. Even though the Secular Education Network has protested, rules that have endured in New Zealand since the 19th century still allow religious instruction if schools are "closed" when that information is delivered. Polish law is clear that educational officials in public schools have the right to offer religious education classes consistent with the wishes of parents or legal guardians, who are free to request that their children be excused from attending such instruction. South Africa's adoption of the co-operative model between the state and public schools, coupled with the principle of subsidiarity, both of which promote tolerance for other beliefs, has proven successful and practicable in allowing teaching about religion in the multireligious heterogeneity in most of its schools.

Spain permits teaching about denominational perspectives on religion in state schools. To this end, educators must provide instruction on the Catholic religion as an optional subject for both parents and pupils in all state schools. Spain must also allow teaching in compliance with the agreements signed with the Protestant, Jewish, and Muslim communities about those faiths at the option of students and their parents. The Spanish government does subsidize private, religious schools, which are overwhelmingly Catholic, allowing religion to be taught in these publicly funded institutions. Sweden, which prohibits schools from being confessional in nature, mandates that all students must receive equal education about religions, and no religious aspects may "spill over" into any other subjects or classes. Accordingly, educators in Swedish schools can teach about religion as long as they remain within these parameters.

Taiwan, which guarantees religious freedom for all, adopted the principle of separation of church and state coupled with the equal treatment of religion. Under this principle, the state must maintain religious neutrality. As such, while officials in public schools in Taiwan cannot offer classes in religious education about particular religions, they can provide instruction about religion in different classes to help students understand this important topic. Religious education in Turkey, which is compulsory in grades 4–12, is offered under state supervision and control in order to prevent improper instruction about the practices and the interpretations or distortions of different faiths. Religious education takes place in Religious Culture and Moral Knowledge, a class that teaches Islam and other religions by using a descriptive approach. Parents who are not members of Islam can request that their children be exempted from this course; if officials grant the requests, these students then do not participate in the class.

Starting in the 1960s, the US Supreme Court entered what is now ongoing debate on teaching about religion in public school curricula. The Court has ruled that while educators in public schools could walk a fine line in teaching about religion, they must be careful to balance issues arising pursuant to the Free Exercise Clause rights of students while simultaneously guarding against Establishment Clause violations if the actions of educators favor (or can be perceived as favoring) one faith or faiths over others. Lower courts in the United States regularly address a wide array of cases debating the different ways religious issues can make their way into instruction and curricula in public schools.

Emerging Issues

Rather than identify an array of issues, including those pointed out in the introduction to this chapter, that may be of limited general interest, this section highlights the most significant topic emerging broadly in public schools in the nations studied herein with regard to teaching about religion and related controversial, but important, subjects in public schools. This matter can also be described as demonstrating a concern over freedom of religion and belief for the purposes of this brief discussion. This issue is singled out for attention because it has surfaced explicitly in Australia, Canada, England, Hungary, Italy, Mexico, the Netherlands, South Africa, Spain, Taiwan, and the United States.

This nascent, but widespread, controversy focuses broadly on who can, or should, control curricular content when dealing with important topics with regard to human sexuality, broadly defined. More specifically, this far-reaching, brewing dispute concerns how national and local educational leaders, lawyers, political leaders, and policymakers can balance tensions on both sides of the issue dealing with human sexuality.

On the one hand, leaders must certainly teach respect for and tolerance of those whose lives and beliefs, particularly those in the LGBTQ community, may differ from what appear to be prevailing, often religion-based, views in their larger societies. On the other hand, the challenge for these leaders is to help foster respect for and safeguarding of the beliefs and values of people of faith. The trick for these leaders is to mediate this often heated dispute in a way that can satisfy individuals on both sides of what is becoming a growing divide, even a chasm.

As questions related to human sexuality come to the fore, struggles are emerging because both sides seek to add instruction on this and related topics in curricula. In so doing, educators, in consultation with experts in the different fields, should provide instruction that is age-appropriate, factual, neutral, and not advocating or proselytizing. For younger students, it may also be wise to inform parents and obtain their consent prior to instructing students. The hope, then, is that individuals on both sides of these difficult questions can demonstrate that as important as it is to be able to disagree with one another – even vociferously – in free and open debate, these discussions can be done in a way that is neither personally disagreeable nor disrespectful.

Recommendations

As reflected by the review of the legal issues addressed in this volume associated with teaching about religion in public schools, this is a subject of significant concern to many people around the globe. The challenge is finding the proper balance so that educators can avoid the appearance of preferring one set of faith-based values over another when religion is included in public school curricula. Educators, lawyers, political leaders, policymakers, and other interested parties may thus wish to consider the following recommendations:[1]

1. In line with the internationally instruments identified throughout this volume, educational, legal, religious, and political leaders, both nationally and locally, must take explicit steps to recognize and safeguard the twin rights to education and freedom of religion as fundamental human rights for all children, particularly those from minority races, ethnic groups, and/or faiths. Put another way, all sorts of national leaders should work to develop laws and policies designed to protect the status of teaching about religion in public schools in order to enhance understanding and tolerance between and among all students regardless of their faiths and those of their families.

At the same time, because teaching about religion can present a challenge in parts of the world that have been slow to extend full rights to historically underrepresented racial, ethnic, and/or religious groups, especially in locations where religious freedom and plurality have not been at a premium, leaders from all backgrounds must step up to ensure that as all children grow into adulthood, they will reach their full potential.

Educational leaders, in particular, should encourage parents to become more involved in the schooling of their children and to take steps to make certain that their school governing bodies, or boards, truly represent community interests while maintaining appropriate educational standards.

2. National leaders must provide adequate funding to create schools to provide children of all faiths with world-class education on the objective, rather than proselytizing or advocacy-based, study of religions other than their own. This is especially important during a time when there seems to be a growing cynicism about the need for education as a tool to help promote intellectual diversity, whether in religion,[2] a focal point of this book, or more broadly as extended to culture as reflected through one's beliefs. This is important so that as students grow into adulthood, their understandings of others can move beyond concerns over resources or capacity in order to focus on how educational systems can not only be better funded but also be made accessible to all. Funding must cover not only construction of facilities and purchasing up-to-date culturally and religiously sensitive instructional materials but also paying salaries designed to enhance the "best and brightest" to enter the field of education.
3. Treat education, whether religious or secular, as an integrative factor, one designed to help prepare all children to become productive members of their societies rather than set them apart from one another based on religion and/or other personal characteristics such as race and/or ethnicity. If acceptance of the religious beliefs of others is encouraged as a form of intellectual diversity, it should be embedded throughout curricula via such courses that include, but are not necessarily limited to, world and/or comparative religions, literature, and history. Unless educators adopt such an approach, it is unlikely that such acceptance of different perspectives can be present in the rest of societies.
4. Reconceptualized school systems must be open to all children in which educators teach respect for religiously pluralistic, cross-cultural principles operating in conjunction with internationally accepted norms and national laws. Put another way, educational systems and institutions must be inclusive, not exclusive, in teaching about religion and other belief systems in public school curricula.
5. Depending on the level at which educational standards are created, leaders should work to adopt laws and accompanying policies meeting the needs of religious minorities, particularly those who are immigrants. Of course, laws and policies must also teach members of religious minorities who are immigrants to respect both the laws of host nations and internationally accepted norms about the treatment of individuals, whether inside or outside of their own faith communities.
6. Institutions of higher learning must work to improve their teacher and administrator preparation programs by including instruction

about how educators can teach objectively about religion in public schools in order to better prepare children for living in religiously diverse communities.

7. Educational leaders in elementary and secondary institutions should adopt proactive policies. These policies should be designed to encourage the creation of shared values among all groups, whether students, parents, faculty members, administrators, or other staff, in developing educational or curricular standards for teaching about religion by ensuring that schools offer courses such as comparative religions and others identified above. These programs should avoid the imposition of mandatory sectarian teaching of or about singular religious perspectives in public schools, even in nations where those beliefs are dominant. Depending on the structure of how educational systems are configured, officials in central governmental ministries or departments at the state or national levels must maintain leadership roles in developing curricular content when teaching about religion in order to ensure uniformity in all schools.
8. Educators, whether at the state or local levels, particularly in such federal republics as Australia, Malaysia, Mexico, and the United States, where centralized control is not a priority, should develop curricular content and accompanying materials about religion and the advancement of religious freedom drafted by professionals who can call on outside experts for assistance.

Individuals from respective governmental and educational ministries or departments as well as professionals from higher, or tertiary, education should provide leadership on this important task. Additionally, even as educational leaders work to develop curricula with an eye primarily toward protecting religious freedom, they must simultaneously teach students to develop critical thinking skills intended to challenge their own established beliefs while walking a tightrope by not necessarily asking them to abandon, alter, or change aspects of their faiths that may be inconsistent with the acceptance of religious freedom and plurality.

9. Leaders should implement curricular programs addressing religion in a manner that can be widely accepted by parents whose children attend public schools as well as by members of their local faith communities. In so doing, educational leaders should give some consideration to permitting groups to preserve their independent religious heritages in the schools within the boundaries of domestic law and internationally accepted civil rights covenants, respectful of the rights of women and members of minority religions.
10. Members of committees assigned the task of developing curricular materials to be used in teaching about religion should be selected

from among a broad representation of stakeholders. These committees should include, but not necessarily be limited to, administrators at the central office and building level, teachers, other staff members such as counselors who interact with pupils, professionals from local institutions of higher education who can help to insure that instruction is both factually objective and non-proselytizing, parents, students (especially those in secondary schools), and perhaps local civic and/or religious leaders interested in helping to ensure equal educational opportunities for all children.

11. Governing bodies should provide mandatory professional development sessions for teachers and other staff members to keep them informed on the importance of, and new or emerging trends on, teaching about religion in public schools.
12. Leaders should schedule information or instructional sessions on the twin rights to education and religious freedom open to parents, community members, and others interested in helping to ensure equal educational opportunities on these topics for all children. These sessions should be sure to include invitations to members of underrepresented and/or minority religions to help them develop a sense of acceptance in the learning communities of their children.
13. Educational leaders should include information on teaching about religion in public schools in teacher and student handbooks as well as on school websites and in information sent home to parents in order to keep them informed about their rights in helping to oversee the educational rights of their children.
14. In light of the rapid pace at which change occurs, leaders, whether nationally and/or locally, should review, and if necessary, revise their internal policies and procedures annually to make certain that they comply with best practices in education in order to ensure that they are meeting the intellectual needs of all of their students.

Conclusion

As religious conflict continues to spread throughout the world, keeping in mind the maxim attributed to Sir Francis Bacon that "knowledge is power," it is important to remember that education is a means that can hopefully help to stem such violence. As idealistic as it may sound, then – not that there is anything improper with idealism – perhaps school curricula hold the key to stemming senseless violence and lead to a brighter tomorrow.

If educators, lawyers, political leaders, and policymakers can agree to work together to expand curricula to teach students about religion, not only to provide them with well-grounded knowledge to help them to have basic understands the faiths of others but also to respect those whose beliefs are different, then perhaps the proverbial "little child will lead them."[3] In so doing, perhaps a single child or a generation of children can lead a revolution of sorts by example to help society to help create a better future respecting the religious beliefs of those whose are different from their own through the power of education for the betterment of all.

Notes

1. These recommendations are adapted, and expanded on, those presented in Charles J. Russo (ed.), *International Perspectives on Education, Law, and Religion* (New York: Routledge, 2014), 216–218.
2. See, e.g., Charles J. Russo, Is Religion the Lost Diversity in Education in an Era of "Militant Secularists?" *The University of Notre Dame Australia Law Review*, 21 (2020), 1–21. Retrieved from https://researchonline.nd.edu.au/undalr/.
3. Isaiah 11.6.

Index

Note: Page numbers followed by 'n' indicate a note on the corresponding page.

For Product Safety Concerns and Information please contact our EU
representative GPSR@taylorandfrancis.com
Taylor & Francis Verlag GmbH, Kaufingerstraße 24, 80331 München, Germany

www.ingramcontent.com/pod-product-compliance
Lightning Source LLC
LaVergne TN
LVHW021118300926
849160LV00010B/775

* 9 7 8 1 0 3 2 0 6 4 4 8 2 *